A CELEBRATION
OF POETS

CALIFORNIA
GRADES 7-12
SPRING 2008

creativeCOMMUNICATION
A CELEBRATION OF TODAY'S WRITERS

A CELEBRATION OF POETS
CALIFORNIA
GRADES 7-12
SPRING 2008

AN ANTHOLOGY COMPILED BY CREATIVE COMMUNICATION, INC.

Published by:

creativeCOMMUNICATION
A CELEBRATION OF TODAY'S WRITERS

1488 NORTH 200 WEST · LOGAN, UTAH 84341
TEL. 435-713-4411 · WWW.POETICPOWER.COM

Copyright © 2008 by Creative Communication, Inc.
Printed in the United States of America

ISBN: 978-1-60050-206-4

FOREWORD

This edition of our poetry anthology is an important transition for Creative Communication. Since our beginning in 1993, we have called our contest "A Celebration of Young Poets." Having worked with student poets for over 15 years, we realized that the writers who have been accepted to be published are not "young" poets. They are poets. Young or old, they are writers who have proven their worth as poets. These are the poets we celebrate.

We also start this year with a new cover for the anthologies. We are excited about this new look and our new logo of a hand releasing stars. Our logo can represent different things. It could be a teacher or mentor releasing a writer to the world through our publication. It could represent the fact that the stars are limitless and these writers are just starting to shine with their potential. We have become the starting point for thousands of writers and we hope each poet continues to make writing a part of their lives.

What is recorded between these pages is unique. It exists nowhere else in the world and is now recorded forever. Take the time to read what these poets have shared. A part of themselves and their world exists in each poem. Savor it. Enjoy.

Sincerely,
Thomas Kenne Worthen, Ph.D.
Editor
Creative Communication

WRITING CONTESTS!

Enter our next POETRY contest!
Enter our next ESSAY contest!

Why should I enter?
Win prizes and get published! Each year thousands of dollars in prizes are awarded in each region and tens of thousands of dollars in prizes are awarded throughout North America. The top writers in each division receive a monetary award and a free book that includes their published poem or essay. Entries of merit are also selected to be published in our anthology.

Who may enter?
There are four divisions in the poetry and essay contests. The divisions are grades K-3, 4-6, 7-9, and 10-12.

What is needed to enter the contest?
To enter the poetry contest send in one original poem, 21 lines or less. To enter the essay contest send in one original essay, 250 words or less, on any topic. Each entry must include the student's name, grade, address, city, state, and zip code, and the student's school name and school address. Students who include their teacher's name may help the teacher qualify for a free copy of the anthology.

How do I enter?
Enter a poem online at:
www.poeticpower.com
or
Mail your poem to:
   Poetry Contest
   1488 North 200 West
   Logan, UT 84341

Enter an essay online at:
www.studentessaycontest.com
or
Mail your essay to:
   Essay Contest
   1488 North 200 West
   Logan, UT 84341

When is the deadline?
Poetry contest deadlines are December 4th, April 7th, and August 18th. Essay contest deadlines are October 15th, February 17th, and July 15th. You can enter each contest, however, send only one poem or essay for each contest deadline.

Are there benefits for my school?
Yes. We award $15,000 each year in grants to help with Language Arts programs. Schools qualify to apply for a grant by having a large number of entries of which over fifty percent are accepted for publication. This typically tends to be about 15 accepted entries.

Are there benefits for my teacher?
Yes. Teachers with five or more students accepted to be published receive a free anthology that includes their students' writing.

For more information please go to our website at **www.poeticpower.com**, email us at editor@poeticpower.com or call 435-713-4411.

TABLE OF CONTENTS

Spring 2008 Poetic Achievement Honor Schools

* Teachers who had fifteen or more poets accepted to be published

The following schools are recognized as receiving a "Poetic Achievement Award." This award is given to schools who have a large number of entries of which over fifty percent are accepted for publication. With hundreds of schools entering our contest, only a small percent of these schools are honored with this award. The purpose of this award is to recognize schools with excellent Language Arts programs. This award qualifies these schools to receive a complimentary copy of this anthology. In addition, these schools are eligible to apply for a Creative Communication Language Arts Grant. Grants of two hundred and fifty dollars each are awarded to further develop writing in our schools.

Abraham Lincoln High School
San Francisco
Elizabeth N. Raupers*

Almond Tree Middle School
Delano
S. Barkley*
Marla Dike
Ms. Gaines*
Karen Mayberry*
Martina Salas
Mrs. Taylor

Bradshaw Christian High School
Sacramento
Ric Reyes*

Calaveras Hills High School
Milpitas
Karen Brown*

Challenger School – Ardenwood
Newark
Rebecca Arnold*

Chino Valley Christian Schools
Chino
Cindy Byrne*

Citrus Hills Intermediate School
Corona
Jennifer Fleuette*
Mrs. Lenning
Mary Maiden-Umbarger

Corpus Christi School
San Francisco
Theodore R. Langlais*
Sr. Lucia Yuen

EV Cain Middle School
Auburn
Laurel McFarland*

Fountain Valley High School
Fountain Valley
Sara LaFramboise
Patty Muñoz*

Henry T Gage Middle School
Huntington Park
Petra Jones*

Holy Family Catholic School
Citrus Heights
Sherry Moniz*
Mrs. Murray*

Joan MacQueen Middle School
Alpine
LeeAnn Jones*
Bridget Wetton

John Adams Middle School
Los Angeles
Linda Bolibaugh*

La Joya Middle School
Visalia
Debbie Patton*

Las Flores Middle School
Las Flores
Laurie Cummings*
Lisa Hoover
Justine Lang

Linfield Christian School
Temecula
Pat Heckert*
Desirae Jesse
Dr. Ruth Young

Lucerne Valley Jr/Sr High School
Lucerne Valley
Cindy Lazenby
Linda Schlenz

Madrona Middle School
Torrance
Suzan Harper*
Colleen Poelvoorde*

Martin Murphy Middle School
San Jose
Joan Maguire*

Monte Vista Christian School
Watsonville
Janice Renard*

Our Lady of the Rosary School
Paramount
Sr. Ellen Mary Conefrey*

Palm Desert Middle School
Palm Desert
Julie Davis
Nanette Davis-Kirchhevel
Kristin Wagner*

Redlands Sr High School
Redlands
Mr. Murguia*

Richland Jr High School
Shafter
Mrs. Carson-Verrell*

Rolling Hills Country Day School
Rolling Hills Estates
Debby Corette*
Peggy Johns-Campbell*

Sacred Heart School
Saratoga
Heidi Giammona*

Santa Rosa Technology Magnet School
Camarillo
Michelle Bennett*

Sarah McGarvin Intermediate School
Westminster
Cindy Bowers*
Jasmine Chang*

Shadow Hills Intermediate School
Palmdale
Gerald Farrell*

Sierra Vista High School
Baldwin Park
Ted Meyer*

South Tahoe Middle School
South Lake Tahoe
Ms. Songer*

St Alphonsus School
Los Angeles
Margaret Kirby*

St Barbara School
   Santa Ana
      Rhona England*
      Mrs. Walsh

St Ferdinand Elementary School
   San Fernando
      Alicia Ramirez*

St Francis High School
   La Canada
      Rudy Trujillo*

St Hilary Elementary School
   Pico Rivera
      Monica Mendoza*

St Hilary School
   Tiburon
      Linda Lukas*

St Joan of Arc School
   Los Angeles
      Emili Dagher*
      Mrs. Mackanic*

St Joseph's School of the Sacred Heart
   Atherton
      Nitza Agam*
      Michele Turchetti

St Mary of Assumption School
   Santa Maria
      Ellen Muldoon*

St Mary's School
   El Centro
      Dora Barraza*

St Patrick Parish School
   Carlsbad
      John Acquarelli*

St Raphael School
   Santa Barbara
      Barbara Malvinni*
      Diane McClenathen*

St Sebastian School
   Los Angeles
      Ms. Rucker*

St Vincent Elementary School
   Los Angeles
      Ms. Weyek*

Tenaya Middle School
   Fresno
      Marie Meyer*

The Mirman School
   Los Angeles
      Wendy Samson*
      Jane Shimotsu*

Tierra Linda Middle School
   San Carlos
      Jill Nida
      Jorge Zaiden*

Valley Christian High School
   San Jose
      Judy Marc*
      Alexis Reichow*

Valley Oak Middle School
   Visalia
      Serina Richert*

Westview High School
   San Diego
      Catherine Dow*

Wilder's Preparatory Academy
   Inglewood
      Tonya Humes*
      Mrs. Lydon
      Mrs. McGee
      Ms. Modi

Language Arts
Grant Recipients
2007-2008

After receiving a "Poetic Achievement Award" schools are encouraged to apply for a Creative Communication Language Arts Grant. The following is a list of schools who received a two hundred and fifty dollar grant for the 2007-2008 school year.

Acadamie DaVinci, Dunedin, FL
Altamont Elementary School, Altamont, KS
Belle Valley South School, Belleville, IL
Bose Elementary School, Kenosha, WI
Brittany Hill Middle School, Blue Springs, MO
Carver Jr High School, Spartanburg, SC
Cave City Elementary School, Cave City, AR
Central Elementary School, Iron Mountain, MI
Challenger K8 School of Science and Mathematics, Spring Hill, FL
Columbus Middle School, Columbus, MT
Cypress Christian School, Houston, TX
Deer River High School, Deer River, MN
Deweyville Middle School, Deweyville, TX
Four Peaks Elementary School, Fountain Hills, AZ
Fox Chase School, Philadelphia, PA
Fox Creek High School, North Augusta, SC
Grandview Alternative School, Grandview, MO
Hillcrest Elementary School, Lawrence, KS
Holbrook School, Holden, ME
Houston Middle School, Germantown, TN
Independence High School, Elko, NV
International College Preparatory Academy, Cincinnati, OH
John Bowne High School, Flushing, NY
Lorain County Joint Vocational School, Oberlin, OH
Merritt Secondary School, Merritt, BC
Midway Covenant Christian School, Powder Springs, GA
Muir Middle School, Milford, MI
Northlake Christian School, Covington, LA
Northwood Elementary School, Hilton, NY
Place Middle School, Denver, CO
Public School 124, South Ozone Park, NY

Language Arts Grant Winners cont.

Public School 219 Kennedy King, Brooklyn, NY
Rolling Hills Elementary School, San Diego, CA
St Anthony's School, Streator, IL
St Joan Of Arc School, Library, PA
St Joseph Catholic School, York, NE
St Joseph School-Fullerton, Baltimore, MD
St Monica Elementary School, Mishawaka, IN
St Peter Celestine Catholic School, Cherry Hill, NJ
Strasburg High School, Strasburg, VA
Stratton Elementary School, Stratton, ME
Tom Thomson Public School, Burlington, ON
Tremont Elementary School, Tremont, IL
Warren Elementary School, Warren, OR
Webster Elementary School, Hazel Park, MI
West Woods Elementary School, Arvada, CO
West Woods Upper Elementary School, Farmington, CT
White Pine Middle School, Richmond, UT
Winona Elementary School, Winona, TX
Wissahickon Charter School, Philadelphia, PA
Wood County Christian School, Williamstown, WV
Wray High School, Wray, CO

Grades 10-11-12

Top Poem Grades 10-11-12

Inspiration

Pictures of the world untraveled
Laughing as I come unraveled
Painting 'til the morning dawn
Let light in with curtains drawn
Brown and orange trees of fall
Album pictures when I was small
Acts of kindness from a smiling face
Feeling an old friend's embrace
Hearing a new favorite song
Feeling a sense that we belong
Salty foam on ocean shore
New beginning with an open door
Rainy days give freedom to dance
Being given a second chance
Old couples wearing matching sweaters
'Thinking of you' written on letters
Babies first steps, a mother's surprise
A look of desire in a true love's eyes
Inspiration of moments past
Allow memory to longer last

Amanda Deering, Grade 11
Notre Dame High School

Top Poem Grades 10-11-12

Children of the Cosmos

Sun, light of Earth, gives life's mother his hands,
But desert, is harsh, so he scorches its sands.
Ocean, water's empress, with Earth, she resides,
While moon, slowly waltzes, and changes her tides.
The stars in the night, twinkling ever so lightly,
Moon, right beside them, shines ever more brightly.
Wind, being gentle, with soothing kind breeze,
Then shifts to the whirlwinds, and tears down the trees.
White clouds ever silent, so blissfully drift,
Beneath the grand sky, as they shelter the rift.
Dark clouds call forth rain, giving water, and life,
With thunder, and lightning, who bring pain and strife.
Children of the cosmos; sun, moon, and rain,
Stars, Earth, and whirlwinds, bring both joy and pain,
Thunder and lightning, clouds, ocean, sky,
To dear Mother Earth, they all share a tie.
Children of the cosmos, we watch as they dance,
And forever life shows us, their endless romance.

Nathan Eroles, Grade 10
Pacific Coast High School

Top Poem Grades 10-11-12

My Favorite Place

Through blankets of dripping leaves I fall,
Hearing dancing tambourines.
As ghosts whisper their secrets all;
Echoes wielding in my dreams.
A dance becomes my nightly prayer, in covers warmly bound,
And I am gone from dusk to dusk, in stories tightly wound.
Night and day, night and day,
In my forest of beige and blue
Where I have seen both sun and moon together;
Have taken the forest path all the way through.
From mountainsides I've jumped without fear, landing swiftly on the ground,
And have listened to the wolves call out their names, marveling at the sound.
In mansions hidden deep in secret, have immortals come to rest,
Their eyes scanning reverently over dark skies, their eyes I love the best.
Lost in a world of small magnitude, do the adventures write themselves away,
In a journal kept beside my bed, do I make it clear that they will stay.
With devotion do I sleep so sound, and wake to write the tale,
Of every new place I visit each night, and each night I never fail.
My favorite place, my blanket of leaves, the dreams of which I speak,
Are all found in one quick blink, the moment I fall asleep.

Neda Hawkins, Grade 12
Malibu High School

Top Poem Grades 10-11-12

Autumn

The crisp, chilly weather
Marks the end of summer
Autumn is imminent

Leaves that once embodied a vivid green hue
Turn red, orange, brown, and yellow
An intermixture of vivacious and dull pigments
Which beautify the tranquil landscape

Leaves waver down surreptitiously
One after another, in emulation of each other
Gusts of wind blow periodically
Leaving the earth littered with leaves

Trees are bare and exposed
Casting a silhouette upon the sidewalk
Weeping at their unappealing appearance

Autumn is the cycle of life
The season transitions as time progresses
It reposes when winter approaches
It begins once summer ends
And the perpetual cycle continues

Rebecca Liu, Grade 10
South Pasadena Sr High School

Top Poem Grades 10-11-12

Once

Once we ran in this meadow
Caught ladybugs
Fell and rolled in the sweet knee-high grass
And laughed at a hundred jokes only we two knew.
Once we climbed these trees
At first timidly, then with careless ease
Swung up to our high perches
And surveyed the whole world.
From that vantage
The sky was so big and bright and blue it hurt our eyes.

Now I walk the meadow alone
Ankle-deep weeds waving at my feet
Silent with thought on laughter that's gone.
Saplings have surrounded our climbing trees
And ivy grown to ensnare wanderers' feet.
I lay a hand where I used to perch on high.
So small! How did they bear our weight?
Here in the grove of memory
Where once two little ones played and laughed
An adult stands alone, silent and somber.
The sky from here is still the bluest thing I've ever seen.

Kathryn Mogk, Grade 10
Henry Sr High School

Top Poem Grades 10-11-12

The Great Mourner

As in my childhood days I used to recall,
    Azure leaves descending upon my dainty head.
        The transient wind cracking my breath into feathers,
            As celestial snow drops like cotton in air,
The sea of white kneels before my feet,
    With evergreens surrounding me juxtaposed,
        And grandfather mountains in demure sleep.
I dance to this whimsical fantasy
    Where rich green leaves taste of mints,
        Spitting tongues of fire onto the rustling branches.
While tundra tigers chase forest sprites exuberantly,
    For hours while the joyous mermaids,
        Arise to laud in obsequious cheer,
Though tortured by frostbite and icy water,
    I played happily until that fateful day.
        'Til adolescence had shone its bearing teeth,
A bittersweet fate of destiny,
    My struggles having now lost their way,
        I wished to return back to that place,
            But I know these friends have gone away.

Thomas Nguyen, Grade 10
St. Michael's College Preparatory School

Top Poem Grades 10-11-12

The Painting

She lay collapsed in the corner
A beautiful face once worth seeing
Now cracks outlined her dusty face and the vibrant color was beginning to fade
She was my father's only love
And I, his first-born creation
Often sat and watched him as he sculpted her triangle nose,
Her sparkling eyes, her subtle smile hidden behind the strands of flowing red hair
She seemed to be everything I was not
So I would dress in white and pull my dangling hair across my face
I wanted to be loved, to be held, to be cared for
Father died silent and submissive, fading away like the wind blowing across his canvases
Holding my hand as he took his last breath
I collected his paintings
Mountains and oceans, flowers and trees, and the familiar face of the girl on the swing
Though tattered and worn, the scene captured a moment long forgotten
And as I picked up the portrait I recognized familiar writing through the layered dust
"With what I could not say in words — I painted
With the love I could not share — I give to you now
My first creation, my only love"
And as I outlined the heart of her innocent face and graced my own recognizable dimple
I suddenly realized that she, was me

Lauren Penticuff, Grade 12
University High School

Top Poem Grades 10-11-12

Rain

I hear a melody, in the rain,
A gentle, soothing sound.
The droplets pitter-patter
As they softly hit the ground.

And as I listen from within
My peaceful domicile,
Memories flood my heart with joy
And I cannot help but smile.

Raindrops, beating, growing louder,
Rage inside my head.
I long to join their party — No —
I should stay warm instead.

But their calls are far too great
To even consider resistance.
I abandon my blanket, run outside,
And dance off into the distance.

Alexandra Perry, Grade 11
Valley Christian High School

Top Poem Grades 10-11-12

Universal Language

It runs through your body,
Bends into a shot of adrenaline,
Before you know it, it has you moving,
At the moment it takes you to a much better place,
Is this a new drug?
Most days when you are stressed it relieves your pain.

It is what bonds us together,
Much more than just body language,
One's diversity makes no difference to others,
An instant and you are in another world where there are
No rules, no obligations, no gravity
A place where there is no such thing as problems.

It is a never-ending resource,
A resource that is as important as water,
Unlimited like the air in your lungs,
I feel it is the bread of every day.

It is the language everyone uses,
No need for words,
Use the rhythm in you,
It is what we call music.

Edwin Salgado, Grade 10
Sierra Vista High School

Top Poem Grades 10-11-12

What Matters Most

The road to life, much like the night
Dimly lit by the moon
You can't be too sure if the path ahead
Will bring you from the gloom

The stars above give you hope
In the darkest of the times
They may be small but band together
To make the skies sublime

Though the stars may light the sky
The glow down here is dim
You'll need some strength to make it through
Else hope dangles on a limb

And there is a hand that warms your soul
When strength is at its end
It points to the stars to renew your hope
For in darkness, you need a friend

Melissa Walters, Grade 11
Ukiah High School

I'll Be Waiting

We can stay together
You can go on with your life
You can do what you do
I do my thing.

When you're ready to settle down
I'll be here, waiting for you
Meantime I'll remember,
The memories we had together.

Sheila Ruiz, Grade 10
Sierra Vista High School

Tried to Write It

I tried writing your name in the sky
The wind blew is away.
I tried writing your name in the sand
The waves washed it away.
At least I have your love in my heart
Where it will always stay.
I love you.

Bobby Merrick, Grade 11
Prospect Continuation High School

wiping tables with songs

life ain't that simple.
your brows stitch thin
and fine. oily tips lay

flat like plains, where
as a girl, you sang
steep sopranos and climbed. now mild
you tie aprons with crows
feet, when you grin
taut and tell:

"life
ain't simple, girl.
it ain't.
it ain't."

Ou Rowen Jin, Grade 12
Washington High School

Done

Done lying to ourselves
To the people we care about
To everyone that surrounds us.
Done.
Time to take the mask off
Reveal who we really are
Show our true identities.
Done.
Starting over
A new beginning
A different way of life.

Iris I. Zelaya, Grade 11
Wilson High School

That Old Building in the Future

I stand here with my old feet stuck
    on this broken cement
                    Waiting alone
For my own death
Those buildings in the background that spring to life
       Barely knowing how to walk the wobbles of life
    And yet how I must stand pretty for my little strife
          Waiting for *the man* and his knife
To cut my breath within the life, I stagger through
      Yet, they stand tall in the face of it too
    But here I am, within in the few
         Next to my friend's grave

        He too was as old as I, but I shall not forget
    His little company of silence between
      As we were both glorious and keen
Oh! How I wish I was still seen that time of so heavenly
      By the same little children that sat at my window
        As they chase, play, and follow
Oh! How it grows deep inside me, that immense black sorrow
    I take a sigh — I can hear the bulldozers coming
    My *death* is imminent

Charles Cruz, Grade 10
Helix High School

Summer

A time for a kid to let loose, have fun,
  and not worry about school.
A time when there is always sun,
  and the weather is never too cool.
A time to relax at home during the day,
  but stay out with friends all night.
A time to go to the beach and play,
  or go to an amusement park to get a good fright.
Summer is an amazing season where kids don't have a care in their mind,
  we can sleep all day and have no worries to find.

Andrea Bumbaca, Grade 10
Notre Dame High School

My Life I Lead

The life I lead isn't the life people see.
When time comes I will have to pay,
Because statistics say I will go away,
To prison or end up in a hearse before my 21st birthday.
The law wants me to play by their rules,
But if I do I'm gonna' lose the duel.
They don't understand that guns and knives save my life.
The county don't like me because what I speak and feel is real.
They say my money is ill-gotten,
And they'd rather have me starve on my back in a coffin.
When I'm free people claim I'm a menace to society.
If you're not white in this county, you're automatically a target.
Never forget they're quick to put you in a cell, lock it and throw away the key.
That is why this is the life I lead.

Jordan Pepper, Grade 10
Crossroads School

Shadowed Sky, Hidden Highway
Sunset penetrates a shadowed sky,
Figures of darkness soon disappear
Trees sway in the north wind,
What darkness hides, light cannot reach,
The lone highway emerges into view,
The view of a dream, standing tall and proud,
So many of us do not dare to believe,
For it is this highway we seek,
To balance our lives hidden in shadow.

Hunter Kennelly, Grade 10
Helix High School

Best Friends
Through the tears and the laughs
You have always been there by my side.
You're the sister I never had
And the friend I always wanted.
Our deepest secrets and silliest moments
Are something only we will ever understand.
When the whole world seems to turn it's back on me,
I know I can look next to me and see your smiling face.
In the darkest moments of my life
You are the light at the end of the tunnel,
Always showing me the way.
Our late night talks and ice cream socials
Never get old to me.
But most of all,
Your loyalty and love is what has got us through the years.
You're my confidante, my anchor, my other half,
My best friend.

Alexandra Guerrero, Grade 12
Linfield Christian School

The Flag Fluttered in the Deep Red Sky
Beyond the translucent wall,
Fashioned with aged red tints of contempt
Lays a faded face in wait
With likeness to you, to me
Who are we to blame?

Why, we ask, are their faces the same?
Their colours may fade to a different grey
But this guise hides no weary eyes, no bleeding thoughts.
Worn by authority, to fight, we willingly do
For glory? For power? Honor?
We say we are patriots. Unceasingly.
Who are we to blame?

We lay these lives down, this costly carpet
For these angry leaders. We sigh.
If walls were permeable, we see, we learn, we live.

I wait for the forlorn end in vain
Who are we to blame?

Cora Chong, Grade 10
El Segundo High School

The Castle in the Sky
You've been doing this all your life.
Amidst your pain and all your strife.
And since you have no wings to fly.
You've been looking for the castle in the sky.
All your friends fell to the ground.
Their bodies piled in a mound.
Watch their souls burn in the pyre.
And at its peak you'll find your desire.
You see the castle in the sky.
You see it's ten-thousand miles high.
Your path isn't long enough right now.
So stand yourself and make your vow.
You need more souls to build your path.
So even you can do the math.
And if your friends must provide the way.
Keep them close so they will stay.
Their purpose had been defined.
Ever since the moment your destinies intertwined.
Keep on going your time is nigh.
To reach the castle in the sky.

Lincoln Mitchell, Grade 10
St Francis High School

Lonely Birthday
Dancing lights,
spin in the twilight lit night.
Gorgeous ornaments,
adorn the simplistic elegance of the house.
Fancy preparations,
the food piled up high.
Presents presents!
stacked in every corner.
Friends galore,
special attention on one person.
Loving feeling,
other's let you know they care.
Soft music,
accompanies the pacifying night.
Endless joy,
make this last.

And with that finished, she opens her eyes,
and finishes the traditional process,
blowing out that one candle.
Happy birthday to me.

Claire Yee, Grade 10
American High School

Ode to Sleep
Oh sleep you are what I love to do.
In the night and in the day.
When I sleep I dream and I see the peace always in my sleep.
Oh sleeping is a time where I can rest and think about life.

Michael Rosiles, Grade 12
El Camino High School

The Fat Lady Gave Me a Big Fat "F"

The fat lady waddles toward me,
With the paper in her hand,
With red marks all over it,
Bad news certain to be.

I see her coming closer,
Until she is next to me,
She slams the paper on my desk,
And my heart begins to beat.

I flip it over and there it is,
A clear message of what I've missed,
Like the cow murdered by the wolf,
And dragged across the field,
Crimson red is everywhere,
On this little piece of paper.

The wolf is gone, the cow lies still,
Motionless with his eyes wide open,
On the paper is a big fat F,
Centered and in plain view.

The farmer laments over his dead friend,
While the fat lady waddles away.
Raymond Ngu, Grade 10
Abraham Lincoln High School

Passionate Ruby

Passion
Burns like a ruby's fire
A glistening treasure
Shining light in jubilant pupils
Adoring, radiant;
Enlivens
Souls in flames
Until the bittersweet farewell.
Danielle Maddix, Grade 12
St Joseph Notre Dame High School

Poetry

Defines existence
And the world
It lies within our souls

It exists in our life
It's in our words
It's in our music

We use it to celebrate
We use it to heal
We use it to mourn

Poetry exists in us
And we exist in poetry
Trevor Andrews, Grade 12
San Lorenzo Valley High School

Havoc and Thrills

My world is full of havoc and thrills,
My world is full of flash and dollar bills.

Unfortunately this is where I live,
My world takes until there is nothing left to give.

My world is a world full of lives and deaths,
My world makes you think…
You will only make it if you are the best.

My world makes you always want to give up,
The tricks and persuasions make you think that there is no luck.

But you need to remember that we have the gift of FREE WILL,
And you don't have to buy into the havoc and thrills.
Charlotte Ross, Grade 11
Jack Weaver School

Love at Its Best

I had a friend who was a real bathing beauty
A casualty in every lady killer's eyes
Heartsick and thrown over and she comes to me with her latest tragedies
Over and over and each time she was surprised
The kisses from Judas from every desire of her heart
Left her more and more skeptical of each of her sweethearts
Then came more cadets that flew by night that made her mean
Sad for her, mad for her, she gave them gorgeous dreams
So typical and colorful she makes both the words rhyme
She can still be a catastrophe and an epiphany at the same time
Holly Lyons, Grade 11
JSerra Catholic High School

Fight the Fight

The wind licks at my back like a frightening scream
I feel the eyes of death looking at me like the unblinking light of the moon
I know now what I must do

I ought to pull my socks up
Get out of my funk
I cannot beat something I cannot touch
What must I do to wrestle with the dark?

I must have the heart of a lion!

The strength of a falling boulder
The courage of a single mother trying to keep her head above water
The wit of a slam poet

Yet life is not fair

I am not as open as a mountain pass
I am not as strong as an iron gate

To succeed, I must metaphor the metaphor
Matthew Jekowsky, Grade 12
The Marin School

She

She looked to be quite old
Ancient, thick, and dense,
Yet the sun shone on her
In an unnatural and peculiarly wrong way.

She has seen ending.
All the loss and pain she has felt,
She feels it every day
She can remember each loss.

There is no replacing those gone
Sisters and sons, brothers and husbands,
Taken at the hands of another,
And they left her as the sole witness.

We must remember them
If not for them, then for her sake.

Elena Kohn, Grade 12
Redlands Sr High School

Love

I love it when you whisper in my ear
because you always seem to know
exactly what I want to hear
to make me grin and glow

I love hugging you
because you're always warm
I love everything you do
because you don't conform

I love it when we kiss
because you hold me tight
and there's so much that I miss
when you leave my sight

It's not that I've never loved before
It's just that I've never loved anyone more

Nicole Stephenson, Grade 12
Redlands Sr High School

Presents

Long after children placed milk and cookies
For Santa and echoes of *Jingle Bells* faded,
A plump bunny, fearful of Holiday lights,
Hopped up icy steps. she nestled on the mat
Of a house with no wreath or flashing bulbs.

Day broke to opened gifts, save in one home
Where an old man spending Christmas alone,
Peered out to view bundles of fluff, snuggling.
As the new mother kissed each with her nose,
His wise lips grinned at the best present of all.

Sara Gambord, Grade 11
Saratoga High School

Far Away

They seemed far away.
Too far,
Out of reach,
Almost obsolete.
"Where did they go?" I asked my mother.
And she replied, "Far away."
I looked out my window.
Far away was like the mountain in the distance.
Far away was like the sun and the moon.
Far away was…not near me.
They were gone,
They were forever gone.

Why are people taken away when you need them the most?
No one can answer that.
Because you'll always need them.
They'll always be needed the most, to you that is,
To someone else, they were strangers walking on the sidewalk.
To you, they were life.

Amber McIntire, Grade 10
Gridley High School

When You

When you look at me what do you see
Do you truly see me or what you want me to be
When I catch your eye what are you thinking
Do you think about me
And what we could be
We tried this game twice but three times the charm
I know I hurt you but I'm better than before
When my eyes catch your gaze
it feels like a daze
I'm almost amazed
By the way I feel for you
I like you but afraid to make the first move
So I sit back and watch you from afar
It seems this "we" will never be
I write this out for eyes to see
These feelings are weird they grow strong they grow weak
I guess it's better to wait and not speak

Tonie Oglesby, Grade 11
Los Angeles Adventist Academy

Gateway to Heaven

Dance, it consumes my body as I lead with my soul.
It is the driving force that keeps me whole.
My fears and worries all fade away,
As I release the storms of life I face today.
I use my movements to cast these storms
And cry to myself releasing life's harm.
No one can hear my cry or see my pain,
So I dance to my own beat to keep me sane.
Completely fulfilled I dance through life,
Confusing by day but tranquil by night.

Celestine Denson, Grade 12
Los Angeles County High School-Arts School

Far Away

Loneliness is a curse
a way to a great depression
brought upon us
when we choose to live
a life that brings pain.
Hurtful it is
like burning flames
and small sharp tacks
or little blades.
Painful to the mind
and deadly to the heart
gloomy and dark,
a cold alleyway
away from all light
no where near warmth,
far away from home.

Mesang Clayborne, Grade 11
Summit High School

Us

Our limiting bodies
Souls entombed
Trapped forever
A broken womb

Our consciences dictating
Our souls inside
Giving birth
To a stream of lies

For it is spoken
Gone always unheard
So try to embrace it
Maybe let forth a word

Matthew Hemphill, Grade 10
Fall River Jr/Sr High School

The Fruits of the Spirit

Love bursts into a hospital,
Where a brand new baby is born.
Peace flows into a funeral home,
Where a death is being mourned.
Patience is stuck in a traffic jam
That seems backed up for miles.
Kindness is on a face,
With a sweet old woman's smile.
Gentleness is holding a child,
Caught within affliction.
Self-control is hidden,
Inside a man with an addiction.
Goodness and Joy are clearly heard,
From the church across the street.
Faithfulness is newly found,
As a lost man kneels at Jesus' feet.

Aubrey Newton, Grade 10
Calvary Christian High School

To Another Land

My supple skin withered into a dried fruit perched on a tree.
Eyes like a deepened honey shifted into a color of a cloudy gray,
But still hold the horrors of the prison like a lock to its key.
I will tell the agonizing story today.
I took a ship and crossed many leagues to find a greater light,
Only to be shut down by men in black.
They stole my name, belongings, and my sight.
They threw me like a doll into a cramped shack.
Time passed until time was all I had.
I was an abandoned dog waiting to be picked up by a stranger.
I wrote my heart on the wall like a pad.
The Black Men asked me questions as if I was a danger.
But, surely, I couldn't be? I don't remember.
They finally let me breathe the crisp air after a fierce interrogation.
By the time I reached the land of light, it was late November.
I became revitalized, looking at the world with new admiration

Jacalyn Ho, Grade 10
Abraham Lincoln High School

Wishes

Do you ever wish you didn't have to go home?
Do you ever wish for a different life?
Do you wish to escape what you've been through?
All that's handed to you?

Is the weight on your shoulders pulling you down?
Slowly pulling you down?
As you twist the knob on the door, do you wish for something else?

Love? Appreciation? Is that what you ask for?
Look within and it will be looking back.

Suman Mattu, Grade 10
Gridley High School

Silver String

I've been told that always there is someone offering sweeter drinks;
Someone promising to keep them on a silver string.
Always there is something better, something grander.
Always there is something to look forward to.
But is that something really there?
Can life get better with no end in sight?
Are promises real?
Will sweeter things come with no end?
Reality says no —
But, I do believe
There is something grander than the things I see.
I've heard,
I've felt,
I've seen,
I've thought
I know of sweeter things to come.
It's the retrieval that is tricky.
To escape from the usual and indulge in the sweeter drinks,
Never ending on a silver string.

Mellissa Barton, Grade 10
Gridley High School

Nature's Beauty

Softly caressed by a crisp evening breeze,
I gaze upon the stars in the sky
as leaves sway in perpetual motion above me.
The calming depths of the mysterious forest
cast a spell on my mind
and I am suddenly smothered
by nothing more than the absence of light.

Perspiration seeps out my pores
like fresh dew on a morning rose.
Echoing throughout the vast forest,
my piercing cries are recognized
by no one other than the savage beasts,
which roam the unforgiving night.

It is a typical sight for highest of mountains,
as well as the smallest of even the most
delicate of flowers —
that of yet another victim
succumbing to the horrifying perils
of nature.

Tyler Uyehara, Grade 10
St Francis High School

Someone

Always there is someone promising to end suffering.
Someone offering sweeter drinks,
To bring an end to pain as if it were a dream.

Always there is someone who has a solution,
But you must look.

Always there is someone who will break your heart,
But then there will be someone to repair it.

Always there is someone who will help you after a fall,
Someone is always there.

Always there is someone to rely on, to lean on,
Someone who will help you through tough times.
Keeping dreams on a silver string.

That someone is you.

McKenna Cox, Grade 10
Gridley High School

Freckles

She has freckles about which I have heard her speak
Only once when we were drunk,
And even then she spoke with disdain.

I had meant to say 'trash' when
I told her one person's treasure is another person's treasure —
But she understood.

Will Mullaney, Grade 12
Albany High School

We Forget

Sometimes we forget — life is not just a reality,
It is a gift.
Sometimes we forget, and kill,
The innocent babies gifted with a soul, mind and will.
Sometimes we forget the lives of tiny children,
And try to save the diminishing whale population.
Sometimes we forget — murder is a choice,
Children are a gift to be received or rejected.
Sometimes we forget — a mother on the operating table,
Glimpses her stillborn baby.
Sometimes we forget — in a building not far away,
Another gift was thrown away.
Sometimes we forget — choices have consequences,
Guilt and sorrow come swiftly and never depart.
Sometimes we forget — life is precious,
Life is a gift.

Marilla DiNatale, Grade 10
Legacy Academy

Tick, Tock

"Tick, tock," goes the clock.
Will class never end?
I sit and stare and stare and stare.
I want to scream, but wouldn't dare.

"Tick, tock," goes the clock.
This is UNBELIEVABLY dire!
The teacher's voice drones on and on.
Will she *never* tire?!

"Tick, tock," goes the clock.
It reads "11:59."
"Just 37 seconds left,"
I tell that hungry stomach of mine.

"Tick, tock," goes the clock.
Lunch time's excitement I can hardly bear.
Ten more seconds,
And I'll be there.

"Ring-ding-ding," goes the bell.
Run!!!
'Cuz man, have I got gossip to tell!

Whitney Brown, Grade 10
Calvary Chapel Christian School

Waves

Waves are much like life, crashing on the beach.
They rise, and then they break,
Much as life has its ups and downs.
They always crash on the sand,
Yet they retrace their steps
And form into magnificent waves again.

Greg Thompson, Grade 10
St Francis High School

My Nation

My nation was where I was born, and I will die for my nation wrapped up in the red, white, and the blue flag. My dog tag hung around my neck and I am in my USMC suit, my gun on my side. They gave me my freedom, my family, my school I found love in my nation to be in the hall of fame. If it means I will die so my little brother and sister and my baby girl can grow up without having to watch what they say to people so we don't have to be slaves to some other nation. I came into this world and people cried. Now I hope they will cry when I leave this world. Then enter those golden gates in my USMC suit with my flag hung over one of my shoulders with my dog tags shinier than ever. With my sword on my side and everyone will cry when I come I will be with all the rest of the people who died for their nation The United States.

Kenneth C. Pavlovich, Grade 11
Riverside County High School

My Love

Feelings of love, sadness, and happiness flow deeply between us.
There are billions of words that express the way I feel, who you are, why we're here, what we are.
I love you, I care about every beautiful word that comes out of your mouth.
Your voice is like the sweet songs of birds in spring. Your beauty is unmatched to anything on Earth.
The things you say are like music to my love stricken ears. You're the best thing that God created.
You overwhelm me with joy and sadness.
Your eyes are like beautiful gems shining in the light and staring, piercing my heart with your love.
When we fight sadness strickens me to the point I can't go on. Seeing, hearing you're sad kills me slowly.
I'm giving you all my love.
You changed my live for the better.
I love you.

Izzy Zavala, Grade 10
Shasta High School

"Fifty Years Ago"

The sun has risen once again.
It's time for me to work in the rice fields,
I remember the days when I was here as a young and spirited teenager
When I was younger, I could have cultivated a lot more than I could nowadays.
Working days and nights was not a problem for me when I was younger,
but as time goes on, my bones grow weaker and my arms tire out faster,
I hope that my kids will grow big and strong.
For when my time is up, they can take over working in the rice fields,
Or perhaps they will find a better life in America.
For I have heard of a land that has gold paving its streets,
I have once heard of this land
Anyone who has lived there called it the "American Dream."
Where anyone can live, eat, and breathe this dream.
For this is where people can truly live as equals
I dream for a time when Chinese people can work as hard and get paid as much as Americans.
I dream for a future in which my kids and my grandkids will be able to get a good education and live a long and prosperous life.
But for now, all I can do is wait for the future to come and continue my work in the fields.
Hoping that one day, Chinese people have the courage and strength to take what is rightfully theirs in America.

Philip Su, Grade 10
Abraham Lincoln High School

Ups and Downs

As you cross over into heaven don't forget to look down and wave upon the sight of me as I wave right back for all the tears I've shed have come and gone but memories still linger on the smell, the smile, and your eyes. I will never forget the comfortness of your gentle eyes, and the sweetness of your smile. Even though your spirit is gone, the memories will live on until I join you in the holy place of heaven until we meet again, when the crimson light fades the dark shadows of your face appear on my wall and memories begin to haunt my dreams of sad memories of the past. As strong as I may be the thoughts and feelings get to me over time and the wound never heals.

Emily Martinez, Grade 10
Shoreline Independent Study

Poet's Despair

What do I have to do with this?
This thing is such a bore.
Each thought I've had has been dismissed.
This is like none before.

I cannot think of anything.
Why do you mock me so!
This white sheet is a scary thing;
It's still as pale as snow!

I feel like I'm about to faint.
I am so deathly weak.
Another way to work, there ain't.
The outlook sure seems bleak.

I think my work is finally done.
Two lines are what remains.
I do not think that this was fun,
But I feel this was not in vain.

James Krasner, Grade 10
St Francis High School

Safe and Secure

A burning light, a burning plan,
Safe and secure in the palm of His hand.
Safe and secure in the palm of His hand,
Leading us on to the Promised Land.
Expedition of the faithful and few,
Journey to the land of the brave and the true.
A healing touch, a healing hand,
Safe and secure in the palm of His hand.
Make a stand for the right command,
Safe and secure in the palm of His hand.
Glory and honor go to His name,
Healing the blind, the sick, the lame.
Safe and secure in the palm of His hand.
Leading His child through dangerous land
Leading His child with a loving hand,
Safe and secure in the palm of His hand.
Bright North Star guiding us at night,
Keeping the way safe and bright.
Safe and secure in the palm of His hand.
Learning to trust, learning to care,
Safe and secure in the palm of His hand.

Julia Garcia, Grade 11
Heritage Christian School

The Way I Feel

The lights in my street
Are always on
But they can be
A little annoying to my heartbeat
The neighbors say, who cares they're free

Jerry Mendoza, Grade 10
Academic/Vocational Institute

Memory Lane

The kids in the street playing happily,
Going skinny-dipping in the river,
Singing Christmas carols beautifully,
And sledding quickly in sleds of cedar.

Running in their short pants through the small grass,
Playing hide-and-seek, perhaps even tag,
Running and pulling their wagons of brass,
But then having to wash them with a rag.

Studying English in the one-roomed school house,
Paying close attention to the teacher,
Chasing grey squirrels and maybe a mouse,
Around the church and around the preacher.

And when thinking back on the good-old days,
Many-a-time it's like I'm in a daze.

Ronald Radut, Grade 12
Redlands Sr High School

When I Die...

When I die
Even though I may not be alive
Don't let me see you cry
Yes I was happy to be alive
Love to see all of you
With the joy you held inside
Wish I would be there when things aren't all right
Embrace you with a touch of my hug
Look into your eyes and say things will brighten up
Wipe the empty tears that fall from those gorgeous eyes
When you need a helping hand don't feel alone
The touch of a cool breeze is to let you know it's me
When you feel like you can't budge from missing me
I will always send you a sign
To let you know my presence is still alive
I'm happier now
I'm in a place where I can finally be at ease
Nothing can bother me
Heaven is where I have to be
A soldier of God is the road I must lead.

Joanna Urratio, Grade 12
Options for Youth - Victorville 4

This Is My Letter to the Waves

This is my letter to the saves
That never broke for me —
The only thing I longed for —
With many marvelous dreams

Her power is devoted
To artists of the wave —
For awe of her — rad — surfer dudes —
Bring some waves — to me

Kelsey Byrd, Grade 11
Valley Christian High School

Tennis

Walking onto the court
Is like walking into an alternate universe
Where hours become minutes,
Obstacles spur new goals,
And failures inspire determination.
Cries of exhaustion and anguish
Echo through the air.
Internal embers ignite a massive inferno,
Sparked by passion,
Fueled by desire,
A desire to win.

Norman Xie, Grade 11
St Joseph Notre Dame High School

Open the Window

Open the window
And let out all of the sadness
The people being mad at me
Let out night school and crazy ex's
Let out trying to graduate

Open the window
To let in ones I love
All my friends, Julie and Aaron
Let education and my job expand
Let in the food I like

Open the window
I want my grandma back
I want a husband and kids
Let come in happiness
A house that's all mine

Now close the window
Leticia Mendoza, Grade 11
Prospect Continuation High School

Silent Fear

Lurking under your feet
Pitch black
Tickling your toes
No air

Glowing in the distance
Nibbling your fingers
Picking your hair
No air

Chills all over
Stinging your body
Noise of an unknown
No air

No air…
Samantha Chavez, Grade 12
Redlands Sr High School

Lady

I'll walk to the sun; see me burn
I'll keep walking; I'm alone
You're dancing to the moon; I'm eating up the sun
It's burning in my mouth; our souls are going south
Lady death awaits; I'm burning in my head
The perfect lady in my bed; your voice soothes my soul
I want you whole and all I'm keeping me in shame, perfect time for feeling lame
The heat is greater near you; the fire is hotter near you
I'll walk into the sun, alone; seems no more fun
I'm burning in my head; you're gone and having fun; I'll wait for your return
Your beauty is high by far; so am I
Your flame corrupts my mind; it leaves me like oh so blind
I'm eating up the sun; you and I are one
You are my girl, my only girl
Ruby, silver or gold; you're better than a pearl
Never seen eyes like yours, only in dreams
Your voice takes all souls; you and the fire; some heat makes you hotter
Sun and stars, deep fire; it's so nice; hotter than the stars stars of your shining eyes
Deeper than the sea; with you I roam free
I love lady flame; I love you lady shame
I love you in my mind; I love you lady beauty; love like yours is hard to find

Angel Sanchez, Grade 11
San Ysidro High School

War!

The pain in the eyes of a loved one
Caused by the stupidity of a selfish one.
Rapid bullets bring rapid deaths,
And leave the innocent ones with their final breath.
Day after day filled with sorrow,
Now the people must pray it will be better tomorrow.
Soldiers as monsters killing; only thinking of completing their evil task,
Makes me think of a question to ask.
What good does this killing do for anyone?
War!
What is it good for?

Justin Ballatore, Grade 10
South Pasadena Sr High School

North Korean Life

Living as a North Korean farmer is not very hard.
We work during the day and then at night gaze at the stars.
I have a hard working wife and five wonderful children.
Never had the thought of becoming Southern Korean.
We lived under Japanese rule but it was not so bad.
But over the years people like Kim Il Sung were getting mad.
Until one day Kim Il Sung came to town.
And turned everyone's smile into a frown.
He took wounded North Korea as if it was his own.
And killed many people who tried to stop him after Japan was overthrown.
Now my wife is dead and my sons have fled.
Now all my hard work like blood has been shed.
Living as a North Korean is very hard.
I never knew living here would tear my life apart.

John Park, Grade 10
Abraham Lincoln High School

One Long Nightmare

My life's a nightmare, I still can't believe it's true,
I pray so much, I might as well glue my hands.
The way I am being treated, I just can't understand.
People ignore and don't care,
About the positive things I achieve and do,
All because the color of my skin and the city I live in.
Hell they have put me through,
365 days and 365 nights.
I have been falsely imprisoned and violated for my rights.
Missing out on my teenage years, too angry to even shed tears.
Steadily missing my family.
For no reason these people can't stand me.
They want to see negative, but that will never happen.
Shoot! They wish I would.
Denying that they're prejudice,
But they don't want to see the good.
They got me feeling pain, every day is rain.
Can't even look me in the eyes because they feel ashamed.
Marquis Douglas is my name,
And I will continue praying for their hearts to change.

Marquis Douglas, Grade 12
Crossroads School

Until That Day

I want to hold your hand,
I want to rest my head on your shoulder,
As we could sing our emotions together
But we are separated by years,
"Love is patient," we say
To assure this could be true someday.
Forced to pretend,
Forced to keep silent,
Forced to think this is our end,
But inside we know the truth.
I would wait forever
Just to hold your hand,
Just to rest my head on your shoulder,
Just to say "hello."
We look up to this same night sky
And I know we're going to make this,
I will always wait here
Until that day.

Cachet Whitman, Grade 11
Valley Christian High School

There Is No Journey, Like High School

There is no journey, like high school,
To prepare us for college,
Nor any leaders, like a teacher,
Of helpful knowledge,
This road which the seekers take,
Without limits of mind,
How frugal is the adventure,
That bears the desired find.

CJ Standridge, Grade 11
Valley Christian High School

My Illusions

On my shoulders, hundred pound concrete bags,
On my feet, blisters and calluses.
In my stomach, bread digests from yesterday night,
but in my mind is the thought of my wife and children fed.
This was what I lived on, what I based my dreams upon,
that one day my family will live in the grandest house.
In all of Canton.
That unlike now, my children will have the education they need.
I remember the days when I would wake up
and decide that today would be the day where I
pretend that the concrete was gold,
my bitterness, sweetness instead.
That my feet does not hurt
and we live in a palace
and those thoughts have led me to where I am now,
Paradise.

Michelle Tang, Grade 10
Abraham Lincoln High School

Writer's Block

The clock on the wall keeps on tick-tick-ticking,
In a thunderous reminder time is slowly slipping.
The clock doesn't stop, even for one with writer's block.
My focus is on naught, save for this poem…or so I thought.
I tap the pen on the notebook in my lap,
But no ink spills forth, nor the words I know are in my head.
The muffled murmurs of a story on a distant TV,
Distract once again from this poetry.
I close my eyes, and sigghhh in frustration,
Hoping for some poetic inspiration.

Christina Garvin, Grade 11
St Bonaventure High School

From Land to the Sea

The land is like a kind mother
Carefully watching with a hawk's eye;
The sea is like a quiet king
Who never lets anything pass him by.

The land's rhythm is like a soloist
Quiet yet clearly heard;
The sea's tune is like a spring day,
Sprinkled with the tunes of a singing bird.

The land is infinite
The sea is forever
The land's design is like a simple picture
The sea's a bit more clever

The land has never known calm
The sea is its balm
As it ripples against the edge of danger,
Longing for the forgotten sight of a stranger.

Lucy Zheng, Grade 12
Redlands Sr High School

Was Once

In a room where memories drift
love and fantasy was once remained.
Stains of love were once placed
upon the bed that she laid.
No more were they one,
no more were they love.
Alone she was on the bed she laid upon.

Nights drift with bleak memories of you.
Rebecca Williams, Grade 11
Valley Christian High School

Shadow

Dreaming to feel
Forever stalking behind
Wishing to be real
A puppet bound
Forever mocking movements
Its master found
Put in a trance
Forever cursed to follow
Always shackled to this endless dance
Hiding away from light
Forever cast in shade
Its presence locked in eternal blight
Its world is bleak
Forever seeing what could be
Powerless and weak
Forever wishing to strive
Forever wishing to stay
Forever wishing to be alive
Forever the shadow
Eric Magsayo, Grade 11
Anderson W Clark Magnet High School

Wasting Away

I am wasting away.
Bones crumbling,
the pain elevating.
Sick in my bed,
my age makes me
close to dead.
So many wishes
floating in my head.
So many uncompleted tasks,
so many things I haven't done.
So, as I sit here
and this daydream passes,
A new one forms,
of me and my friends
living life to the fullest,
so that it isn't me wasting away,
daydreaming about the things
I should have done.
Meriel Blum, Grade 10
South Pasadena Sr High School

Matthew Xavier Garvey

I was the youngest of six.
Born in the Bronx, NY in 1928.
My parents came from Ireland looking for a better life,
Away from poverty.
Maybe that's why I started working so hard at an early age.
My first job was at the Yankee Stadium.
Popcorn, peanuts, crackerjacks anyone?
I've been working hard ever since.
In the army at 18, the first in my family to go to college.
Landed a corporate job which took me to many places,
Asia, Europe, South America, and Australia.
I raised seven wonderful girls and wanted to grow old with my beautiful wife.
Life didn't give us that much time to do that.
But I did a lot of living in 59 years.
December 18, 1928-September 11, 1988.

Alana Barrueto, Grade 10
Abraham Lincoln High School

My Inspiration

You are my inspiration, the one who pushes me through.
Everyone saw the bad in me but you saw the good.
You were there through thick and thin and you never gave in.
You are my heart who knows me within.
You are the one who believes in my dreams.
You are the one who believes me when I say it's not as bad as it seems.
You would do anything to make me smile.
I would do anything to talk to you even for a little while.
Then you grew sick but you said you were strong.
For once I thought you were wrong.
You were my grandmother and I love you.
I know God took you to heaven because he needs you.

Alexandra Garcia, Grade 12
Redlands Sr High School

Advice

To try and distinguish rich between poor is easy
Their characteristics give it away
Although we are all human
We are not the same
Challenging it is for her to merely work
And not ruin her nails
But not for her to have sown in a company
To be paid a misery and have sown herself away
And for him to have been eaten up by hunger
but for him to have merely touched the plate
So he can only have it as a decor for the thoughts of his fellow friends
But we are all people,
So we must not think ill of each other
She may be poor, she may be rich
He may be self centered and he may be caring
But so may be the case
We must learn from each other
And we must help each other
Because I remember once that you helped me.

Elaine Gutierrez, Grade 12
Yuba County Career Preparatory Charter School

Rain

Sitting alone in the dark of the night
Charcoal grey clouds closing in from all sides
Everyone left, running away in fright
Forgetting that I sat among the tides

Their feet palpitating in the distance
When suddenly the rain began to pour
Oblivious of my own existence
I ran through the rain along the cold shore

I wish the rain would wash away my fears
And fill my life to the brim with comfort
But it is simply the source of fake tears
And a variety of discomfort

Accompanied by cold winds and lightning
But deeper within is enlightening

Johana Lin, Grade 12
Redlands Sr High School

Living in China

Living in China, taking care of my kids
Having them realize of everything I did
Earning money with my husband at work
Although sometimes he may be a jerk
With his boss yelling at him for not doing a good job
I go home every day and start to sob
Feeling useless and weak
There's no one left to seek
Now I am coming to America for good
Living there for as long as I could
Don't know how long I will last
At least I've got great memories from the past

Judy Yin, Grade 10
Abraham Lincoln High School

Life

When the time comes,
The road will end and the sun will set for me.
I want no sadness and no tears,
Why cry for a soul that's free?
This is the life we live one chance for a dream,
Live it while you can one day we will live free!

We have that journey,
We all must take and each must go alone.
With memories that will never fade away.
Sadly, we all go through it and feel the pain
Wishing it could be easy enough for it to wash away.

It's all a part of life,
Live it and give up your look but never your soul.
Think of it as another step to home.

Erica Zambrano, Grade 11
Soquel High School

Families

Families,
You can't pick them but
You can always trust them
No matter what happens they are there
Even when you just can't bear anything
They teach you lessons, they get on your nerves
But they're always yours
Families
Some are big and some are small
But we still love them all
Stay together don't ever break apart
Because you'll be breaking too many hearts
Love them, cherish them
Tomorrow is not guaranteed
But you can always have your family's memories

Mercedes Hobbs-Hovda, Grade 11
Inderkum High School

Ball Game

The pitcher steps on the rubber with two outs in the ninth,
This is the end of the ball game the out of his life.
As he focuses on the crowd so he can hear,
All the champion chants loud and clear.
The catcher gives the sign low and away,
The pitcher gives a nod to say okay.
Aggressively he winds up to throw the pitch,
It hits the catcher's glove a swing and a miss.
The fans jump onto their feet,
Knowing their team got a victory not a defeat.
The ball game is over the champions are crowned,
The whole team loves the scene and the sound.

Gregory Monson, Grade 11
Bradshaw Christian High School

A Hazy Shade of Radiance

The sky is a hazy shade of radiance
It matches the color I find behind your eyes
Don't you see the devastating beauty?
The exhilarating rush of engulfing emptiness?
Would you dance in oceans of red and gold?
I would
With the luminescent clouds through which the sun peers out
And the stark and jagged trees
Like the taste of wonder behind your angry words
Their meaning melds with the tall purple grass
That has been painted green by lying hands and tortured eyes
Even the birds are fooled by your red-golden laugh

But I see behind the blueness of your eyes
Beyond your words and your laughter
To find your meticulously placed truths
Your angry words melt and your laughter fades
Now you see the devastating beauty
As the sky turns a hazy shade of radiance

Amber Shettler, Grade 12
San Lorenzo Valley High School

Chemo

It ravages the person in the inside
Yet they are all smiles on the outside
Inside there is something that eats them
Yet they keep laughing on the outside
Slowly and quietly it fills them up
Yet loud and fast they remain
Inside they feel pain
Yet on the outside no pain can be seen
Inside all there is, is worry
yet on the outside they are carefree
Inside their heart beats slower
Yet on the outside they make hearts race
Inside they know that they can beat it
Outside shows that they will beat it

Genesis Artiga, Grade 10
Sierra Vista High School

The Door

White and bright
With many window panes
Transmitting gentle afternoon light
Into the interior. It opens gently.
It closes without a sound.
I am Home.

Nick Matsumoto, Grade 11
Valley Christian High School

I Used To

I used to think that
I would stay little forever
And I would never see the world
But I was wrong

Tiffany Nguyen, Grade 11
Calaveras Hills High School

He Who Spoke in Words Unspoken

A mind, untuned and out of key,
dreams listless dreams of majesty.
Translucent lights shine broken beams.
Reflections of something unseen.

A poet, born without a face,
described to me a space-less place
beyond the reach of Heaven's eye.
The darkest corner of the sky.
His sentence was a symphony
of melodious emotion.
Gradually, it ebbed and flowed
like the tides of the evening ocean.

A man, alive in memory,
lies all alone and broken.
He searched for what no one could see
and spoke in words unspoken.

Rick Veloz, Grade 12
Hiram W Johnson High School

Life of a Farmer

Clear plains.
Shiny skies.
Growing grains.
Working guys.
When did life get so complicated?
When the water stopped falling,
the seeds stopped growing,
the guys have nothing to work with,
and the plains weren't big in width.
An idea of an American life was a goal,
to never feel cold,
to never worry,
and to never ever fear.
We will not drop another tear.
The life in America sounds so great.

Christina Lim, Grade 11
Abraham Lincoln High School

I Am Here

I am here,
But I go unseen.
I hear your words,
But I do not make a sound.
I see your love,
But I do nothing in return.
I smell your fear,
But do nothing to comfort.
I feel your pain,
But do not shed a tear.
I am here,
But I go unseen.

Cassie Castaneda, Grade 11
Chowchilla High School

Sweet Drinks

She drinks coconut and papaya juice
Only on Tuesdays
Wishing there were sweeter drinks
Not bitter like an empty room
Sweet like cotton candy
Sweet like a tropical breeze
Sweet like freedom

She's always wanted freedom
To feel the wind in her hair
The sun on her skin
But she's trapped
Lonely
Sad
Afraid
Waiting for her prince to set her free
To grant her her sweet, happy ending
Her freedom

Mayra Puga, Grade 10
Gridley High School

Save Our Environment

Suddenly,
Slowly,
The Earth goes around the Sun;
Carefully, with responsibility
The Earth takes care of all of us.

Its surface, full of wonders
makes life possible.
Fresh water, hydrates our bodies
while fields feed our hunger.

The Earth is our home.
it's here where we live.
You and many others live here, too.
The Earth is our home.
The Earth is our mom.

You must keep it clean
for the animals to live.
You must protect it
so our nature will not disappear,
Suddenly,
Slowly.

Jesus Duran, Grade 12
Citrus Hill High School

Time

I watch as Time plods slowly by
a rhythmic thunk-thunk-thunk
like the weary hooves
on a horse well passed his prime.
Slowly onwards he journeys,
but from a beaten path
he does not stray.
And with each annular turn he takes
is one less moment, chance, opportunity
I have to be carried away.

Liz Fleming, Grade 11
Valley Christian High School

Basketball

An orange ball
That I call a basketball
A ball so big but yet so small
I shot it up
I hoped and prayed
That it would come back down
In that perfectly shaped orange hole
Now I am just three points closer
To my number one goal
Three, two, one
I just won
That championship game of basketball

Sherine Zahra, Grade 12
Valley Christian High School

The Missing Frame

To break down, and cease all feeling
Burn now, what once was breathing
Imperfect cry, and scream in ecstasy
Look what I've built, it shines so beautifully

To cry out, and begin my healing
Breathe now, which was appealing
Listen softly, and ponder in laughter
Look what I've built, no friends ever after

I know now, my distractions
Distaste my, no reactions
Touch costly, and dream of youth
Look what I've built, another search for truth

To wake up, and feel no glory
Feel now, my lonely story
Painful cry, in a fight of rage
Look what I've built, another turn of the page

Eric Amparan, Grade 10
St Francis High School

Sunset

The sunset is a beautiful thing to sight,
The shades of red, orange, and yellow light.
Behind the horizon you can see,
The beautiful colors hiding behind the blue sea.

Jeannet Gonzalez, Grade 12
Calaveras Hills High School

Time Goes On*

Tick-tock goes the clock,
Never stopping for a break.
Tick-tock, it's 8 o' clock.
Time to get up and start the day!
Another day starting the same old way.
Tick-tock it's 11 o' clock.
Something is wrong, an ominous haze,
But people endure through work in their days.
Tick-tock it's 8 o' clock.
Fire burns through the town,
Firemen's strong-minded efforts scorched in flames,
Helpless cries from women and children,
There is no one around to answer,
Tick-tock, it's 12 o' clock.
Silence through the town.
Nothing moves.
Tick-tock, it's 8 o' clock.
Another day starting the same old way,
No one exists to know the troubles of yesterday.
Tick-tock goes the clock,
Never stopping for a break.

Crystal Lam, Grade 11
Schurr High School
In response to "There Will Come Soft Rains"
by Ray Bradbury

Vigilante

One step
One set of feet walking to a beat
Two hands close to his sides
Balled up fists with blood dripping as his two eyes cry
One tear coming down when his old man died
One block
Around the corner is where he lay
Two doors down from where his mother used to stay
Same corner where his brother got slain
These deaths have been like vultures eating at his brain
One problem
Officers tend to give chase
But what of the day he turns and shows them his true face
Death becomes the officer
When a demon gets put in place
One life
Is all he has, no wife no kids
And no mom and dad
No grip on what he grabs
He's a boy looking at the world through tempered glass

Jared Murray-Bruce, Grade 10
Dunn School

These I've Loved

These I've loved since I was three,
Sitting on my parents' knee,
Climbing monkey bars at my school,
Learning how to obey a rule.

Waiting for Mommy to pick me up,
Telling her how much I want a pup,
Playing Hide-and-Seek with my dad,
Sharing feelings, happy or sad.

Having fun with my neighbor's dog,
Crawling through a rolling log,
Going back home to pray to my Lord,
Thanking Him that I didn't trip over the cord.

Up the stairs, to my bed
Watching for my little head,
My parents come to kiss me good night,
And wish me that I will sleep tight.

Dawning Wu, Grade 11
Valley Christian High School

Fire

She destroys, but eyes can't pull away.
Confused by the gaiety with which she razes.
Her joyous wrath consuming all it touches,
Captivating and astounding all who behold it.
Spark her fury and be afraid,
She is blind in her vengeance.

Tim Johnson, Grade 12
Bishop Montgomery High School

Ordinary Day

Dip your hair in rubies
Paint your face with fire —
A sparkle here,
A flare there —
Dressed in black silk, velvet red
Eyes masked by the color of the stars —
You're ready for the ball.

Keep your head high
And your glittered eyes low;
Gloved hands at your side
And a smirk at your lips.
Keep them waiting, wanting,
Keep them guessing —
They'll treat you like a queen.

Dance and twirl to the minstrel's song
But not too much
(Simply hum quietly along)
Greet those you love
But not too warmly —
Smile wide, eyes guarded
You'll do just fine.

Jordan Tao, Grade 11
Valley Christian High School

Home Is a House…

Home is a house in a photograph
A place where your family resides
Home is a house in a photograph
Forcing fears to run a nd hide

In this place
No harm there will be
In this place
Enemies you will not see

Only loved ones
Teaching wrong from right
Only loved ones
Forever in your sight

Home is a house in a photograph

Daniel Reeder, Grade 10
Gridley High School

Impression

Death
Unbelievable at first
Shocking
Everyone experience it
The start of a new world
The ending and
The beginning

Sean Munshower, Grade 11
Calaveras Hills High School

Through the Window Panes*

I feel my hands, cracked and dry;
calluses on my feet, ripping and turning rye.
My heart has numbed over the years,
My eyes drowning in a sea of illustrious tears.
The sun beats down against my wrinkled, tanned face;
Through the window, standing at just a few feet's pace.
Sitting on this beaten, wood floor.
Touching the fragments where the panels were torn.
I think about the pain and the suffering my friends have endured,
As I lay waiting, for my dreams to be restored.

Meg Zabriskie, Grade 10
Helix High School
*Based on "Untitled" by Miguel Rio Branco

Alora Grace

Pitter Patter.
The sound she makes when she walks.
It's been a year since birth and she's grown so much since then;
both physically and mentally.
One can see the change just by looking at her.
Her once tiny hands, now the size of my palm.
And her body, once so frail and small,
now full of strength and with many rolls.
Her hazel eyes shine with excitement
while she smiles with a crinkled up nose.
Trouble brewing, in her head full of brunette curls.
No one can resist a feeling of happiness
when watching her play; waddling back and forth between toys.
It brings a smile to my face, to be so honored as to have her as a sister.
In future years, we'll be good friends,
and I'll tell her stories of when she was young.
But for now, those stories must wait.
And until that time, I'll watch her grow,
listening to that soft
Pitter Patter.

Kayla Cole, Grade 11
Galt High School

The Day and Night Hard Working

It is an early dawn and we still haven't made a penny,
It is hard these days to make money, but we haven't given up these days.
The weather isn't as sunny as it used to be,
But has it ever changed these years?
The sky isn't as blue as it has been,
Perhaps a storm, or thunder coming?
We struggled through day and night,
Day by day and night by night.
But nevertheless we never stopped planting our plantation,
In China these days many people depend on planting.
Growing out this and that, a little over there and here,
So we can put food on the table for our children and family.
China these days are nothing without hard working people,
We should all be hardworking for many generations to come.

Lily Huang, Grade 10
Abraham Lincoln High School

New Lands and Obstacles

I came to America for China to reach my destination
I will work hard to make it easier on the future generations
I will work all night
Even until it is so dark I cannot see anything in sight
How I can survive here is 100% unclear…
But the difficulty working is something I will bear
I will get a major in chemistry
It is something I like as you can see
There will be many hurdles, both big and small…
But I will conquer them all, I will not fall

Victor Owyang, Grade 10
Abraham Lincoln High School

I'm Stronger Than This

I threw down all the walls for you,
now look what I'm going through.
It seems I don't belong here,
so I gotta move on and forget the fear.
It seems I always let myself fall,
but now I know it's just wrong.
I will be the strong person I'm known to be,
and I ask you to please forget me.
I will forgive you for your mistakes,
I just hope you can forgive yourself.
Russian roulette is a game I like to play,
but this time like all the rest you played me.
So I'm gonna move on,
and try to forget you my dear.
And maybe when the time is right,
we will find each other in true peace and light.

Amber Beideman, Grade 11
Inderkum High School

Meaning of Life

The sun starts shining,
Another wonderful day
Filled with new successes
And new promises are underway.

The world is here
Dreams can be chased
They can be reached
And special moments won't come to waste.

Always go after what you believe in
Keep an optimistic view
Keep your goals reality
Don't let your successes be few.

The stars are emerging
Just another something life can bring
Everything is worthwhile
And you can do anything.

Christine Nguyen, Grade 11
Saugus High School

My Perfect Morning

I open my eyes.
I can hear the birds outside
Singing their song of life.
And my neighbor mowing his lawn,
And my fan softly whirling,
And sometimes, to my dismay,
My little brother and sister
Yelling downstairs.
I can smell pancakes cooking
Or, on a special day, cinnamon rolls.
It's not often that I wake up like this,
With no help from my alarm or Mom.
Just my body telling me I've had enough sleep.
I enjoy this feeling.
I touch my soft, comforting bedding,
Grab my familiar teddy bear,
And revel in this rare state of calmness.

Jenny Weber, Grade 11
Bradshaw Christian High School

It Did Not Happen Long Ago

It did not happen long ago,
When my love became a foe.
She felt at times it would be at last,
If only I had known that in the past.
This though is what I do not get,
If how after this event I will not regret
That by and by through the months,
Not twice but only once
I had a chance to redeem myself,
Before she put me back on the shelf.
But my chance was soon lost,
But why, I have not walked on roads that were crossed.
I guess our times together are done for,
My hands tremble against the wooden floor.
She said she still wants to be my friend,
But our friendship will never truly mend.
Time and time I see her walking in the halls,
I run to the bathroom and cry in the stalls,
It did not happen long ago,
When my love became a foe.

Gregory Kealey, Grade 10
Arcadia High School

Life

Life is given freely,
We choose how to live,
Give greatness and share of how you lived,
Life we share we learn from others, and pass
To and fro from one another,
New habits form to form each other,
Life is give and take,
Practice to share to make life in the stakes,
For life is give and take

Ashley Adkins, Grade 10
Jack Weaver School

Untitled

China has given my pockets holes.
No matter how much I dropped into my pockets,
They'd all seem to fall right out.
With hopes of mending my torn pockets, I set off to Indonesia.
There I found myself in fear of a tribe
That didn't give any insight to what others thought and saw them as.
Their princess became my heart's very own desire,
And I hoped and wished for her to be unlike the others and take sight of me.
Her father questioned my love for her, but nothing puzzled me for I found the answer, *her.*
The question marks soon turned into exclamation points.
From "You're going to marry her?" to "You're going to marry her!"
My life from there just began,
And we shared our love for each other with our 7 children,
But love was not the only treasure shared with one another.
Trying to support our family was not so easy, but *she* made it not so hard.
Indonesia not only helped in mending my torn pockets,
But also helped to fill my pockets with treasure.

Eveline Junaedy, Grade 12
Abraham Lincoln High School

I Am Confused...

I am confused.
The though of her will flip my world. What can I do for the one I love to show her how I feel, and how sorry I am? Can I bring her flowers, can I take her somewhere? I am confused. I did what I did in the past but this is the present. Why is she so angry? Is it the fact that I did the unspeakable, or is it the fact that she is jealous?
I am confused.

I thought I loved her. I thought she loved me. Is it true that there is no love for me in her heart or her in my heart? Am I showing her love? Is there room for her in my life, or is she pushing me down, or do I just love her so much that the thought of her just makes my whole mind just go crazy?
I am so confused.

What should I do? Should I look for another girl and show her how I feel? Would I even remember that girl the one I once loved, or will I forget I ever met her? Would I ever hurt another girl or will the next one I find be the one for me and one to enjoy being around? I think sometimes that if I had never met the one I once loved would my mind, body, and spirit be hurt? Or should I have never done the unspeakable thing? My life is now over and
I AM FREE.

Robert Guilbault, Grade 12
Riverside County High School

Germany Live

G ray plains afar in the distance, that is the background I see before me
E ach and every person running, fleeing from this place, this wretched place that used to be home
R unning to a place of peace, far from here, far from the evil we see before us now
M any dying to this evil, and though I am not a target to this demon I must flee
A nd run from here I shall to the East
N ot to hide, but to born a child to these troubled times, and share my experience
Y earning for a resolution within my soul I will do what I must

L earning to live again after such a massacre will be a great obstacle
I mmigration to the Oriental land is all there is left
V ying for something more is out of my grasp now
E verything I have left, I shall put upon my daughter
    While hoping someday she will be able to go to the land of hope in my place

Alvin Liu, Grade 10
Abraham Lincoln High School

Ancestry of the Past
Our ancestry from the past,
From southeast Asia has,
Made us who we are now,
Evolved and modernized,
They suffered through many,
Generations of agony and poverty,
And all they want was a meal.
Working from sunrise to sunset,
And now that we moved on from that lifestyle,
We are now living the American lifestyle.
John Wong, Grade 10
Abraham Lincoln High School

Like a Rose in the Middle of the Snow
I met you sometime ago
With the moon in your nose
From first sight I fell in love
I only love you without a thought
I didn't wanted to be alone
So I decided to confess you all
I even wrote you a song
To tell you that I'm all yours
But for my sorrow you said NO
Now there is no more hope
I can't laugh any more
Since you gave me that NO
I'm like a bird without a song
Without you I'm lost
I don't have any more joy
I'm like a rose in the middle of the snow
Please tell me when I went wrong
My heart is all broke
I need you my love
I beg you to come
Save me before I'm gone
Tiffany Vides, Grade 10
Huntington Park College Ready Academy High School

The Most Confusing Problem
Love is annoying,
A real big pest,
How can anyone get out of this mess?

Love is nagging, strange,
Yet kind,
It is an inner conflict that will never unwind.

Love is a monster
That's full of deceiving sin,
But still appears a dazzling angel from within.

Love is full of hope, caring,
And trust,
Which is really scary for the most of us.
Rose Rutherford, Grade 11
Grossmont High School

Music
Music is more than just loud instruments
It is something that you feel
Music helps me express my emotions
Music has something that reaches inside of me
It can make me feel like I'm coming alive

Music can be something that brings me strength
It is also something that can bring me hope
Music can brighten a dark day
Music is an influence
Music influences me

Music is something that I can create
Making music can be fun
Making good music can be hard
Music also tells stories
Stories of good times and bad times

Music can be whatever I make it
It can be my clay
I am the sculptor
I can influence others with music
For me, music is a passion
Music can make me feel alive
Michael Saragoza, Grade 11
Bradshaw Christian High School

The Royal Tragedy
It was about that time when all were sleeping,
When all clangs of clatter were gone,
That Amelia of the Royal family,
Was murdered before dawn.

How the deed was done is rather simple to say,
The item found was clear —
The creamy rope that strangled her,
Was hung from her bedroom chandelier.

Yes it was he who did the deed,
He who committed the crime,
Out of pure jealousy and rage,
When she did not fall in love with him a second time.

A gallant knight had come to town,
And swept Amelia off her feet,
Our murderer implored her to remember the past,
But he always met defeat.

"I tried to warn you Amelia,
I tried to make you understand,
But because you have rejected me,
I can now do this with mine own hands."
Briana Robell, Grade 12
Academy of Our Lady of Peace

Choices Made

Your choices made today,
Form the days that proceed,
No one knows the future,
But you may just impede.
Be careful where you go today,
Because where you end up,
Could straighten out your future,
Or empty your life cup.
Make friendships that will last,
And establish your belief,
So when the future comes,
You will be free of grief.
Remember to work hard,
And always give your best,
So when the trumpets sound,
God will give you rest.

CJ Wrye, Grade 11
Valley Christian High School

Mom, Thank You

You get out of your comfortable bed
You say you're tired of beans and rice
You say you want new clothes
Do you even say thank you?

She comes home exhausted
She sees the television on
She sees dishes in the sink
Do you even say thank you?

Beatriz Barrett, Grade 10
Sierra Vista High School

Home

Darkness now surrounds me,
Cutting off my air.
Panic sets in and I start to scream
But I don't know why I'm scared.
This is what I've always wanted,
To finally end the pain.
But suddenly, when I'm about to let go,
I faintly hear your name.
Perhaps the reason I'm terrified
Of being set free,
Is that I don't want you to go,
Through the process of mourning me.
So I'll try to find the candle
In my darkened place
But none can be so radiant,
As the glory of your grace.
I will keep on trudging,
Down this lonely road
Until at last I'm in your arms
And I can finally say:
I'm home.

Jared Thornton, Grade 12
Yuba City High School

Love

Well, love isn't always a fairy tale
It always has its ups and downs
And it always ends up in tears
And memories
And a broken heart
But at the end you learn from your mistakes
And you realize love isn't always a fairy tale
And you realize that love isn't always happiness
And love isn't always everything
When you find love make sure you know who you're falling for
So you won't end up regretting something that you know was the best thing in your life
And always remember that love doesn't always end up with a happily ever after

Monica Cruz, Grade 10
Sierra Vista High School

Silent Sound

In every little town filled with quiet sleepers echoes a loud silence
In the ears of those who wake,
In the dead of quiet night each feeling has a voice,
Each voice comes alive, each ear awake and wide takes in the sound:
Cars that pass and lights that play on the walls through blinds into
Minds pondering about the coming day,
Each new day as it dawns bringing along another continuation of habitual ritual,
To each man, and then to these — on lots, in queue, by highways,
Passing through each one as he completes his custom,
Reverberating sound —
While he toils this day, while he waits for the next,
Though he finds him self-same, he awaits a new day, a new sound,
Forward echoing through the night, waiting loudly, to help quiet sleepers waken,
Beckoned into restlessness by impress of silent beckoning.

Amber Clark, Grade 11
Westmont High School

The Myth

Addiction is taking over the habit
The past has been erased yet still braggin'
Too much the same at the starter line with they're groove theories
Close my eyes to wake up to bad memories
Too much confidence and high maintenance clouded minds
Like smoking the herbal essence ending up on cloud nine
We all plan to get rich in this life or the next one
Clearing mental space for less not the best one
Virtual insanity in high times I live
We always can take but never give
Mother and child chooses a color to avoid
Their feelings and understandings being toyed
Still you can't break me only add pieces
My good vibe zone they try to hold on leashes
So I approach them quietly like the grim reaper
Breathing is much deeper and now love is much cheaper
If you can't stay ahead you're finding forever
Low self-esteem got me low? Never
Rhythm and beats I am affiliated with
Others are just overweighted of my gift cause I lift

Shirle Howard, Grade 12
Buena Vista High School

'Til Love

Of such warmth and passion I knew not
'Til the day love held me to his heart.
From my friend I never wish to part
Who by Cupid's bow was to me brought.
Winter's jealous wind may strongly blow;
Summer's heat dares not to cross my way.
I from sweet love's path shall never stray.
Tempests cannot cool my fired soul.
Love has held me in his strong embrace,
The passion I once ignorant of has been
Placed within my heart. Mine eyes have seen
His love divine. How glorious is his face!
I do so yearn to hold him close to me
While hoping that my love he'll brightly see.

Lea Negrin, Grade 11
Marysville Charter Academy for the Arts

Who Am I?

Who am I?
Am I a man?
Or just an instrument of neo-expressionism
Sent here by the big guy
To express the modern arts
Or maybe I'm just a boy
Born into a rebellion of freedom
When this land is already "free"
Sent by myself to bomb these streets
Like Hiroshima in a spray can
But no
I'm just a kid
With a dream
A passion
Maybe —

Robert Chavarria, Grade 11
Calaveras Hills High School

Promises

You promised me heaven,
but you gave me hell.
You promised me love,
but you brought me sorrow.
You promised me tomorrow,
but it ended today.
You promised me happiness,
but you made my life a mess.
Stop making me promises,
that you can't keep.
Stop making me promises,
that weren't meant to be.
Stop making me promises,
cause you never intended
to love me.

Rebecca Chaqueco, Grade 10
Huntington Park College Ready Academy High School

Vietnam Life

My grandparents adapting in the life of Vietnam.
Living in the hot weather with not much money.
Hard working place to make money.
Hard jobs, hard to handle, and very tiring.
Praying every day to have best wishes.
Keeping their culture without letting go.
Buddhist is the Vietnamese way to go.
Going to temple to pray for ancestors and Buddha.
Getting awfully old with health problems.
Wishing to get better and praying for our family.
To keep the family going with a better life.
Wanting everyone to work hard and a better future.

Larry Pho, Grade 10
Abraham Lincoln High School

Memories

Memories are all I have left of you,
Without memories, I wouldn't know you are.

Your departure seems like it was yesterday
So suddenly
So unexpected.

When I am alone,
I cry and sob
As you appear vividly in my mind.

Everything in my mind is intact,
And I wish I could travel back in time
To replay the joyful moments of our past.

The pain that I bear is starting to hurt
As I long for your love
Yet, I know it might not be possible.

Even though we might never meet again,
My memories of you will remain in my mind
Forever.

Frankie Wong, Grade 11
Gretchen Whitney High School

He Makes Me Wonder

He stares into my eyes;
    I wonder if there's something on my face.
He looks me up and down;
    I wonder if there's something wrong with me.
He says, "I love you."
    I wonder if he really means it.
But then,
    He holds me tight in his arms,
        And kisses me sweetly,
            And I wonder,
                How I could not have realized,
                    That he truly loves me.

Alisha Jonas, Grade 10
Bella Vista High School

Moving On

No one ever said that love is easy
No one ever told me that love hurts
And when you left me
That's when I knew
You took your heart and went with her
All I have is just your shirt
I can't move on
What is wrong?
I've never met anyone like you
I miss you
That's true
Every time I go to sleep
I always think of you
No matter how hard I tried to let you go
Your name will always be in my heart
Why are we apart?
I finally put your shirt away
That's the only way I could move on
Now that you're gone
I'm moving on…

See Lor, Grade 12
Grant Union High School

Forget Me

Why can't you forget me
There is no love no more
My dreams had faded
Who are you waiting for

Forget all the love we shared
And those once special hugs
Just let go of me
As I turn and run

Roxann Pickett, Grade 11
Lucerne Valley Jr/Sr High School

Cherish

Once a starry night
So filled with delight
A beautiful time
Earth is so sublime

Trees shake and begin
As moon shows a grin
Reflect off river
Fish start to quiver

Moon sits in the skies
She looks in my eyes
This surely is bliss
As I share a kiss

With my one excite
Once a starry night

Ricky Rhodes, Grade 10
St Francis High School

The Long Path

She takes the long path.
No fiend, no friend will she hither cross.
She is alone, serene, yet filled with humans of all sorts.
Their voices in her head, she is unable to walk in solitude.
She takes the long path,
Not wanting to offend, solely searching to please.
She avoids contact, making sure the distance between her heart
and her mind remains lengthy.
She takes the long path
where obstacles are not kind,
where simplicities become intricate, but the trail ahead is always clear.
Always waiting.
She takes the long path
setting down each foot with caution,
But taking only as much time as is allowed.
Her submission to protocol results
in a clear prediction of each of her steps.
She takes the long path, looking to the future to guide her,
keeping her goal in mind, concerned only with what lies ahead.
She takes the long path
for the short one does not exist.

Amy Horowitz, Grade 11
Miramonte High School

As I Lie Awake

As I lie awake I think of you.
Wondering if you're thinking of me too.
I lie awake wanting you to be mine,
Though I know there's someone else on your mind
The love I want from you, you're giving to someone else.
That's why I tried to hide how I felt.
When I try to win you over it doesn't help
because I feel guilty I'm taking you from someone else.
During the day I try to take away the pain by finding something to do.
But when I lay my head on the pillow I lie awake thinking of you.

Laina Shaw, Grade 12
Jack Weaver School

Discipleship

Immense zeal and oblique passion for divinity.
Condemned, ridiculed, and forsaken for our perception of faith.
Contemplating my actions or lack of the Trinity.
Compromising my time to witness; who am I making safe?
A lazy will; undedicated motive will corrupt our soul.
My mouth is still; declining morals guarantees conformity to sin.
Questions will go unanswered; flesh will burn fast as coal.
Our sinful nature will prevail, and then who do you think will win?
Our faith is a ray of extremely bright light.
It challenges majority, it challenges the conformity of the Earth.
The Bible is our weapon that gives our souls insight.
The Savior is calling us all to be warmed in his saving hearth.
True discipleship is imminent if our zeal is raised high.
True discipleship is imminent so we don't live a hypocritical life.

Jonathan Oliva, Grade 10
Calvary Christian High School

Fairy Tale

As years pass…
I learn that the older I get,
The more problems I gain.
The more tears I shed,
More pain I feel, for more reasons.
I slowly wake up from a fairy tale.
No more sun shines,
No more magic spells to solve problems.
There's no Prince Charming to come and rescue you.
It's reality,
It's the world,
It's my life.
More pain,
More problems,
More suffering,
More loneliness,
More tears and
More grief around the corner.
The fairy tale is over; it has been over a long time ago.
It's real life now.

Mayra Piceno, Grade 11
Calaveras Hills High School

No Speak

No speak English,
she says to the child
who sings in a language that sounds like tin.

It is not our language,
or where we belong.

This is not our culture,
or where we should live.

Our language is beautiful,
and belongs to where our home is
and shall always be.

Home is where the heart is,
but I have lost my heart,
for it is home,
where I came from,
and where I belong.

Kayla Casillas, Grade 10
Gridley High School

Sunrise

S un gives us light.
U nder certain conditions,
N ever will we see it hide from the world.
R eflecting its bright yellow smile upon us,
I t brings a new day.
S urprisingly,
E veryone wants it to come out later.

Bao Dao, Grade 11
Mira Loma High School

"The" Picture

Pictures and memories
they come and go,
but not for me.
I have a memory of everything,
but they're sitting in a corner inside my head.
I see an image,
I look at the picture
and I see the exact moment it was taken.
Nobody can see what I see and feel.
They hear it, but they cannot connect
I am being absorbed into the picture, slower and slower.
Outside, it's sunny and warm
I let my thoughts run; someone calls to me
but I am in the picture now
experiencing the past that I never could see
I hear laughter, shouts, and cries
Why are they so loud?
Next to me, I see a mirror.
Suddenly, I see myself older, back in present time,
gripping the picture I was just in.

Daphne Chien, Grade 10
South Pasadena Sr High School

A Dream

I have a dream
A dream that I will love.
Or a dream that will be hard.
But a dream that I would want.
A dream that I will do forever.
It might be hard.
But if you put your mind to it you will do it.
I can do anything I want.
I can climb to the top of a high rock.
So just push through
If you put your mind to it you can do anything you want.
So never say never.
Just do it.
I know you can.

Heather Schwitkis, Grade 11
The Winston School

He Left Us!!

He left us without saying good-bye,
Just closed his eyes,
Left in peace
Leaving us behind.

Things happen for a reason
Yet I still don't understand.
I went through my mom's and dad's death,
Now my grandpa's?
The question is why?

Marisol Cabral, Grade 10
Sierra Vista High School

Beauty Is More Than Skin Deep

Beauty is more than just looks
It is more than being pretty
It is thinking of others before yourself
And beauty is more than skin deep

Beauty is not about looking hot
It is more than being glamorous
It can be found beyond the make-up
And beauty is more than skin deep

Beauty is not about what you wear
It is not about being "all that"
It is about your outlook on life
And beauty is more than skin deep

Beauty is more than your appearance
It is more than being sexy
It is what is on the inside
And beauty is more than skin deep
Hannah Dahlke, Grade 11
Jack Weaver School

The Enchantress

Her lips are like roses
But poisoned ones.
Death lies on her mouth.
A seductive smile
And a small little gestures
To attract the unsuspecting soul.
Beware, my brothers
For there is danger within
The arms of the silver-haired maiden.
Her beauty is great
And her words the most pleasing
But the soul of a demon is within her.
One night with the lady
Will be your last
If you are foolish enough to join her.
Her bed is covered in roses
Her sheets are silky and red
Perfume lingers on her neck.
A snare for the unwitting man.
Beware, my brothers, beware.
Beware of the silver-haired maiden.
Jacob Webb, Grade 10
Calvary Christian High School

Family

Family is a blessing
Filling my life with precious jewels
Family is so important
So much I know it's real
Family is my life
Who makes me who I am?
Rocio Rangel, Grade 12
Academic/Vocational Institute

Faces

I see faces stretching down the city lanes;
The burning sun reflects their hidden pains,
They walk around with boxes connected to their fingertips,
Boxes full of hidden fears and worldly conflicts,
Can you see the stars melting in the sky?
The burning of cities or Mother Nature's decaying cry?
Yes, these faces do see it, but they turn their backs on it,
Believing other solutions as to why their world is falling apart.
Man conjures ideas of life for these faces' perceptions,
Allowing them to dwell in the shadows of deception,
If only we could open these boxes making them hollow,
The death of the world would be an easier concept for us to swallow.
Joe Flores, Grade 12
Bradshaw Christian High School

Anabel

I am a caring and loving person.
I wonder what I'll be when I grow up.
I hear a sad melody that symbolizes all the violence in wars and the damage it causes.
I see a world where racism doesn't exist.
I want to succeed in life.

I pretend that I am a vet.
I feel that mankind will destroy the earth.
I touch a cloud of smoke representing all the bad and wrong things of the world.
I worry about my family.
I cry when I see homeless people.
I am a caring and loving person.

I understand the many races in this world.
I say no matter what race you are we're all the same and equal.
I dream of traveling the world.
I try to give to the less fortunate.
I hope poverty ends soon.
I am a caring and loving person.
Anabel Gomez, Grade 11
William Finch Charter School

A Black and White Rainbow

Fifty-nine years back my life was not a colorful dream.
But a tale of lost hope and desire is what it seemed.
Six brothers and sisters in a house with rice not enough to feed the family.
Bombing, screaming, yelling as the Japanese invaded our territory.
They took away our money and the lives of our friends and families.
Nowhere to run, it was just a complete devastating state.
Nowhere to hide, they have eyes everywhere.
Trapped around a room with four corners of walls,
Where cried and sorrows cannot escape for all eternity.
Five years later, farms began to recover and people's lives restored.
A blind marriage came to me with the kid next door.
We married and had two children with food enough for all.
And that was that, what can I say more.
After the rainy days in my life, with no hope and desire to fill me full.
I look up to the sky, and a single black and white rainbow reflected on my life so.
Cindy Liu, Grade 10
Abraham Lincoln High School

A Cloudy Sky with a Rainbow

A dark cloudy sky looming over me
Threatening to burst into tears at any moment.
With a flash and a crash
Driving every soul away.
But I, a lonely wonderer in an empty street
With grief so heavy pulling on my tender heart.
Which will never soar again! All hope vanished!
Darkness surrounds me
Forever following me like my own shadow.
But what's this I see?
A rainbow it must be!
Such perfection!
What bright colors against the gloomy gray.
Oh! The beauty shining through the darkness.
My love, shall you be as such?
Coming to me during my time of pain?
So unexpectedly?
A flicker of hope,
A speck of light,
Like fire it spreads through me.

Elizabeth Chan Lee, Grade 10
Lowell High School

A Girl Whose Name I Blank

A girl I love whose name I blank
Has more beauty than a regiment does rank
Her light-colored eyes looking sensitive and sweet
But pierce the heart with much deceit
Her lips bright red but mostly pink
Who commands a soul with a simple blink
Skin of gold both soft and smooth
Which calms the soul and also soothes
Her smile radiant and luminous too
Her emotions high she's never blue
Her hair a color dark but bright
Which shines in the sun's rays of light
All of these beautiful things I say
Will belong to a girl I soon shall name

Joe Castro, Grade 10
Montclair High School

The Oriental Hellbroth

From Asia came unappetizing gruel,
Concocted from those sickening soybeans,
Smashed and fermented into awful drool,
To form the worst soup worlds have ever seen.
With its gross slimy slices of seaweed,
And cubes of that inedible tofu,
To those not drinking that soup are envied,
For one sip can make nausea come anew.
Adding sprinkles of green onion to hide,
The disgusting bland flavor of that broth,
Console from tang of spice my tongue denied,
At smell of that bad taste my mouth shall froth.
  Compared to miso soup that can give ill,
  Of witches' hellbroth, I'll have a refill.

Elizabeth Wu, Grade 11
Davis Sr High School

Those Desks

Bodies sitting in wood and metal desks;
The flat, smooth wood holds books and papers.
Days, weeks, and months of sitting;
Those desks stand in rows and columns.
Engraved with words from notes and papers;
Tired from the weight of students and books.
Lectures and lessons heard over and over;
Those desks stand in rows and columns.

Priscilla Shen, Grade 11
Valley Christian High School

Alive

"Hooray for the Madness!" we sing.
A single tear in our eye,
The Beauty cannot last,
Like all — it dies.

Before the music fades,
And reality grips our throats,
We shall laugh and be merry —
Vulgar and crude,
Crazy and rude.

But who is to stop us?
We are still young,
Though venerable and vulnerable inside,
Eyes widened — forever learning,
We know not all, but we know Truth —
He is our best friend,
Setting us apart —
He is our worst enemy,
Tearing at our Heart.
Young and restless, we entertain ourselves,
Clinging to what we Love —
We shall Live.

Veronica Campbell, Grade 10
Jack Weaver School

The Burning House

The house was burning.
Smoke fuming through the air,
The screaming child trapped in heat.
The cackling flames dancing in the room.
People were frantically running,
The sirens blared across the sky,
The fire trucks blazed speedily by,
And the fighters came out for war.
A dramatic brawl ensued,
An age old conflict raged on,
As water ferociously battled fire.
Finally the flamebeasts were extinguished,
The warriors searched through the house.
The whimpering child found unscathed,
Surviving.

Victor Chang, Grade 11
Valley Christian High School

Cold War Between My Mind and Heart

They say, the eye's are the windows to a man's soul, look at mine, all you see is a black hole, trying to maintain, the things I let control, playing life's game, with the cards that I hold, trying to live my life, in the mold of the man's code, I was told, never to fold, stand bold on the hard road, cause your future's untold only God knows, and when you start to fall, get up, and continue to ball, till God calls, I got to be tall, cause I'm in it for the long hall, in my body and soul, it feels like World War 2 again, will this cold war ever end, My mind says forget love, I'm as free as a dove, But my heart says no, cause it feels like heavens above, but you just don't know what it's like being alone, could be with someone and still feel alone, cause they just don't know, your trials or struggles, all they see is another trying to make hustle, while they on the outside looking in, you on the inside looking out, trying to figure out, what the world is all about, I understand with hard times come doubts, but you see that's what faith, is all about, it feels like World War 2 again, will this cold war ever end, I once thought of ending it all, then I heard a voice call, say don't you fall, be strong for a little longer, you never know, I may use you, to end world hunger, I wonder, is my mind playing tricks or is my heart not trying to quit, so you telling me some place in this world I fit, never forget, a purpose you was born with, I don't know, maybe one day I'll understand, how to be a better man, but until then at least I know that my plan's in God's hands, In my body and soul it fills like World War 2 again will this cold war ever end.

Ottis Smith, Grade 11
Renaissance High School for the Arts

Music

Even the visuals of the TV flashing as the basketball being played outside
Were not as enjoying. Family members chattering
As they smiled not you. In your house that seemed to have everything
You sat alone as everyone else was having fun
In their own little party in the living room. Your father comes into your room
As it seemed like he was an officer of your room. You never dared to look at him
And say anything to him. You tried hard to find something fun to do.
The video games were still there in your room, though I said it's boring and pointless now
You liked going outside. You liked feeling the fresh winter breeze.
You liked the peacefulness surrounding you. "What can I do now?" you ask me now. "What can I do
When my parents did not like me going out?"
The saying your mom says is that music is the lullaby of a baby, relaxing as a comfy chair.
Her sayings drift through the family.
You told me once you were in a car to go to Las Vegas.
Your family quiet like you'd be in prison alone. You looked around and there was nothing to do.
You wanted to just jump out of the car. Outside was just the dry land with no grass.
You, who was bored to death, finally took out your iPod
Like it was treasure. You put on your earphone.
"Time to pass time," You said. You closed your eyes and you sang along in your head.
This is what you used to pass through time and have fun
In places of silence. You smile through the whole trip like a baby sleeping to its lullaby.

Eugene Dalaten, Grade 10
Sierra Vista High School

The Fear of Me

I went to school with fear and shame, worrying about the presentation as I came.
The heavy burden I carried increasingly gained, I was feeling as if I were going insane.
Watching presentations weren't so bad, until my time came, I felt so sad.
It was time for me to come up now, I felt so naked without a towel.
Shaking with fearfulness as I went, I felt like someone snatched away my confidence.
It took a moment for me to start,
So I looked apprehensive as I swallowed and gulped for me to depart.
Deep down, I know I have the courage, I just need to bring that out to nourish.
I spoke inside so loud and clear, that some courage came upon me to appear.
I won't let fear stay to rule, because I have the courage as a bull.
Then as I started the presentation, I gave the conclusion with understood information.
When the fear extremely departed from me, I had many presentations in my class tease.

MaryAnn Davis, Grade 11
Grant Union High School

I Am

I am a smart guy who loves to dance
I wonder how things will be once I am dead
I hear the voice of angels calling my name
I see the doors of heaven opening
I want to become very successful
I am a smart guy who loves to dance.

I pretend I am an astronaut going to the moon
I feel like lions will begin to rule the world
I touch the highest clouds in the sky
I worry where my life will be ten years from now
I cry because my family is falling apart
I am a smart guy who loves to dance.

I understand that I have control over my life
I say that I will follow God but tend to stray
I dream about becoming a professional choreographer
I try to do my best when in school
I hope that I change my life around
I am a smart guy who loves to dance.

Antwan Rowel, Grade 12
Redwood High School

Horrific Patterns

Since when don't you deserve
to have have everything
that you have wanted?
But no, you are tortured and abused
mistreated and threatened
held against your will
Lies and confusion fill your head
hoping for the pain to subside
Day after day a constant reminder
of what happened time after time
You have grown stronger to accept the past
which makes you willing to change the future
For you and all the countless children like yourself
break free of the chains that
secured you in that dungeon
and live your life to receive everything you ever wanted
Change the pattern to save a life

Courtney Small, Grade 12
San Lorenzo Valley High School

You Will See

We're all alone in this world we know
Too many things are holding us back
To say the truth or watch it fall
Nothing and nobody can tell us how to act
Sometimes we wonder how we can live
Then we think about all the good times we had
And much more will come
As the days go by you will see
We're all alone in this world we know.

Anjie Pineda, Grade 10
Oakdale Charter High School

Afraid of Dying

I'm not afraid of standing still.
I'm just afraid of being bored.
I'm not afraid of speaking my mind.
I'm just afraid of being ignored.

I'm not afraid of feeling and I'm not afraid of trying…
I'm just afraid of losing and I am afraid of DYING!

I'm not afraid of being sick.
I'm more afraid of being healthy.
I'm not afraid…give me what you've got…
I'm just afraid that it will hurt ridiculously.

I'm not afraid of screaming and I'm not afraid of crying
I'm just afraid of being forgotten and I am afraid of DYING!

I'm not afraid of looking ugly.
I couldn't care less what they say.
I'm not afraid of happy endings…
I'm just afraid it won't work that way.

I'm not afraid of forgiveness…I'll absolve your everything.
I'm not afraid of lying but I am afraid of DYING!

Heather Larson, Grade 11
Bradshaw Christian High School

Free Again

We look around,
There is an aroma of smiling faces.
So sweet and innocent,
As we all were.

Running for freedom,
And running for joy.
Across an imaginary meadow,
That should have been there.

Picking the delicate flowers of hope,
Later to be pressed into
Dirty pages of their new prison.

While the butterflies of the next generation fly by.
We catch a few,
To remind them that their freedom
They once had, was not free.

We cram them into jars.
Wings flashing bright,
To hide their dulling hearts.

Hearts that had one wish remaining,
To be free again.

Evelyn Brewster, Grade 10
Calvary Christian High School

Sealed Off Door

They bolted you shut,
Closed you real tight
Made you over,
Turned out the light.

You were locked twice,
They buried the key,
But they forgot something,
They forgot me.

I glimpsed your shadow from behind
The stained fading paint,
I peeked inside,
And I liked what they hate.

Others thought you were through,
You were gone for good,
But I'll chip off the concealer,
They never knew I could.

We'll go back to your past,
Just for old time's sake,
To dream of a better yesterday,
And in the morning, sorrowfully awake.

Danielle Drogos, Grade 11
Presentation High School

Stars

I'm like a rock star
Dance like a superstar
But it's not a dream
It's about how you look
Act like a star
And I'll take you to the stars

Dulce Serrano, Grade 10
Academic/Vocational Institute

Miles and Miles

Miles and miles
May keep us apart,
But no distance can divide
The bond of our hearts.
Our bodies may be
Separated by a vast ocean,
But we are connected
By a bridge of our love and devotion.
You see temptation
Each and every day,
Yet you vow that
With me you will stay.
And I hope you can see
From my point of view,
That I will always
Love, honor and cherish you.

Angel Zavala, Grade 10
Sierra Vista High School

Vigorous Father

The person I name when observing my personality,
My father gave life to my thoughts with his brutal delicacy,
Turning a kid into a potentially effective mind,
Teaching how to face the world avoiding a hit from behind,
Picked me up when hopes were dragged and weary,
Opening wounds enough to hurt but closed enough to not kill me,
He planted the first frozen icicle into my heart,
Continuously making it cold so I can tear worlds apart,
Facing the world with a sharp perspective as if it was a blade,
Without my father my enlightened world could not have been made,
For this fact I owe him the proper gratitude,
I honor my father with my strongest attitude.

Ricardo Contreras, Grade 11
Lawndale High School

The American Dream

Who decides which man will walk tall in his three piece suit,
While another bows his head, sweating in the sun,
Singing a song of backache, dirt and blistered hands?
The politician speaks of merit and strength of the soul,
But anyone who has felt the pain in their limbs, or saw the rats in their homes,
Or heard the metallic click of the jail cell door knows better.
The poor laugh at the myth painted by Horatio Alger
And the American flag with its empty stars and its empty stripes
And its empty dreams and its empty gold
With dreams blown up thick and full,
Only to be smashed by greed and corrupted control.
And here I am, with big visions of fists clenched tight,
Raised into the air with a cry of strength,
Longing to take the hands of the hurt and lead them,
Though I don't know where to go.
Wishing to be able to run and catch the fallen dreams
Before they slam to the ground like broken birds of prey
And lift them up again into the sky.

Alysha Aziz, Grade 12
Castro Valley High School

Simply Just Me!

I am a simple person. Yes, a simple person I am.
Since I am strong, intelligent, beautiful and most importantly, I stay true to myself.
The arrogance and judgment in this world is the last thing stopping me
from being who I want to be or who I am.
I am just simply me, I have nothing to lose and nothing to gain,
It will take all you can give to keep me away.
So if you try to stop me, you will not succeed because I am a fighter
and it would take a whole troop to keep me down.
It would take the whole world to keep me down. I am just simply me,
I am a girl, no I am a women transitioning into the adult world.
Realizing how cruel and selfish this planet we call Earth really is.
I am one to always speak her mind and always stand up for what is right.
I am me and I never forget who I am. where I come from or my roots,
but yet I wait to see who I will become.
I am just simply me.

Monica Rodarte, Grade 10
Sierra Vista High School

Time in the System

The weather is right,
and the sun is bright.
Sometimes the sun likes to go so high,
the wings of birds that fly by, up in the sky.

A great time to start school,
to swim in a pool,
and time to play with friends that are cool.

If you do not skip school,
you will not be a fool.
I hated school so much,
that every day I got up to flee.

When I fled so much,
the school was afraid,
that I was going to fail that grade,
because my teachers didn't like what I played.

I needed to be super brave,
not to think about my deathly grave,
or be someone's slave — hey,
that happens to be the lead singer
on a band called the wave.

Jeremiah Maurer, Grade 10
Milhous School

War

Take me to the field
where strangers gather in dissolution.
Let me feel the bloody tears of Earth
burn me
beyond flesh and bone.
Sickly pale, raw, pure.

In my dreams I see only shadows.
Death
calling for me to be caged,
wanting me to be its prisoner.

I see him there straight above the wheat,
wild and untamed among the morning fog
like Bacchus on a brannigan.
Oh Death!
Transform me into an animal —
Force me to feed upon the grass —
Lay with me at the center of the path —
Slaughter me.

I close my eyes as if in a nightmare,
feeling you delude me,
waiting for you to rupture my stained heart.

Amanda Licato, Grade 11
Torrey Pines High School

Life

Well, life is not always fair
It's sometimes how you want it,
And sometimes not.
And maybe it will someday be fair.
And maybe it will never be fair.
But we live life the way it is
And we should never give up
And if we fall in life we need to get back up.
Where there is faith life will be good
So always live life to the fullest.
Don't let anything bring you down,
And even if life is not always fair
We should never give up.

Gladys Artiga, Grade 10
Sierra Vista High School

Same Old Thing

Same thing every day.
I wish that I could go away.
Not too far from here for I'll fear,
That my life wouldn't seem as clear.

I want to go to Paris, France.
So I can get a whole new chance.
Or is it better I go to Boston?
I could meet a man named Austin!

I could go to Delaware.
I'll catch up with my old pal Cher.
Or I could go to swell Utah.
Plan a meeting with the Grand-Pooh-Bah.

Now that I come to think of it,
My daily life's just fine.
I'm not that tired of the same old thing.
I'll just sit here and I will sing.

Ashley Scott, Grade 10
Lodi Academy

Everlasting

Roses are red violets are blue
If only you knew how much I care about you
I smile when you're near
You make me tear when you're away
As you come to me day by day
You take my pain away
You make me laugh in a certain way
You wipe these tears from my face
As long as you're near me these fears get swept away
If only you knew how much I care about you
You know you're my everything
And this will definitely last
Forget the past because it surely will be you and me
Let's make the future amazing for us to see

Brittany Brown, Grade 10
Jack Weaver School

Melodious

I would like to be
a symphony.
to be every note,
to tug at heartstrings,
to strike fear into ears,
to sail across every staff.
to draw people
closer
and closer
until they can hear
the whisper of the dulcet violin,
the chirp of the sweet triangle,
the whistle of the silvery flute.
let the music wash over them until,
they would like to be a symphony.

Lindsay Winkler, Grade 12
San Lorenzo Valley High School

Shy of Swimming

No running leap
Cautiously approaching the edge
Toes curling over
Reaching out
Absorbing the scattered spray of splashes
Yearning to take the plunge
Yet watching
Always watching
Momentarily pulled in by
"Hey watch this"
Ready
Though skeptical of staying afloat
Pushed in
Immersed
Reluctant and relieved
To have broken the surface
I remember to breathe and kick

Stephanie Armstrong, Grade 12
Central Catholic High School

Crayola

Splashes of brilliant color
Animate the page.
Who could have known
That these tiny sticks of color
Could bring such wond'rous forms
To the stage.

Dancing wild flowers
And magnificently plumed birds
Doth it display.
But who could have known
That such awe striking beauty
Could be contained
In such a simple page.

Elizabeth Vogt, Grade 12
Redlands Sr High School

Life

People live a thousand lives and die a thousand ways,
And yet never learn how to stop their decay.
They can fly higher than any mountain's peak
And cry for that eternal secret that the gods keep.
Continue to strive to control natures way,
But they won't know how to stop their decay.
The sky darkened by their towers of smoke,
Lakes and creeks turned to muck by the filth of these common folk.
They cut down their forests, they brought drought to their rivers.
They tore into the earth to get their gems, gold, and silvers.
All species bow to their tyrannical rule
Even the strongest and the fastest became their tools.
But they still don't know why they decay
Or how to prevent their ending day.

Quereno Sevilla, Grade 12
Sweetwater High School

Lola

Lola…
Lola consisting of two syllables
Lola is the Tagalog term for grandmother
Lola is the term used by grandchildren meaning eradicator of all sorrow

Lola is the one you run to when you want homemade cookies
Lola is the one you hide behind when a monster is coming to attack
Lola is the one you turn to when your parents are being "bad guys"
Lola is the one you want present in both good times and bad

Lola never has to forgive because she is never mad at you
Lola never has to forgive because she understands you
Lola never has to forgive because you are the apple of her eye
Lola never has to forgive because she loves you

Lola starts with the letter "l" just as love does
Lola…
She is one of the ultimate meanings of love

Mercielynd Rejoice Hernandez, Grade 12
Redlands Sr High School

Recollection

In the United States, I have passed the 50th spring.
During these years, there are a lot of memories in my life.
50 years ago, I moved to United States alone because of the war.
My family died in the war and I lost all I have.
I felt like a fish that leaps out of water,
Like an that leaves its team,
And totally lost…
No food to eat, no house to live… it was difficult.
To survive, I had to leave the country that I was born in — China
And took the ship to here…
In here, I started my new life.
In recalled a lot of happiness,
I have seen the changes of San Francisco…
I have seen my children and grandsons growing…

Rachel Yang, Grade 12
Abraham Lincoln High School

Staying Away

Back in the day we had to stay away
Moving south towards the border of Myanmar
In this time China and Japan did not get along
Using Chinese as experiments was not right
Finding mine and my family's life a way out
Calling everyone I knew, passing some money around
We got out
These days I look back, glad to be alive
Sacrificed everything for the life of my family
It was all worth it

Kurt Kyauk, Grade 11
Abraham Lincoln High School

Our Lost World

Days pass by
Years bade good bye
And time continues running
Changing every being
From a baby to a teen
Everyone is keen
Of rushing and leaving the world unseen
So, don't close your eyes
Rather open them and live because in this world there lies
A beautiful world with joy and happiness
Ready to be shared without any restlessness
So, for the days that everyone has left to live
Let's not take, but instead give
Either compliments, time or a smile
Let's make it worth so that it will go a mile
Let us make a difference in this world of ours
That has nature: animals, human beings, and flowers
So that the rest of the world will appreciate us
And create a place without any fuss
Let's make peace as common as bread
And let joy live and spread

Nikita Bedi, Grade 10
Westmont High School

Harvest Moon

The sweet songs, of the farmers' voices —
Makes a wondrous chant — it flows through the fields.
The swollen moon, smiling brightly —
Lights a path, for the beautiful melodies.

The luscious grapes — shine under the moonlight —
And the crimson strawberries — emit sweet fragrances.
Fireflies dance — swaying to the festive music —
Owls crone — flying over the fields.
Stars sparkle, twinkling in the midnight sky

Farmers joyce — it is a festive time —
Time of harvest — time of life.
Under the luminous moon — the farmers embrace —
The sweet absolution — of Harvest Moon.

Sophia Roland, Grade 11
Arcadia High School

What If?

What if you had one day left to live?
What would you do?
Where would you go?
If I had one day left to live
I would say goodbye to everyone I loved and
I would hop on my horse and
Race into the sunset as fast as I could
I would ride faster and faster
Through deserts
Over mountains and
Swim through rivers
Until I could go no farther
To feel the wind one
Last time in my face is what I
Would do

Theresa Smrt, Grade 12
San Lorenzo Valley High School

Face It

Face it.
A mirror is a piece of glass.
Nothing that can tell the past,
Nothing that can make people see
What it is like to be you or me.
A mirror can't tell you if I'm lovely,
It can't tell you if I'm harsh,
It can't tell you if I'm euphoric,
Or mired in a marsh.
A mirror can't look into you,
To show people what is true.
Face it.
A mirror is just a piece of glass,
Don't make it your mask.

Sarah Su, Grade 10
St Joseph Notre Dame High School

Rerun

Pages run dry and get old,
This text rots away like mold.
Routines we no longer adore.
Much more meaning, but now no more.
Soft hands, old hands,
All different plans.
Familiar faces, but never really seen in places.
Tape being played in front of eyes;
What they want me to see, in disguise.
Hide the truth, from the blind.
Play the tape for you.
It's all reruns, the show of reality.
Just like on TV.
Rewind it, wait stop!
Play it back again.

Jimmy Dane, Grade 10
Grace Brethren Jr/Sr High School

Driving

Being sixteen
Is a cool age
Wanted to drive so bad
Can't hardly wait
Took written test
Flunked it twice
But then the 3rd time
I made it right
Behind the wheel
With a strange and smelly teacher
6 months later I had
A piece of paper
Took it to the DMV
And paid my fee
April 1st took the test
Best day ever because I passed
Left the car looking doom and gloom
Made a face like I was in a classroom
Started to smile like I'm leaving school
"Tricked you Dad, April Fool"
Oh, how happy I am!!

Andrew Tu, Grade 12
Bradshaw Christian High School

A Cascade of Petals

Cherry blossoms
Elegantly blooming on an ancient tree
Glistening radiantly under a full moon
Swirling blissfully upon a playful breeze
Falling gently,
Like pure pink snow,
Before the next day begins.

Christopher Duong, Grade 10
St Joseph Notre Dame High School

Thought

If the world was flat,
around where would it end?

If the mind could flex itself,
where would it bend?

If a broken heart fixed itself,
how would it mend?

If laughter was currency,
what more could we spend?

If true love is infinite,
where is its trend?

If God has a plan for you,
why not befriend?

Peter Olson, Grade 11
Villanova Preparatory School

Christmas

Our Savior was born on December 25.
Many deny it, some say it's a myth.
Many traveled from lands afar.
They were led by a star.

He was born in a manger,
And He grew up a stranger.
He preached to the priests,
In what is now the Middle East.

When He was arrested,
His followers were tested.
He was nailed to a cross,
But His life was not lost.

He rose from the grave,
He still had lives to save.
We'll be raised up to heaven,
Some at age one-hundred,
Some at age eleven.

Jarrett Reynolds, Grade 12
Linfield Christian School

My Garden

Relaxation is like going to the moon
And feeling the absences of gravity.
When I put my head down
In the colorful soft pillows I
Can smell the plants and the lemon.
I get the smell of nature
Stuck in my head.
I never want to leave this place
I wish I could stay here
Forever until I fade away with the wind.
I can hear the birds sing
With their beautiful voices
So I close my eyes and let
Myself go and fly away.

Mariel Pineda, Grade 11
Academic/Vocational Institute

The Coming

Ethereal thoughts
Turn my stomach to knots
Are we wasting time on Earth?
And what's in a second birth?
When my time runs out
There'll be no more doubt
Now that life seems to fade
All ahead is not but shade
How is heaven or hell?
This, only time can tell.

Rachel Weerth, Grade 11
Valley Christian High School

I Wish

I wish
You were here
To hold me and tell me you care
Or to tell me it's all right
Maybe if you didn't get cancer
Everything would be better

Sarah Babcock, Grade 11
Calaveras Hills High School

Blazing Race, Saving Grace

Here I am
Running this race
Wondering, will I get first place?

Here I go
Walk, jog, or run,
There is no fun under the sun

I cry out
Shouting in grief
Is there someone who can hear me?

I look up
Seeking relief
I see a light purer than me

I reach out
He takes my hand
He takes my fears, and wipes my tears

Now I see
O could it be?
The Sacred Lamb, who died for me

Daniel Chance, Grade 10
Christian Life Academy

The Leopard

Eagles soaring far below
Water rushing quickly by
The sun has risen soon to fall
The leafy canopy high above
Protecting all from harsh light
Animals are all below
Soon the day will come to end
Along with the suns heat
And cold will take once again
Standing here on this high cliff
I reign over the land
For I am king
As of royal blood
Nothing defies me
A leopard I stand

Liam Savage, Grade 12
Redlands Sr High School

Life Not Spent on a Dime

Life is a dream.
To dream is to live,
To live is to love.

Love and friendship are the wind.
You cannot see it with your eyes,
But you see with your heart.

Love is as true as a breeze that caresses your face.
So soft, gentle, and kind.
A touch of heaven one touch at a time.

A cloud of truth floats on a sigh.
Smooth as silk and lost in the skies of time.

Friendship is a breath of beauty and essence.
It is a raindrop that tastes of peace and patience.

This is life not spent on a dime.

Marissa Gomez, Grade 12
Redlands Sr High School

Time

Time is a grumpy old man;
mad at the world,
trapped in clocks since time was born.

Time doesn't rest;
He lives for impatience.
If we want the minutes and hours to fly,
time will roll them slowly by.
And if we don't want something to end,
Time will trick us.
Time will start slow, but as we tread down the hill,
the minutes will pass faster and faster
until it's over.

That's how he is, Time;
If he can't be happy, he'll make it rough for us too.
And that's how it's going to be
Because Time, himself, knows no end.

Vicente Fuentes, Grade 10
Gridley High School

My Birthday

Today is my birthday so
today is my day
it's mine and only mine and
don't care what anyone has to say
it's raining outside for goodness sake
but I hope that the rain doesn't ruin my cake.

Keith Holland, Grade 11
Downey High School

A Look into My Heart

About to see his passionate, rugged face,
Scared and hurt, how I missed his warm embrace.
As he walked into the room all righteous and aglow,
That closeness we had darkened long ago.
Dodging, stooping, finally hiding in curtaining shadows,
Overcome with the urge, to run through sage meadows.
With a pounding in my heart, loudly hearing an inner voice,
"Recall the courage you asked for, remember it is your choice?"
Looking deep into myself, where finally I found,
That aplomb and strength, and womanly sound.
I approached him with grace and softly I said,
"I can't wait for the life that faces us ahead."
Talking for hours and recalling feelings of past,
This strong bond and love was truly meant to last.
My hand in marriage he asked one more time,
The life with him, was the mountain I would climb.
Our future was warm, with love and compassion,
Like a fairy tale ending in style and fashion.
Two children made our family so happy you know,
His love on me he truly did bestow.
The result of the courage, I prayed for long ago.

Amanda Sahm, Grade 11
Saugus High School

The Sojourn

To walk away from what we were,
To walk away from what we've left,
To walk away, and stray not a step,
To the right nor to the left.

To walk past treasures which bring false joy,
To walk past dreams which distract and destroy,
To walk past mirrors which reflect our old shame,
We walk free at last for Christ bore our blame.

Elias Larimer, Grade 10
Home Educator's Resource Center

Change

Change can be tough for the faint of heart
the homesick women and patriotic men
To move to a country without knowing the language
They stay where they are as their children grow
Always hoping for that day to go "home"
Mi casa, mi pueblo, mi tierra
Never thinking of where they are at
Always of where they would be
The memories left behind
The family, friends they miss
the money sent and never seen again
Cuando regresaré?
They work and work but never change
Their children grown and stay the same
Always wishing to go home
Always

Jose Orozco, Grade 10
Gridley High School

Woodlands

Snow mountains border
A golden forest bustling
With squirrels and birds
Waking after winter nights.

Bounteous berry bushes
Treat robins to breakfast
While crystal droplets fall,
Spring showers arriving.

Steven McLellan, Grade 11
Saratoga High School

Wishes

If I wished upon a star
Wished on something out so far
Twirling in the sky's deep blue
Would that little wish come true?

If I tightly held your hand
Eyes squeezed shut, my heart expands
Bursting with three words within
The world around me swiftly spins.

And if I wished upon that star
Wished on something out so far…
And if I let those three words ring
All held so high on fragile strings?

What would you do in the fading light
Under that beautiful, stunning sight?

Jennifer Tsao, Grade 11
Jack Weaver School

A World of Dark and Light

Hold me tight, through eternity.
Keep me close
As the world swings by.
I can't see through the stars
What really is to be.

You say, "All's well"
And yet I get the feeling
It isn't meant to be.
So we'll close our eyes to the darkness
Of the gradual dawn.
Don't look past our memories,
Into the light of the sunset.

Don't let me go.
Even if it might be best for me.
I would live condemned for you.
As the world goes 'round
We'd meet again anyway.
Two dark stars in a world of light.

Lauren Young, Grade 11
Mira Loma High School

Sister

There isn't a time that I can remember without you here
There isn't a person who means more to me than you do
There isn't a time that you have given up on me
You have stuck with me through it all
The good times which were great
And there were the bad times in which I learned something new from you
No one else knows how to make me smile the way you do
No one else understands what is on my mind like you
There is no one else who is as close to me as you
You are an angel who saves me every time I fall
You are the one who carries me when I can't walk
You always help me through those times when I feel there is no point to life
By watching you I learn too
By hearing your voice I know that I can make it through
By loving you I am loved too
You are the one and only person
You are the one who I am not afraid to say
I love you too and it will be okay

Crystal Poublon, Grade 11
Jack Weaver School

Enumerating Your Memories

Time passes by as does the memory of our loved ones
Drifts closer towards forsaken thoughts and soon forgotten,
But the strongest of these memories will burn deeply in the mind
To commemorate the input on your life which this person has left behind.
No matter how far apart we may live from each other
The good times remembered will always keep us together
Our friendship is strong, even without the presence of one another
For in our hearts, we'll always know that what we share will last forever.

Catalina Mele, Grade 11
Mira Loma High School

Have Faith

I look out at the fields of China.
As I sip my cup of tea in the morning,
the steam of the tea rises up to my face.
I feel the pain through my skin,
and in my blood, because I know my dream
of making a better living was slowly drifting away.
I walked outside to the little farm my family owned.
I start to work early in the morning
at 5 AM since I was six years old.
I worked eleven hours a day and
as I stand outside in the bitter cold of winter,
the cold wind numbs my whole body
and I sense nothing in the world.
I try to regain my strength,
but it seems as if hope slowly dies away each day.
My mother told me to never give up.
She said faith is all I need to survive.
So I try my best to trust and listen to her.
Then all of a sudden, it feels as if all my worries were lifted away.

Elaine Wong, Grade 10
Abraham Lincoln High School

Our First Time

Grinning faces, and butterfly stomachs,
Dressing nicely for that one special day,
Her hair pinned up, his shirt buttoned up tight,
Racing to the car, impatient to see that Mr. or Mrs. Right.
Taking that second and last look in the mirror,
Bringing a special red gift for that other person,
Feeling jittery and heart skips,
Feeling uncomfortable and stomach dips.
Sweaty palms and all,
Waiting for what is in store,
Cannot believe the things your mind is thinking,
Because first impression means everything.

"Mrs. Hooks is my name," she said with a smile,
Accepting that red apple gift from the little child.
Parents slowly leaving at the door,
Kicking screaming just can't take it anymore.
"Mom dad where are you going!" screaming with a fright.
Now believe the actuality…
That the first day of school does not seem quite right.

Anthony Brooks, Grade 12
Redlands Sr High School

Shines Through Clouds

Like a saber,
Glorious, high above
Bright hope
Parts the gray gloom of a storm past.
As if the hand of God touches the dark Earth.

Jonathan Chue, Grade 11
Valley Christian High School

Her and I

her sitting in the far distance,
Shivering and drowning in pain inflicted.
Her sitting and watching,
Wondering why I do nothing.
her sitting and staring to feel,
A change for the good a change to forget.

I not sitting or standing realize,
I've been walking the wrong path.
I not sitting nor standing come to a halt,
To turn around and begin to walk the walk intended to.

Her sitting in the far distance,
Shivering no more and granted with hope.
Her sitting and watching,
As I do something.
her sitting and starting to feel;
A chance for good and a chance to forget.

Her and I not sitting nor standing,
Searching for love inviting yet not demanding.

Kevin Bran, Grade 10
Sierra Vista High School

Any Day Can Be That Day

The jungle's czar has preemptive strikes
And young Hamlet planned for weeks.
But Professor Keating practiced the idea of Carpe Diem,
Accomplishing day by day all that he seeks.

Any day can be *that* day

The president elect is a title given over night,
As was the length of time in which Romeo and Juliet fell in love.
And one choice can decide whether one goes to the pit of hell,
Or if they will continue their quest for the paradise above.

Any day can be *that* day

Fitzgerald Darcy wrote Elizabeth Bennett a letter
While George Bailey gave Mary the moon
And neither made their move a moment too late,
As did neither make it just too soon

Any day can be *that* day
Why not vanquish *it* today?

Bradley Jay Evans, Grade 12
Redlands Sr High School

Evanston

Ethereal flakes tumble from cumulus clouds,
They waltz on invisible planes,
Sprinkling sloped rooftops with glistening frost.
Drifting by tidy lawns,
They rest on dewy windowsills.
Every kiss blesses powdered houses,
While Heaven and nature sing
Silent Night.

Teresa Mooney, Grade 11
St Joseph Notre Dame High School

The Sign on the Hill

More than just a boulevard.
More than just a sign on a hill.
9 simple letters: H.O.L.L.Y.W.O.O.D.
Nine letters that makes the name,
that makes the world what it is.
Most do not even realize that every day,
they see the sign on the hill, they drive down the boulevard.
Those who do realize try hard to fight it and say they don't.
Then, there are those who desire to BE the boulevard.
They will do whatever it takes to have their name
put next to the sign on the hill, they do whatever it takes.
Even if it means exchanging integrity for interviews
or exchanging a conscience for a corvette.
Am I one of these people? I certainly hope not.
Yet, I'll be there one day.
Script in one hand scripture in the other.
Do I want my name in lights? That would be nice.
But not at the expense of the exchange.

Jonathon Murillo, Grade 11
Bradshaw Christian High School

A Ball Field

A ball field rests peacefully; it is quiet, and still.
Its serene slumber holds many memories and dreams.
Wood and metal bleachers once filled with cheering fans,
now stand bare and naked in the cold winter wind.

Its green grass envelopes me with a sweet, distinctive scent.
Rich, red earth at home plate clings to my feet and crunches under my weight.
The wind in my ears echoes the sound a bat sings as it commands the ball to take flight.
Closing my eyes, I envision a player rounding third base and sprinting for a score.
The dugout empties onto the field as teammates erupt in a shower of cheers.

Come spring, this field's solace will be roused once more
as another quiet winter, retreat concludes.
The now empty field will awaken and invite teams of boys to play the game they love.
The field's eyes and ears will watch and see
as more memories and dreams are made on its green grass and red clay.

John A. Moe III, Grade 10
St Francis High School

My Grandfather the Robot

The year comes and goes.
My gears have been long rusted from age.
They groan with every little twitch I make.
My fuel source is constantly low.
Just barely enough to keep me up during the day.
Unfortunately, I have contracted a virus.
One that is incurable.
Soon, I will become just another part of the scrap yard.
As my time draws near, I cannot help looking over my past experiences.
I remember being born in China.
I remember seeing the love of my life for the very first time, who would later become my wife.
Remembering these moments makes me feel regretful,
For all the missed chances, missed experiences, and past feelings.
For once my time as passed, none of it will come with me.
As I lay in my death bed.
I give my last breath, my last words
And I leave this world for good and move onto the next.

Julian Wong, Grade 10
Abraham Lincoln High School

The Greatest Mother

Every night I lay down in my bed, and I think about the wonderful roof you put over my head.
I could never ask for anymore from you, so it's my turn to show you what I can do.
I could never explain to you how I truly feel, because my emotion I speak wouldn't sound so real.
You put me on this earth to let me shine, the emotions in my heart portray through this rose vine.

As my head is spinning like a wheel, I'm only trying to explain how I truly feel.
It's a hard time when death does us part, but you're the only key that unlocks my heart
It breaks my heart when you're disappointed at me, even you know you should never be.
I'm growing up now and I think you should know, that you're parenting skills will really show.

When I depart from the house it will be a sad day, but just remember I'm only one call away.
I know we will always be here for each other, that's why you are the world's greatest mother.
Mom you are the one that I look up to, so I want to say I love you.

Jesse Matheny, Grade 12
Redlands Sr High School

A Forever Gaze

Lost within the complexities of the mind, a forever gaze
Mesmerized, it was as if time stood still
Everything silent, the whole world had become mute
The only sound to be heard was the beating of a forsaken heart
A statue frozen in time as the world keeps moving forward
A soul longing to fill an empty void
Standing in the epicenter of this so called planet
Watching its inhabitants thoughtlessly live out their lives
Tongue tied and words all jumbled
Hoping life would be so much simpler
Stuck in a forever gaze never to be broken

Pamela Escobar, Grade 12
Saddleback Valley Christian Schools

Every Time

every time he sees her,
he stops and stares.
he finally realizes
how much he truly cares.
they spent every minute together,
in perfect bliss.
he misses everything about her,
especially her kiss.
no one cared about him
more than she could
she would do anything for him
for him, she would.
he took advantage of her love,
and always put her down.
she always stayed around, waiting for him
while he ran around town.
now, she has moved on
and found someone who
cares for her
the same as i did for you.

Mona Ruiz, Grade 12
Monache High School

Blue Twin

We resemble so much, you and I
Yet we differ in many ways
The fact that we are close was a lie
In our ambitions is where the truth lays

You're cold and harsh and hunger for power
Thinking of ways to get strong
You look down at us from the decrepit old tower
Not realizing what you do is wrong

We resemble so much, you and I
Seeing as how you are my twin,
You want to be different and you can try
But remember you'll always be kin

Sydney Breanne Clark, Grade 12
Redlands Sr High School

A Story I Have to Tell

I have six brothers and sisters, and we all live together,
I thought this kind of life would be forever.
Since I was born, I have to work in the farm,
from the bright morning till dawn.
One night when I was at home,
a man showed up and talked to my father alone.
I knew at that point that the decision is made,
I don't love him, nor hate him, but he's now my soul mate.
We have two kids and they changed our lives.
Our relationship deepened as time flew by.
But happy times always goes by fast,
not you are in heaven but our love will grow and last.

Amy Liu, Grade 10
Abraham Lincoln High School

True Friends

The thought of a good friend may never end
for there are so few of them.

You will never lose a true friend because
your bond is strong with them.

These are the friends that really care
they are special and very rare.

You don't need to tease, you don't need to stare.
You just need to be the friend that's there.

As trees grow tall and begin to sway
As flowers bloom and fade away
As things change from day to day.
A true friend will always stay.

Ilene M. Kruger, Grade 11
Round Valley High School

Where the Wild Things Play

The end of the day
I crash into you

You embrace me with soft springy open arms
I rest my noggin on your pillows
to drown myself in Z'ss

Barely 10 seconds pass and I am gone
into a world of flying microwaves
and a pink elephant named Horton

Your silk smooth covers engulf the entirety of me
keep out the chill keep in the hope
you seduce me every night with promises
of nothing but comfort

Beneath your sheets I'm in nirvana
the only thing left to desire is you

Jeremy Shriver-Munsch, Grade 12
San Lorenzo Valley High School

Grow Up

the fiercest thing in life
is to swing on the swings in the night
a cool April night at the church playground,
with wood chips like before
stars tilt and slide as you rise and fall

it's mere weeks before this changes
before we can't be free as easily
soon there will be nothing to resist,
no seat belt to leave unbuckled and taut
drinking Slurpees and speeding away

it's somewhere between, isn't it?
not the sea change or the buffalo stampede,
the most refreshing liberation carries with it
a newer sharper slavery to be tolerated.

Andrew Chapman, Grade 12
Clovis East High School

My Story

I am Liu, Gun
I was a dedicated worker and mother.

Growing up in Canton, China,
life as a farmer was hard.
Born to grow rice and vegetables,
to raise chickens and pigs,
just to make food and money.

As you can see, a poor life
with houses made from brick.
How hard it was at dinner
to start fires with grass.

While the main goal was to work in factories,
to become successful and have a good life.

Hannah Kong, Grade 10
Abraham Lincoln High School

The Man Dressed in Red

Have you heard of the Man Dressed in Red?
Have you heard of the deeds he has done?
Have you heard of the son born of Sparta?
The man who, against demons, has won.

Or had you not realized there was something to win?
Did you not know that there was struggle behind?
We owe thanks to this skilled man in red,
Who helped remove the evil that was intertwined.

The evil which was born from the same place as him
But encompassed all he refused to become
Who looked just like him, and was just as skilled
But was not enough to take over where the first man was from.

Breanna Northway, Grade 12
Redlands Sr High School

Innocence

We come here every day
Playing and trading cards.
All that we ever do is play and
Trade
Play and
Trade.

Sitting around waiting for
Someone or something interesting
To come around to play with us.
Blowing bubbles as we wait.
All that we ever do is play and
Trade
Play and
Trade.

The fun comes to an end,
As the sun is setting and going down.
Until tomorrow Tommy, Jane, and Billy
All that we ever do is play and
Trade
Play and
Trade all day.

Lleseña TeJeda, Grade 10
Helix High School

Swing Sets

Sitting on this swing set,
I can't help but look up at the sky
An endless sea of diamonds gazing back at me,
Glittering,
Winking
Mocking the heaviness in my heart.

This dull ache can't seem to go away
Thumping,
Beating
Tearing at the remnants of my soul.

It's quiet,
Desolate.
The sounds of a creaking swing,
Of sneakers brushing gravel
They entwine to form an anomalous symphony,
A symphony that only we can understand.

Sitting on this swing set,
I can't help but look up at the sky
Sitting,
Wondering,
Are you looking at the same sky I am?

Clare Nguyen, Grade 11
Valley Christian High School

A Darker Time

Let me tell you a story about a time way back when,
a time where life was much simpler.
I lived on an island of South Vietnam,
it goes by the name of "Dao Phu Quy"
It was all good, just fishing from day to day,
earning just enough to put food on the table for family and kids.
One day I came back from a trip of fishing,
I heard the news and my world went black.
"VIETNAM AT WAR"
I ran home to hide my family from the troops.
Soldiers storming all about the island, looking for new recruits.
I turned to my eldest son,
told him to run away to America with the rest of the refugees,
try your best to do well and come back for us.
My son left for the land of new beginnings.
From that day on, I did my best to keep my family safe.
Fast forward a couple years into the future,
sure enough he got us out of the war zone.
My family and I finally made it to the safety of America.
To have a safer place to live.
To have a better life.

Andrew Dang, Grade 10
Abraham Lincoln High School

Love for Him from Love for Me

People ask me why I say,
I live for Him, all the way,
I turn to them to tell them why,
I live for Him, because he died,
They ask what he did for me,
I live for him, HE DIED FOR ME,
The truth is that I do not know,
How he could love a sinner so,
I turn to him to ask for a sign,
How could you trade your life for mine?
He answered me that very night,
And now I tell others of His might,
He died for you too, let your love show,
So I ask you, no, I beg you, stay on the right track,
Turn to Jesus, and love him back.

Matthew Nomicos, Grade 11
Chowchilla High School

That August Day

That August day was not one of laughter or play.
It was not a day for welcome and stay.
This was a day that would cause great sorrow and pain.
On this cold and gloomy day there was nothing to gain.
Instead this was a day of heartbreak and loss.
On such a day one can only turn and toss.
One could only wish that such a day did not exist.
Yet there are so many that one could even make a list.
So life goes on and so do the August days.
Where she had to go and you had to stay.

Josh Tractenberg, Grade 11
St. Michael's College Preparatory School

Sonnet I

When affection overwhelms one's reason
And desire outperforms the pure mind
The true heart, which sometimes leans to treason
Holds hostage rationale, they speak combined.
So the tongue is tied and the mouth confused
So that what should be heard must now be read
What simply should not be must be excused
What should be said must fester here instead.
Unless, as time has shown itself to be
With lengthy passage such it can effect
Words, mind and heart in perfect harmony
And then what must be heard is said direct.
 So if hand and heart may work together
 Purest love you'll find in ev'ry letter.

Max Sutton-Smolin, Grade 12
Torrey Pines High School

young prisoner

panhandler of my dreams
my past invading the present
rancid magic
a vast subdivision
over the meaningless sky
i'm life proof
but shut out
dragged in and let down
and only the young, they bring anything in
but they are not young very long
hit hard! you put fire in my chest
through the bars lies the dead frontier
groveling
cruel and ugly
dead end horror

Briezi Beauchamp, Grade 11
Rancho Cucamonga High School

Liberate

I am mentally homeless,
Allow me to introduce myself into reality,
For I live in a dream world,
Whether it be better or worse.
I need someone to dream of.
To walk me back, so I can wake up alive.
I don't want to die in a world of war,
Where people destroy everything in their path.
To see a human killed because of their religion,
An animal killed for make up,
A country killed for oil.
I am one alive, a world away,
For those who fight and lose.
I'm being beaten down by those with no cause,
Who take up space and criticize a movement
A movement for life,
Walk with me
Liberate liberate liberate

Alicia Ortiz, Grade 12
Patriot High School

Mirror

I look into a shiny piece of glass
What do I see?
All I see is a girl
Staring back at me
Does she have a face of sorrow?
Does she have a face of shame?
Why does she look sad
Does anyone know her name?
She feels as if no one cares
She doesn't feel loved
What she doesn't realize
Is that she is watched from up above
He will continue to be with her
These hard times will soon pass
So build up some courage
And break that shiny piece of glass
Ashley Mauro, Grade 11
Valley Christian High School

The Shore

Look at the mysterious shore.
Colorful pebbles and shells
Decorate the bare sand.

The small smooth pebbles
Rest in the sand's grooves
Like honeybees in their
Honeycombs buzzing in the summer.

The sound of the ocean
Fills the ear with pelting mystique.

Nature's musk of sand
And salty ocean
Arises the senses.

Look at the mysterious shore.
Lavinia Ruxandra Mitroi, Grade 12
Redlands Sr High School

Life

Scared and cold
First night on the street
Your body hurt from you
Head to your feet
You miss school
Not the work but the friends
Wondering when they ask
Where you been?
Got a dollar fifty?
Every penny gotta spend
Make a wrong move
BOOM…
"Your life comes to an end"
Jasmine Perry, Grade 11
Calaveras Hills High School

From East to West and Back

The bombs struck China many years ago
When Japanese soldiers invaded the city
My grandparents were frightened to go
Everyone was scared of the calamity.
They walked many miles to Hong Kong
Where they boarded a ship to the United States
After the journey that was long
Their children found their mates
But after staying in America for several years
My grandfather wanted to go back to his homeland
The traffic and hustle of the city was too much for his ears.
He wanted to go back to where things were originally made by hand.
His children did not want to see him go back
He said he didn't understand English
And that going back to China was his one wish
So back to his homeland where he stayed till he was 92
The funeral was held in China and I could not attend
By then I wanted to make amends
That's how my grandfather was,
Going from east to west and back.
Ashley Yee, Grade 10
Abraham Lincoln High School

The Guide to Being Insane

To be insane does not mean to be in an insane asylum.
To be insane you must view things in a different perspective than the normal view.
You must see the possibilities not the obstacles
You must throw away all the sadness and reach for the happiness
To be insane is to be out of the ordinary and not afraid to admit it.
To be insane you must let your imagination flow like a river
And you must never let that river be blocked.
To be insane you mush face the sunrise with a smile
And face the sunset with the same smile.
To be insane is not a bad thing.
To be insane means you see life with a different point of view than normal people.
To be insane you must never let others put you down
And always keep to the sunny side of things.
Louis Solis, Grade 10
Abraham Lincoln High School

Football

Fighting for the man to your left, to your right, behind you,
But vowing to destroy the person in front of you.
The ball is released; the bullets have been fired,
However, the only injuries come from the perspired.
You charge, retreat, and fight for your life,
Fight for the players you play with, their souls, and their sacrifice.
It is a violent competition for glory and fame,
Yet all it comes down to is having fun playing the game.
But the thing that separates the game from any other match,
Is the fact that you are fighting for your survival,
For every play could be your last.
So fight to the end you gallant men!
You brave souls of football, you players unsurpassed.
Keenan Welsh, Grade 10
St Francis High School

Glory

To you, yes you, glory will be held
Through duels, gambits, and combat
Through persistence and pleasure of gain
The glory of the sword can be yours

There exists another glory which may be held
Through riches, fame, and power
By acts that may contradict chivalrous play
The glory of gold can be yours

The third glory, for you, can be held
Through education and studies
Which progress your prowess
The glory of the pen can be yours

Only you will know if this glory shall be held
Through devotion, love, and charity
By selflessness and your sacrifice
The glory of the heart can be yours

One glory is easy to reach but hardest to hold
Throw away the anger of the sword and greed of the gold
Grasp the pen and work with pure love for God, Lord above all
The glory of the soul, greatest of all, can be yours

Michael DiPietro, Grade 10
St Francis High School

I Love You

I sat down thinking to myself today
When will all this unhappiness go away?

Sometimes I think I have something important to say,
Until all of my vocabulary just goes away

I sit staring blankly at the wall that I see,
'Til I see a picture of just you and me.

Your pretty face and long black hair,
Sometimes I wish that I just could be there.

But these walls that have me locked up inside,
Brings out feelings that I just can't hide.

Some days I sit when I'm all alone
And dream of the day I will soon be home.

I write like this when I think of you
I write to let you know my feelings are true.

I Love You.

Dewayne Shepherd, Grade 12
Redwood High School

The Fear Rises the Fear Falls*

The fear rises, the fear falls,
Fluorescent light, three shadowed walls,
A girl who cannot help but frown
Bemoans the weights which hold her down
And the fear rises, the fear falls.
Silence settles the outside halls
But she dares, she dares to make no calls
With an aching heart she decides to bear
The heavy load wrought by fear,
And the fear rises, the fear falls
Freedom through respite calls
Swiftly she flit through all the halls
Daily movement masks from the eye
Signs of weakness she would deny
And the fear rises, the fear falls.

Anna-Kay Richards, Grade 11
Valley Christian High School
*Patterned after Henry Wadsworth Longfellow's
"The Tide Rises, The Tide Falls"

Rainy Days

My life seems to be in constant rain,
And so full of pain.
There's so much confusion in my brain,
It makes me go insane.
Time seems to be so slow,
And what might happen to my future, I just don't know.
If this sadness doesn't stop to grow,
Then I just might blow.
These rainy days just seem so gray.

Edgar Aguilar, Grade 10
Crossroads School

Worcester v Georgia

God only knows what
made the Red Man red
instead of peach, ebony, or cream.
Yet such a difference made no difference;
like the others, he turned blue.
Hope, home, health, his breaths could not
continue to pretend the World was Old.

O cloudless drought, the salty
flood filled stoic rivers
full to the crest;
crashing over, breaking proud
banks, falling to the dust.
Unheeded. No eyes to see his eyes' levies break.
Ill-mannered conqu'rors; victory
but such a loss.
Drums no longer beat to bring rain; rhythm
Of tight skin still clinging to
flesh echoes in the mourning wind.
Westward, Ho!

Katie Donovan, Grade 12
Clovis East High School

Lost

Lost and alone
Hunger has taken me down to the bone
Running in circles all around
My possibilities never bound
Trying to find a place of reason
But hiding from the traces of treason

Where do I go?
Who do I see?
No one knows
'Cus I have only foes
I'm alone in the world
And never heard

Logan Benge, Grade 12
Redlands Sr High School

That's All

Hatred, silence
That's all I hear
My heart, it slows down
I feel no life
That heart, I use
To suffer, and love
Yet no one knows.

Jessica Hernandez, Grade 10
American Indian Public High School

There Is No Burden Like Homework

There is no burden like homework
To take my time away
Nor any sight like my planner
Of taunting words to me
This adventure all must take
And endure the timeless toll
How futile is the teacher's class
That bears the student's soul

Macie McMillan, Grade 11
Valley Christian High School

I Write About

I write about the bright days of summer,
Of swimming in the deep pool.
About the lemonade that I sip,
And burning under the hot sun.

I write about chocolate milk,
Of yummy food that I eat.
About raspberries and strawberries,
And tasty banana splits.

I write about friends,
Of going to the mall.
About seeing a good movie,
And laughing about it all.

Alla Kalyuta, Grade 10
Bella Vista High School

My Day

7:00 my eyes open just like every day of the week.
I sit and stare for just a moment at what the weather today might be.
7:10 my mouth opens eating eggs and ham.
7:45 locker opens grabbing binders in a rush.
12:15 my lunch bag opens and I get excited when I see a cookie.
After lunch I go to talk and almost forgot my bookie'.
2:48 bell rings and I go over to practice.
During practice we have to run, man my coach is one tough son of a gun.
6:00 pm I arrive home hungry as could be.
I jump for joy when I heard my dad cooked steak.
I ate so much I had a stomachache.
One half an hour later I take a shower before I watch Jack Bauer.
10:00 my day was good luckily I don't live in the hood.

Michael Cunningham, Grade 10
Ponderosa High School

The Wondrous Mutt!

The crossing of the sea to me

Is a trivial imagination of glee

As I see the shores of sand

I've returned to my place, home on land.

To leave the salty air behind

Over hills, stones and rocks on foot

Live with the trees entwined

Dig in the snow because I could

Walk the mountains for life

Swim the rivers for travel

Take to the skies in sight

Seeing the world in ten different sights.

Cortney Edwards, Grade 11
Marysville Charter Academy for the Arts

Genesis

I am from the religious town of Sahuayo and the streets of Oakland.
I am from the sounds of Mexican music and laughter.
I am from the sayings
   "That's life,"
    "You tell me, Grandpa,"
     "Don't tell your dad we went shopping," and
      "Look where I used to work."
I am from the nicknames of relative, cousin, countryman.
I am from the games of lottery, cards, and dominos.
I am from the large family of Mom, Dad, Erik, Aunt Maria, Miriam, Laura, Mayra, Fernanda, Sofia, Arturo, David, Aryanna, Daniel, Aunt Berta, Uncle David, grandma Eva…

I am from the bad picture days,
   the first day of school,
    and Sunday afternoon baseball games.
I am from the Mexican food of tamales, tacos, burritos, enchiladas, and salsa.
I am from the traditional birthday song and grandma's homemade birthday cakes.

I am me.

Tracy Castillo, Grade 10
St Joseph Notre Dame High School

Something I Love

Happiness you and I together always.
You and I forever and ever.
We will always keep the memories.
We will always be together.
When I am happy, shall I love.
That I will grater than be.
Times when I'm sad,
Memories of happiness make me glad again.

Bianca Jimenez, Grade 10
Sierra Vista High School

The Bronx, NY

My origin
My homeland, unlike any other.
A ghetto in the eyes of the nation;
My pride, my culture, my heritage.

New York, the center of all nations,
Superior to all other cities,
Pugsley Avenue is like a street of gold;
A borough like no other.

Not like LA, Chicago, or Oakland,
Different from Brooklyn and Harlem.
We go to eat pizza and cheer for Los Jankees,
And view all things Boston with hate.

Accents we have, though I have none,
Proud we are and New Yorkers we stand,
Draping the flags of our nations on our backs,
Melding together in what we call the Bronx.

Some people say, "I'm from such and such a place,
Give me the respect I want."
I say, "Yeah, sure, that sounds okay,
But I was 'born and raised' in the Bronx."

Nelson R. Miranda, Grade 11
Bradshaw Christian High School

Raging San Diego Fires

The children cry what happened to their home,
Reminding us the last time flames went by,
Oh, what has happened to that place, my home,
The flames engulfed and soar into the sky,
The firefighters try to put it out,
The flames attack destroying as they pass,
The man in yellow I can hear him shout,
In sadness he retreats and leaves his task,
More help has come to rid the town from wreck,
To stop the path the scorching fire has made,
More firefighters race on top the deck,
The fam'lies mourn and start to bury their dead,
At last it's safe to go back home and see,
The aftermath the flames have brought on me.

Yosif Al-Sharrak, Grade 12
Granite Hills High School

Two Weeks

You are the lucky ones,
though you do not know it.
You see things as they were,
not as they are, not as they will be.
You do not feel the fear.
For that you are lucky.
Spared from the regret,
the shudders of the future,
which screams its heat
as might the sun's rays,
as might a burning fire,
as might a desperate, pained heart,
inspiring only a desperate desire to look away —
You are spared from the Earth
falling from beneath you.
Because there is no soul more terrified,
no soul less aching, less anxious and angry
than that of he who must wait.

Daniel Gross, Grade 11
Los Alamitos High School

What I Fear

I fear of what may become of me,
And I fear I may not succeed
I am afraid I may not move on,
I am afraid of what might possibly go wrong
So I sit here watching the people go by,
I look up and watch the stars in the sky
I am dreaming everything will be all right
I am watching the view of the city-lights
I fear everything might go out of place,
So I'll walk through it all at an even pace

Patricia Urena, Grade 11
Calaveras Hills High School

Where Are You?

Who's my mother I think I know
The woman that gave me birth
To see me accomplish all my goals.
She's the woman I didn't get to know.

Even though I didn't get to see her
I ask if she thinks there was some mistake
Traveling without a child she left behind
Hoping she gives her head a big shake.

And turn around and see she's traveling without me
A child that she won't see accomplish all her goals
I hope I see her stopping here on a rainy day,
Like the day she gave me birth.

I think I will see myself full of joy
The day that I see my mother walking through that door
And miles before she let me explore the world,
And miles before she let me explore the world.

Daisy Salgado, Grade 10
Sierra Vista High School

Think, Evaluate, Do or Don't

I have for all my life been incredible self-aware,
unforgivably self-concerned, and irrevocably self-something or other.
My attention to everyone else's attention to me has been keen, and my interpretation of them,
regrettable undoubtedly misconstrued.
I am aware you are looking at me. I can feel you listening to me.
I hope to impress you without looking like I care to impress you at all.
Over and over again until the day's through.
My free-spiritedness is well thought out, as well as it could be in seconds.
I think I will tell a joke.
It's really pretty witty.
They'll laugh — and I'll make myself believe that I really didn't think they would.
I'll laugh too.

Elaine Kathryn Andres, Grade 12
Redlands Sr High School

To My Niece or Nephew

I've loved you from the moment I found out about you, to the moment I see you, to the moment I die. I will always love you!
You're not born yet, but it's nice to know you're loved, by all of us. And we will love you no matter what you do.
And I want you to know I will be the best auntie a kid could have!
No matter if you're a boy or girl, I will love and protect you as much as possible
I count the months until you're born, right now it's 8 but those 8 months will fly by, for your mom, dad, and all of us.
I was ecstatic the moment I found out! And will be the day you're born.
I can't wait to find out if it's a niece or nephew I'm getting.
Then I can't wait to see your face, because for that moment, there will be nothing better to happen or be seen, by anybody.
And to watch you grow up! That's going to be a blast.
The day I find out if you're a boy or a girl, I'm going to buy you the cutest clothes and toys a baby can get!
And in your family's eyes you will be the most beautiful baby ever, because you're ours, our family.
You will have the greatest parents, grandparents, aunties and uncles.
We will pack your mind with all our knowledge.
I just want you to know for the next 80 years I will love you.
We are all so excited for you to join our family,
And to see this beautiful creation God has given to your mom, dad, and the rest of us.
I promise I will be the best auntie I can be!

Emily Wade, Grade 11
Dixon High School

World War I

Of course it was inevitable that we would go to war again
With such a big country, someone's liable to go mess things up
And of course, we get into a war with some of the biggest countries
In a continent which we at first wished to ignore no matter what happened
But not all is lost, for this war has done something for this country
As a farmer one may not think it to be true, but I know much
of what is going on in this country, and with the coming of this war
there has been a sense of togetherness that as not been felt in this country in a long time.
Many are working side by side for the betterment of our country,
where in the past we would have scoffed at one another
for even attempting to make eye contact with the other.
Everywhere I go I see campaigns asking me to buy war bonds, to join the Navy,
to support the women who traveled overseas to accompany the fine young gentlemen
who would risk their lives for the country they were raised in.
I have thought it over time and time again, for I would join the Army
if it weren't for my wife, who would kill me if I made it back alive
Though we may lose lives, I will miss this sense.

John Elam, Grade 10
Abraham Lincoln High School

The Coma

Never waking,
    Not fully conscious.
Never living,
    Yet not passed away.
Not yet deceased,
    Somehow still breathing.

Anything is possible,
    But you have to believe.
Things aren't always the worst,
    Though not the best.

Wandering in the playground of your mind,
    Not realizing life is passing you buy.
As it goes on without you,
    Aging,
        Withering,
            Decaying.

There's not much you can do,
    When your life is in the hands
        Of the people you care about most.

Kimberly A. Dameri, Grade 12
Wilson High School

Nothing

Why? Why on earth would you say that, do that?
Make me doubt all our past.
Was it real? Did you ever really care?
I want to punch, kick, scream,
Release this inferno inside me, but I can't.
I can't.
I can't hurt you, make you feel bad,
Because I like you.
I hate those words, what do they even mean?
They meant nothing to you.

I made myself vulnerable, threw myself at you,
But you left me out in the cold, and I crawled back.
Why? Why? Why?
I took a chance, but only to fail,
Only to die inside, lose all hope.
Emotions like a flurry of snow.
No, a blizzard, a tormenting blizzard.
Yet, I'm numb.
No feelings. Nothing.

I feel nothing.
Nothing for you.

Linnea Wier, Grade 11
Grossmont High School

Then and Now

I used to play in imaginary worlds
But now my realm is reality

I used to be shy
But now I seek the boldness of life

I used to hide from fears
But now I decide to face them

I used to long for warm summer days
But now I cherish the delicate frosts of winter

I used to hold a paintbrush with no inspiration
But now art fills my life and spirit every day

I used to dream in beautiful shades of blue
But now I love elegant greens instead

I used to try and count the stars at night
But now I just enjoy their splendor

Sarah Kate Johnson, Grade 11
Gridley High School

Love Is a Dream

Love is a deal I'm willing to take.
It always occurred to me that love is fake,
An illusion of the mind, it's impossible to find.

It's only but a dream, it's not what it seems.
The day I met you I began to see love is real and exists in me.

William Mochidome, Grade 10
Opportunities for Learning Center

Desert Bliss

Why does my heart cave in?
When it's all undone
Feeling the weight of this
No help or bliss, just feeling amiss

Holding the letter in her hand
Letting it drop to the ground
News of his descent was not to be found

A thousand miles away
With disappointment on his face
Head dropped low with hands empty
Receiving the letter she had sent he
In this place of war and pain
No sadness cast, but only a frown upside down

News of a baby boy so precious and small
Sent from Heaven's womb to bless them all
All said and done, home from desert plains
Bright is this day the Lord has made!

Andrew Alfaro, Grade 11
Christian Life Academy

Location of Enlightenment

How do we find
Someone else's mind?

What's the goal
For our immortal souls?

How do we blame
That which has no name?

I can see it now,
It's all just a game.
Peter Czupil, Grade 12
Wilson High School

Music

With every note playing loudly now
And everyone listening
All of the small dogs baying
While the moon is glistening

A wonderful and happy player plays
Shows his great talent playing
With his partner accompanying
They entertain with saying

As the guests arrive on quick time
More enjoy themselves as thoroughly
And as ignorance is deprived
More enlighten themselves

The music has ended
And all has been said
The people depart
As the musicians go to bed
Arthur Aivazian, Grade 10
St Francis High School

The Subway

Do you see me?
I am where people meet.
Day after day
They come.
Do you notice my filth?
I am dirty, contaminated
With the odors
Of crowds like livestock.
Do you catch the hopelessness?
I am filled with broken dreams.
My passengers stare,
Worn down.
Do you see them?
Forced onto this subway
They are tired of drudgery,
But no one stands forth.
Amanda Chase, Grade 10
Helix High School

From China to the Dominican Republic

My grandfather's uncle went overseas from China.
From China he went to the Dominican Republic.
The reason he moved to the Dominican Republic,
Is to live a better life.
Life in China was difficult in the early 1900s,
that is why my grandfather's uncle went to the Dominican Republic.
Later my grandfather's brother follow his uncle,
to live in the Dominican Republic.
It was always hard moving to a new country,
and adapt an entirely different culture into their life.
They went to the Dominican Republic to work.
Also it was not easy for them to work right away,
because they needed to learn the language of the country.
My grandfather's brother and uncle sometimes went back to China,
to visit their family and their relatives.
Jacky Joa, Grade 10
Abraham Lincoln High School

Emotion

I wake up with a feeling,
One that gets me excited.
It starts with the night before,
the Fellowship with my brothers is the start of one exciting end.
The end of the week is one night away.
I sit and enjoy the company of my brothers.
I get the rest that is necessary for the task ahead.
I can't sleep with what's burning inside.
7 o'clock rolls around, I jump out of bed and get ready for the day.
The day goes slow but 3 comes around.
My team meets up and eats. Enjoy each other's company.
Game time! We walk out heart in my throat looking at my enemy.
The taste of sweat and blood.
Bruises and cuts all around. Five four three two one.
The game is done. Victory at hand, standing with my brothers.
I thank God for this last game. My feeling released. Satisfaction in my heart.
The team gives one last prayer and breaks forever.
I am so lucky to have the chance to be apart of something bigger then me.
And the legacy will carry on forever.
Collin Van Bruggen, Grade 12
Linfield Christian School

The Untouchable

I am the untouchable, I'm the frozen one.
You may call me ice queen, or the girl with the gun.
'Cause no one's allowed to come,
And try to touch my heart.
I am the untouchable, the one who builds walls,
That surround my hardened soul, to ensure I won't fall,
For the first one who comes and tries
To touch my heart.
Oh, it hurts, to be so strong, all life long, and in the dark I cry sometimes,
Fear attacks me, feel as though I'll never learn to feel.
Oh, and how it hurts to be,
The untouchable me.
Becca Snider, Grade 11
Centennial High School

Basketball

This is my world
This is my life
This is the only thing that's
Keeping me alive.
It's basketball. Yes, I said it
Loud and clear.
Don't know where I would be without it
And I'm glad of what I did with it.
I love the way it takes all my problems away
And my worries.
It's like a second parent
Just without the talking and the demands.
Basketball — thank the man who made it
And respect the man who mastered it.
My heart beating so hard that it feels like exploding
When I hit the floor preparing.
Love that it treats me good,
But sometimes we have our fights.

Cristian Diaz, Grade 12
Monache High School

Final Approach

Damp grass, freshly cut,
All you hope is to make that one putt,
The air is calm,
Sweat fills your palm,
Walking to the tee of the eighteenth hole,
Only hoping not to drill a light pole,
Birdie on your mind, par in your heart,
First shot is a bulls-eyes dart,
The second shot feels as if the ground starts to quake,
The ball soars over that very large lake,
Hit the green in two,
Nothing more you can really do,
You read your line, you felt the grass,
Please don't hit it too far past,
You hit the putt; it sits on the brim,
Like a basketball rolling around a rim,
The crowd starts to gasp,
You start to cringe,
But here comes a nice wind patch,
Suddenly, you win the match.

Patrick Shatkus, Grade 11
Saugus High School

Great Losses

Important things in my life I eventually lose
Why I lose them seems to confuse
Just when everything feels just right
It is gone as fast as a flash of light
Hurts more every day knowing it's gone
Tell myself I must somehow move on
Even if these losses have torn me apart
Good times will always live on in my heart

Araceli Cervantes, Grade 11
Sweetwater High School

Explain…

Why do you do what has been done?
Why do you say what has been said?
Why do you make what has been made?
Why, yes, why is this so fashionable?

Well explain to me, try and say to me
How you can be "new"
If it has been all done, said, and made before
You are so far from comprehension

Do me a favor and just keep quiet
They always said that "Actions speak louder than words"
You always told me to "Be what you are"
"Just shut up and listen to yourself"
That's what you said

Well please explain to me, try to say to me
How you can be "new"
If this too has been said before
If this too has all happened before

Can anything truly be new?
Or, is new just reinvented, re-improved versions of old.
How about we just strive to be (not new, not old, just be…)

Matthew Brendan Powell, Grade 12
Redlands Sr High School

Letter from the Left Hand to the Right Hand

To My Friend on the Right:
When writing, I'm dragged across the page,
smearing the words I just wrote like painting in the rain.
On guitar, you envy my flexibility, but
on piano, the tinkling flourish of the melody is yours.
I am mere backup, unnecessary.
Guitar is silent without your rhythmic plunge,
while on piano you can dance alone.
You say you envy my grunt work with fork and spoon?
Just once I'd like to cut a steak.
On computers, you control the mouse
and can type "jumpin'"
pressing delete if you change your mind.
Ask yourself, even if you are still willing to sacrifice these things
(and I've pointed out an awful lot of things)
For all the things I do, would you give up
Being offered first to clasp another hand in greeting?

By the way,
I would have written this by hand
If you were there to hold the paper down.

Brandon Young, Grade 12
Torrey Pines High School

All I Can Do

I wish I could take your hardships
Wipe the tears that you shed
Heal the scars of life's infliction
I want to hold you close to my heart
So you could feel it beat
And hear it scream your pain
I wish I could chase the darkness
Bring a little light to your weary eyes
I wish that with one sweep of my hand
You would forget the labor and duty
Forget the anxiety of instability
More then anything, all I wish
All I wish, with all my heart,
Is to believe, believe that things
Will get better
Becky Xu Hua Fu, Grade 12
Inderkum High School

Passing of Time

The clock ticks, the clock tocks
A moment too long in deadened locks
So much to do, so little time
All in a lonely pantomime
And the clock ticks, the clock tocks

Dismal pouring rain mocks
As the pitter-patter beat rocks
Washing, washing to mend
Never, never to end
And the clock ticks, the clock tocks

The warm sun is in a blissful box
Stress-filled times only mock
But I look forward to the day
When my work is less than my pay
And the clock ticks, the clock tocks
Robyn Bayless, Grade 11
Valley Christian High School

Trenches*

I sit with my best friend
Crouching, hiding
In a hole of burden
We have been through everything
He has saved my life
And taken others
A monster rolls overhead
Out to destroy
Another family
Another soul
I wait with my best friend
And I wait for the end
Olivia Drummond, Grade 10
Helix High School
*Inspired by Mark Markog-Grinberg's
"In the Trenches" near Korsk

Take My Hand

Walk with me through this life.
Carry me when my feet grow weary,
and I will hold you together, in your times of strife
Take my hand

Cry with me when my heart is broken.
And I will mourn with you, when your dreams are stolen
Take my hand

Laugh with me, as we behold the beauty in this world.
and I will sing, and dance with you, as we experience the splendor in growing old
Take my hand

Remember me, if before you I am gone
And I will remember you, if you leave me here, alone
Take my hand
Jesaka Chanel Davitt, Grade 12
Redlands Sr High School

Freedom

Wide white wings brutally beat the sky.
Brutally.
The anomalous animal ripped from its home in the African savanna.
Such a wide savanna.
With wide open ranges. Plenty of running room. Plenty.
But now, such a graceful animal,
With the candied eyes,
beat against the sky desperate for a way out
of animal slavery
of hatred
of an enmeshed life.
It had to fly away.
Pierce the sky with invisible tears.
Kiss the Earth with tears from its mother
and break free.
Mariah Farris, Grade 11
Elk Grove High School

Alone

He walks alone in the darkest hours, never wishing to stop.
The darker it gets, the easier he hides, but from what he does not know.
He wishes he could stop and sit, or maybe get some rest,
But he cannot stop he must not stop, it's his mind he's running from.

Long ago he walked in the day when the world was bright with sunlight;
The brilliance echoed how he felt inside and even made it stronger.
But now he cannot stand the light, not since she was forced to darkness.
So he cannot stop he must not stop, it's her he's running to.

Sometimes he thinks he feels her touch; she whispers "Please let go,"
But he gave her his life, he gave her his all; he does not wish to fill the void she left.
And darkness, he cannot be blind in darkness, for a veil already covers all.
So he cannot stop he will not stop, until he rests once more with her.
Jilly Jefferson, Grade 12
William Finch Charter School

While in a Meadow

I am in an endless meadow,
I remember my past,
Recall my present,
I look to my future.
Although I stand in my own way,
I will continue to push myself along
Further and further to my eventual end.
I would never accept myself if I were to ever give up.
Even though I will not be able to
Prevent the ending of my chapter;
Being a chapter in the Book of All Life,
I will live every day like it were my last.
I watch the clouds float by
Without a care for anything or anyone;
Oblivious to life below,
It continues along.
I had a chance to reflect
Upon my life,
I have learned to accept the past,
Move on and not look back,
I wander to a new place.

Jacob Evans, Grade 10
Saddleback High School

A Face Unrecognized

At the eve of time, when beasts turned to man;
And man into beasts.
There were
One kind which remained the same
Never changing,
Never growing.

Only waiting for the time to show itself.
As if it was shy,
A culture that flourishes in the deep
Jungles of Laos.
Just like our elders of long ago…

Roaming the plains from here to there
Only to end up from one place to the next.
A lifetime of wandering:
Is a lifetime of memories.
My ancestors have given me roots,
Where I must stand my ground
For if I leave,
I will collapse and die.

Wither away like I was never here
I am proud to be Hmong…

Chue Yang, Grade 11
Marysville Charter Academy for the Arts

I Wish

I wish
I were the Moon
Floating in the orbit
Looking deep into the solar system
Maybe even show an eclipse once in a while

Austin Adams, Grade 12
Calaveras Hills High School

Inspiration

Inspiration is a spider web wet with dew
Glistening against the morning sky's blue.

Inspiration is the fireworks on Independence night
In cascading colors and bursts of light.

Inspiration is a river churning white
Below flocks of sparrows taking flight.

Inspiration is a flag above a battlefield
Stern determination not to yield.

Inspiration is the sunlight hitting a snowy hill
A majestic jewel breathing wintry chill.

Inspiration can be found in everything
Keep your eyes open, there's much worth discovering!

Michelle Fang, Grade 11
Irvine High School

Forever Love

I am thinking of you,
since that's what I do every day.
Keeping your memory in me
by the passes of the day.
It's just like a tattoo
that I can't take away.

I have nothing else to say,
so my feelings are so powerful
just like the warmth you gave me
on a cold winter day.

You tucked me in your arms
and told me "Everything's gonna be okay."
Wow, wouldn't I have known
that that would be the last day.

It's all gone now,
but I'm sure the memories still live,
and I know I have to go on, just like you did.
But even though you might be with another woman,
and might see me with another man
always remember that
I love you.

Mari Castillo, Grade 10
Sierra Vista High School

Certainty

Bound with love,
Bound with fear,
Bound with hate,
We all seem to dissipate,
Into the force that is life,
Our path unable to be seen.
Dangerous this situation is,
For here we are confused,
Unsure of which road to take,
Or whether our stamina will break.
Suddenly it becomes clear,
The heavenly glow that is the end,
To our confusion and disorientation,
And the beginning of our assent,
Our assent to certainty.

Molli Fanchar, Grade 10
El Camino Fundamental High School

Like Helen

A poet is a blind girl learning to see:
She starts with but thoughts of light,

Fumbles along walls of nightmares
Caging her mind in dullest night;

Yet someone takes her pen, dips it
Into a fountain of inspiration —

Understanding — streams of water,
A wellspring of crystal sensation;

Joy — liquid running over fingers,
And laughter like a rushing tide.

Faith — in the brush of cool cotton
As the Muse floats by her side.

A poet now, she envisions words
In a vast expanse, bright as day;

For poets can know without seeing
When they let truth lead the way.

Connie Shang, Grade 11
Saratoga High School

Bond

By the look of your eyes
As we both stand here
Within this space
That defines our emptiness
I can assure you
That you are the girl for me.

Lisa Marin, Grade 12
Academic/Vocational Institute

Facts of the Past

He sits there alone
Thinking of what to say
The days go by
She doesn't know till this day

How much she means
To him he cannot say
He doesn't want to know
What she just might say

The facts of the past
Keep him bottled up inside
Like a man with no courage
Or one who's lost his pride

He wants her to know
That he loves her so
But the facts of the past
He cannot let go

He loves her to death
No one can interfere
But the facts of the past
Is his only fear

Jose Monge, Grade 11
Downey High School

The Day the Music Died

A cruel thing happened one winter day
On The Day the Music Died
For Three Musicians have passed away
Many of their fans have cried

Tired of long car rides in the cold snow
Holly, Valens, Richardson
To the Winter Dance Party they go
But go on a plane instead

Richie Valens, youngest of the three
Fate decided by coin toss
He won, and able to get a seat
Did not know the life he lost

The little plane took off with the Stars
With only room for the three
They took the plane instead of the cars
Cars were as cold as can be

Soon after takeoff, the plane went down
Certain Death for those inside
No more La Bamba, or Peggy Sue
On The Day the Music Died

Daniel Martinez, Grade 10
St Francis High School

Thanksgiving

They release the nails that bind him.
They scatter around to catch him
Carrying the king away.
Holding our lifeless pale father
The tears drop like a waterfall
But the blood still falls like a stream,
All hope is lost for the children.
BUT NO!
It cannot stop him
For death is his ally
He is the one who created it.
Raise your head.
Children of God must taste the courage.
His rise is more beautiful than his fall.

Collin Masteller, Grade 10
Calvary Christian High School

Our Children

In time
We watch children grow
We prepare for the youth
As one whole
To read and write
That's what we teach
No thugs no drugs
It's what we preach
For them, we hope
And wish for the best
Like birds it's nature
To take care of the nest
We go through goods
And go through bads
God bless the many
Moms and dads

Ashton White, Grade 12
Monache High School

Ode to Life

Life is a clock
Ticking with time
Life is a song
Without a rhyme

Life is happiness
That is enjoyed
Life is something
Not to be destroyed

Life is tranquil
Like a stream
Life is a place
To fulfill your dream

Patriya Pilouk, Grade 12
Redlands Sr High School

Life in the Slow Fast Lane

You're innocent, you're curious
You want to be able to relate
So you become spontaneous
And begin to feel hate.

You always wanted to know,
Now you do,
Now you begin your show,
Not knowing what to do.

You think you have control
Because you're having fun,
But you always have to be on patrol
Unless you're the one with the gun.

Flashing lights
Glowing through the darkness,
Causing fights
While you're blinded from the blankness.

Amy Griffith, Grade 11
Valley Christian High School

Taken Away*

The day you were taken away,
Was the eleventh of May.
My heart was split,
I couldn't sit.
I couldn't even talk,
I just needed to walk.
My heart was pounding,
In my head I could here the fire engine sounding.
I didn't want it to be true,
I didn't want to realize I would now have to live without you.
All I could say was, "Why?"
And, of course, cry, cry, cry.
Because I know I can't bring you back,
I want you to know the memories of you, I will never lack.
I love you.

Kimberly Vieyra, Grade 10
Saddleback High School
*Dedicated to my grandmother Maria Guadalupe Vieyra

Racing

Starting your engine,
First gear, let's go,
Appears like a hawk chasing after its prey,
Waiting for an opening, hoping for a mistake,
Getting sick of looking at the same bumper,
Step it up a notch or two by taking a risk,
Passing him with a sigh of relief,
Checking your rearview mirror
While smiling at the finish line,
Shifting to fifth gear,
Sounds like victory!

Jason Huang, Grade 12
Calaveras Hills High School

Left Broken

I am lost, feel disgrace, and can't bear to look into her face,
Seeing that smile that filled me with joy,
Now I realized all she did was toy,
I can't help it, don't know what to do,
All I wanted was to be alone with you,
But now is done, I will go,
But before I leave there is something I want you to know,
I've been watching from far apart,
Wondering, thinking of ways to your heart,
Now I am here with heartbreak,
Feeling this pain that nobody can take,
But now I pray to God to help me forget,
To take away this emotional threat,
I can't run and I can't hide,
From memories of you by my side,
Now I feel as if I have no soul.
Heartbreak and anger have taken their toll,
What can I say and what can I do,
But say I no longer have feelings for you,
Deep inside I know I lie,
Because these feelings for you will never die.

Victor Marquez, Grade 11
Downey High School

In My House

In my house
There is a girl
She follows me every day

She looks at me when I look at her
She dresses like I do
And speaks when I speak

She sees her brother dancing in his room
Her mom busy in the kitchen
And her dad nowhere in sight

She plays outside with my dog
And goes to my friend's house
She does my chores every day and wears me out

To her, my life is perfect
To me, her life is perfect
We want our paths to cross

Each in our own worlds
Thinking our own thoughts
But in reality we are one individual
Staring at the same reflection

Xochilt Azpilcueta, Grade 10
North Salinas High School

Music Is My Drug

Music is my drug
It's my antidepressant
With the power to warm cold hearts
A little light in life filled with dark
David Olivares, Grade 11
Academic/Vocational Institute

Pessimistic Soul

Criticize the world
And the soul will forget
All that is peaceful.
Then sadness will be met.
Nina Lam, Grade 11
Downey High School

Sitting on the Rocks

Waves
Crashing
On the
Rocks
Where I
Sit
Gazing
At the
Beautiful
Colors
Disappearing
In the
Sky
Wind that
Gives me a
Chill
Lets me know
Autumn
Is just
Around
The Corner
Alesia Jacobs, Grade 10
Balboa City School

The Trees Stand Tall

The trees stand tall with their
Dark-charred bark and
Blush-toned blossoms.

A rustle,
Hands grab and shake the limbs, then
Jagged wood defends its stillness
And the hands come loose.

But the petals on the edge
Fly softly with
Nowhere else to go
But down.
Chris Hohl, Grade 11
Valley Christian High School

Voyage

Whoever made the voyage up the Hudson
must remember the Catskill Mountains,
where the weather is fair and settled
and the mountains clothed in blue and purple.

At the foot of these fairy mountains,
the voyager may have described the light smoke
curling up from a village, whose shingle roofs gleam among the trees,
just where the blue tints of the upland melt away,
into the fresh green of the nearer landscape.
David Kauffman, Grade 11
Gridley High School

My Angel

As I was wandering aimlessly, without help of any kind,
All my fears crept up from every dark corner of my mind.
Shining in the darkness, I saw a brilliant light.
"So beautiful, so elegant, so radiant," I said in mesmerized delight.
So I hastened to see it closer, dodged everything in my sight.
I was an insignificant fly drawn to this everlasting sight.
When I realized what it was, my heart began to soar.
It was an angel, the angel, my angel, whom I adore.
"She's beautiful," I said in an awestruck pose.
How long did I gaze at her truly only God knows.
We run to each other lovingly, now we both bear a glow.
Our hearts were filled with love for one another, surely this was so.
I prayed to remain with her forever, to God did I beseech.
She was as gorgeous as watching a sunset, a sunset on the beach.
But like all sunsets, my sun was setting fast.
"So cherishing, so memorable, I knew it couldn't last."
I woke up…she wasn't there…tears began to pour.
I moaned…I groaned…I wanted her. I missed her evermore.
I hope to see her one day, for this I'll never be sure.
I pray to look upon the face of my angel whom I adore.
Chibuzor Ejiaga, Grade 11
St. Michael's College Preparatory School

Taking the Risk

Our village was simple and yet poor in China.
I was the housewife in the family.
Many responsibilities were weighing down on me.
My husband is now too busy finding a better job elsewhere.
Hmm, I wonder if he ever thought about me since the day he left.
I looked at my rough and dirty fingers and felt disgusted.
I know, I know, I should not complain.
Every day, my schedule was the same.
The food was scare and barely enough to feed all nine of us.
There were times I wished to be spoiled rotten,
then my siblings would soon be forgotten.
I decided to come to America and started all over from scratch.
I have worked my hardest,
but dirt still lay underneath my fingernails.
Knowing all the things I did from the beginning,
would be repaid in the end.
Serena Tsang, Grade 10
Abraham Lincoln High School

To Persephone's Mother

I am no poet. The eternal source has faded.
Crumbled shadows
Like a weed at Exbury
Emanate from its arid hollow.

The echo of a distant wind,
Parched azaleas, rusted sleep.
Perhaps in April, I'll revive again.

Yet, windows veiled in grime
At the violet hour,
And veins that follow like a map
To the canker of Reason.

Should I but for a moment
Escape the withering pestilence,
Night falls again.

Let Clarity bear fruit among the ruin,
Particles that wander toward their other mate
Until head and tail become one.

I am she who dared to confront
The assiduous quarrel of drought and plenty.
I am the author of the Wheel.

Vy-Vy Dang-Tran, Grade 12
Mission Viejo High School

Husband and Father

I see my wife cry and
hear my children complain,
"Dad, we are hungry!"
Life is difficult here, with barely any food,
we live in a small shelter.
No clean water, no stove, no bathroom.
I dream about living in America,
to find a job and make money.
Until one day this finally came true.
So I came to America,
leaving everyone behind,
I made more than I ever imagined.
But having all this money
means nothing without them here.
So I return home to be with my family.
Together we will starve,
together we will complain,
together we will deal with poverty.
But all this doesn't matter,
because my family makes me happy.

Ellen Cruz, Grade 10
Abraham Lincoln High School

Gossip

I can taste the whispers in my ears,
And the disappointment in people's eyes.
Each word that passes each face,
Causes more sweat to run down my body.

I can smell the rage in people's voices.
Each gab of stories that hurts someone's feelings.

I can hear colors rush past my face.
The word keeps spreading faster and faster each minute.
Each word makes people shriek with terror.

It looks as if there is no escape.
The hurtful words are blinding our eyes
With the bright white light.

It feels like a bunch of nails jumping in my soul.
Each saying haunts your every step.

It feels, tastes, smells, looks, and
Sounds like gossip.

Shanae Kavanaugh, Grade 10
Ponderosa High School

Rejuvenation

Tears kiss the morning grass, flickering fields of dew,
Reflecting the unfolding dawn as serene voices coo,

Where squalls of grief had cried trembling life is sown,
Wan whispers of healing where the storms of night had blown,

And the winds whisper a melody, silent and fluid as a stream,
Singing across the grasses, the skies are lit with golden dream,

On ageless hills of memory written is a past,
And ecstasy blesses tearstained eyes as they see the light at last.

Gold upon the grasses, the mantle of the dawn,
The anguish is relieved, the plight of fear is gone.

In the starlit reverie of dew, spread across meadows of light,
We all find peace through agony as memory forgives the night.

Mark Runyan, Grade 10
Marysville Charter Academy for the Arts

Loving You

Loving you is waking up in the morning
and smelling that good ole breakfast Mama used to make.
Loving you is the feeling you get when all your
friends surprise you on your birthday.
Loving you is winning in a war after working
so damn hard.
Loving you is a check coming in the mail
after being broke for so long.

Luis Lopez, Grade 11
Wilson High School

Blossoming Chaos

Tears, joy, devastation and perseverance is what has become of our world now.
Parched throats unable to grasp the bit of juice that comes from the fruit they admire so dearly.
You say you hear the blood scream and the anger ooze from your own heart.
Did you ever take the time to wonder why dueling seems to be the answer to everything we breathe?

You are too oblivious to your surroundings to notice the truth.
Like a glass of wine sitting on the table, you do not know where you got where you stand,
You tend to forget where you come from, supposedly a place of a more peaceful nature.

BOOM! There's the defending gunshot blown by the soldier. BOOM! There is the shot created by the enemy.
Chaos flies as an angel up in Heaven. Death approaches, taking the lives of many.
Loved ones are gone and people are torn away with angry fear,
Piercing the mind from the blossomed birth of the intellectual and naive flower;
Blooming with grace, unaware of the negative environment it will be a part of once discovered.

Alyssa Reaves, Grade 10
Wildwood School - Secondary Campus

Hidden in Plain View

I am disabled. My appearance has told on me.
The outside that I have come to know mocks me, day and night.
How come I'm slower than the rest? What if I was normal?
And I'm behind closed doors not wanting the world to see me, because I don't think that they'll understand.

I should be learning how to apply makeup, but instead I'm being taught how to tie my shoes.
My hands are shriveled and weak.
If I were to wake up one day and was normal would they still say, "There goes the retard"
And treat me as though I was invisible.
I should be able to speak up for myself, but I'm too scared.
And I'm behind closed doors not wanting the world to see me, because I don't think that they'll understand.

Nobody stops to put themselves in my position.
I should have stayed at the home, at least there people get me.
Why do I have to be the one wearing leg braces.
I have no STD's or skin diseases.
So why am I isolated from the other kids during P.E.
And I'm behind closed doors not wanting the world to see me, because I don't think that they'll understand.

Michelle Elizabeth Torres, Grade 10
Sierra Vista High School

We Are a Family at AIPHS

Every day, I see them and smile
each one of them so different and special
some are shy, some are loud, some are sarcastic, and some are hilarious
but one characteristic we all have in common is our intelligence
we all care for one another and we look out for each other
we're a team and we help each other
even though our personalities are so varied, we think as one when we come together in the classroom
we learn our Pre-calculus skills from a brilliant math master
we learn how to write beautiful essays and how to closely analyze published works from a clever English teacher
we learn how to impress outsiders with our Mandarin from a knowledgeable educator
we learn the history of our nation from a talented instructor
we learn physics lessons from a bright college professor
although every single one of us is a minority, we have a chance to learn and we cherish it
we will shine together as bright as the sun for the entire nation to see who we are.

Carmen La, Grade 11
American Indian Public High School

Forever and Always

I am here for you and I always will be,
Because you are so very special to me.
To stop caring for you and loving you I will never,
For this love between the two of us will last forever.

I will be there if you have something for me to do,
Because I would do absolutely anything to please you.
And when moments come where you and I are apart,
You will continue to hold a place in my heart.

If you may ever be in grief or denial,
I will be around to make you smile.
I will be there for you whenever you may fall,
Because a life without you is no life at all.

Though our time together is ceased by the end of days.
I will love you forever and always.

Giovanni Rivas, Grade 12
Pioneer High School

Be Yourself

I remember growing up with a mom who was so sweet,
We were poor, but she tried to give me everything.
It would be raining, but she would still
Be playing softball with me in the street,

When I was thirteen,
I found out she had a hole in her heart.
And that really hurt me.

I might not have showed it, but inside I was crying.
I didn't want anybody to think I was a baby,
So I held it all inside.

I'm sixteen now, and I'm doing a lot better.
I still struggle, but my mom has taught me to believe in myself
And not care what anybody thinks.

Just be yourself,
That's all that counts.

John Balderas, Grade 10
Redwood High School

Untitled

Japan, boring, spacious, repetition of daily life,
Spring is the season to plant the crops
Harvest them with a razor sharp knife
Wail till the day that our lives come to a complete stop
Sit back and watch the days pass by
Leaving this country felt nice
Reunited with my family once again
Feels good to plant another grain of rice
Hearing the roosters sing in the morning once again
To rest in peace in the soil of America.

Evan Motoshige, Grade 10
Abraham Lincoln High School

One Too Many

Trying to keep up with what this generation calls the norm,
Always searching for mayhem that will slightly amuse,
Looking up from this path, only seeing a foul storm,
Spiraling down, ignorant of lives being abused.

Kids filling their lives with poison and pleasure,
Speeding towards an aimless existence,
Craving a dose for what they truly treasure,
Falling deeper and deeper without any sign of resistance.

Going through life, only knowing stimulation,
Following the crowd on a path that seems fitting,
No desire to stop, lacking all consideration,
Hooked in a world that is always spinning.

Round and round the years go by,
Trying to cease this senseless fun,
Realizing their lives were only a lie,
No place to go, turning towards a gun.

Now at the bottom of everything due to this addiction,
On the wrong path, unable to control their fate,
Speeding down a road only towards perdition,
Struggling to get free but one choice too late.

Joseph Stack, Grade 10
St. Michael's College Preparatory School

Past Memories

Walking the streets of dear China,
Looking from side to side.
The people, their faces powdered in brown,
Wearing clothes less than what they deserve.
I pray that one day will be a better day,
That my descendants will live a better life.
Not needing to put through these fragile years
Is a decision that is to be made.
A dangerous war broke out! Run!
Escaping the chaos, with everyone safe,
We moved down to poor little Burma,
Experiencing conditions worse than before.
For the better of the future, we signed some papers,
And went our separate ways.
I dropped by in Taiwan, to be with my son,
Separated from my other children in the safety of America.
Soon reunited with all my loved ones,
I settled down in America that I now call home.
I come to the point where my story will end,
But generation after generation,
Will the future share the greatest of memories.

Kassandra Lau, Grade 10
Abraham Lincoln High School

Music

M y way to block the world out.
U nique beats, memorable rhymes.
S mooth rhythm to my ears.
I ntense lyrics that flow.
C areless rhymes they speak.

Melissa DeGuzman, Grade 12
Calaveras Hills High School

Lucifer's Tears

Heaven;s gates slamming shut,
Clouds flashing by,
My wings cut,
By god in the sky.

Tears floating all around me,
Arms outstretched wide,
Reaching for his majesty,
Whom I did not abide.

Now reaching the fiery lake,
Horns sprouting form my head,
For my won sake,
Why can't some angel take my stead?

My father,
Is this how it's supposed to be?
How much farther,
Will this war go between you and me?

Wade Washington, Grade 10
Milhous School

Waiting

The anticipation begins in the car
"Maybe today" my heart beats
Palms sweat
Head aches

Light stays red too long
"Almost there" my heart echoes
Palms pour
Head pounds

We round the corner
There sits the mailbox
Innocently closed, concealing
"Maybe today" my heart cries

Finally the car stops
I run out
"Maybe today" my heart faints
Empty, like my heart

"Maybe tomorrow"
The beat goes on.

Farah Ereiqat, Grade 12
Fairfield High School

Channels

I see you in pain. I want to take it away.
I watch it ooze out of your skin I want to take it away.
But there is a wall.
Sometimes I see a ray of light shine through.
Sometimes you reach out. You let me in.
It is not easy for anyone. Not just you.
You are not alone. We all fight the pain.

But there are channels, tunnels, ways and ways.
One is through your skin.
One is through your mouth. One is through your hand. One is through your ears.
The pain must go.
The pain has many names. Lonely, heartbroken, feeling unloved.
Feeling abandoned, feeling like there is no hope.
But the pain must go. It is poison.

It all gets better when it hits the air.
It must go through channels. You pick the channel.
The channel is the way out. For me it is the mouth: I talk it out.
It took me years to make the easiest channel for me. It is the least painful.
I see you use your hand to write.
I see you use your ears to listen. I see the pain coming out on your skin.
And it is still easier for me to use my mouth and just talk it out.

Brittany Woodard, Grade 10
Springall Academy

Fly

It seems I've been falling and there's no one around
Even though I'm flying high, all I see is the ground
I try to lift my eyes up, with all my might
But it seems that my goals are just out of my sight
Every time I try to grasp a dream or aspiration
There is something there to push down my hand, and add more aggravation

I know that without trials and failures, I will never grow
But I've been waiting to reap after so much has been sown
I'm tired of seeing just attempts, not followed by results
And after all this effort, nothing's clear but all my faults
I've tried to seek you, Lord, for truth and guidance in my life
But it seems that all you do is add failures to my strife

And so in my life I fall lower, and lower still
And the ground comes closer, and even closer, until
Your hand reaches down, from heaven above
And for the first time in a while, I can clearly see Your love

So you see, it was at these lowest times when I was inches from the floor
When I felt like I don't think I can take anymore
Just as I'm falling and the blades of grass become clear
You take the wheel of my life, and begin to steer

Kimberly Kawamoto, Grade 11
Valley Christian High School

Hate

Its ravaged path through time is seen
Through blood and tears and symphonies
Of angry cries and mocking stares,
Piercing words and scornful glares.

It's brought millions to their graves,
It's made wars, and it's made slaves.
It's brought tyrants into power
And it's seen them to their final hours.

It's pitted people against one another,
Whether sister and sister, or brother and brother.
It nailed our Lord upon the cross,
Who wanted naught but to save the lost.

It makes racial divisions get worse and worse,
And it makes men avoid those who are diverse.
Jew and Muslim, Korean and Japanese,
Many can loathe each other with ease.

It destroys all who stand in its path,
For none are safe from its mighty wrath.
And all who hold it dear shall fade,
Their legacy marred with an eternal shade.

Melissa Marcussen, Grade 10
Visalia Christian Academy

Accepting Yourself

You cannot run away from yourself.
You cannot lie to yourself.
Do not fear of who you are,
And do not fear of who you have become.
Be happy of who you are,
And for what you have accomplished.
You don't have to hide behind that mask.
The mask that you wear every time,
For fear of being rejected from peers,
Just to have a place to belong.
Remember, true friends —
Accept you for who you are.
If you believe no one understands you,
Think again, for there is always —
Someone that does.
It is time to take off that mask,
And show your true colors,
For the game of pretending,
Is now over.
You cannot lie to yourself,
Be happy for who you are.

Diana Palomares, Grade 12
San Clemente High School

That Special Place Is Here

Have no fear,
Steer the wheel,
Either right or left you'll come near,
To that one special place where there's no need for tears,
Express yourself loud and clear,
With no one there who's there to hear,
The thoughts that bring you to tears,
Can be expressed right here,
There should be no smears, because everything's so clear,
The atmosphere is so fierce,
A soul inside of you gets pierced,
From the ocean breeze to the sun kissed heat you'll see
There's no where else to be.

Shabnm Asady, Grade 11
Torrey Pines High School

We Once Shared a Heart

I once shared her heart
Now all I have are memories.
The notes and poems mean nothing now.
I can't bear to read them.
My Heart Weeps…

We once shared hands and lips
Too much to bear
My legs tremble as I fall to my knees.
All I can do is pray for forgiveness.
My Heart Weeps…

I see her in the halls; the void in my heart screams her name.
Tears swell in my eyes
I try to fill that void, but there is only her
She is the one.
My Heart Weeps…

Brynt Campbell, Grade 12
Gridley High School

Orchids

All
these Orchids
                    kill me.
                              In the middle of the aisle,
                    all of a sudden,
        a voice
              like giving
                    my whole life
                    paradise.
        Pretty
              rocks
                              look up at me and smile
              a nice smile.
Very sensitive
              but
                                        slightly insane.

Kelsey Humphreys, Grade 10
Balboa City School

Mother

Dear mother of mine,
It was only you and I then,
Ever since you brought me here.
Although it hasn't been a steady ride,
We both knew things were falling apart,
As I see tears dripping from your eyes.
You told me to stay strong,
And I have always been
Putting that same smile on my face,
Still trying to forget the past,
Yet the very same story plays,
Every time I look deeply into your eyes.

Kim Pahimulin, Grade 12
Calaveras Hills High School

Skateboarding

Skateboarding
Is excitement on wheels
Always rolling.

Tyler Kavanagh, Grade 10
Lucerne Valley Jr/Sr High School

Redemption

The brightest light,
The blackest night,
Virtue and sin,
Black and white,
All depends on our choices in life.

As a flame brings warmth
And a sword protects,
So can a flame destroy
And a sword bring death.

The path of Redemption is narrow,
The road grueling and long,
Rife with hardship and sorrow,
The only ones to succeed are the strong.

Do not hesitate nor falter!
Stay strong and resolute!
For those determined and faithful
Awaits pure and absolute
Salvation.

Jan Alexis Salandanan, Grade 11
Valley Christian High School

Luna

Majestic and rare
The moon hides
A secret pristine world
Of endless dreams
As she captivates the soul
Drifting away

Emily Dobrzanowski, Grade 10
St Joseph Notre Dame High School

Letter to the Ghetto

If you think talkin' loud, mouthin' off to your teachers and cussin' nonstop is cute.
What in the name of Hera is your definition of cute?

Quit! Rollin' your eyes.
Stop! Smackin' your lips.

Act! As though you were raised to have a little class.
Pretend! You have some manners.

Don't! Let your Upbringing Handicap you. Define yourself.

Let the world Know! Who! You are.
Let them Know! Where! You're going.

And Let them Know! You are More! Than some Ghetto girl From the hood.

Save being
Ghetto
for your friends.

Ashlei Kelly, Grade 10
Grant Union High School

Hate That I Love You!!!

We were once together, but now we are apart
the love I felt for you grew and grew
but before I knew, we were through.

When I first met you, I knew you were the one
you charmed and amazed me with those things you do
all the things you did got me closer and closer to you.

When we walked together hand in hand
you made me feel I was the only one
but I guess I was so damn wrong.

Everything was going good until you played me wrong
I did not know what to do when you asked me for another chance
all I knew was that my heart was broken like a piece of glass.
I hate that I love you.

You make it so hard to get over you because you didn't have the slightest clue
that I was completely in love with you. I hate that I love you.

Now you're making it harder every day because I just can't get up and say:
"I never loved you, anyway!" I hate that I love you.

Jeannette Bravo, Grade 10
Sierra Vista High School

Nature

Mountains a far as I can see
I love the view of all the trees.
Snow tops all of them making it only feel like Christmas is here.
But it's almost spring.
Every day I see a bunch of beautiful trees and mountains as far as I can see.

Cheyenne Robinson, Grade 10
William Finch Charter School

Who Am I?

Who am I?
Am I a rock?
A rock on another rocky road
Or am I a piece of candy
Sorted amongst other sweet candies
Am I as sweet as candy or as rough
As a rock?
Who am I?
I am the boulder scattered among pebbles
On a river of gold
And you?
You are the bean stock amongst a field of daisies
Leading to the heavens above
Who are we?
We are all different.

Anthony Garcia, Grade 12
Calaveras Hills High School

What a Difference

Stuck here for the best
I have an aching pain in my chest
I miss the ones at home
But I need to be on my own
This place is so surreal
Saying what I feel
I'm scared to be here for so long
Because my hurt will be prolonged
I can't see the one I love
But what can I do about it? Tough
I'll stay here and try to change
And be the best I can be

Bianca Eisenberg, Grade 11
Jack Weaver School

The Song of the Thrush

The barren hill that sits of there
Seems but a lonely chair,
For one small tree and prickly bush,
Upon which sits a singing thrush.

The hill once covered by the trees
Now perishes in eternal weeds.
Years pass by its balding head
And even weeds and thorns grow dead.

Where once the great birds paused to perch
On a cedar or a birch,
No more do loving hands reach high
To give rest to those who fly.

The sun is setting in the west,
And now the simple, singing guest,
In no apparent rush at all,
Finds another place, from which to call.

John Oven, Grade 11
St. Michael's College Preparatory School

My Tragedy

I am coming to realize that nothing is as it seems
and nobody is who they say they are or be.
The people I trusted ended up just taking advantage of me
How come I always do the same thing?
What can I do or say to make it stop.
A person is dying, and all I can do is watch.

I have to learn how to just say no.
In time I'm going to make it show.
My problems aren't going to just disappear.
Suppose I stand up for what I believe in.
They will all rise in sight.
But I can't
The truth is, I'm just a kid
There is too much I have to say
And nobody to listen.
My friend is dying, and all I can do is watch.

Nobody listens to my part of this tragedy
I should have been the one on that bed.
My best friend got me out of it.
Why does he have to be the one to suffer this?
He was the one that stood up for me when I couldn't.
My best friend is dying, and I just can't watch.

Jesse Lona, Grade 10
Sierra Vista High School

Day's Soul

Waking up in the morning,
Standing behind a locked door,
Watching the rain pouring,
I never did this before.
Something inside is ignoring,
Having no kind of feeling.
Wondering why this life?
Falling on my back looking up at the ceiling.
Never take a second to think twice.
Every minute someone is passing by.
So I continue on my stride,
Glaring out the window,
Hoping to see sunlight.
No more incoming mail.
Surrounded by walls in juvenile jail.
The opposite of good turns to bad.
The days of my soul hurt.
Doing something wrong and I get mad.
Having a crazy mortality,
Of the days of my soul,
But it's all reality.

Victor Lueras, Grade 10
Crossroads School

Artist

A crylic paints are used constantly.
R ough textures give feelings.
T iles are used in pottery.
I deas of art will never end.
S ketches are key to portraits.
T ime is the strongest tool.

Racquel Chagoya, Grade 10
Lucerne Valley Jr/Sr High School

I Dreamt a Little Dream

I dreamt a little dream,
That all was fair and well.
White feathers fluttered everywhere —
Where the happy creatures fell.

I dreamt a little dream,
That all was faded and gone.
Red ribbons curled everywhere —
Where realizations dawned.

I dreamt a little dream,
That all was warm and bright.
Yellow sparkles glinted everywhere —
Where civilizations took flight.

I dreamt a little dream,
That all was frost and cold.
Mighty ice shattered everywhere —
Where the weary heart became bold.

I dreamt a little dream,
That all was sun and moon.
Twinkling dust scattered everywhere —
Where a lord gave his servants a boon.

I dreamt a little reality.

Hillary Nguyen, Grade 10
Saddleback High School

Unbreakable Truths

Words
Shake the foundations of the Earth
They are everything
The unknown in every equation

Absolutes that are incontrovertible
Declarations that are unascertainable
Universes that are beyond imaginations
Dimensions that have no origin

Unconditional mortal love
Freedom and hatred for mankind
Planets and galaxies light years away
Portals to all heavens and hells

Denis Everett, Grade 10
Coronado High School

One in the Same

I laugh when you laugh I cry when you cry
Your success is my success without you I die

It's because we're one in the same

Most people don't know you think you're the only one
When two are connected and near separated the damage is close to permanently done

When one is divided in half, the number ceases to exist.
It's the same with you and me

If one member of a team messes up the team's winning opportunity will be missed
If we mess up completely we will cease to exist

It's bigger than two; it's as big as one

I've realized that looking out for me kills me and looking out for you kills you
But when we look out for us as one there's nothing we can't do

Without one, there is zero.
Without one, there can be no numbers after it.
When we are one in the same, everything else follows.

Jordan Smallwood, Grade 11
Valley Christian High School

The Rush of Darkness

I am at this unknown place in the middle of nowhere.
I hear my fellow mates running, playing tag, yelling, I want to control them.

I feel the cold salty water rinsing my feet,
It feels as if I was taking a much needed shower.
I feel something crash into my feet.
A shell, I pick it up and wipe off the cool wet sand.
I wear the shell as an eye patch,
I throw some mud on my face.
Who am I? I can be anyone I want to be!

I run back to the others.
As power hungry as ever.
I am the king of the Jungle.
"Where are my weapons? Where are my servants?
I am the soul of this land!
I am its sky, water, and wind!"

I feel the darkness taking over my body, I feel chills crawl up my spine.
I feel the rush of darkness.
WAIT! STOP! Who am I? Who is this two faced person?
Just a mere schoolboy that evolved into a barbaric emperor.
I have become savage, I take off my mask
Who am I?

Annapreet Athwal, Grade 10
Bella Vista High School

My Fairest Adored

My evening dream and morning thought
Consumed by what is sought
My fairest adored
The search for glimmering starlight
In this forever endless night
My fairest adored
Spirit of eternal mercy
A prayer of beauty
My fairest adored
Thou hearkened to a sinner's cries
Ascending to limitless skies
Thou heard the coward's mournful moan
Raised him upon thy graceful throne
My fairest, you are adored
Entranced by your stunning gaze
Until the end of glorious days
My search is no longer in vain
Love is no longer pain
My fairest adored
No reason for love to be further explored
My fairest, you are adored

Bret Sears, Grade 11
Nordhoff High School

Sun and Moon

Singing softly to the fading light
Whispering secrets to the growing night
The shelves contain a legend of old
A tale of love that's about to unfold

Her family of light, his kin of dark
Together their journey is about to embark
On Destiny's path of passion and pain
Through the war of their families' desire to reign

A clash of differences, silver and gold
The feeling of warmth in a battle with cold
But setting aside their lives of contrast
Their hearts were the same, these lovers of past

They met in secret as the war raged on
The setting sun and the approaching dawn
But soon their secret was discovered
A warning of fire and ice was uttered

The lovers knew they could not exist
Without the other and so they kissed
Silently dying to a star-crossed tune
They now rule over Earth as the Sun and Moon

Jennifer Rowlett, Grade 10
Kern Valley High School

Past My Image

Why do you act like you don't like me.
When you know that you do.
Maybe it's because I'm a size 26 and not a size 2.
If you look past my image, you'll see what lies inside.
The true and beautiful me.
What you're missing will soon fly free.
Too bad you're looking but you can't see.
You're side blinded but I'm strong minded.
I'll always love you.
And you know that it's true.
When I'm around you I never feel blue.
Hopefully your true colors will show.
And you'll love me too.
Maybe when you see this token of my love.
You'll see past my image and get the clue.
That I'm so deeply in love with you.
And I'm dying for you to feel it too.

Angelina Villalobos, Grade 11
Charles Zupanic Alternative High School

Lost Love of One's Self

Time has just stopped, chaos everywhere
I'm restless and my soul is lonely
Your face behind my eyes
Nights pass, and I can't imagine life alone
How can I explain my pain when I'm here and you're there?

A noise at the door makes me bloom like a flower,
But silence talks to me
Once there was a time we were always together
But now there's distance between you and I
I'm here and you're there…

It's been a decade since the last time I smiled,
My story is written in my tears
Everywhere I look, I see you, my love
But, I'm here and you're there…

Rifat Khan, Grade 12
Gridley High School

Love Is Heaven and Hell

Love is like heaven
It's a real great feeling
It is great when two come together but not with seven
Love is not for telling
Saying how many you dated or got into bed
Love is also like hell
It's not a great thing to do, say, or have in the head
Much pain and suffering may come ringing a bell
Love can be good or bad but not be for sale
Don't look for it just wait
Wishing in a wishing well
Waiting for that love to finally come having so much faith
The one for you is out there don't ever give up

Mark Aldapa, Grade 12
South East High School

There Lay the Horizon

I made the mistake of letting myself get too comfortable.
I lay there engulfed by my blankets of security and warmth.
My head heavy on a perforated pillow.
I took my dreams for granted.
And dream I did; in every direction.
I let my guard down.
When morning came, light particles that rested on dust particles ripped the dark from my eyes.
And winter's breath seeped through my white pained window, finding home on my feet.
I pushed and they pushed back.
Relentless in their effort to make me feel.
I stood before the day, leaving sleep to fend for itself, and for a moment I gave into fear.
Because there lay the horizon to my world.
An untouched portrait of adventure.
A caricature of change.

Alysia Alex, Grade 11
Louisville High School

The Disease of the Seas, the Disguise of the Skies

Having now found the source of imminent surprises, I cautiously wade, waiting on a sign.
No coincidence, mere chance? Or something beyond the wealth of my knowledge,
and when attained, I escalate to the status of the Grand Master Himself?
I ought to dwell on this perplexity, for there is no greater security than the doubtfulness we all experience.
The Candymaker will heed the call. He will distribute the token to Eternal Happiness
for I who seek, for I who question, for I who love.
Refer to a previous incantation and then, your light bulb of recollections will ignite and all will be left for you.
I allow The Candymaker to let me view Paradise,
I permit myself to shrink and enter the glass, the glass yet to be filled with wine.
Once inside, He explains that there is but one button left to press.
With all to gain and questions aside, I gallantly push, the index the focal point.
TIXE! TIXE! TIXE! We are racing the Universe, having yet to be caught, breaking all barriers.
The eyes are the soul's scouts, acting like Kamadeva. I see Her. I see Me.
Everything we both had doubted had halted and retreated, retracing demon-steps and leaving us be.
Our souls had resurrected from The Extinguishing.
Suddenly, I became the man who had everything he wished for.
No more disease of the seas, no more disguise of the skies,
for the lies are merely unsold truth, and the truth be simply done told lies.

Alex Alvarez, Grade 11
Downey High School

Puzzled by Life?

How come our hearts can be torn in so many pieces to completely different things? How come it's so hard for us to choose something? How come even when we try not to, we hurt the ones we love the most? How come the truth is not always followed by the action? How come we push our limits? And how come everyone's way of fixing things is walking away? How come growing up involves so much heartache and pain? How come no matter how many tears have been shed there are always more to cry? How come it's so hard to stick up for what's right? How come no one follows their heart — the happiness within? And how come life is so complicated?

Do we long for different things cuz we can't find it all within one? If we find everything within one would that make it easier to choose? Do we say things to make our loved ones feel good only to tear them down by not following through and do we push the limits just to see how far they can be thrown? Does the pain we experience or difficulties we go through make us stronger? Do the tears we cry prepare us for the heartaches ahead? Is it sticking up for what's right that's hard or not believing in it that's the problem? It's not that we don't follow our hearts, it's all that we do! Everything we do is out of love and we get so caught-up in all of it we ignore and hurt those we care so much about! Those closest to us will wait for us to change, the key is for us to realize this in time cuz nobody will wait forever!

Life is simple, our emotions are what complicates it!

Natasha Hart, Grade 11
Shasta High School

July 6, 2007

From the movies to the car,
there was no mistake at all.
We knew what was coming up next,
because we had talked about it over a text.
This was going to be something original,
that would lead others to think you were a criminal.
You leaned over and whispered to me,
"So are you my honey bee?"
There was so much tension
that I answered back with a question.
We looked into each other's eyes
and knew we would be together till we died.
We made it official with a kiss
and thought the world should know about this.
On July six two thousand seven
we were a match made from heaven.

Jennifer Zermeno, Grade 10
Saddleback High School

With You I Laughed

With you I laughed, long time ago
We used to dream, places to go.
Italy, London, France, and Spain
— Maybe some more along the way.

Remember talking about snow?
And of so many things we didn't know?
Of life and love when sun was low?
I remember wanting to stay
With you. I laughed

At all the jokes aplenty shown.
We swam in rivers, played with toads.
But now all the things we never say
Have stopped the laughs and stopped the games.
I ne'er wanted it to end, so
With you I laughed.

Alannah Myers, Grade 11
Marysville Charter Academy for the Arts

Onboard to America

The boat rocked like a baby's cradle.
Diseases traveled faster than sound.
Day by day, I dream of finally reaching America.
To my right and left are seniors.
Every wrinkle on their face represents a moment in time.
Their face expression tells it all.
Their only goal is to reach America.
Shriek! The boat comes to a sudden stop.
Everybody young and old stampedes their way to the exit.
I am last to leave the dreadful boat.
I took my last glance and headed towards the light.
I took my first step into California, the golden state.

Derek Chen, Grade 10
Abraham Lincoln High School

My Fear

I look upon his face but fear to see his eyes.
Fear that if I look into them he'll look into me.
Fear that wanders my body and mind
Trapping what is my soul,
And that my heart does possess
Everything he shall find.
Eyes are the doorway to the heart, and everything it sees.
Fear that if he looks into mine
He will see all of me.
And what my heart does possess
The will to strive and live
But the deeds I've done to know his heart
I cannot forgive.
Fear that if he looks into my eyes
He will see the truth,
And all that lays underneath
Its solid layer of youth.
My heart forgetting how to protect itself
Quickly rising to fall
Pray that he'll never see into me
For my fear will say it all...

Claire Ngoon, Grade 12
George Washington High School

After Annabel Lee*

After my love Annabel Lee had left me
She is still within me.
I can still hear her lovely voice callin' my name
I can still see her, I miss her.
After she had left me
I had never loved again.
One day I saw her ghost.
She was as beautiful as when she had left this world
My face goes pale, I had fainted.

I hear her whispering in my ear, WAKE UP!
I'm sorry that I had left you in this cruel world
I didn't want to leave you, but I had to
I love you n' always will,
I will always be there.
Good-bye my love, forever.

As I woke up, she was fading away from me
I said good bye my love
I love you too, always
My dear I will miss you a lot
I can't believe that you had left me,
My love.

Ali Drew, Grade 10
The Winston School
*Inspired by "Annabel Lee" by Edgar Allan Poe

My Pie

The green and white wrapping paper
Rests silently on the table.
Its fruity smell seduces every nose.
I long to rip it open
And enjoy every bite,
Just thinking about
My Hostess Apple Pie.
David Romanchuk, Grade 11
Valley Christian High School

Nature's Answer

I thought of you today
— I know I shouldn't.
But I did and realized
I'm at a loss of words.

A flower blooms in spring
but it is the rain
that lets it sprout.
The rain is forgotten.

A spring runs wild
through a sea
of oversimplified beauty.
But the rocks are its protection
a guiding force.

I don't do much
I think too hard
our lives aren't together
but something is.
Daniel Lombardo, Grade 12
Newbury Park High School

Did You Ever Really Care?

You said you would love
Forever and a day
You said you would love
In a very caring way

You made me think
That I would always be yours
You made me think
There was no more

You said you would love
On a cold winter night
You said you would love
Even if I were out of sight

You made me believe
That I could trust you
You made me believe
In nothing because nothing is you
Ashley Wall, Grade 12
San Lorenzo Valley High School

Paradise

My wishes are paradise, in my mind I can see it,
Then reality hits and I'm in a cage and there's no way to leave it.
My girlfriend's crying, I seen the tears on the letter.
Every night I get on my hands and knees praying to God for things to get better.
I want to grow up to be a man, have a wife, a house, and a son.
My heart is saying get out of this life and don't look back when you run.
I want to be something better than what I've become.
Months of my life thrown away because of a bad choice.
I want to see what Heaven's like and hear God's voice.
I look at the stars, wishing for the world to be nice,
I'm tired of all this hatred and pain throughout my life.
I'm hoping the end of this road leads to paradise.
Matthew Carbajal, Grade 11
Crossroads School

Irony

Oh how ironic is it that:
Wars are created to bring peace into the world,
Political candidates constantly criticize one another and promise citizens a better life,
Minimum wage laws force more people into unemployment,
Obesity is a major problem when the other side of the world is starving to death,
The government has to use tax write offs as incentives for people to donate to charity.

Oh how ironic is it:
Seeing people rush by at the sight of stop signs,
Surround lies are the only remains of true hope,
Calling friends back stabbers behind their backs,
Doubting yourself when everyone else has faith in you,
Having sight but not being able to see the beauty of life.
Esha Nuzhat, Grade 12
Redlands Sr High School

Suffocated from My Dreams

Most say the key to success is the gripping of hope
I'm twisted in a whirlpool of heartaches expecting a rope
I can write my lyrics of thoughts, but I lack to reach further
Optimistic isn't even an option, I'm clouded with hearted murder
I'm buried under pessimistic barriers, which there's no retreat
Soon to be discovered in confusion to eyes, while extinct
I shed tears from my soul, most don't understand my pain
Tried stopping the habit of negative attention, but I'm still shamed
Resting my head on my pillow, yet my sleep holds balled fist
Because my vision is blinded, my ground, sight is just mist
Family, I don't hold onto them because they're gone
My sensitivity toward no family, makes me make figured clones
I look in eyes of worry, so my tears aren't the wettest
Expressing my feelings to my companions, gets others jealous
I wish to the day of my dreams being realistic with every breath
I wish to look to my other side with my partner saying yes
I look forward to the day of happiness, and rain to light
I only fear God, but at times I think I have feeling frights
So, I wait for my dreams patiently, every single night
It's like the devil was hungry, so my life he took a bite
I'm suffocated from my dreams, to the highest limit of height
Jonathan J., Grade 12
Vista Del Rio Jr/Sr High School

I Am the Ocean

I am the ocean
And my waves are soothing
My current can be gentle
My waves can be full of sounds
I am a home full of life
How come I am always so joyful
Why do I seem so unhappy?
And I am the ocean proclaiming my smile

I have to be a home
Many things depend on me
I feel my joy is not enough
What if I can't provide what they need
My blue body of water is flowing
Is it enough for every species
And I am the ocean proclaiming my smile

I have to be strong
My soul feels polluted
Is my joy enough
I should be strong
I should flow and work with my currents
And I am the ocean proclaiming my smile

Ashley Carranza, Grade 10
Sierra Vista High School

The Dog

A shadow that swept across the ground
A mutt, a rover, a dirty hound
The fur that stuck onto his back
Was shiny but a greasy black

Crusted over was dirt and age-old food
Come here little doggy I softly cooed
A jolt of happiness sprang into his eyes
It took all his strength just to rise

I knelt down beside this creature of sorrow
I patted his head, sorry I wouldn't be there tomorrow
He closed his eyes in peace and comfort
For that split second he forgot his hurt

I lifted my hand with tender care
And knew in my heart it wasn't fair
He walked away as soon as he came
With his head slumping down in sorrow and shame

Oh how life differs for every boy and girl
One with a plastic gem one with a pearl

Hailley Hukill, Grade 11
San Clemente High School

Fish

I wish
I was a fish
Careless and free
Not a care in the world
Just me under the sea
Swimming, swimming
I go as fast as I can
Jumping in and out of the water
The joy I get no one can understand

Samantha Alvarado, Grade 11
Calaveras Hills High School

Homework

Homework is grumpy, homework is mean
Homework is dirty, impure, and unclean.
It sneaks up to you during the day unseen
And makes you stay up late, that old fiend.

It takes away fun, your favorite game
And when your friends come up and say
"Hey! Want to play ball?"
You know what to say
That you have your old friend, Homework to blame
And when parties come to call
Homework is the only party you can attend at all.

But even though Homework's a beast
Maybe you could finish it at least
Besides, it's only all for the best.
Because tomorrow…
Tomorrow, you have a test.

Charles Lam, Grade 10
St Francis High School

Repressed Memories

The appalling memories that I repress,
till this day causes me distress.
My story may come as a shock to you,
but young people need to see what I've been through.
My family lived in poverty,
and we were lucky if any of us reached thirty.
We never knew when our next meal would be,
so each night I would pray for God's mercy.
God never answered my prayers
but instead challenged me with world affairs.
When the Japanese attacked my homeland,
our only two caribous were their demand.
Caribou was what was keeping us alive,
without it, we wouldn't be able to survive,
so my brave father fought till he was out of breath,
but in the end, they ended up beating him to death.
No home, no food, no money,
life was so hard, it's not even funny.

Lana Salvador, Grade 10
Abraham Lincoln High School

The Rain

The rain, the rain, comes pouring down,
There is no end to the same sound.
The lakes are deep for one to drown,
The drought has gone, the water round.

Again there's life in every sight,
There is no more, no deathly state.
For life now lives on ground and flight,
The loss of water is no fate.

The weeks pass by with no more rain,
The life is dying once again.
The birds are chirping in much pain,
The hope to see it once again.

The rain, the rain, is nowhere yet,
The land, it waits with much intent.
The clouds, they owe the land a debt,
This debt be paid when rain descent.

Nick Lupica, Grade 10
St Francis High School

Stephanie

S low in the mornings
T ough in the evenings
E asy to find me
P erfect to hide
H appy in moments
A lmost always on time
N ever too negative
I mpossible as it may seem
E nough about me what about you?

Stephanie Dukes, Grade 12
Calaveras Hills High School

Freedom…

Putting on the cold, leather jacket
Strapping on the worn out gloves,
Lacing the battered boots,
It's our time.

Saddling on the empty seat,
Twisting open the throttle,
Listening to the crackling engine,
It's our time.

Speeding down the highway,
Shifting through the gears,
Winding down the fuel,
Looking back only to
Remember, what was then
And to know what's now.

Now is freedom…

Michael Giron, Grade 10
Helix High School

Sad Girl

Sad Girl…
Dang ain't that a shame always in pain…
Always alone…can remain in a world of fear…
Without shedding a single tear…
Until the darkness begins to reappear…

She feels the heartache that no one seems to know how to cure…
Smile by day tear by night…
Wipe her tears they are her kryptonite…
When they drop she loses her cool she loses all patience that she saved
all for you…

You make her smile but it seems that they don't last…
She feels your heart…but she aches the past…
It hurts her to think…
To breathe…to smile…
It hurts her to feel…
She has no sympathy…

Sad girl…
It is a code name…
It hides the true her that she is inside…
Touch her soul and she begins to cry…for this is why…
Her code name of pain…SAD Girl

Ann Low, Grade 12
Options for Youth School - North Highlands

Glimpses

And I awake with groggy eyes to an alarm that electrifies,
My body and soul are alert and quickly the secondhand flies
I rush to brush and wash myself and look for my wallet on the shelf
Then, my eye is caught by the colors of sunlight illuminating the horizon.

Dressed, I fly out the door five minutes passed my preconceived time
I drive often higher than the legal suggestion
As the food I just ate begins digestion
Then, I get out and admire the wondrous valley-city surrounding.

The teachers drone on and on,
I think I just slept through that lecture,
Oh gee another test,
Then, I walk down the halls I see a perfect smile.

The bell has rung, finally the worst has passed
I go to lift and play rugby,
Hard work, sweat, and passion combined,
Then, my trip home, a tree in bloom, dressed in pink.

I drag to the door, exhaustion all the way through.

Daniel Huffman, Grade 11
Valley Christian High School

Voice in a Crowd

Her heart is screaming with love for you.
She always wondered if you ever knew.
This heart full of love isn't just the case.
Can't you see the tear's streaming from her face?

She smiles to hide the pain from you.
You walk by not knowing just what you do.
This girl you've broken to many times to say.
It's a wonder how she gets through the day.

Her heart is shattered, there's no doubt of that.
And yet, she'll keep loving you after that.
The years go by and her heart screams loud.
But to you, she's just a voice in a crowd.

Vanessa Thedford, Grade 11
Peter Johansen High School

Scraped Knees and Sore Bums

Some call it dull, simple, and slow,
but I know the game is tough to follow.
There's always that something that needs to be learned,
a game that is tough and harder to earn.

Straightforward games give me no fun.
Nothing beats crushing a game winning run.
Many large factors tell the game's fate.
Nothing beats sprinting and stealing home plate.

The scrapes and the sores will all go away,
winning it all is bigger any day.
Making mistakes but still standing tall,
Love it for life, it's fast-pitch softball.

Krislyn Li, Grade 10
Abraham Lincoln High School

The Stress Rises, the Stress Falls

The stress rises, the stress falls
The homework comes, the problems call
With all the work to do each night
The student tries to win the fight
And the stress rises, the stress falls.

Essays appear during winters and falls,
But the sleep, the sleep midst the homework calls:
The tempting bed, soft and warm instead
Efface attention from my head
And the stress rises, the stress falls.

The morning comes; bells ring in the halls
Sent to class, behind those empty walls:
The class is done, it never leaves
The homework comes like other eves,
And the stress rises, the stress falls.

Timothy Lin, Grade 11
Valley Christian High School

Parlors

In parlors darkened, black and poor,
Chairs creak in the silence;
Men hover round the centerpiece,
A woman howls in defiance:
"I walked along an endless road"
(Her whispers filled the room).
"Over hills and mountains, crawling underground,
And through the coldest streams, the warmest streams,
Streams rippling through the woods
And, drying up in valleys broad,
Sucked up, spat out with 'coulds'.
I passed many on this weary way,
Most broken with despair,
So I sat with them and looked through them —
Their eyes held in their stare
The vastness of the universe —
Colored brightly, purple, blue —
Containing within a window frame
That idea, still far removed:
That in the end, we all are dead;
We're mourned and we're buried and we're done."

Michael Forsyth, Grade 11
St. Michael's College Preparatory School

Women

They are the feminine part of society,
the ones who bring creativity and variety,
No one can match their own originality,
While they hold the truth in each of their personality

They are unique in their own way,
Complicated is the word people can say,
Sometimes understanding them is like a puzzle or a maze,
In which you're trapped, and try to solve for days

They are not only brave, intelligent, and confident
But also generous and benevolent,
All struggling to get respect,
That many neglect.

Now imagine the world without them,
It would all be plain,
Many wouldn't know what to do
And order would not be maintained.

A day without women on hand
would be day without restore,
A day a man cannot endure,
And a time the world would not be able to stand any more...

Omar Rojas, Grade 10
Sierra Vista High School

Decisions

Love, she is my unfamiliar stranger.
The one I am willing to meet.
But as I quest for her,
She eludes me quite stealthily.

Hate, she is my constant companion.
The fuel to my pride.
The reason for my nature.
My future in her eyes.

Heart, you are my center.
The one that resides.
You, the ruler of my fate
Only you can decide.

So please sleep my Heart
And wait for her.
Wait for my mystery.
Or face my companion.

Remember your right.
Your choice.
Only you can decide.
Only you can decide.

Lauren Ashley Nallie, Grade 10
Northwood High School

Procrastination

Just ten more minutes
I didn't hear the alarm
This bed I'm laying on
Is holding me down
I swear, it's not me.

Just one more show
Only thirty more minutes
This TV with magical powers
Is hypnotizing
I swear, it's not me.

Just checking my email
Oh, my friend's asking
'Bout homework
This computer monitor
Is pulling me in
I swear, it's not me.

Just after this song
It's my all-time favorite
These cheap earphones
Are clinging on
I swear, it's not me.

Grace Shin, Grade 10
Cypress High School

My Gramma

She started out
Like a budding rose
Beautiful for all to see
But as time went on
The flower bent closer
To the ground with a plea
A plea for strength
For endurance and power
So that she might be free
And finish to the end
But even as she pled
This wilted flower shriveled
And fell fell fell
To the ground below
Cut from her support
She found at length
Her body's true strength.

Grace Anderson, Grade 11
Valley Christian High School

Goodnight

Dreams
Can be happy
Where they help you
Sleep through the night
Where you just don't want to
Wake up
So
Sweet dreams
Dreams can be scary
Where they wake you up
Through the night
Sometimes you scream
Sometimes you cry
Sometimes you smile
But then you realize
It's just a dream
So
Sweet dreams

Annalee Kintz, Grade 11
The Winston School

Only Nature

Trees at night reflect the bright moon
Stars twinkle and light the dark sky
Cold mist overlaps the night soon
Shooting stars pass before our eye

The forest is quiet and still
Just enjoying the peaceful sound
Only nature gives us the thrill
No limits, no boundaries, calm

Kristi McBain, Grade 11
Valley Christian High School

The Honest Lyric

I am a truly honest one,
I'm truthful as can be.
If ever someone asks something
I respond with integrity.

If e'er I lie, I feel remorse,
It overwhelms me so,
I go forth and apologize,
In a voice that's meek and low.

Sebastian Certik, Grade 12
Balboa City School

Garden of Dreams

Everybody has their own dreams
Some people hang on to them
And some let them go.

My wildest dream is
To be with my mom again,
And my simplest dream
Is to always be there
For my family.

Every single person has their
Own Garden of Dreams.
I know I have mine.
Some bloom and some wither.

Maria Casillas, Grade 10
Knight High School

The Voice Inside

The voice inside,
It's waiting to burst out.

The voice inside,
It wants everyone to hear it,
But I won't let it.

The voice inside,
It's trapped
And wants to be let out.

The voice inside,
It wants to show everybody
Who I really am.

The voice inside,
It wants everyone to hear it,
But I won't let it.

The voice inside,
It's waiting to burst out.

Julianne Obregon, Grade 11
Lone Pine High School

What a Gang Banger Will Like the World to Be Like

Every day in the pad is filled with sadness and pains.
For I long to be with my loved ones,
But instead I am on streets just doing nothing.
With my heart broken and nothing to release my pains.
My heart doesn't cry,
But my tears swell up inside.
People they said, "grown men don't cry."
But what keeps me on my feet is my family and dreams.

I dream of a happy place where nobody is two-faced,
A place where we all get along, somewhere nice and very calm
Where money is not an issue, no crying eyes needing a tissue.

I dream of a special girl.
That she's loyal to me and I'm loyal to her,
A girl that I'm able to trust in
One that is beautiful from within,
That our love for each other is unconditional
And together we go and conquer the world.

I have many dreams,
So many that most is unseen.
Dreams don't lie and I'm a fiend for the truth.
My biggest dream is that all my dreams come true.

Arturo De Haro, Grade 12
Sweetwater High School

Holding a Wall

Something there is that doesn't love a wall
Something that keeps me from you
That sends me signs pointing the other direction
Gaps have been made by hunters in the past
As I work to make repairs
I find it harder and harder to get through to you
Which makes it hard to make two into one
As we bring back the wall it makes it easier to stay close
I suppose the saying is right
"Good fences make good neighbors."
My question is what is the wall hiding?
I hope you know I'll work my fingers to the bone
To keep you safe like a caterpillar in its cocoon
To watch our relationship bloom
If you are all pine and I am all apple orchard
Always know my tree will never
Wander into unmarked territory
Then you remind me
"Good fences make good neighbors."
However spring is the mischief in me
And I can't help but wonder why?

Cailyn Gryder, Grade 10
Sierra Vista High School

Paradise

A Man once walked this Earth,
Like we walk every day,
He let men come out of their lame birth,
While others saw the world in a whole new way.
He taught us to live,
He taught us to love,
He taught us to give,
He taught us of the One above.
Why did He pay the terrible price,
Yet to come back three days later,
So we could live in paradise,
If we take part in this gift from our Creator.

Emily Huntsinger, Grade 12
Redlands Sr High School

The Audacity of Lovesickness

She stares at me with her baby blue eyes
I ask myself does she really like me?
I feel lonely as I look at the skies
Every night I wonder if we could be…
More than all the things I could ever want
She is brilliant, clever and sarcastic
Her amazing voice is the type that will haunt
A mere thought of her can make me lovesick
Her hair is like beautiful long brown ropes
That sparkle, and shine with sheer excitement
Just being with her is one of my hopes
My love for her will always remain constant
Every night before bed I wonder if she
Feels exactly the same way about me

James Mbacho, Grade 12
La Jolla Sr High School

Stopping at the Coliseum on a Sunny Evening

Whose coliseum is this I think I know.
His shot at fame doesn't lie on a chair though;
Now he will not see me stopping here
To watch his dreams in the coliseum fill up with fame.

My friend must think it's weird
To stop without a crowd near
Between the coliseum and the big city
The sunniest evening of the year.

He gives his friend a look
To ask if there is some mistake.
The only other sound's the ball
Of a nice kick and easy goal.

The coliseum is big, nice, and bright,
Waiting for him to shine,
But he must get out of the chair and kick the ball to get a start,
But he must get out of the chair and kick the ball to get a start.

Elizabeth Rivera, Grade 10
Sierra Vista High School

Work of Art, Art of Work

Art is an expression,
An expression that I draw,
Art is a treasure in the mind,
With lots of wealth that it offers,
Art is my soul and spirit,
Art is what I do.

Alfredo Renteria, Grade 11
Academic/Vocational Institute

Mother Earth

Mother Earth is full;
Unique in every way
She is never dull
She is free.

Mother Earth is eternal;
As each thing passes another
To take its place
The scars she will always bear.

Mother Earth is beautiful;
Each person with their own story
And role to play
Roles change.

Mother Earth.
Mother.
Earth.
ME.

Tommy Maher, Grade 12
Balboa City School

I Will Stand

The world can crumble,
But I will stand.
The skies may fall,
But I will find shade.
My heart may hurt,
But it will not break.
My trust may be betrayed,
But my confidence will stay in tact.
My hopes may be far,
But I have all the directions.
My dreams may seem impossible,
But I see them every day.
Even when:
My lips shiver,
My hands tremble,
My eyes swell, and my heart pounds,
I will not falter.
I will not weep.
I will not fall.
I will stand.
I will stand.

Priscilla Ah Fook, Grade 12
Buena Vista High School

A Piece of Me

I stare absent-mindedly through the window
Into the waves crashing beside the boat
As the boat slowly chugs along, I can feel my dreams approaching
With each wave I know this journey is a test.
The past, present, and future become a haze
It feels as if all the struggles in the past have led up to this moment
Sitting here pondering at all the chances
The chance of a better life
Maybe I can experience those feelings again
The joy of accomplishment, dignity, and happiness
I've spent my entire life trying to accomplish something meaningful
Now I'm heading towards a future where all will be just
I'll help my family back home.
I could hear shouts above me and excited whispers
I got up and went outside; blinded by the sunlight
Through the light I could see a foggy stretch of land
I was glad it was foggy that day
Because I might not have had the courage to continue,
If I saw the long road ahead.

Jordan Ng, Grade 10
Abraham Lincoln High School

Broken Heart Again

I should have known this would happen to me again,
I think we were better off just being friends

I could talk to you about anything, cry on your shoulder,
lay my head on your chest to take my pain away, just until time got older

What happened to the person I fell in love with?
The person I felt a passion for when we kissed?
The person that I loved no matter what you did,
I thought we would grow old and have a kid.

I had to let you go, I had to be set free, but
letting you go wasn't easy for me, 'cuz you were my first in everything

Well now it's the end, and like Chris Brown said it's never a right time to say good-bye,
but good-bye, and my love for you will never die.

Janae Jones, Grade 10
American High School

Feelings

Sadness is like leaving the one you love.
Happiness is like finding the one you feel like you've known forever.
Relaxing is like a summer day.
Building mud pies and sand castles is like an old forgotten dog.
Excitement is when you get something new.
Boredom is being alone all day.
Depression can be like drowning in a pool of water.
Joy is spending time with people you love.
Hate is the root of all evil.
Love is like never wanting to let go, because without that
person in your life you are missing a piece of yourself.

Alicia Hale, Grade 11
Prospect Continuation High School

Perfect

It surprised me one day
as my friend spoke to say,
"In all ways, I am perfect."
I only looked and stared,
confounded by these words.
"But you cannot walk."
I gently reminded.
"No, I am perfect,"
my friend responded.
"Though unable to move,
and never will I run;
It's a gift from God.
It is my burden, my cross to bear."
"Then God is cruel, to force
that on you," I answered.
But to confusion, my friend only laughed.
"No He knew I was strong.
He knew I could carry this burden."
"And how would He know?" I asked.
And with a smile my friend answered.
"Because He made me."

Janel Raab, Grade 10
Santa Clara High School

Hope

Hope…the feeling that drives
The feeling that lets you know your soul is alive
The feeling that motivates
The feeling that we continuously contemplate
Hope is what makes us break free
From anything that tries to stop us deliberately
It's what makes us continue to thrive
When everyone else doubts us on the outside
Hope…The greatest motivation there could ever be
Hope…The only thing that won't abandon you completely

Christopher Garcia, Grade 12
Wilson High School

Summer Breeze

Up and down the brown leaf sways,
Across the patio and down to the never ending meadow,
Some might say that father time likes to run away,
While others have all the time to play,
Life has not one straight path,
But with many twists and turns,
That even the wisest sparrows might go astray.
When one looks back it all seems to be a blur,
Mix images of great times, happy times, and delightful times,
But it is what one does with his life now
That changes the best of boys into men.
So we try our best to maintain the right course,
And hope that will all our strong work and determination,
We will conquer our dreams.

Sevan Demirdji, Grade 12
Redlands Sr High School

Las Vegas Lights

Nighttime streets are lit,
the town awake all hours,
when do they ever sleep?
Everyone's gone crazy.
Las Vegas Lights.

Cha, cha, cha ching…slot machines a few rows down.
Cha, cha, cha ching, people win lots of dough,
and spend, spend, spend, like there's no end.
Las Vegas Lights.

Party, party, party,
Friends, family, and lovers,
Party, party, party,
Never-ending nights, never-ending lights
'til the crack of dawn.

Las Vegas Lights…

Brittney Blaylock, Grade 12
Gridley High School

A Heavens' Glance

What are these slow pulses I feel,
Or the half breathing I sigh,
What is this gentle lull I must have,
Or the soft lit sky?

When may I see the end,
Or even a glance,
When can I seize this moment,
Or just reach for this feeling that will never pretend?

Why must we go on,
Who will be there,
Why must we trust in something we don't comprehend,
But I'll be there waiting…

In some distant moonlight…
In a place so familiar,
So right.

Katy Sullivan, Grade 11
Valley Christian High School

Don't Look Back

Some people smiled every day, like it was their last.
Some frowned as if they had nothing left.
Some graduated early, Other's didn't at all.
This passing year's been like a reality TV show.
It's been a year of anger, a year of loss
A year of forgiveness, and finding who you are.
A year of relationships, from good to bad.
A year of confusion, laughter, and love.
Oh, and don't forget,
All the things we should, or shouldn't have done.

Breanna Bybee, Grade 11
Albert Powell Alternative High School

Expressing Myself

By expressing myself, I wear my heart on my sleeve
By speaking out, though my voice never heard
By letting those tears fall, so my eyes can create anew
By being myself, knowing that what I really want isn't always true
By loving him, but not him loving me
See expressing myself, is what I can never see
By expressing myself, I grant you the chance to hurt me
But letting you in to love me, it's the fairy tale ending story…

Shani Anderson, Grade 10
Opportunities for Learning Charter School

Where My Heart Resides

My heart stops,
Nerves climb my spine until they reach the thoughts of my mind,
Grabbing at each rung of the perpetual ladder with a stutter in each step,
Shaking, shuddering, the simulations flow on,
This river of fluctuating moods, fluctuating minds,
Held back by the drunken gates of fear,
Pushed on by the tiresome flames of pursuit,
Where this trail of everlasting battles
May wither away in the calm settled air,
How life can be a war of truths;
It's overcoming the balance of desperation and consciousness.
Never docile is the heavy weight of life, nor sailed on, across a sea of anguish with ease,
For where the secret happiness floats on a crystal lake of dreams,
That is where my heart desires to reside.
Where the agile breeze carries frivolous petals,
Of pastels and vivid brights painting the sky,
Life flying by,
My heart stops,
And the short breaths linger.

Samantha Harrison, Grade 10
South Pasadena Sr High School

Second by Second

Second by second, minute by minute, thoughts race through my mind.
The happiness you once gave me to fill my heart has left,
Now my heart is filled with pain and sorrow.
All the fun times we had do not compare, will not compare to how much pain you have put me through.
I thought you said you loved me, but now I know you don't.
I used to be your prized possession, now you've traded me for dope.
I used to look up to you, you used to be my hero.
But now I know what you really do. I just can't help to think I don't EVER want to be like you.
Daddy why do you hurt me so? I never did anything wrong!
Daddy you talk to people who aren't there.
You hear voices, does that mean I'll hear them too?
Every time I look at you, I look into your eyes,
I see nothing but emptiness and hatred inside.
Daddy when I get older am I going to be like you?
Mommy says if I get help I won't be like you. But to tell you the truth I already am.
Maybe, if I stay away, you won't put me through so much pain.
But no matter how far away we are from each other,
The pain you put me through will never go away!

Hillary Hall, Grade 12
Monache High School

Why Love

Why should I love someone who doesn't love me back?
But I love him so much; I can't keep on track.
Who can control their heart?
Someone please teach me that great art.

Why do I go through this pain?
It is making me go insane.
I know he will never love me,
Because he is just a friend to me.

Every time I see him, I feel the pain again and again.
I don't know how long in love I've been.
I hate the way he only says "HEY!"
That is the whole conversation every day.

Why should I love someone who doesn't love me back?
But I love him so much; I can't keep on track.

Melissa Schwolow, Grade 12
Clovis East High School

Believe

Poor, old man with your tired hands.
Your greasy hair smothers your neck,
while your eyes squint from the harsh, morning light.

Your face tells a story;
the universal one of a broken heart.
You sink into despair
as your kind heart grows cold.

Your intelligent mind begins to melt
as you let that liquid consume you.
Your stench seeks new heights,
your body slowly disintegrates.

You have changed,
but I still love you,
I know that young man is in there.

You may seem dead to some,
but you are still alive to me.

Betsy Simonson, Grade 12
San Lorenzo Valley High School

Never Settle

Out of all the things that this small planet holds,
The jungle is one, and it's green and it's bold.
The trees are tall, they tangle and twist.
Like the tentacle of an octopus snaring fish.
Like the claws of a tiger grasping its prey,
They're cold and they're sharp and there's no getting away.
So if you are lost in this traitorous deep,
Just close you eyes and go to sleep.
Go to sleep and pretend you are gone,
Because life's just a game, and you're just a pawn.

Cory Lopez, Grade 11
Prospect Continuation High School

The Ant and Its Seasons

Winter has come, the ant is praying for warmth,
It is winter, the ant is sustaining his protection,
It is winter, the ant is very alone and hungry,
It is winter, the ant goes out without hesitation.

Now it is spring, the ant is warmin' up,
It is spring, the ant tired from havin' fun,
It is spring, the ant enjoys the beautiful weather,
It is spring, the ant, happy, under the scorching sun.

Next is summer, the ant it too hot,
It is summer, the ant tries to find shade,
It is summer, the ant gathers his food,
It is summer, the ant ends it with a wonderful parade.

Fall is finally here, the ant begins to organize,
It is fall, the ant rests to prepare,
It is fall, the ant gets ready for another winter,
It is fall, the ant feels winter arrive in the air.

George Janji, Grade 10
St Francis High School

Their Present, Our Future

Another bright day,
Another restless night.
We wake up for our family;
Our parents, our future.
Shake off the sleep; time to wake up.
Today is one more day to work

Two jobs, two children, too much to do.
Every day is exhausting just to get up.
To relax and just dream. That is the dream.
But for them, our children,
We must persevere.

At night, we sleep.
We rest; we dream.
We see our future, our children's, and theirs.

Jae Woo Lee, Grade 10
Abraham Lincoln High School

Backscratcher

A wooden backscratcher
Is laying on the table
Long and stiff,
It has a thick handle
But the stem gets thinner,
Like an arm, a wrist and a hand at the end,
Flat, rectangular boxes curve up

I want to grab the handle
Lift it up, and scratch my back with the hand.

Kevin Wang, Grade 11
Valley Christian High School

Snow

The soft white blanket lies
With tiny feathers falling from the sky
The cold wind gives a loud sigh
Isn't this a perfect paradise?

The songbird gives a musical cry
The tree's tears now unfreeze
The sun comes out, no more breeze
Spring is here, now it's time to die.

Natasha Lie, Grade 11
Valley Christian High School

Comparisons

I need you like a heart needs a beat
Just like a baby needs its mother
And the summer needs its heat
The only thing we need is each other.

You're the lyrics to my song
It plays endlessly for you
Without you, my nights are forever long
Without you, my heart becomes so blue.

But you ignore my whispering call
And I finally notice as I forever fall
That you're steadily becoming my vice
And you've become the fire to my ice.

Eric Kim, Grade 11
Valley Christian High School

Autumn Array

I remember

When royal butterflies shed
A stream of crystalline tears,
Telling a tale of tired wings;

When crystalline tears rained
From arms of wrinkled trees,
Purged jet hair in dewy drops;

When wrinkled trees blazed
In flames of crackling leaves
Burning with gold and scarlet;

When crackling leaves flew
Upon a rush of autumn wind,
Dancing in a fancy flurry;

When autumn wind brought
Royal butterflies whispering
To me a tale of tired wings.

Yes, I remember!

Aaron Garg, Grade 11
Saratoga High School

A Hundred Years Ago

Growing up in an era of communism and Chairman Mao,
I couldn't predict my future, what'll be life, where and how.
My father's side was rich, one of the few that were wealthy,
He demanded the importance of education and staying healthy.
Now my mom always wanted me to become a doctor,
So when I was successful, you could've guessed it shocked her.
Between the two of them, they never knew what I had in mind,
I wanted to become a writer, they said I never had the time.
I was sadly fine, so I only wondered what I could've been,
Never to find happiness, so I never felt good within.
I'd try to predict the future and how it seemed ahead,
But somehow, I always ended up with a dream instead.
Only knew a few rules: family first, health, and intelligence,
Maybe 100 years from now, I can tell you how well it went.

Cynthia Tran, Grade 10
Abraham Lincoln High School

Have You Ever?

Have you ever cried when you were sad?
Have you ever wished for something you never had?
Have you even felt pain for others?
Have you ever been there for someone?
Have you ever had a life in your hands?
Have you ever tried to walk on the other side of the fence?
Have you ever walked in someone else's shoes for a change?
Have you ever seen someone die?
Have you ever judged when you shouldn't?
Have you ever seen someone lose their loved one?
Have you ever tried to stop the bleeding of a broken heart?
Have you ever tried to bring someone back that's down too far?
Have you?

Michael Guerra, Grade 11
Prospect Continuation High School

I Remember

I remember when my life was simple.
When I was five I never had to deal with this.
When I was ten I was a sweet honor student.
When I was twelve I had to deal with all that was coming after me.
I remember the first time I really stopped and thought about it all.
I remember when my mom realized I knew it all.
I believe that yesterday was better than today.
I wish I hadn't done all the bad things I did.
I remember when my life was so much happier.
I cannot remember when my life was so much happier.
I cannot remember when I was ever this upset.
I cannot remember when I was ever this messed up.
I want to remember when I had fun.
I remember the day I was playing and not crying.
My parents remember when I was their little girl.
I remember my life never being fun.
I know that it will get better.
I remember when I was really living.

Amanda Easton, Grade 11
Prospect Continuation High School

You (Me)

Feeling of pain and feeling of hate.
All the confusion that's been brought my way.
Being hurt and being put down
You always turn my smile to a frown.
Things you've done and the things you'll do
Why do I let you play me for a fool???
You lie and you manipulate
Tricking me into following your ways.
You're deceiving and it's so believing.
The words you've spoken still remain.
You follow me around and you're stuck in my head;
I wish you would hurry up, and be dead.
But, you'll never leave and I'll never be free.
You're my shadow during the day and my
Reflection at night.
You're under my skin and you'll always
Flow through my veins.
We make one person with two
Different minds.
Who would have ever guessed…
You were me this whole time.

Serenity Navarro, Grade 12
Pioneer Technical Center

Something Lacking

Black Book I ask to keep your cover shut.
Your white pages have not had time to rust.
And while I weather on I'm in disgust.

I lack the motivation.

I am beset with fear to have you near.
Atop my shoulder goblins try to peer.
Please hold my secrets dear that I hold dear.

I lack the realization.

A lack of sun has left your ridgerows blind.
I leave you shut with influence I find.
And in the snowstorm nothing springs to mind.

Since I lack the expectation.

Conor McRae, Grade 12
Pacific Collegiate School

Grades 7-8-9

Top Poem Grades 7-8-9

In My Window

My windowsill is great for me
To sit and watch the birds and trees
I think of how they sing their songs,
The beauty that the leaves give off

The music they bring reminds me of you
When I try to forget — it fills up my mind;
You make it so hard to forget
All of our problems, all my regret…

Now, I sit here all alone
Wishing I could go back to that night
On the porch knowing what I had done
Having *this* deep, deep in my heart

I'll never do it again, never!
I swear that I love you, I do!
I did it, I admit it. I am not proud.
I tried to apologize, but you wouldn't let me

Now, I sit here all alone
Wishing you would come find me
Sitting in my windowsill
Watching the birds and trees.

Hannah Akman, Grade 9
University Preparatory School

Top Poem Grades 7-8-9

The Rain

How does the rain fall?
Like a butterfly carried softly by the gentle north wind?
Or pitter, patter, pitter, patter against my windowpane?
Or clash, splash, splash, clash against my roof?
Maybe even drop, drop, pat, drop, pat, pat on my glasses?
How does the rain fall?
Like a baby being rocked to sleep by a gentle lullaby?
Like a leaf in the harsh south wind?
I know how the rain falls.
It goes tap, tap, tap very softly on all the walls around me until I fall asleep.

Emily Fowler, Grade 7
Rancho Del Rey Middle School

Top Poem Grades 7-8-9

Miracle

As I reside on an old, grimy boulder deep in the forest,
I watch the innocence of spring surround me.

Silvery white birches shield me
From the strong afternoon sun.
Their branches, once bent by the heavy snow of winter,
Exert new life for spring.

In a pond nearby, I see my reflection slowly come into focus.
Koi fish swim around my head like a halo.
And moss, floating by, acts as a mustache.
A dry, dead leaf floats into view, and now it's an eyebrow.

I spend my time watching a family of ducks
March towards the welcoming, sapphire pond;
Breathing in the clean, crisp air the emerald trees have to offer;
And skipping smooth, shiny, speckled pebbles into the pond.

Spring is a blessing, a miracle in itself.
Spring is a renewed, strong, energetic life.

Camille Jacobson, Grade 7
Rolling Hills Country Day School

Top Poem Grades 7-8-9

One White Canvas

One white canvas,
Freshly opened tubes of paint,
Each a different color
Squeezed separately onto the palette
Isolated from each other
Until one brush stroke combines them
For one vision, one cause
Until it is complete,
Until the once white canvas is no longer blank,
And you see a playground
With kids laughing, giggling, playing
But what you do not realize is that
We are those individual colors
Those isolated colors on a palette
With no purpose,
Until one brush stroke brings us together
To create a beautiful painting on our one white canvas

Laura Li, Grade 9
Mount Carmel High School

Top Poem Grades 7-8-9

Grace Everywhere*

A car in the dark, driving on black ice
on the twisting canyon road, it nearly crashes twice.
Swerving frantically, barely staying on its path,
only a matter of time 'til it yields to nature's wrath.
From a parting in the clouds comes the faintest ray of light.
A faint glimmer, but it saves him from a terrifying plight.
The driver peers out, spying some thawed ground.
He must steer carefully now, but at least his course is sound.

A solitary rose against the prison wall
like moonlight was to the driver, there to temper Hester's fall.
Having lost it all, the rose gives her heart
to navigate the fateful course some learned man saw fit to chart.
It brings a simple beauty to her harsh and graceless days.
It weaves rich golden fibers in amongst the pallid grays.
It gives us, the readers, a mast to which to cling
throughout her grueling epic, whatever it may bring.

No matter whether or not this gracious symbol truly grows,
it is far more real than what you'll find in any of your garden's rows.
It is in the moonlight, in the dewy morning air.
In the spirit of all people, the rose of graces thrives everywhere.

Anne Mathews, Grade 8
Gaspar De Portola Middle School
Based upon "The Scarlet Letter"

Top Poem Grades 7-8-9

Rain

Shrouded in darkness
I feel the mist
The soft dew drops
Rest softly upon my hand
Like the memory of an old friend
I open my arms
Waiting for the warm embrace
Of the gentle rain that will cool my face
I see the ominous clouds stretched before me
Soon I will be set free
I hear the thunderous echo in reply
I watch as lightning fills the sky
Soon drenched in the rapture of thundershowers
I hear my heartbeat
As the water falls quickly at my feet
My soul beckons for more
Hoping the heavens will hear my plea
I stare upward eagerly waiting to see
If promises will be made to me
Suddenly without effort the clouds burst
Painting ardently its beauty upon the Earth

Avery A. McGrath, Grade 8
Holy Family Catholic School

Top Poem Grades 7-8-9

Ellen's Story

Ellen Moore was in a terrible fate, for she was fatally ill
Life was no store of cashmere sweaters for her to touch and feel
She received the news that she had three months to live
So her parents gave to her all they could give
But she had a dream, the dream to fly
Among the birds and the clouds in the sky
So her parents asked for Make-a-Wish's aid
And soon they had all the arrangements made
She arrived at the private airport right on time
And my dad, the pilot, said he didn't want a dime
All he wanted was for her to give a single smile
He said, "To see her happy would make everything worthwhile."
Indeed, Ellen more than smiled; she beamed like the sun
She was no longer in pain, it seemed; she was having fun
And an hour later when she got back down again
She exclaimed, "I give that flight a one-hundred out of ten!"
Three weeks later, I'm sorry to say
Ellen's spirit went even farther away
Past the birds and past the sky
Why God took her so soon, no one knows why

Stephanie Narlesky, Grade 8
Valley Christian Jr High School

Top Poem Grades 7-8-9

The Fleeing Night

The wind whispered, the leaves fluttered;
No sound could be heard from east or west.
In the dark the spirits muttered,
Listless from their deep Earth's rest.

Suddenly in dark, a sound could be heard like
the swift beating of wild drums.
Then out of the deep night, like a racing gale, on,
on the rider comes.
Shadow's his mantle and moonlight his steed,
Never halting his onward race.
Winds rushed down with the strength of his speed,
Fleeing from the eternal chase.

Then, behind him another came,
Cloaked in light with horse of flame.
Spirits fled,
All but some.
Night is dead.
Day has come!

Aysha Robinson, Grade 9
Golden Eagle Charter School

Top Poem Grades 7-8-9

Sings of a Winter to Come

Tall green figures that reach the sky
Dark clouds with a silver lining,
And a ring of yellow, orange and red
Hitting against the hills.

Cold breezes through the day
Shadows casting in the distance,
Leaves rustling through grassy plains
Patience for nature can't be rushed.

Desperately seeking peaceful and quiet streams
Searching for water lilies along the banks,
Awaiting for their magnificent glory
Birds nesting beyond the meadows.

Squirrels gathering nuts before winter's frost
The beginning of a creature's hibernation
A rampage of preparation
Patience for nature can't be rushed.

Mercedes Wenz, Grade 8
Chino Valley Christian Schools

Top Poem Grades 7-8-9

Strength

Raining from heaven
The brilliance leapt in my heart
Lighting a candle

Too soon, it left me
Off to warm needier souls
While my candle dimmed

Doubt clouded my mind
Taking root and chilling me
My dim glow snuffed out

Sensing my distress
The radiance blazed to me
Clear and beautiful

Scolding the darkness
It re-lit my heart, sighing
Taking flight once more

It still warms others
Flitting back only briefly
To me, it's enough

Janelle Wong, Grade 8
Madrona Middle School

Falling

Falling, falling, falling,
Falling into nothing,
There is only me,
Only I am falling,
Nobody to keep me company,
Nobody but me,
I don't know if it is day,
Or if it is night,
I see nothing,
Not a single drop of light,
Falling, falling, falling,
Falling into nothing.

Colby Wells, Grade 7
Carden School of Sacramento

Solemn Truth

I dare not break
These chains of bondage
That bind my soul
To you forever more

You are my destiny
The only one that can set me free
So still I lie here
Waiting for you
I'm awaiting
Your
Solemn Truth

Duston Gragg, Grade 8
La Joya Middle School

It's Finally Here

when they hear the sound
everyone can shout
it's good to be free with no doubt

the wait is over
so let's go hang out
now matter where
just be there

now we can be loud
no worries about the crowd

lovin' every minute we share
just living life without a care

no fighting allowed
we just got to stand up and be proud

as long as we have friends there
we can take it anywhere
because summer is finally here
until next school year

Ashley Cook, Grade 8
EV Cain Middle School

Learning

Disappointments come our way
Just live life to the fullest and never regret
Cherish your youth and have fun!
Dance in the rain
Don't be afraid!
Live in the moment forget the past!
Take every chance you get!
Aim to the highest
If you don't make it where you wanted to it's fine at least you tried!
Be friends with the people who treat you right
and forget about the ones that don't

Jessica Sanchez, Grade 7
Sarah McGarvin Intermediate School

Track

T he crowd roars and their eyes soar,
R eady to race, you take a deep breath,
A nd then you decide to stretch,
C ourses of hurdles in front of you,
K nowing that you could easily hurt a knee,

A nd then the gun blows and we are off to a start,
N o, you must not get tired, you must go as fast as you were when you started,
D on't ever look at the crowd or you will fall to your lost,

F inishing only half of the race you think to yourself is "faster,"
I n the end of the race the crowd is cheering much louder,
E ven if the race did not come out as you wanted, at least you did not place last,
L ast is not bad, and it does not mean that you are not fast,
D one the race is, relieved you are.

Victoria Flores, Grade 8
Santa Rosa Technology Magnet School

A Letter to a Familiar Friend

Dear Familiar Stranger,
Time is wasted trying to think about you
At least, you being a good person
Or being there for the one you say you love
For how long I struggle to make things right
You turn away and my trust for you has shortened,
Keep telling yourself that you love me
You're the only one who still believes that
You have always told me "actions speak louder than words."
You should start to practice what you preach
My friend, you have become my foe
My partner, you have become my enemy
You used to be the hero in my life
But now you have become the villain
I would tell you I'm sorry for these harsh words
But I'm too tired of making sure you're happy
When it seems you didn't care about my own bliss
Even though I love you,
Sometimes it's a mystery if you even think about me through your day.
Yours truly, A Memory.

Emily Miller, Grade 8
Palm Desert Middle School

The Key to Adventure

I open my eyes and look downward to find,
A book by my side with its pages open wide,
Then close your eyes and open your heart,
Believe in yourself, because that's how it starts,

A world full of wonder and mystics galore,
With everything you can dream of all lie in store,
A deserted island, the ocean bottom, the seashore,
A flight in outer space, the North Pole, and even more,

One dangerous yet gripping adventure on top of a skyscraper,
The villain escapes but you shall take him to justice later,
Unbelievable treasures and hidden secrets under the seas,
Among sea urchins, dolphins, and many creatures you can see,

In outer space the spaceship collapses in a pile or rubble,
And desperately trying to fix it before you are in trouble,
Deserted islands with pirates and buried treasure,
Many parrots, pieces of eight and better,

A dim and feeble streak of light flashes,
As your world of wonder turns into ashes,
You set the book back down on to the floor,
Because this is just the beginning of so much more.

May Young, Grade 8
Challenger School – Ardenwood

Yourself

You might say that you are cool,
But others might think you're a fool.
Show those people who you really are,
The prize won't really be that far.
Maybe you'll be in their crew,
So hurry up because the time is almost due.

Lourdes Sanchez, Grade 7
Sarah McGarvin Intermediate School

The Perfect Teen

I always wonder why I get dirty looks from my family.
My mother always asks, will we survive?
I do not understand her, I am the perfect child.
My father always says, why me Lord, why?
I just look at it as another bad day at work for Dad.
My brother is always in trouble because of me.
I do what I am told with a mad undertone.
I slam the door of my bedroom at least four times a day.
I yell, why don't they understand, I need my privacy!
I love to talk on the phone and IM.
School is not as important as my friends.
I am so embarrassed to be with my mom.
My father is even worse.
My brother is a nuisance.
I wish I was an only child.
Can't they see it is hard to be me, the perfect teen.

Rebecca Idolor, Grade 8
Nobel Middle School

Every Day

Every day I stare at the star
and imagine me and you
I take a deep breath and close my eyes
I see your face.
Every day I daydream of this love
growing bigger each day.
Every day I think of you
I ask myself is he thinking of me.
Every day I know you and I will be together forever
So as I stay here in the deep breeze
I will think of you every day.

Sonia Perez, Grade 8
St Vincent Elementary School

I Need You with Me

I see your face every day
I don't know why my heart beats faster
My hands sweat
I know now I have fallen in love with you
I care for you
I need you to make me whole
I need you to save me
You to be by my side
To hold when I am sad
To put a smile on my face
Come back to me I need you

Korine Sherman, Grade 7
Orville Wright Middle School

Love Is Beautiful

Love is a beautiful thing
It is a lovely sight
Love is so wonderful, it makes my heart sing

To see us together under God's wing
We are forever in His light
Love is a beautiful thing

Our love is like birds in the spring
It makes a dark day seem so bright
Love is so wonderful, it makes my heart sing

In God we trust, and to God we cling
Through the good and bad we hang on tight
Love is a beautiful thing

With every day we are together, joy we bring
With God in our hearts we get through a hard night
Love is so wonderful, it makes my heart sing

Love brings us hope for the next day coming
With Him I know I will be all right
Love is a beautiful thing
Love is so wonderful, it makes my heart sing

Angelina Wills, Grade 8
CORE Butte Charter School

Animals

I like some types of animals
I'll name a few for you:
Dogs, cats, lions, and tigers
dolphins, snakes, but not spiders.
Although dogs and cats are my favorite,
I am like the lions and tigers
never scared of the dark.
I like the water as much as dolphins do
and sometimes I am like a snake,
very clever and slick.
I like some types of animals
I'll name a few for you.

Jessica Mayer, Grade 7
Renuevo School

Natural Earth

Trees, wind
branches, air
the sweet nature
soil, sun, water
Earth, fire
the naturality
things of God,
creator of Earth,
thanks to Him
we live today

Denisse Lopez, Grade 8
St Vincent Elementary School

This Mystery Called Life

Give me a second,
and I'll walk you through,
this mystery called life,
that you thought you knew.

We live to die,
and die to live,
and when it's over,
there's nothing left to give.

There's black for death,
and a rose for love,
beyond the blue sky,
are the heavens above.

But there's a sad, sad truth,
that the beauty hides,
because there's a black abyss,
behind the lies.

But there is a bright side,
behind all the lies,
but only you can solve,
this mystery called life.

Bradly Bounds, Grade 8
Andros Karperos Middle School

I'm Sorry

Remember your shoes…the ones that you just got and really liked
Well…I had "accidentally" got the hose and filled up your shoes with water
You really did make me mad when you ruined my picture
I'm sorry…I hope you can forgive me
I really didn't mean to
But you should have seen how funny you looked…
When you had to walk into the store barefoot

Nicka Deldjoui, Grade 8
Madrona Middle School

We're Not the Only Ones

We think we're the only one to go through tough times.
God doesn't know what it's like, He wouldn't understand.
We think we have it so rough, we're late to school and miss the bus.
We have too much homework, or someone has been unkind.
But I know someone, Jesus is His name,
He's gone through it all and He knows our troubles.
King of all Kings, Lord of Lords, came down to this world,
in the form of a baby, humble from birth.
He grew up like we did, with school and friends.
He grew up teaching God's word, and a perfect child He was.
But some did not like him, for he taught the truth.
And King of all Kings, Lord of Lords died a criminal's death.
Nailed to a cross with a crown of thorns on His brow,
they beat Him and whipped Him until He was dead.
Placed in a tomb so small and dark,
He rose from the dead, three days from then!
Why Jesus did this, we all may ask,
He did this to pay for all the bad sins we've done!
So when you begin to think that God doesn't know,
remember that Jesus came from Heaven, and walked in your shoes.

Elise Herrscher, Grade 7
Linfield Christian School

Anything for You

When I see you sad, it makes me feel bad.
When I see you cry, it makes me sad.
When I see you in pain, it makes me so mad.
I don't want you sad because it makes me want to cry
and tell you everything's all right.
I don't want you to cry
because it makes me want to hold you until your tears run dry.
I don't want you in pain
because it makes my heart ache.
I'll do anything you want to stop the sadness.
I'll say anything you want to stop the pain of blackness.
Anything just to stop those tears of darkness.
It hurts me deeply when your in pain, like an open wound that can go away
but leaves a scar to be remembered of that hurtful day.
Please don't cry. Don't be sad. Don't feel bad.
Because I'm here and I'll stay by your side until you're all right.
Just like you stayed with me to stop my agony.
Now it's my turn to help you because you're my friend and I want you to be happy.

Mariah Valdez, Grade 9
Greenfield High School

The Exact Moment

I remember the exact moment I found out
April 5, 2008, I got the worst news ever.
I walk inside the house and my brother's crying.
"What happened?"
"Cristian's dead!"
I stood there in shock, until it finally hit me
Cristian's gone, no longer with us.
I started crying and walked to my room
I just didn't know what to do.

I couldn't breathe so I went outside
Looking out into the street
I remembered Cristian forgot his sweater at our house.
Holding the sweater in my hands just broke me in half.
He was like my little brother
He and my eldest brother, Andy, were really close
As Cristian would say, he was his brother from another mother.
Now Andy sleeps with that sweater every night.

Cristian was the sweetest boy you could ever meet,
Never argued,
Always smiling, enjoying life as it was,
Cristian will always be in my heart.

Emily Quezada, Grade 8
McCabe Elementary School

A French Morning

Seize the French morning.
For life may turn out to be boring.
Wake up happy for a brighter day.
And don't live with dismay.
Walk down Champs-Elysées.
Where all the smiles are aimed towards you.

Carla Torres, Grade 7
John Adams Middle School

My Sisters

My sisters will be there for me
during good times and bad times.
When I'm in trouble
they will always help me.
When I'm feeling sad
they will always help me.
When I feel happy
they will be there and celebrate with me.
When I feel like I'm not worth anything
they will always be there.
When I can't decide on what I want
they will decide with me.
When I won't listen to what I'm told
they will help me go through it.
When I can't think straight
they will be there to help me.
My sisters will always find a way to help me.

Alma Ayala, Grade 7
Almond Tree Middle School

Nature

As I walk down a path
Oh see the sun shining down like the lights of heaven

The wet mud on the ground
Looks like a giant chocolate pudding

What part of nature do I take in this world

I see a turtle sleeping in a mossy cove
Makes me feel like drifting away

Alec Sorensen, Grade 8
Citrus Hills Intermediate School

Flawless Execution

My legs quake underneath my dress.
My knees uncontrollably knock together.
My eyes burn from the bright significance of the lights.
I somehow walk, fearing I'll collapse,
On my way from the steps to my assigned spot.
I can feel thousands of pairs of eyes,
Ready to mock any wrong move.
I finally reach my destination,
My heart pounding and my mind spinning,
As if I've just finished a 100-yard dash.
I can hear faint music from behind me,
And, just as I've practiced a thousand times before,
I join in on the third measure, fourth beat,
Singing better than I ever have before.
When I finish,
I turn confidently on my heel, back to the steps.
The crowd is calling my name, over and over!
With each step, the applause grows louder than one can bear!
My director whispers in my ear.
"Encore, my dear."
So I return.

Sarah Mighell, Grade 7
Joshua Springs Academy

The Beach

Where the children play in the soft warm sand
Where the adults sit and get a tan
    The Beach
Where the sun sets and the sky is pretty
Where the waves crash on the smooth shoreline
    The Beach
Where the teens play volleyball on the sandy shore
Where the big light house is on the rocky shore
    The Beach
Where the boats dock after a very long journey
Where the sea shells lay what a pretty sight to see
    The beach
Where the people ride horses on the shoreline
Where Jesus walked on that sun set evening
    THE BEACH!

Moises Kristich, Grade 7
Monte Vista Christian School

You Broke My Heart

You broke my heart
And I wanted you back
but you didn't
I pray to God
We'll get back together
But he said it wouldn't happen

Yessenia Gamez, Grade 7
Richland Jr High School

The Sun

The sun is rising
As I lay on the cool grass
I watch the night pass

Mariah Valdivia, Grade 8
South Tahoe Middle School

Family

A family sticks together
No matter how difficult
A situation we are in.
They give us tips
How to be better.
They want us to be our best,
Achieve our goals,
Grow up to achieve great things
Making our life happy and easy.

Aharron Alvarez, Grade 7
St Alphonsus School

Jake the Hamster

Oh Jake the hamster
Jake the cuddly hamster
Soft as silk he was
The months we had him.

Oh Jake the hamster
Jake the playful hamster
Wandering creature in a small land
The months we had him.

Oh Jake the hamster
Jake the friendly hamster
His cage had called to me
The last night we had him.

Oh Jake the hamster
Jake the lone hamster
Lie down kept quiet
The last minute we had him.

Oh Jake the hamster
Jake the best hamster
Our favorite memories
The months after his soul went away.

Holly Danielle Rodriguez, Grade 8
Valley Oak Middle School

Because of You

Because of you, I learned that life is only one,
but you could only live it once.
Because of you, I learn it's okay to make mistakes
everybody does that and that's okay.
Because of you, I learned that love is precious,
but you must learn how to appreciate.
Because of you, I learned how to respect others and myself at all times.
Because of you, I learned how the world takes action in life
For all that and much more I have learned
Thank you Mom!

Daniela Espinoza, Grade 8
Almond Tree Middle School

The Wind

The wind
The wind
It calls to me
It's like the sea, it rolls on by
Never to see that same cloud in the sky
The wind is a flute player playing in the night
And the birds are like a piccolo singing away
Its applause is the leaves crunching under my feet
My hair is blowing in the wind
They never know, they never say when the wind is on its way
Night or day, the wind goes by, sometimes leaving its mark behind
It could be weak or at its peak
No need to speak, just listen, listen closely
The wind
The wind
It calls to me

Jennifer Santos, Grade 8
Valley Oak Middle School

An Ode to School

"School was fine"
I say to my parents when it really isn't
Going to school facing those gossipers
Hanging with someone and then being labeled
So much drama
"Yeah, school is great"
Who's going out with whom?
Did you hear what SHE did?
"School was okay"
Going home feeling bad
Hoping tomorrow will be better
Going home crying
Getting into another fight with your friend, or maybe your boyfriend?
You know, the one who cheated on you with your friend?
Or maybe hearing another rumor (whatever it is) about yourself
Yet, all you can say to your parents each day is
"Yeah, school was cool"
You know they won't understand
You think no one does
You just go home and cry.

Marie Nguyen, Grade 8
Crittenden Middle School

Ode to Music

Oh, my Lord how I love my music.
It's relaxing and fun and my number one.
Blasting my music so the speakers blow out,
My mom says to stop it and turn it down.
Music is my stress reliever,
Especially the songs that give you dancing fever,
Even though my sister says to stop,
I say go away you little snot!
Today I think I'll sing aloud
To the music that makes me wild and loud!

Jordyn Loyd, Grade 8
Citrus Hills Intermediate School

I Am

I am a twelve year old girl
I wonder will I go to college
I hear a lot of people tell me I won't
I see a lot of bad things happening
I want to go to college but school is hard
I am going to go no matter what
I pretend that I go away
I feel good things happening
I touch my baby sister
I worry that I will have to go back
I am just that kind of girl
I understand that sometimes I am bad
I dream that I will finish school
I hope one day I will
I am a dream and one day it will come true

Keyondra Young, Grade 7
Richland Jr High School

House of Glass and Tears

Alone in that thick glass house you sit
With tears clouding your vision.
You think you're alone and nobody cares.
You cannot see all the people you've locked out.
Each time you despair of the loneliness, we drown.
All people who love you can only watch
Through your glass walls
Swallowed in your grief.
Love nor hate can sway you
Only the emptiness is there.
Our love can't penetrate your walls
You don't feel it.
We reach out to you, but you lock us away.
We call to you, but you hear nothing.
All we can do for you
Is watch and weep.
You bear your pain
No one can help.
While you live in your world
With only glass and tears.
Alone.

Ellen Webre, Grade 8
Lakeside Middle School

Baseball

Baseball is my favorite sport
In baseball it doesn't matter if you're tall or short
Strong or weak
I love baseball because you can work as a team
Sometimes you need other people to help you
Because you can't take on the world alone

Juan Carlos Gómez, Grade 7
St Mary's School

The Wild

Someday somehow what will I do, go into the wild
Where the flowers bloom from day to day
And rivers run a mile away
From the ground all the way to the trees
From the beautiful butterflies to the bees
Where wild horses run free
And little baby blue birds fly and flee
Pretty little patterns in the sky
Go passing by
I wonder if this is where I belong
In my heart plays a mellow song
Someday somehow what will I do, go into the wild

Brianna Edwards, Grade 8
Robert E Peary Middle School

A Lifetime

What comes today
Will go tomorrow
For all your life, you'll sit in sorrow
A place in this world so strong and bold
A time for giving with nothing to hold
The time has come when you'll be free
Your spirit will rise with nowhere to flee
A choice to be made
It will never be the same
So make your choice and write your claim

Sophia Gonzalez, Grade 8
Manton School

The Last in Line

Auschwitz, waiting in line.
If you cried, you died.
The place where families
were forced to say goodbye.
All brought there by a clever lie.
Waiting and working, trying to survive.
Why? Did they enjoy watching people cry?
It started with one mind.
Feeling the rest of humankind
was somewhere far behind.
Looking back, we clearly see he was blind.
But be careful, you may one day find
You, yourself, the last in line.

Dakota Flores, Grade 9
Visalia Christian Academy

A Sense of Spring

Can you feel the breeze?
Can you hear the wind blowing?
Can you smell the air?

The ice is melting
The flowers are soon to bloom
Spring has left its mark.

Margarita Arreola, Grade 7
South Tahoe Middle School

Creamy Peanut Butter

Peanut butter for lunch,
With milk or some punch.

So sticky, so creamy,
Mix it with jam, and oh so dreamy.

Eat it alone or with bread,
or with some chocolate instead!

Sweet and delicious,
and also very nutritious.

Like love birds so sweet.
It can never be beat.

Katrina Avena, Grade 8
Madrona Middle School

A Trip to France

I'd like to go to France someday
I just cannot wait
Food to eat, people to meet
It's going to be so great
So many things to do and say
And oh! So many reasons
To go to France someday

Isabel Torres, Grade 7
John Adams Middle School

Swim

Once that gun goes off
You've already started the race
Once you hit that water
Try not to hit your face

You're in it
Give it all you've got
The water is so cold
But your body feels so hot

You're on your last lap!
Maybe one day you'll be Michael Phelps
And win by .01 of a second
Well, I hoped that helps

Kenny Nguyen, Grade 7
Sarah McGarvin Intermediate School

I Have a Friend

I have a friend
He is a Redwood tree
Ask him a foggy question and
He will answer in streaks of light

I have a friend
Whose branches are long like
A wizard's tail
Shading his blemished face
Faith is howling to him
Trying to
Grasp his unsophisticated knowledge

I have a friend
Who seems a shy blue
But is bursting with excitement
Inside
His blank gazes will confuse you
His ancient songs hush you to sleep
His rugged wood will
Smooth out your
Dreams
I have a friend

Matthew Waxman, Grade 7
Adaline E Kent Middle School

Raindrops

A drop of rain hit my window
Tap, tap, tap,
Is someone there?
Oh, it is nothing more
Than the cloud's tears.

A drop of rain hit the grass
Squish squash
Is someone there?
Oh, it is nothing more
Than the clouds waters its garden.

A drop of rain hits the earth
Pouring, pouring, pouring
Is someone there?
Oh, it is the rain and nothing more.

Natalie Woerner, Grade 8
Madrona Middle School

The Bright Sky

The moon was bright
And so were the stars
The bird was singing
And it was there
All by himself and in
The late bright night
Singing.

Ana Torres, Grade 7
Richland Jr High School

Looking at My Mom

Looking at my mom
I saw tears in her eyes
I cannot stand it
When I see her cry

I asked her
What are you crying for ?
She said
I can't go to work anymore

She told me
To work hard and don't stop
So when I grew up
I can get a better job

Now that I graduated from college
My smile filled with glee
I looked at my mom
She was proud of me

Danh Le, Grade 7
Sarah McGarvin Intermediate School

Sun

Bright, shiny, yellow
Floats happily in the sky
Giving us light
Makes plants grow
Seems to be moving
Makes people warm
When they are cold.

Destiny Duran, Grade 7
St Alphonsus School

Hurricane

A hurricane is approaching
A flurry of activity,
As the people prepare
The meteorologists rant on
About its strength
And our impending doom
Cars parked in front of the garage door
I stand out front and see
The invasion coming
The dark horsemen
The Calvary thundering forward
Their war cries carried in the wind
I shiver and run back in for cover
And as they draw nearer
Their arrows strain to hit us
Nicking all obstructions as they pass
The horses now near
They slam into the trees
The houses, the telephone poles
And now reaching the city.

Kyle Hallsten, Grade 8
Madrona Middle School

France

French is an essential feeling in your skin
It cannot be even kept in a bin
To learn French is a privilege to me
I don't think it even has a fee
Going to France will be exciting and fun
It just makes me want to run
Selling the land and receiving donations
I think France is my favorite nation
So going to France is my dream
Even though its not how it might seem

Raphael Reyes, Grade 7
John Adams Middle School

Ode to Gunner

If I haven't traveled to this far distant home,
Then I wouldn't have written this very poem.
We picked him up, in an old dog house,
Filled with bugs and one dead mouse.
We saved him from the awful place,
And now he wears a smile on his face.
We bought him home to his new land,
Full of kids and petting hands.
My dad thought that life was too short,
And without a dog, it would be to distort.
We then had conflict about his new name,
That soon should bring him much great fame.
We came to an end and named him Gunner,
Now life with him is so much funner.

Brad Walker, Grade 7
Santa Rosa Technology Magnet School

Fun All Day

Sports are fun,
Especially with a lot of sun
So come and play
On this sunny day
Have a great time
Enjoy your life
Because you only get one life to enjoy,
So use it as best as you can
Play all day
In a sunny May
Let your skin feel the sun's heat
Like fresh roasted meat
Don't let your time be a waste
Kids have fun all day
But adults should make some time to play
Enjoyment is a key thing in life
So let your inner fun out
And give a big shout
That you are great and want to have fun
Live your life
And don't let it go to waste

Aakash Kadakia, Grade 7
Thornton Jr High School

An Ode to Dogs

Furry, grimy, big or small
Give enjoyment to one and all
Make you happy, make you sad
Understand when you are mad
Very cute or very gross, never even try to boast
They never speak, they never shout
But always know what you're thinking about
Never cry, never complain
Love it when you call their name
They may be playful, they may be boring
But it is funny when they are snoring
May be anxious, may be calm
But always love to lick your palm
Make them sit or make them shake
But remember to give them a break
Can't do homework, can't do math
But always hate to get a bath
Love it when you scratch their ears
But hate it when you shed your tears
They may be fat, they may be small
But I make sure to love them all.

Evan Marshall, Grade 7
Santa Rosa Technology Magnet School

Ocean Air

I sit on the fence, while watching the sea.
The ocean is beautiful; it seems so kind.
I wish to be a dolphin; I want to swim freely.
But I never will be; it must stay in my mind.

Brian Hertz, Grade 8
Kadima Heschel West Middle School

Raindrop

What is your secret?
Why is it that you so quickly come and go?
Do you perhaps conceal something from my limited sight?
Why do you hide your beauty from the sun's glow?
Does the wind command your every little move?
Or do you get to choose your own path to take?
Where would you go, if only you knew?
Are you an enchanted teardrop being cried?
Why else do you appear as a crystal shard?
Is that a rainbow I glimpse inside?
Do you capture the essence of light?
Are you golden by the sun? Silver by the moon?
Or do you change your color during flight?
What are you really attempting to show me?
Is that a memory or a reflection of myself?
Are you a window to something I can't see?

What is your secret?
Are you real or something that I imagined?
Is your glitter and sparkle just a part of that magic?
Or are you something much more significant?

Amanda Trinh, Grade 9
Notre Dame High School

Life

Life is given by God
Life is all
Life is precious
Life is grateful
Life is everything to me
Life is only to be taken away by God

Cecie Puente, Grade 8
Our Lady of the Rosary School

Baseball

Baseball is not just a game
It is much more
You can play even if you're poor

When I step on that field
I am a changed person
And when I step in that batter's box
I feel invincible

When I am on the base
I am as still as a vase
And when I am prepared
It's not even fair

Win or lose
I play my hardest
So I have no shame
Because I have love for the game.

Nathan Murray, Grade 7
Joan MacQueen Middle School

My Dream

To play like a madman is my dream,
To play the guitar as good as B.B. King,
Like Eric Clapton or Steve Windwood,
To play like the best is my dream.

Fingers burning and hurting,
With a never-ending pain,
But that's the price to pay
To play like the best.

The day I play "catfish blues"
To be the best that it can be,
Like the way Jimi used to play.
To play like the best is my dream.

Richard Christman, Grade 7
Linfield Christian School

Rain

There is lots of rain
And now it's cold
It's such a pain
Now I've found mold

Selena Coronado, Grade 7
Richland Jr High School

A Teddy's Story

There was a time when you took me everywhere you went.
You never let go.
There was a time when you and I were best friends.
You never left me.
Then there was a time when they laughed and you hated me.
You never smiled.
There was another time when you hid me and loved me in secret.
You never told them.
There was a time when you forgot me and packed me away.
You never needed me.
Much later there was a time when you picked me up again.
You'd always missed me.
Then came the time when you stuck me on the shelf.
You always glanced there.
There was a time when all I did was watch from that shelf.
You never glanced anymore.
But then came the day, many years later, when you picked me up and hugged me.
You never forgot me again.
The rest of our time you glanced and you smiled and up on my shelf I smiled back.
You'd let go of me, and found yourself.

Maren Fichter, Grade 9
Westview High School

The Avenue

Lights are flashing.
All the nice cars, gases are smashing, radios blaring
Driving by slowly revving in neutral, people staring.
Restaurants filled, people laughing, eating and talking
Couples just watching them and continue walking.
Benzes Bimmers, Lamborghinis and Bentleys roar down the avenue
Showing off the watches, the glasses and of all…their money.
The avenue is filled with people saying "I love you honey."
Sounds of engines, people talking and laughing, getting away from it all for one special night on the avenue.
On the avenue, there is no need to speed through, you want to tip
Slow and be loud so everyone can hear and see you.
Classy rich people stroll down from their avenue apartments, jewelry and couture from the designer departments.
Life is good for people on the avenue.

Reza Mirgoli, Grade 8
Tierra Linda Middle School

My Awesome Middle School

Through all my years at my middle school
There's been days that have been exciting, challenging, and just plain cool
A ride of its own since 6th grade
Where we explored our new beginnings as elementary school faded
Then came 7th grade day by day
Yet now we were familiar with our campus in our own way
And finally came 8th grade the best of them all
To see how we've grown through rise and fall
Oh, I'm going to miss these days where I walked through my school that were the best
All because I attended my awesome middle school…WEST!!!

Marina George, Grade 8
West Middle School

Junior High

Junior high is crazy,
It's been really hard for those who are lazy,
Full of Homework and Drama,
And lame jokes about "yo momma,"
Junior high is crazy,
All of the teachers both good and the bad,
Loading us with homework and making us mad,
Junior high sports are wicked fun too,
Especially while watching Markham boo hoo,
Junior high is crazy,
Junior high has been full of laughter,
But we're all looking forward to high school thereafter
Junior high is crazy.

Jim Hansen, Grade 8
Northside Elementary School

The Win

I'm standing at the starting line.
My adrenaline is pumping.
I'm waiting for the gun to fire.
I think I hear people jumping.

I begin running.
I can't see anyone in front of me or beside me.
I can hear people in the stands jumping.
I feel like I'm the queen bee.

The wind is blinding me.
I can barely see.
And no one can stop me.
I won! And I'm the queen bee.

Mika Klitsch, Grade 7
South Tahoe Middle School

Jessica

Intelligent
Nice
Beautiful
Wishes to be a college student
Dreams of a sweet life
Wants to be a house owner
Who wonders about life
Who fears about gangsters
Who is afraid of monkeys
Who likes to hang out with friends
Who believes in myself
Who loves to talk to boys
Who loves her family
Who loves shopping
Who loves music
Who plans to be a teacher
Who plans to not do drugs
Who plans to be a successful student
Whose final destination is Universal Studios

Jessica Arredondo, Grade 7
Almond Tree Middle School

Regrets

From the moment you let go of your loved one,
the food you eat will have no taste,
your body will have no warmth,
and your heart will have no beats.
Till the day you die,
you will regret.

Ngoc Nguyen, Grade 7
Sarah McGarvin Intermediate School

Life Is Not Fair

As I open the tinted glass door
I enter a stone room covered in tile
I turn the metal faucet to the left
Quickly retreating from the small room
In minutes steam appears
Seeping through the top of the door
the sound of rain pours down
Hitting the ground with a big splash
As I open the door, heat expands around me
Smothering me with steam
The water seeps out of the shower head
Creating a burning sensation on my skin
As I wash my hair
I stood in thought about all the children in Uganda
Walking miles to find a fresh water source
When all I have to do is turn a knob
And like magic, water appears

Kelsey Hemm, Grade 8
St Joseph's School of the Sacred Heart

Unchanged Time

We try to think of many ways
To fix what is already done
We try to change the past
Even though the battle has been won

What's done is done many have said
The battle is fought, the water runs red
Mangled bodies have fallen from the sky
Many people scream their last goodbye

Hearts slain and souls are killed
Lives are taken, fates are sealed
But still we try to rewrite old stories
Change old cares, replace all worries

Change the past day by day
Try to turn the future away
But we must remember that in the course of destiny
Forever is not eternally

Even as the wind bells chime
The past will forever remain unchanged time

Veronica Carr, Grade 8
Antioch Middle School

Friendship

The only time you can be obnoxious, weird, and fun too, no one would even consider judging you
Everyone is nice to each other, they are the ones who push you to do your best like your mother
Lots of sunshine all around, time for friends can always be found
Feel the cool wind rush through your hair, as you fly up in the air
Staying up all night is the test, a three day long movie fest
Eat junk food all day, we are all smart idiots in our own way
Softly she sings so kind it stings
We all have the same track spikes, love to dance around and eat Mike and Ikes
Bad things may happen both big and small, but we will help each other through it all
It will take time to heal, no matter how bad you really feel
You must never fear, because you have me my dear

Sarah Haydock, Grade 9
Fountain Valley High School

Visualizations of Life

Life is full of diversity. It can cause conflict or harmony.
But that's the beauty of it all. Some symbolize strength and stand tall.
They're emancipated to make their own choices. We can all represent that and display our voices.

Life is a river rippling on in various ways. We shall make it pure even on those bad days.
The divergent creatures portray our world's differences. Hopefully we can respect each other and come to our senses.
Let us choose wisely as we can for our hearts to mend. We must try before our river comes to its end.

Life is the tremendous sky-blue and with any kind of weather. We all wish our problems were easy and light as a feather.
Birds serenade the sun and fly freely away. "If only they can give us their wings!" I say.
We have to face obstacles sometimes though. When your sky rains, always believe in the appearance of a rainbow.

Life is a road — open and smooth, or split in two. It has numerous opportunities waiting for you.
Follow your own path that guides you to your success. Never let anything reprimand you from your happiness.
A river, a road, and the sky. What is your visualization of life?

Decie Jean Reyes, Grade 9
Westview High School

Icy Raindrops

A scattered slate cloud roofing the Earth's atmosphere.
Reviving raindrops come from the pacifying ocean, blue ridge mountains, and a rippling river.
Those teardrops from the sky build up on my window,
Forming muddy puddles in my backyard.

I run my hands down the dulled window from the numbing chill outside.
Drops from the ceiling descend upon my head,
From the leak made by the treacherous downpour.

The pitter patter of the raindrops are a running sink.
From my bedroom I hear a lonesome dog,
Howling in the rain for its owner.

My hazy breath forms from the loathsome icy breeze.
I can almost taste the rain seeping through the window.

The salty cerulean sea lies before me,
Getting punched blow by blow by the rain.
In the next room I faintly smell a pot of chicken noodle soup simmering,
Tempting me to rush to the kitchen for a welcoming of heat and happiness.

Justin Uesugi, Grade 8
Rolling Hills Country Day School

Basketball

Playing on a court
or playing outside
Basketball is really fun
you have to give it a try.

Playing a basketball game
is like taking candy from a baby
When a stranger asks me to play
I have to say maybe.

Sometimes before playing
I get really nervous
But my coach says "Keep trying"
and I get focused.

I love playing basketball so much
and I hope other people do too
I've got a basketball so come over and play
Trust me, I'll go easy on you!

Rachel Beasley, Grade 7
Joan MacQueen Middle School

I Am the Past

I am the past,
Known from the mind.
Child of present, daughter of time.
I am the past,
Friend of future.
Live to be remembered,
Dream to be forever.
I am the past,
That loves to be shared.
I fear to be forgotten for I want to be cared.
I am the past.

Theresa Tran, Grade 7
St Barbara School

No One Meant for Us to Lose

No one meant for us to lose
We are born to choose
to use our voice
We are given options with no choice
Pity our potential known only to others
Rise against
Conquer your fear you have yet to weather
Drift as weightless as a feather
Run your fingers through the Earth
Retrieve the flower from the dirt
Open the road you created yourself
Find your path seen to no one else
An open road suddenly split in two
Choose the path still clean and new
There is nothing out of view

Angela Yuan, Grade 9
Westview High School

May

Month of celebration
Time of joy and happiness
Happy, colorful, and great
Cinco De Mayo

Maria Avalos, Grade 7
John Charles Fremont Intermediate School

Kaytlin Elizabeth Lee

Why did He do it?
You just got here, you had to leave.
I never even knew you.
I see you in pictures
It's like they say don't forget.
So little and fragile,
Fragile like the butterflies that fly in the sky.
A shining star that is always there
But not always seen.
You're gone forever, so they say
But to me you are everywhere.
You're there when I laugh
And there when I cry
You're there when I breathe
And there when I try.
I try so hard to remember
Someone I never met.
If only I was there to catch you
The day you had to fall.
I will forever love you
Kaytlin Elizabeth Lee.

Chelsea Harbison, Grade 8
Valley Oak Middle School

A Day in the Life of the Horde

Listen my friends and you shall hear,
Of the battle of might and fear;
A Tauren by the name of Borris,
Walking along the Barrens witnessing,
A raid on the Crossroads which is horrifying.

He quickly mounted and went to the next city on their way,
The great Orgimmar a major city of the Horde on that day;
He ran in as fast as he can,
Everyone not knowing,
Of the fate becoming.

He exclaimed the Alliance is coming,
They mounted their force for the battle which is forming,
Everyone went out awaiting their fate,
Not knowing of what's coming,
They fought until they made them start running.

A victorious day for the Horde this is,
Killing the Alliance is,
A day's work.

Steven Pytel, Grade 8
Palm Desert Middle School

Loving Mother

You are small in size but,
Big in heart,
You are cool with friends,
But awesome with us,
You are nice to him,
But beautiful to us,
You are faithful to him,
And also to us,
But you have one thing others don't have
lovable to all,
Who are you?
My Loving Mother!

Hector Guerra, Grade 7
St Mary's School

Old Days

I miss the old days
The days back then
The sun's rays shining
Again and again
When all was well
Nothing wrong
The ringing of the school bell
Sounding just like a song
I miss the old days
When I could go out
Jump around and play
Go about
Singing and dancing
Showing my soul
Wearing my cool bling
Reaching my goals
Those days are gone
Never to be seen
All seems to go wrong
Everyone mean

Lucy Guo, Grade 8
William Hopkins Jr High School

Hatred

I hate you, you hate me,
there's nothing much to say,
— beside the fact that you are ugly,
you scare me throughout the day.

I hate you, you hate me,
we're best enemies for life,
to you I'm just a hideous monster,
more ruthless than a knife.

But deep, deep, down inside our hearts,
we know someday we'll face,
— there's a very, very, very thin line,
between love and hate

Kimlynn Do, Grade 7
Sarah McGarvin Intermediate School

So Sorry

I'm sorry for the time when you were about to sit and I pulled your chair
Got everyone to laugh and stare.
You get up, then sock my arm
But you laugh too cause I caused no harm.
You got up, but didn't tell.
You'd laugh too, if it was me that fell.
So I'm sorry for pulling out your chair, but what can I say
I'll probably do it again, anyway!

Gabriel Cueva, Grade 8
Saint Sebastian School

Hitsuzen

Walking along an endless road, that is fated to someday end.
Hearts become lonely and cold, as the road begins to bend.
It's foolish to wait 'til tomorrow, what if nothing happens that day?
Life will be filled with sorrow, if you waste the days away.
The future laid out in front of me, is cast in iron stone.
If I searched for the future restlessly, I would end up all alone.
The path was already chosen, and destiny takes its place.
The future was always frozen, it's something I don't need to chase.
Everything happens for a reason, because this world revolves around fate.
So whichever road I choose this season, was already set for me to take.
I won't bother trying to change it, it will happen as foretold.
There's no point worrying which, fate has formed the destined road.
I will not act for the future, I'll do what my realities allow.
I don't have the need to be secure, don't want to regret the time spent now.
So let me have my fun, I won't let the present drown.
When there are two roads I'll just pick one, 'cause fate won't let me down.
Naturally foreordained events, time and time again.
Doesn't matter who dissents, hitsuzen.

Fifi Tran, Grade 9
Westview High School

Secrets of the Sky

As I raise my head from the water, and straight past the trees,
I feel the warmth of the sun, yet the coolness of the breeze.
Laying on my back, I stare directly at the sky,
Where the clouds take on odd shapes and the birds fly by.
To me, the white fluffs represent each day of my unique life,
Whether it include happiness, sadness, celebration, or strife.
The sky appears and endless timeline — future, present, and past,
Yet I consider it all the while mysterious, just as it is vast.
Present looks back down at me, and future in the distance.
I am looking forward to it, not at all in fear of its presence.
The movement of the cloud above represents the day in progress,
And you see that one little bird? It is I, and nothing less.
There I am, constantly and conscientiously soaring this way and that;
I could change my flight's direction, my mind, at the drop of a hat.
Do you see me now? I am human, on the stairs to the cloud,
Climbing step-by-step, reaching a goal that I know I will be proud.
Every one of those once-in-a-while storm clouds is an obstacle,
Just to be quickly overcome before it becomes a debacle.
I figure that this is enough sky gazing for one day,
Instead of asking the sky for answers, I'll go my own way.

Justine Law, Grade 8
Challenger School – Ardenwood

Heroes

They crashed into the Towers
Because they were cowards
For it was Al Quaida who had attacked our Freedom
We are fighting back
And we do not lack
This is why we are now in Iraq
And lets not forget the brave men and women in Iraq
I hope they will all come back
For it's America the brave
Who always lets their flag wave

Kyle McCarthy, Grade 7
Citrus Hills Intermediate School

A Strive for the Moon

There once was a man with a peculiar plan
He wanted to walk on the moon
He trained every day with one goal in his mind
And he knew it would be coming soon
It's finally the day. He preparing for launch
His chance was upon him, but he still had a hunch
That his trip would end badly
But he got over it quick
And took his spree gladly
His conscience still thick.
It happened so slow that time was a snail,
He needed to be sure that there was perfect detail
His historic takeoff was to occur at noon
Like an explosion, a terrible "BOOM!"
The rocket waved goodbye, and left for the moon.

Joey Mancinelli and Terry Elliott, Grade 8
St Patrick Parish School

Slipping Away

They keep slipping further away
More and more each day
I'm still standing on the edge
That's on the ledge of righteousness
Watching them slip farther away
Is there nothing I can say

They're slipping farther away
A little more each day
I'm yelling from the edge
To just stop and use their heads

I just want them back again
Why won't they give me their hand
So I can pull them back
Stop the craziness
Running around my head
I want things the way they used to be
The hide-and-seek days that were so carefree.
I miss those days
But everything's slipping away

Emily Jones, Grade 8
EV Cain Middle School

Snow of July

It is snowing now.
Today is not December.
Today is not January.
It is July.

Someone is waiting for sunshine.
Someone is waiting for the feeling of warmth.
But it is snowing now.
And today is July.

It seems like the snow is ignoring them.
And the snow is falling heavier.
Every second of air getting colder and colder.
Today is July.

Someone is waiting for sunshine
Instead of the feeling of freezing.
And they are waiting for July
Without the snow.

Diana Ko, Grade 8
Madrona Middle School

Where I'm From

I am from fun in the swimming pool
To playing guitar which is really cool
From playing tag
And carrying books in a bag
From playing the cello
To being really mellow.

I am from learning to write
And flying a kite
From going on Myspace
To getting first place
From shooting hoops
And making homemade soup.

I am from s'mores
To shopping at electronic stores
From playing football
And reciting verses by Paul
I am from the colors of red, white, and blue
To sitting on a pew
This is where I am from.

Matthew Im, Grade 7
Linfield Christian School

Ode to Friends

My friends are the ones I see every day,
They listen to what I have to say.
Some people say you can't always depend on your friends,
But I think of friends as stars
You may not always see them but you know they're there!

Brenna Lallande, Grade 8
Citrus Hills Intermediate School

Pollution

There is not just one
Pollution is made famous
It can kill the world

It goes in the air
It can get people very sick
It can hurt anyone

It is around us
It can be easy to stop
If all people help

Emmanuel Ortiz, Grade 8
Almond Tree Middle School

Spring

They say it is
a time for happiness
a time for blossom.
Everyone is happy
everyone blossoms into
a beautiful flower.
People change
colors change
the world
becomes beautiful.
The sound of the wind
is softer more peaceful
and calm.

Brandi Gonzales, Grade 8
St Hilary Elementary School

The Lonely Chair

The soft sand sparkles
Under the scorching sun
That slowly burns the ground
Cool mellow waves slowly crash
Blowing light mist around them
Soft gentle breezes
Whistle through the air
Tossing bits of sand
While fearful clouds shrink
Fleeing from the everlasting sun
Leaving only a patch
Of blue-gray sky

Fins of dolphins sway in the water
Up and down, back and forth,
Being the only company
For the dull-colored torn up chair
That sits alone in the middle
Of the gray sand,
And in it is where she sits,
Lonely, hiding,
Like every other day.

Rachel Grau, Grade 8
St Joseph's School of the Sacred Heart

Smile

A smile costs nothing, but gives much.
It enriches those who receive, without making poorer those who give.
It takes but a moment, but the memory of it sometimes lasts forever.
None is so rich or might that he can get along without it,
and none is so poor, but that he can be made rich by it.

Eric Tran, Grade 7
Holy Family Catholic School

Secrets

What is a secret if the secret is told?
What is the meaning what does it hold?
Why do we have them? Why do we care?
If all we're going to do is spread them and share!

Secrets should be kept in the back of the mind. Somewhere in a safe place
With no hidden want, and no hidden trace.
You know it's been spread
When someone has said.

Or when he looks at you with deepest eyes
And she looks at you with deepest despise.
So what is a secret if the secret is told?
What is the meaning? What does it hold?

Well, I won't tell you my friend,
It is for you to find out, and for you to mend.
You must keep your secrets, you must learn!
To not let them wonder, don't let them yearn!

Leah Barten, Grade 8
Madrona Middle School

Without Their Love

Every day, I am proud to have them by my side.
Without their love, I am lost and cannot live.

Start with my aunt, fallen through a trapdoor of depression
Without a key; she walks with her head held high.
Her heart, a broken mirror, is suffering through a landslide of lost hope.
Stronger than a rock is her faith, but weaker than a snail is her devotion.

Listen to my mother's pain for she has seen the impossible.
To some, she is a smart aleck who never seems to succeed;
Though, to me she is a diamond, never rusting away.
Her face filled with warmth, yet her heart filled with sorrow.

To all, my grandmother is the queen of "cleanliness."
Look at her hands, so jagged and burned, cleaning her way to the end of the world.
She is the fairy godmother, you see, helping those in need.

Before I bid thee farewell, I want you to gaze at the auspicious side; my grandfather.
He is the Cheshire Cat always mysterious and gleeful.
My grandmother and grandfather, a cat and a mouse, bicker
At the crack of dawn to the end of time.

Lorita Boghospor, Grade 9
Gunderson High School

Ode to Soccer

The cheer of a loud crowd
Players trying to get the ball
The ball being passed back and forth
Spectators on the edge of their seat, quiet
A player kicks the ball sending like a rocket to the goal
The goalie flings himself into the air as if he was
Launched from a catapult
Suspended in mid-air he catches the ball
The cheer of the loud crowd

Tyler Salinas, Grade 7
Santa Rosa Technology Magnet School

The Beach

Salty ocean breeze blowing through my hair
Ready to have fun
The cool blue ocean is calling me
I want to feel the sun

Beach chairs and umbrellas everywhere
I find a place to sit
All the people crammed together
My chair can barely fit

My legs are cold as ice
As I wade into the water
The waves lift me off the ground
In my bathing suit from Hollister

I love the beach
It is my favorite place to be
When I lay there on the sand
My problems can all flee

Meghan Fallan, Grade 9
Fountain Valley High School

I'm Sorry

I'm sorry he came along,
You liked it just us two,
I didn't think it would be so wrong,
But I guess you wanted just me and you.

I'm sorry he's what I care for,
What am I supposed to do?
He's all I want plus more,
But I promise I won't forget you.

I'm sorry but I found someone new,
But we can still be friends,
I've moved on and so must you,
Don't worry your heart will someday mend.

I really don't feel the same way I used to,
So now I'm sorry to say, I don't love you.

Krista Garcia, Grade 8
Almond Tree Middle School

Wishing I Can Be...

I want to be a superstar.
I want to be a person I always dream of.
I know my dream will come true,
Because if you believe in it,
It will come true.
Life isn't the way you want.
But if you hold your dream tight,
It will come true.
I'm not a somebody,
But I will be soon.
Someday people will lift their head and see
How much this mean to me.
I can't give up now,
But I know someday my dream will come true.
I won't lose.
I can't let someone step on my head,
Even if it means hurting my feelings.
I can be someone.
I have to reach for the star.
If I pray from the bottom of my heart,
Someday I can be a superstar.

Jennifer Lysaythong, Grade 9
Hiram W Johnson High School

Your Most Treasured Friend

I lay up in the closet discarded,
patiently waiting for you to return to me.
My hair remains knotted,
and my dress is gathering up dust.
That little rip on my hand,
still remains untended to.
I wonder to myself if you may have forgotten me,
I dash that silly thought out of my head as fast as it comes.
You still love me right?
You would never forget about me,
your most treasured friend.

Ashley Rockwell, Grade 9
Gunderson High School

I Don't Understand...

I don't understand,
Why the world is round,
Why dreams seem so real,
Why nightmares feel like a wisp of darkness.

But most of all,
Why life can't be fun,
Why everyone is judged by their appearance,
Why the human race can be so fickle.

What I understand the most is,
Why everyone has a breaking point,
Why letting my voice be heard is hard,
Why I think everyone deserves a second chance.

Kevin Zhang, Grade 8
Dorris-Eaton School

Fall

The tree is shedding
And its leaves are falling
Some red, some orange, some yellow
The rake is calling!

Leaves in the street
All over the place
Leaves in the garden
Just more to rake!

The trash bag is full
Full of leaves
How could one tree
Have so many leaves!

Gabriel Reynolds, Grade 8
Madrona Middle School

Stars

Shiny and sparkly in the sky
Can make the shape of your favorite pie
They come out at night
To shine their light
You cannot miss
Their feeling of bliss
Like a diamond way up high
Shining light in your eye
See them at camp
And even when it's damp
The midnight shadow shows them off
The moon is jealous so he coughs
Their colors come in white and yellow
Looking soft just like a marshmallow
Scattered around
But never making a sound
Way smaller than a car
They are so far
Sometimes shooting like a gun
Make a wish and then you're done!

Carissa Carnine, Grade 8
Madrona Middle School

Stars, Moon, Future

When I look up at the stars and moon
I wonder how it would be in the future
If anything is going to change
Or if everything is going
To stay the same

Jocelyne Perez, Grade 7
Richland Jr High School

Perseverance

Always persevere
Try your best, then never fear
Success will adhere

Justin Kuntarodjanjun, Grade 7
St Cyprian School

Love

Love is like a battlefield,
Where you will die without a shield.

It will stare you in the eye,
And sometimes even make you cry.

Love can make your emotions run wild,
As if you were just a three year old child.

Love will make you smile on a bad day,
And even wipe your tears away.

It might hurt you just a bit,
Until you find the perfect fit.

In love you might end up heart broken,
If your true feelings aren't spoken.

Jake Renze, Grade 8
Madrona Middle School

The Forest

Squish, squish
Make a wish
Walking through the forest
The darkest night fills all my sight
As I gaze at the stars so bright

The owl's eyes show
And the coyote's cries grow
As the twigs snap below my feet

Squish, squish
I made a wish
To stay here forever and ever

Rachel Roskelley, Grade 8
EV Cain Middle School

Clean Water

Fresh, pure
water.

Crisp and
refreshing.

Cold, on a hot,
humid day.

Cooling me down.
Trickling down my throat.

Aww! Mmm!

So delicious…
it quenches my thirst.

Yolanda Islas, Grade 8
St Sebastian School

The Winter Came

The winter is cold
Snow finally arrived
With snowflakes that frost
So many freezes
Thinking of summer days
But fresh air seems enough
Trees frosted with snow
Wind blowing back and forth
Then sun comes up
Snow melts away
Gets better and better
And go outside and play

Rosa Denis, Grade 7
Richland Jr High School

My Grandpa

To be apart from a grandpa like mine
Shows how much it's not divine
Where comfort was shown
And moments were shared
I can't feel anything, but him impaired
It was him I laughed with
It was him I enjoyed being with
And it was him I could cry with
But now he is gone
And all I'm left with is memories
For now I can't share them
Because he is the only one
He expressed his joy
He expressed his pride
But now his weakened heart
Felt as if it was a roller coaster ride
For he is a grandpa
A bull full of strength
A grandpa full of love
A grandpa I can't touch
That's probably why I miss him so much.

RoseAnne Capillo, Grade 8
Almondale Middle School

Global Warming

Burning hot temperatures
More gases in the air
Overflowing Mother Natures
Does anyone really care?
The Earth will need a fan or two
When the time comes near
When it is as hot as the sun
How are we going to play?
I think that we all must fear
The big industries are not listening
To what we have to say
We must save our Earth
And we must save it today.

Maximiliano Lewis-Radillo, Grade 8
Madrona Middle School

The Way of Life

This life is bursting with pain and debates.
Everything you do appears to be wrong.
You feel as if no one appreciates.
Sometimes you feel like you do not belong.
Why is it that life is a horrid maze?
Why can't life be so great and wonderful?
Sometimes you feel like a turned off blaze.
You can sometimes feel like an immense fool.
Yet, there is almost always a way out.
The key to finding this is to believe.
If you ever feel the need to get out,
You need to find a new way of relief.
There is always another way to deal,
With the feelings just try to appeal.

Carolina Nazarit, Grade 8
John Adams Middle School

More Cloudy Days

There's only one thing
that can stop a cloudy day,
it's the sight of you smiling
that causes me to change the way
I look at things, even the way I feel!
You add so much to my life, you complete me!
So…please…don't move away.
I'll never forget you, you see,
because, suddenly, my days will start to turn grey.

Gaby Cabalza, Grade 7
Monte Vista Christian School

Ode to Hamburger Helper

It is the smell of heaven
It dances around my tongue

It is as if it fell from the skies as a meteor
It is beautiful when made to perfection

It calls me when made
It tastes like food from heaven

It is the soul of food
It puts me in a good mood

When I'm full it puts me to sleep
I dream of pasta and meat

When I wake I want more
But there is no more

I go to buy some more
I am happy there is more

When I eat Hamburger helper
I am glad there is more

Hector Beltran, Grade 8
Valley Oak Middle School

Out of Sight Out of Mind

Friends forever so we thought
Never knew we'd be torn apart

I promised that we'd keep in touch
But I guess that didn't do too much

I sometimes take a stroll down memory lane
Remembering all those times of dancing in the rain

Out of sight out of mind I guess it's true
Because I'm no longer friends with you

Brianna Violet, Grade 8
Holy Family Catholic School

A Breeze in the Sky

The gentle breeze in the sky
It makes me want to sigh

The calm breeze over the ocean waves
I could watch it from a cave

The rugged breeze through the desert dunes
Running over ancient runes

The icy breeze colliding with glaciers
It makes me want to hide under sheets

The breezes that cover our world
Will run forever until it's over

Christopher Susa, Grade 7
Almond Tree Middle School

Funeral Bells

The farmers plow in the field,
The soldiers muster their shields,
And the children play with their toys,
When "toll, toll, toll, toll."
The funeral bell sounds!
Against its sides it pounds!
The men rush in, the women cry,
And "toll, toll toll."
The people gather at the center,
The victim was an old mentor,
The people weep and mourn,
While "toll, toll, toll toll."
Throughout the funeral,
The bells go on,
"Toll, toll, toll, toll."
And when the ceremony is done,
The bells keep tolling all day.
Finally into the night,
Black is the bell ringer's sight
So, "toll, toll, toll, t…"

Jonathan Bonello, Grade 9
St. Michael's College Preparatory School

The Winds of Change

The winds of change blow again,
This way, that way, front and back.
They blow across a desert plain,
This way, that way, front and back.

In ravaged lands of my mind,
Wreaking havoc for all to see.
Tearing up and leaving behind,
Broken hearts and things that could be.

Hollowing what once was there,
Peeling back layers of the heart
Leaving all to cower in fear,
My mind is breaking, tearing apart.

Reshaping hills and moving stone,
Blowing strongly ever more,
Cutting through my flesh and bone
Faster, stronger, away it tore.

It, I can no longer withstand
The times and memories turn to sand.
Forcing me to leave the past,
Dying goals and dreams surpass.

Eve Yuan, Grade 7
Pleasanton Middle School

My Favorites

Soccer is my favorite sport
I guess you're wondering why.
It is because when I play goalie,
I feel like I can fly.

Acting is my favorite hobby.
It is really fun.
But when I put on the costume
I sometimes feel dumb.

When I do these fun things
Some people think I'm weird.
But I just ignore them and think,
"Hey, that's just their deal."

Dillon Daggs, Grade 8
South Tahoe Middle School

My Wish

I once had a wish
I wanted to bake
"that's some wish," said a talking fish
but all I got was a burnt cake
I tried my best,
but it wasn't enough
I must confess
I bake burnt stuff!

Angela Nguyen, Grade 7
Sarah McGarvin Intermediate School

The Things We Want as Teens

We want so much at this stage
We ask for so many privileges even at this young age

What we hear, is it that we don't notice or is it that we don't care
The more privileges the heavier the cross we have to bear

As teens we want so much to fit in
But is it worth leaving the grounds with a frown instead of a grin

Funny that the ones who disappoint you most in the end
To fit in, you turn around and call them friends

There is so much about the world we still don't know
But for some reason we are driven to want to go

We long to be free, leave the nest, grow wings and fly away
But in troubled times we run back to those who love us most
Because in their arms we know it will be okay.

Jude Aka, Grade 8
Holy Family Catholic School

An Ode to Ice Cream

I savor the moment you touch my tongue
the coldness is refreshing
the blast of taste catches me off guard
I haven't tasted you until now
Summertime
I yearn for the fruitiness and the thrill of my mouth being semi-frozen
Every time my taste buds make contact with you
my tongue smiles
The strawberry flavor washes over me as I take another spoonful
All of my worries are forgotten
Until I run out of ice cream.

Nathan Galicia, Grade 8
Tierra Linda Middle School

True Love

Love is but a mere toy that a person keeps for a short time.
It helps in expressing your true feelings,
But also exposes your true identity.
It keeps you sidetracked from the rest of the universe,
Controlling and dictating your every move.
Love is nothing but a mere hindrance that every living thing must overcome.
It is a non permanent state of mind
Distracting lost souls for a certain amount of time,
Then releasing its firm grip.
Love is a mountainous road that a person must take
In order to gain a true sense of peace.
It is a commitment that plans out the rest of your life for you,
So that the balance of life and love may both fall into unity.
Though love is an obstacle almost impossible to overcome,
True Love is a permanent connection between two beings,
Binding the love they have for each other, for eternity.
Oh yes, yes, now that is True Love.

Ryan Ramoneda, Grade 8
Chino Valley Christian Schools

Sky

The sky goes on and on
Turning into many faces
Crying tears when it's sad
Crackling and shaking the ground when mad
Showing clouds when glum
When it's shy, it turns red plum
In the night it glitters itself to a party
It has many faces
The sky goes on and on

Nicole Sato, Grade 8
Madrona Middle School

Time

The shining might of the minute
The melancholy harshness of the hour
The holy sweetness of the second
They are all part of time
Never to stop for no man or thing
Time, which plan the future but never make
Time, which relives the past but never change
Time, man's curse and enemy
However also a friend
Always one but never both
The minute
The hour
The second
In which the hand points
Towards death at hand

Emily Nguyen, Grade 7
Sarah McGarvin Intermediate School

My Friend

I once had a friend
Who lived in animal form
But now he is in a better place,
With God
I know that he was just a dog to some people
But he was more than that to me
He was my friend
His name was Snowy and he was as white as snow
And as nice as can be
I loved him and he loved me
Although his spirit still lives on through me
I wish he was here with me
I do get sad at times but I will still live on
I will do it for my friend
I will always know that he is watching over me
It may not be in animal form
But it is in spiritual form
To my friend, I must now say good bye
I will see you someday and our hearts
Will bind together and I will never forget
MY FRIEND

Courtney Robledo, Grade 7
Holy Family Catholic School

Mother Earth

Our world has changed thanks to the war and hate
Once was beauty but changed into the beast.
Now our mother is used just like bait
And if only once there was a world peace.

I know this world is not what I expect
The greed and hate cannot be explained well
If there is something wrong who would have guessed
Our every day is as if it had rained

As the clock ticks by yet we all still try
To save the Earth and our hope as well
Our hope and peace is something we can't buy
And hopefully we can get rid of hell

It will never be too late to turn around
And all together love is always found.

Delia Melendrez, Grade 8
John Adams Middle School

Crazy San Franciscan Weather

Sometimes, I bask in the sunlight
just to remind myself of the warmth
I feel whenever you're around.
But then the breeze blows around me
and I have to remind myself of the chills
I have to experience when you're not.
Sometimes, I dance in the rain
just to remind myself that it's better
to face adversity with joy rather than sulk.
But then I get sick from my silly actions
and have to remind myself that I hate the rain,
because the sky can cry when I can't.
Sometimes, I sit alone in the cold
just to remind myself that I'd much rather
be stuck here now than on a broiling summer day.
But then I catch a glimpse of a happy couple
walking by, cuddling, and have to remind myself
that I'm alone and can't share warmth like that.
Sometimes, I don't always say it directly,
but I have to remind myself, so you need to hear it,
too, every once in a while: I really miss you.

Tracy Lee, Grade 8
Corpus Christi School

Stars

Stars are bright and shiny,
Some are big, some are tiny,
You can't see them in the city,
But in the forest they're bright and pretty,
You don't have to be near to see a star,
You can see them even if you're far,
To see a star you don't have to try,
Just wait 'till it's dark out and look up in the sky.

Jimmie Cruz, Grade 8
Madrona Middle School

Memorabilia of You

Grant me your amnesty; I never intended it to end this way —
    I still ache for you to need me,
Though I must relinquish these relations, and attempt to abide the inevitability,
    The void yearning for you will persist.
Your rapture will forever be powerful, making it nearly impossible to resist —
    Though I must strive intended for our mutual sakes.
I'll always sincerely commemorate you, despite how potently I try not to;
    I will eternally cherish the moments we once had.
The stars, the skies, are my memorabilia of you, memories from the precedent,
    Back from when we used to gaze at the boundless constellations.
If you remember me, I'll remember you; because I will always ache for you to need me.

Alayna Mitchell, Grade 8
Madrona Middle School

I Remember

I remember the pink play pen where I spent most of my toddler days
Watching for Daddy to walk through the door
I remember that first school day where I made many friends
I remember Mommy coming home with a crying baby
I remember those hot summer days in the pool with Yiggy
and all my friends splashing, yelling and having as much fun as possible
I remember leaving the place I loved to make room for my new baby sister
I remember making new friends at my new home but still longing to go back
To the place I loved
I remember getting up about 5:30 in the morning to watch *Bear in the Big Blue House*
and laughing so hard I woke up my parents
I remember the long car trips to Yosemite and Clark's Fort to go camping
Hiking to the river but if you put your foot in your teeth chatter
I remember the hot summer days at the park where we often had picnics
Eating the crisp watermelon and playing tag by the swings
I remember the year I left all my friends to go to a better school
It was the best school, but I missed the people I grew up with
I will remember that day I walk across the stage to get my diploma
And the butterflies I will get when I look in the crowd
and see my family's excited faces

Ashlee Knoll, Grade 8
Daniel Savage Middle School

Heart Broken

Omi, I love you with all my heart, even as you depart
I will not forget you, as you would not forget me
I will handle your possessions carefully; as you are so fragile you might have broken
We had our moments when we got mad, but we worked them out because it was not worth losing our friendship
We laughed and cried and had good times, because we are alike in many ways
When I heard the bad news I was confused, because I knew that could never happen
I wanted you for myself, to not share you with God
My heart is slowly mending, to what it used to be
All the pain is taken from you, and put into me
So why did God make it this way? Because now when I die I have something to look forward to, seeing you
So now as I close my eyes I think of you, and what you did for me
I wish for you to be back with me, for all eternity
I wish I could see ghosts, that way we could keep in touch
But God has a reason for everything, even if I don't realize what it is just yet
But the most important thing to remember is that I will always and forever be your Cherry Eyes…I will

Kirsti Buckendorf, Grade 7
Marina Village Intermediate School

Dealing with Peer Pressure

Being an outstanding student
Great at sports
Friends asking him to smoke weed
Afraid of what his friends would think
If he said no
Feeling forced into saying yes
H said yes
Once he tried it, he got hooked
Trying new drugs every day
Once he dropped out of high school
His mom kicked him out of their house,
So he started living in the streets.
Willing to give up his life for drugs
A couple of years with meth and more stuff
H died of an overdose
Killing himself and his family's spirit.

Ricardo Picazo, Grade 8
St Alphonsus School

Golden State

I am from
the "Golden State,"
where cars honk
nonstop.
People sing,
dance, and do hip-hop.

I am from
where waves crash against the shore.
Palm trees in front of every door.
McDonald's aroma surround me,
at every corner there's either a Starbucks or Coffee Bean.
Lights shine brightly after dark,
where there are castles inside theme parks.

I am from
a large family tree,
filled with secrets and surprises.
But one thing is for sure,
I know where I came from.
Some people call it the "Golden State,"
but I call it my home.

Kelly Blaney, Grade 8
St Sebastian School

The Constellations' Curse

A storm of hail and drop of rain
Fractious lightning inflicting pain
Tempest blazoned through the midnight sky
The vortex extricates jetsam nigh
To filch the power of nature's own
The heaven's wrath reveals its tone
Celestial rays hindered alone
Controlling halos of g-ds home unknown

Rebecca Aaron, Grade 7
The Mirman School

Metamorphosis

While I'm sitting here alone,
trying to figure out who I really am,
giving you clues
for you to solve this difficult puzzle and ask,
asking why am I not in God's hands?
I left for a little dark vacation,
where death caught your wet eyes.
Seeing chaos has caught in,
it's just a little silly knot.
Attacking me with their loud voices,
trying to walk by and become deaf to the noises
But somehow I can't escape!
I'm trapped in my own body.
Erasing a loving young girl I'd once been.
Willing to give all my tomorrows
just to return and fix that yesterday.
It's a story of my past.
But somehow someone's brought it into my present.
Trying to say goodbye and survive from drowning.
It's a big part of my life but I'm willing to,
forgive and forget the words that create this story.

Eonis Cibrian, Grade 8
Live Oak Middle School

Bad Dream

I walk alone in the dark mist.
With no one to hold and no one to cry with.
Wondering if I will ever get out.
Out of this dark scary place.
Screaming and shouting.
When no one can hear me scream,
I wonder if I'll ever leave.

Celeste Castro, Grade 7
Richland Jr High School

White Winter

It is winter at last
The sky is shaking sprinkles of snowflakes
Chilling the air with pleasures of white snow
Giving the sky a scent of pine trees
Bringing everyone joy

It is winter at last
Nothing in sight except pure whiteness
Children and their parents laughing with joy
Playing on the white fur of a thousand rabbits
Everyone filled with delight as the laughter fills the empty night

It is winter at last
Darkness descends
People make a trail
As they head to their homes
To warm their chilly hands

Jessica Yim, Grade 8
Madrona Middle School

God's Creation

The mountain's so high
It almost touches the sky
When you look down it is deep
As deep as the beautiful sea
When you step on ground it glows
Like winter when it snows
We are a part of this nation
This is called God's creation

Stephen Mamiit, Grade 7
St Joan of Arc School

Mirror Lights

Mirror lights, glowing on the border.
Golden stoplights flickering,
Encouraging and enlightening.
Hope's searchlight

A pre-show limelight,
Not colorful like the Northern Lights,
Though simple as one's headlights,
Urging you

You are on in five,
Time to get the show on the road.
The mirror light will be waiting,
For your return, to applaud you.

Tiffany Walz, Grade 8
Madrona Middle School

To the Death

We marched in rows,
like dominoes, waiting to be toppled.

We stood there waiting,
our hearts beating at our chest.

Waiting for a sound,
that loud booming sound of death.

Standing there,
tense,
in rows,
to the death.

Andrew Listvinsky, Grade 8
Tierra Linda Middle School

Him

What was there to thank Him for?
So much cruelty?
So much anger?
So much war?
So much hate?
Yet it is not Him that creates evil
He just makes machines that create evil.

Kyle Koenig, Grade 8
St Joseph's School of the Sacred Heart

The Eiffel Tower

The Eiffel Tower, makes you smile,
So bright, it makes your eyes shine like shooting stars,
So tall, it makes you want to climb its complex structure,
You can't frown at the precious structure,
The Eiffel Tower, makes you sigh in admiration,
For it was a finalist to be one of the new 7 wonders,
It will leave you breathless,
So never miss a chance to visit the so tall and bright Eiffel Tower.

Josefina Castillo, Grade 7
John Adams Middle School

Past and Present

It was a dark and stormy night
I was alone in my room when I saw IT
It was standing outside in the middle of a storm looking into my room
With every bolt of lightning IT seemed to get closer and closer to my room
Boom went the lightning
It came closer to my window
Boom Boom Boom went the lightning
It was directly in my window
Boom Boom Boom Boom Boom
The lights went out and flashed back on and in an instant IT was in my room,
Staring at me and in that moment I realized that IT was not an it at all
It was a girl a young girl 12 maybe 13 years old, a girl I recognized
She looked bruised and hurt and scared and all at once I realized who she was
She was someone I thought I left behind so long ago someone I fought to escape
Someone I feared
I realized then
That someone
That girl
Was me
Is me

Sherrill Lewis, Grade 9
Del Mar High School

Emotions

Please, someone, tell me who, I really don't know what to do.
All this love and my affection, point me in the right direction.

I need some place to let it out, just shoot it through a giant spout.
My anger that I've bottled up, like the excitement of a cute young pup.

In the death of a good friend, I really cannot see the end.
With the sadness and the crying, in the thought of people dying.

In the joy of it all, you think you can't fall.
With all emotions it's the best, it puts itself above the rest.

With all emotions people feel, some think it is not even real.
With the laughing and the smiling, the happiness is piling.

Love, happy, sad, and mad, emotions really are quite rad.
We really need them to survive, they help us groove, and dance, and jive.

John Hively, Grade 8
Santa Rosa Technology Magnet School

I Guess

I guess
I'm not the best in the softball team.
It seems if I'm not good at anything.
I decided to join the cross-country team,
and I found one of my qualities.
Top of my team I found a sport of my liking.
I guess
I'm just good at running!

Michelle Reynoso, Grade 7
Our Lady of the Rosary School

Golfing

I line up for the flag stick,
I pull the club back as hard as I can,
I bring the club forward,

"Whack" the ball goes flying,
Then the ball lands in the pond that is an ocean,
I felt like dying,

I tried again,
"Whack" the ball is flying once more,
"Thunk" it lands on the green,

I jump for joy,
But I still have to put it in,
If I do I will win,

I line up the putter,
I pull back,
"Tink" I tap the ball,

It stops at the hole…
"Clunk" it falls in,
I went golfing.

Cody Kennel, Grade 7
Joan MacQueen Middle School

My Heart Will Choose…

My love for these two has got me confused!
As each day passes my love grows stronger.
Every time I see them I get amused.
I don't know if my love can last any longer!
Why can't I tell them how I really feel?
Should I keep quiet or tell them the truth?
Just talking to them will make my heart heal.
If only I could stop acting like the youth.
I have now decided what I should do;
My heart belongs to one and only one.
He will discover my love through a clue.
I no longer have a reason to run.
We can now be together forever.
I am sure my choice for him was clever.

Vanessa Lizarraga, Grade 8
John Adams Middle School

Poetry to Me

The way the wind blows when no one listens;
The noise of the sun rising
When no one watches,
The scent of flowers
When no one's there to smell them,
The beauty of the moon rising
When no one's there to enjoy it,
Then, the amazing patience the universe
Has waiting to be explored
The most important thing about poetry is
One must understand himself to truly admire it
That's poetry to me.

David McKeller, Grade 8
Madrona Middle School

A Trip to the Beach

Getting by traffic
Like a mouse in a stampede,
Luck is on your side today
You finally park your beat up bug by a new one,
Everyone rushing out yelling, "Beach!"
While you're grabbing the surfboards.
Walking in the sand with the boards
Like you're on Mt. Everest getting to the top.
You drop everything and listen to the rushing tide of the ocean.
The sun is setting
And the beach goes to sleep.
You pack up your surfboards
Only to end up again, a mouse in a stampede.

Rebecca Reyes, Grade 8
Walter F Dexter Middle School

Heroes

Trying to fit in is a game you will never win.
So when you see those who are marching to their own drum,
You laugh at them because you think they're dumb.
There's that dorky kid getting picked on.
You go along because you want to belong.
Now you feel like you fit, but you just won't quit.
You put more people down, including the true you,
So you can climb higher up your ladder.
So you can be "bigger and better"
What you don't consider is how you made them feel.
The rungs of your ladder. The ones you stepped over.
While you sit high and mighty,
The ones you trampled bear the hurt they can't handle.
Maybe they'll go home that night with a knife at their side.
Because of your words, they give up their life.
But if you had been kind, instead of corrupting their mind,
They'd still be here, and it would all be fine.
Maybe if you had reached out and helped a hurting soul,
They would still have a place in this world, because you
Saved them. Maybe you could have been their Hero.
Heroes are made when you make a choice.

Christine Hansen, Grade 9
Etiwanda High School

Shooting Stars

Shooting across the sky
As you pass my window
I wish for that one wish
Up so far away in the sky
Your yellow glow oh so bright
Like a frozen teardrop
I gaze and watch you slowly fade away
Twinkling beyond the distance
As you shoot away from me
I see your icy trail disappear

Melissa Cunanan, Grade 8
Madrona Middle School

As It Slips and Slides

As it slips and slides,
Flows with the wind.
Its crimson colors
Shimmer through the night.
As it carriers the air,
It shivers with fear.
Its breathless movement
Beams to my heart.
As it twists and turns
It fades away into the glistening night.

Tyler McMurtrie, Grade 7
Round Valley Elementary School

Blue

Blue is the color of a car,
that runs people over and goes very far.

Blue is the color of a blue jay, and if you
keep it in a cage it won't fly away.

Blue is the color of a blueberry,
and the color of my friend's dog, Mary.

Blue is the color when you are sad,
And also when you get really mad.

Lissa Hendrix, Grade 7
St Mary of Assumption School

There

I'm trapped in a sea of my own despair
I keep swimming and swimming,
but I never get there.
There is a place,
where the sun always shines.
There is a place,
full of good times.
I know one day soon
There will arrive
But until then,
I'm trapped in my mind.

Amy Classon, Grade 8
EV Cain Middle School

a silhouette in the wind

am i real?
am i really here?
or am i just
a silhouette in the wind?
blowing through life
without a care
am i really there
when you call me?
am i just a theory
or a memory
or a soul stuck between
heaven and hell?
am i really here…
there?
look.
am i?
am i just
a thing people talk about
or am i just
a silhouette in the wind?

Sydney Bernardo, Grade 8
Corpus Christi School

Friendship

Friends are always there for you
Friends will always love you
Friends are faithful and loyal
Friends will hold on tight
Friends make friendship
And friendship lasts a lifetime

Olivia Sterba, Grade 7
Holy Family Catholic School

The Real World

Hiding in a corner
Darkness all around you,
No one can see you
You're all alone in the world.
No one cares about you.
They walk past you all day long.
They look at you in disgust
They don't offer you a hand
They think they're better than you
They think of you as a filthy animal
They think you're nothing
A worthless piece of life
But they don't even know you
They don't even try
How can they be so cruel
To a person in need of help
You are human too
They're scared of the homeless and poor
So you sit back in the dark
And become invisible again

Ebony Beshears, Grade 8
Shadow Hills Intermediate School

Doors

The only thing that stands in our way
Is doors
And anything
Can be a door

A mother can be a door
Stopping her child from succeeding
But she can open up
And help them to ascend

Money can be a door
Without it, you may not move forward
But when you have it and the door opens
It can lead to trouble

Drugs can be a door
But it goes the other way around
If the door opens
That may be the end for you

Why? You say do I call these doors?
Well, that is pretty simple
Whether it opens or it closes
The choice is up to you

Nikki Wihl, Grade 7
Holy Family Catholic School

The Deepest Treasure

If love was meant for everyone,
Then the sun would set at night,
And rise at dawn,
Moon at dark,
Sun at light,
For love is the true treasure,
Found in the deepest chest,
Your beloved heart

Kayla Hyvonen, Grade 7
Joan MacQueen Middle School

Giving

Gifts can be big,
gifts can be small.
No matter what,
we like them all.

It can be a dog,
it can be a song.
Not like in the movies.
They ruin them all.

They can be cool,
they can be nice.
But what's most important?
It's the sacrifice.

Brandon Bella, Grade 8
Visalia Christian Academy

170,000 Swarmed the Beaches
Brave men fought, others died.
Bullets flew, they tried to hide.
Reinforcements were scarce, they knew their fate.
They thought of the home, the lives destroyed, but wait:

One thought to himself, "Let's go, we're gonna get slaughtered!"
He took his rifle, with the courage he found,
and with one last stand, he took the ground.
Men saw, from all around,
as this brave man stood the line, and refused to be bound.

The men thought in their heads,
"He can do it, so can I!"
Each one jumped to his feet,
for they would not just stand there and die.

They swarmed the beaches with one simple plan,
Flank the left tower with every last man.
With each brave soldier, an army of one,
The Axis had lost, the Allies had won.

Jeff Goss, Grade 8
Visalia Christian Academy

Music
So many great bands.
Can't have a favorite.
Listening to music all night long.
Awesome.

Connor Sipes, Grade 7
John Charles Fremont Intermediate School

Independence Day
every summer our nation celebrates
the fourth day of July
people, parties, parades, picnics
fireworks in the sky

many people have traditions
do the same thing each Independence Day
my family gives my dog a hot dog
but everyone celebrates a different way

some have barbeques at the beach
some go swimming in the pool
the summer sun is blazing
so people wear swimsuits to keep cool

at night the sky is lit up
everyone watches the show
they look up into the bright darkness
to see the fireworks glow

and even after all the summers fly by
I always remember the Fourth of July

Amelia Newman, Grade 9
Fountain Valley High School

Eyes
Exploding with tears in my face
I didn't want to believe it
I needed to face my puppy
Laying dead next to the fence
I saw his eyes shining at me before he left
I didn't want to say goodbye
But his shining eyes told me he left and left forever
I burst into tears
And thought of his glowing eyes

Jasmine Laguna, Grade 8
La Joya Middle School

River of Tears
I see a river of tears flowing to the ground
So gentle and so silent they never make a sound.
From small stream into river from river into lake
Then one more stream appears more tears come in its wake
So hard for me to notice the silent lake of tears
As more of them come faster, but none of them in fear.
So hard to deal with the thought my friend has moved away
No way for me to express it and nothing I can say.
My feelings and my instincts tell me to say goodbye
But she moved without my notice so I just sit and cry.
The lake turns into ocean and soon it is a sea
Of tears flowing down my face for both my friend and me.

Selene Cheong, Grade 7
Whittier Christian Jr High School

The Sinister Sister
Forced to live all by herself,
But it was not her fault,
She cut herself from all her friends,
And is reaping the result

The tears that rarely drip her face
Can bring a man to his knees
One touch of her grieving skin
Will surely spread the disease

She goes by many a name
The most common is depression
She targets those who languish
With a face of no expression

I warn you now, please take a stand,
And face all of your burdens
For if your emotions are what she hungers,
Your life may be uncertain

Crushed, sad, grief, or bland
There's always a solution
So find someone who is there for you,
And STOP the emotional pollution

Mardelano Booc, Grade 8
Almond Tree Middle School

Clouds

Clouds show up on any day
At any time or any place
Clouds show up so in their way
They can help us enjoy the day
In their power they can share
The coolness that is in the air.

Kevin Truong, Grade 7
Sarah McGarvin Intermediate School

Life

Life, is something we all have.
God gives it to us as a gift.
I will never give it up.
It is worth everything to me.
Life, the best gift to ever have.

Janely De Santiago, Grade 8
St Vincent Elementary School

Ode to Volleyball

Volleyball,
You brought many things to me,
Showing me how to be tough,
And not back down.
You swift and sway,
And make my day,
Whenever I get to play!
When I hit you hard,
Like a brick to the head,
I feel your pain,
But oh volleyball,
You make my day!

Michelle Valovcin, Grade 7
Santa Rosa Technology Magnet School

Letter

I bring tears to people's eyes,
I bring smiles to their mouth.
I could tell a lie,
Or travel my way down south.

I don't get torn open,
The envelope does.
I tell people how things are,
And how jail time was.

I can give you information
Or describe his dedication.
I can give you a greeting,
Or the time and place of a meeting.

I am a letter, so you see
Do you now understand?
That great thing I just told you about,
Was me, your letter, the mystery man.

Aryanna Jose, Grade 7
St Barbara School

Ode to My Friends

Laughter, joy, happiness, and love I thank my friends for.
The laughter my friends give me the strength to open my eyes every morning.
Their joy I see every day gives me the strength to jump in the shower.
Their happiness gives me the strength to get in the car.
Their love for I see every day gives me the strength to live my life to the fullest.

Crying, failure, sadness, and hate I thank my friends for.
The crying my friends give me make me want to try harder in life.
Their failure I see tells me never to give up at anything.
Their sadness I get makes me care for others in the world that needs help.
Their hate towards me makes me a better person every day.

So I thank my friends for keeping me loving life, and loving them.
Our friendship is as big as the universe and everlasting.
Thank you friends for being there for me!

Rick Perry, Grade 8
Santa Rosa Technology Magnet School

Memories

Memories come and go as time flows.
Memories exist in everyone.
After we have made a mistake,
The depressing memory lingers.
It stays in my mind for eternity.
I am sad because I can't get rid of my memory.
I cry thinking about it.
I feel an explosion of heat seeping through my skin never to cool.
Time passes; new thoughts intrude my mind.
But agonizing pain remains.
I try to get rid of it but,
Nothing cures the pain.
Setting my mind on something else works
But memories stay forever.

Ashley Tallichet, Grade 8
Rolling Hills Country Day School

Trailblazer

I am a trailblazer.
I burn my way through the dense forest,
Leaving destruction and carnage behind, for I will not be stopped.
But I also leave my one gift;
A chance for new growth among the trees.

I will move on through many new pastures,
And my path shall be paved with ash.
But that dirty trail is the road to greatness,
And so my path will be followed for many generations.
I will be remembered, or nothing will.

By the new moon, the black dust will have blown away,
But the emergent green buds and the scars on the old that will forever remain
Are telltale of that great work that I have done here.
I am that was, I am that is,
I am what is to come.

Hedda Bates, Grade 9
Westview High School

Gumball Machine

A gumball machine is a fishbowl on a tall stump
But instead of water and a fish
Colorful chewy marbles fill the dome
With a lid to keep the cat out
Or the hand of a small boy

Inside the machine are mechanical things
Gears and cogs and clinking parts
So when that quarter hits the bucket
A gumball pops out of the spout
Into the hands of a small boy

Inside it all is a small chamber
Outside space and time
Inside is a happy spirit
Who grabs the ball and tosses it out
It is the spirit of a small boy

Daniel Scott, Grade 8
Crittenden Middle School

Best Friends Forever

Best friends forever no doubt about it
We are always laughing and having fun,
We are like SpongeBob, Sandy, and Patrick.
We are always together like bubble gum.
They are very kind and do me favors
I really appreciate what they do.
But we are different like many flavors,
Sometimes we can be sweet and sour too.
We talk about each other's problems and opinions
Saying we will never be torn apart.
We tell each other our deepest secrets,
I will always keep in my heart.
Friends you can keep and trust honestly,
My best friends Jocelyn and Stephanie.

Crystal Garcia, Grade 8
Henry T Gage Middle School

Epiphany

Why must immigrants be taken away?
Why must they work for lesser pay?
Do you think immigrants should be cared about less?
Do you feel natural born citizens are above the rest?
I say you who believe this is right,
The way that you think is quite a sad sight.
Just think back a few past generations,
You'll realize your family has not always been in this nation.
Ponder these words I give to you,
And know that you're an immigrant too.
Past government has called for equality to all men and women,
So why not treat immigrants as family or friends?
Listen to this and you'll know what to do,
Because deep down inside you know that it's true.

Leonel Con, Grade 8
St Vincent Elementary School

This Moon

Where has this moon gone?
The moon that used to brighten up the sky?
And the moon that used to shine brighter than any star
The moon that used to bring this beautiful light
for this moon used to brighten up my heart
but now this moon is gone
I must rely on the stars to bring me light
This moon left me alone with the stars
And now I know that I am lost
Oh, where has this moon gone?

Hila Alinasab, Grade 8
EV Cain Middle School

I Meant to Do My Work Today*

I meant to do my work today
But the shining sky calling out for me
And the birds flying
And the kites gliding
And the airplane passing by
So what can I do but laugh and go?

I meant to do my work today
But the shining lake was calling me
And the peaceful ducks swimming across me
And the colorful rainbow shining its colors
And the birds singing their melody
So what could I do but laugh and go?

I meant to do my work today
But the jungle singing its melody
And the sound of animals
And the running of tigers
And the shining light of the sun
So what could I do but laugh and go?

Miguel Angel Garcia, Grade 7
Richland Jr High School
*Patterned after "I Meant To Do My Work Today"
by Richard Le Gallienne

Love Song

Go ahead sing me that song
I never knew I could be so wrong
They say that love is blind
So go ahead let me hear that rhyme
Love is just a form of defeat
So go ahead let me hear that beat
Cant even look me in the face
So go ahead let me hear you play that base
You said you loved me at the first hello
So go ahead let me hear you play that cello
You said when you first saw me you were weak at the knees
So go ahead let me hear you hit those keys
Go ahead sing me that song
Then maybe you can tell me what went wrong

Sinclair Cornejo, Grade 8
Wilder's Preparatory Academy

I Love You

You take a breath,
Waiting for the answer,
Not wanting to hear it, but at the same time longing for the response,
Instead of thinking bad thoughts, you drift back to the past…

You start thinking of the early years,
Like when you would get hurt and he would come, pick you up and dust you off,
And how when after you were done visiting, you would go up on your tiptoes
just so you could kiss his soft cheek, and whisper
"I love you"

You start thinking of the later years,
When he couldn't come to anymore of your recitals because he couldn't climb the stairs,
And how when visitation hours were over, you would bend down so you could kiss
his soft cheek, and whisper
"I love you"

A sob brings you back to the present,
You look over to see your mom, cousins, and grandma crying,
You don't even have to ask to know what has happened,
Instead you look up and know that he's watching you right now, and you whisper
"I love you"

Alyssa Matsuhara, Grade 8
Martin Murphy Middle School

Despair

Humiliation is when the flight attendants treat you differently just because you are Indian.
Frustration is when people judge you a different way just because you are smart.
Misery is when your mom will not let you play tennis with the guys just because you are a girl.
Despair is when I am classified as an Indian instead of being judged by my character.
Anger is when the rich white people think they are better than us just because they have lighter skin than us.
Hatred is when you get cheated off of on your tests just because people think you have all the answers.
Aggravation is when your parents are disappointed in you for not being perfect.
Sorrow is when no one pays attention to you because they are too busy with your siblings.
Disappointment is when everyone expects you to be brilliant just because your brother is a genius.
Hurt is when your cheeks get sore at family functions because everyone thinks that you are the baby of the family and pinches your cheeks.
Anguish is when people pressure you by telling you that you have to live up to your sibling's standards.

Meera Reghunathan, Grade 8
Lindero Canyon Middle School

The Stars

As you lie down to watch the stars, do you ever wonder if the stars watch you?
Your crimes and your good deeds? Do you think that stars shine and glimmer with knowledge? I do.
I think stars are more than just a pretty sight.
I think they are scholars; they know all there is to be known.
I think they are people; each an individual, special in their own ways.
Mostly, I think they are actors.
They put on a show every night with us as their audience.
They dazzle us with their tricks and talents, but they become blinded by our lights.
So blinded that they pull a curtain of darkness over themselves and we cannot see them.
Disappointed, we move on. Soon, we forget the show all together.
We need to remember. We get a chance to relive this show every night.
Grab a hold of this chance, and turn off the lights.

Taylor Zelaya, Grade 8
St Hilary Elementary School

Nature

The wind swooshes
Through the forest
Like God blowing
Down on Earth itself
From the heavens above

Lightning strikes the trees
Like an arrow sprung from a powerful bow
It starts a fire
Setting the forest ablaze
The forest burns
And feeds the rapidly growing fire

The trees are like torches
Collapsing all in a bundle
Falling like skyscrapers in the city
Everything is torched to the ground
And turned into ash.

Robin Fukano, Grade 8
Madrona Middle School

The Old Man and the Flower

Look at that old man standing tall,
Holding a flower as beautiful as the stars,
Leaning there against the wall.
Wondering if he will ever find
A perfect wife to live with side by side.

Monica Stofan, Grade 7
Holy Family Catholic School

Ode to the Eagle

A graceful and robust predator
That you are.
Your great wings
Fly you to freedom, and are
A symbol of unity.
Your skills help you
Survive the malicious
Weathers of the four seasons.

Your remarkable eyesight
Lets you catch submerged fish
With your powerful talons.
When I see you glide in the skies,
I get envious of you, but
Half I feel peaceful.
I guess this is the reason

Why I envy such a bird like you,
Because you amaze people without even trying,
And at the same time, you bring peace to them.
Your figure tells the mind that it is safe.
But it tells me
That I am FREE…

Delyn Moua, Grade 8
La Joya Middle School

Open That Door

I've tried to open your door
but I couldn't seem to find it.
You have tried to open my door,
but you were scared to see what's behind it.
I gave up trying to look for your door,
but when I turned around,
there it was, all shiny and tidy.
Now I understand;
your door has been behind me this whole time.
You were scared to open my door
because you saw that I was walking away from it.
As I got closer to the door,
it seemed as if the door grew shinier and shinier.
I touched the knob to open the door
and suddenly, the door grew pink, as did my cheeks.
I open it…
and there he was.

Adriana Martinez, Grade 7
Corpus Christi School

The Ocean

The ocean is deep and blue
The seagulls swoop down and loudly coo
All the creatures of the deep;
Even the ones that to catch their prey, they creep
Fish of every color that are like a traveling rainbow,
They will swim to the ocean's core
The prickly sand that tickles my feet
Is where you and I will meet
Drip! Swish!
There goes the school of the colored fish
Where will they go?
I don't know
But all I can say is,
God created a miracle!

Matt Dickson and Ashley Ray, Grade 7
St Patrick Parish School

My Sister

O, how can I forget those memories.
Those times when me and sister had fun.
The time when we shared happy stories.
Hand by hand below the yellow sun.
Except that she is no longer with me.
The angels took her to the great heaven.
Where she is now only in my sad dreams.
Which I then start to dream at eleven.
But either way the dreams get me happy.
The dreams help me get the sadness away.
Today the heart of mine beats rapidly.
Knowing that my sister is here today.
And so today I see her just in dreams.
Below the yellow sun or so it seems.

Sandra Montejo, Grade 8
John Adams Middle School

Ocean

Sand under my feet
Wind in my hair
Just take a deep breath
Of the salty sea air
I watch in the sea
The seals play
While the crabs hide
For the rest of the day

Rachel Church, Grade 8
EV Cain Middle School

Ode to My Shoes

Always being stepped on,
always being there,
every pair I own,
I will never share.

They are never jealous
with the pair I choose,
for they all know each
will get a turn.
My lovely shoes!

My shoes are always
protecting me from
harmful things on the
ground; such as gum,
rocks, and sharp glass,
wearing my shoes
I will never pass!

Yes, I love my shoes,
I appreciate them very much,
all of them are cute and
always seem to leave the final touch!
Ode to my shoes!

Anissa Orozco, Grade 7
Joan MacQueen Middle School

Fair

Everyone walking past me
I'm begging to be heard
I'm searching and I'm pondering
Why was I so allured?
In this cocoon dry and lonely
Tears are pouring down my face
Though they go on with their merry pace
Scars reopening in my heart
Ripping and tearing seams disappearing
I feel so lost and so confused
Since he's left what can I do?
Trying to gain consciousness
Gasping for air
I don't know how this is fair

LaMaya Swain, Grade 8
Junipero Serra School

Do Your Homework!

As soon as I finished my snack after a long day of school,
My mom cleared her throat and reminded me of the unfair rule,
"You may not watch TV or chat online with your buddies,
Until you have completed all your homework and studies."

I trudged upstairs, giving my mother disappointed looks,
I plopped down at my desk and pulled out all of my textbooks.
For my grammar homework, I identified interjections,
And in my biology notebook, I defined infections.

Because I needed a break from homework, down the stairs I came,
I turned on the television to watch the basketball game.
Out of nowhere and as angry as could be, my mother appeared,
I was forced to go upstairs to do my work, just as I had feared.

History homework was an essay on King George the Third,
Then I read the first chapter of *To Kill a Mockingbird*.
My math teacher assigned us thirty problems of algebra,
And then, I had to study for my test about Arkansas.

After I had finished everything, I let out a long sigh,
As I casually walked downstairs, my spirit soared up high.
Whoo-hoo! I can now do whatever I please, I thought with glee,
And I grabbed the remote to relax in front of the TV.

Sanjana Prasad, Grade 7
Challenger School – Ardenwood

Mother

The worst day I ever had was when my mom died.
I was really mad.
I was really sad.
I had the worst day ever on that day.
I miss her!

I would change it so I could have been there when she died.
I would try to make her live again.
I would try to turn back the hands of time so she could live again.
I would be there when my family saw her.
I wish I could have been there with her the day before she died.

Joseph Esparza, Grade 9
Springall Academy

The First Day of School

I sit at the table and stare at my feet.
Oh, to sleep in would be such a treat.
I sit at the table and stare at my feet.
My dad says, don't be so sad; think of all the people you'll meet!
I sit at the table and stare at my feet.
Why, oh why, do my parents think that the first day of school is so neat?
I sit at the table and stare at my feet.
My mom walks in, and suddenly I turn red as a beet.
She just told me that school doesn't start for another week!

Logan Link, Grade 7
St Hilary School

Tape

There's few things in life that really stick.
Parachute pants and poodle skirts?
Those went out of style quite quick.

I'm here to say there's one thing
That certainly sticks through and through
Its name is tape. Tape is king.

When you need a bond, tape is your man.
The sticky tape keeps it all together
And I'm tape's number one fan.

Tape is like a shiny new folder.
It keeps everything inside
And works even when it gets older

For me, tape is a life saver
I wouldn't survive without it
I know my devotion won't waver.

Emily Hicks, Grade 8
Madrona Middle School

Poetry

Poetry,
Imaginative, beautiful,
Exciting, loving, interesting,
Poetry is a look into a person's inner soul,
Feeling, haunting, hearing,
Creative, lyrical,
Masterpiece

Yuri Pineda, Grade 8
Santa Rosa Technology Magnet School

I Am

I am curious and adventurous — I'll try almost anything.
I wonder how this world is going to turn out.
I hear peace in a noisy world.
I see a paradise earth.
I want everlasting life.

I am curious and adventurous — I'll try almost anything.
I pretend that I'll never die.
I feel excited about my future.
I touch the surface of Mars.
I worry that something bad will happen.
I cry when animals die.

I am curious and adventurous — I'll try almost anything.
I understand life is not going to be easy.
I say life is what you make it.
I dream about tomorrow.
I try to make good decisions.
I hope I will have a good life.

Chandler Lanzarin, Grade 7
William Finch Charter School

Wish

Shall I compare thee to a loving mom?
Thou art as graceful as can be.
You take every blow with great calm,
And I know you will protect me.

Thou art more than just a friend,
More than butterflies and flowers too.
You always have a hand to lend,
And you always know what to do.

However I may long for you this day,
You have gone away forever more.
Now my heart will have to pay,
For there will be no more knocking at this door.

Although you are now long at rest,
My heart will still long for you to smile once more.
Even if this is God's greatest test,
Once more I wish to see you scamper across the floor.

Even though I must let go,
I will always miss thy loving face.
Now my heart is full of sorrow,
Since I now let go of this dreadful chase.

David Lundberg, Grade 7
Old Mission Elementary School

Summer

Summer is like beautiful flowers
Shining from heavenly skies,
It is the time of the flowers to shine and bloom,
And it is the time for trees to grow and sneeze,
Summer will never be the same without flowers
And trees growing and blooming.

Brenda Cervantes, Grade 7
Almond Tree Middle School

The World

The world is an extraordinary place.
There are many countries, races, and religions.
There are many cultures, rituals, and practices.
The world has lots of beautiful scenery.
That brightens our day.
The world is a majestic place
That often doesn't fade away.
There are wars, alliances, treaties.
That keep us safe at night.
The world also has many disadvantages
That saddens my day
Knowing that people out there
Aren't right in their way.
World let us live
Let us breathe.
The world is an extraordinary place.

Sebastian Swietlow, Grade 8
Santa Rosa Technology Magnet School

Love of the Heart

My heart belongs to you
And no one else
I don't know what I would do
If someone tells

My heart belongs to you
But people tell me "No"
I just wonder who
Would have to think so

My heart belongs to you
I know that we are meant to be
They will just have to make do
Because for me it is clear to see

My heart belongs to you
Even as the beat becomes a roar
Because you love me and I love you too
And this love is strong…

Keeping us together forevermore
Theresa Pasion, Grade 7
Holy Family Catholic School

The Moon and Stars

I look at the stars and the moon
I wonder if I'll see them tomorrow
I wait for the next day to come
So I can see the moon and
    The stars
Yasmin Benitez, Grade 7
Richland Jr High School

No Connection

Ever so faint and light as air
It felt like your love wasn't there

Talk, talk, talk that's all you do
Walk, walk, walk because you knew

The world would keep spinning
And you would keep winning

My tears danced on my face
And you saw no trace

Of the love that wasn't there
Of how I really cared

Your heart black and cold
No hand for you to hold

So, how does it feel
To know what was real
Alexis Gonzalez, Grade 8
Valley Oak Middle School

Best Friends

Friends aren't just people
They're people who care
Who stick up for you to show they care
They share stuff with you
You share stuff with them
Because all you do is trust them
They understand the language you speak
Even if it's from planet geek
They can be geeks sometimes
Along with you
Which is a reason you guys make a pair of two
You guys may not have known each other for a long time
Although it feels like you've known each other since you were five
You guys go everywhere together such as the beach and the mall
And have sleepovers together which is the most fun of all
You guys may have little fights
And sometimes they do last long
All because you did something wrong
Although in the end it all works out
Because you guys are best pals

Megan Hobbs, Grade 7
Alta Loma Jr High School

Life with You

I saw you at a park one night, with eyes that shine like moon, so bright
A stroke of luck brought you near, now love struck, I have no fear
We started talking all night long, your words to me were like a song
I spoke to you with such a glee, I knew you were the one for me

Stand by me I need you here, I'll hold you close and keep you near
Embrace the memories that we have shared, thank you for your love and care
And now it is our marriage day, we'll always love each other the same way
Through another's eyes they cannot see, the love that bonds you and me

It has always been you and me, now with this child one and one is three
Love and life is two and one, our love is now within our son
Our son is like a little dove, warmth and kindness shows our love
He slowly learns to write, read, and speak, our passion for him is not at all weak

All the good times that we have cherished
Will go on and will not perish
You and I will always be together
It's considered for always and forever

Son Truong, Grade 7
Sarah McGarvin Intermediate School

Deluge

A cold gust of wind blows from where he stands watching the waterfall.
The cataract spilling like a cup filled with too much water.
The noise drumming in his ears as he silently observes the milky downpour.
The air so filled with moisture he practically drinks instead of breathes.
The great veil mocks the little creature,
showing off its elegant flows
and beckoning him to come and drown in her little white dress.

Thais Alves, Grade 8
South Lake Middle School

Nature Lives Forever

As I walk outside with nature everywhere,
The breezes are calm as they flow through my hair.

As the flowers blossom and are coming alive,
Their beautiful scent, I now smell, shall survive.

As I pick up an orange at the bottom of my feet,
I peel and eat it, and it tastes so sweet.

The life all around, so beautiful and dear,
As I walk about, I know God is near.

All the mountains, trees, and plants of all sort,
They love and protect you like a king and his fort.

They shall live forever and will always stay,
Nature loves everyone and will never go away.

Garrett Stone, Grade 7
St Luke the Evangelist Catholic School

Lone Biker

Wandering to man knows where
He wanders swiftly without emotion or care
His identity is not known
Just rides on that old road carelessly and alone
Dressed in tight jeans, boots, and black leather
Sometimes he rides so fast he is as light as a feather
His only stops are to eat and sleep
See if you can find him on that old dusty street

John Dolan, Grade 7
St Luke the Evangelist Catholic School

Eyes of I

impatience. importance.
the two Eyes of my life: one far-sighted, one nearsighted
why must i wait? and why do you glare?
there is no end to the masquerade
without-patience i overturn every smirking mask
the not-not-pettiness poking the whip at my back
like an immigrant i cannot comprehend this path
of-much-weight blows a tantrum
at my wandering attention: do not question.
can't-see the devilish turns of this road
i search with sodden fingers
the want of tantalizingly-substantial gnawing my gut.
there are no scissors to this word: i'm patient
moment-of-truth groans like lead
cannot be dragged forward sideways anywhere.
kingdom-come-when-i'll-be-still paralyzes my mind
fingers emblazoned in covetous want
i cannot find it. where-what-when-who-how-why
knowledge hides, the subtlety camouflaging
into the broken weave of the world
the two I's of my life, blinded within each other

Clara Fannjiang, Grade 8
Oliver Wendell Holmes Jr High School

I Remember

I remember the first day you fell in love with me
It was so easy to see
It felt so good when you said "I love you"
That's when I knew I was your Boo
I loved the way we held each other's hands
It felt like I was out at the beach touching the sand
It felt so good to fall in love
And I knew right there and then you were the one
I know that he loves me 'cause his feelings show
That's when I remember the first day we fell in love.

Andrianna Penaran, Grade 8
Almond Tree Middle School

My Special Someone

My special someone is the best as can be,
In a sea of people he's the only one I see.

He makes me laugh when I'm down,
I never see him frown, so I'd give him a crown.

Every time I look at him I smile
I can't stand to be away from him for awhile.

Every time he comforts me he's as warm as a bear
That I won from a fair.

He always light up my world
Every time I see him my stomach gets twirled.

Every time I hear his deep voice
My heart will rejoice.

We'll always be together
I'll always love him forever.

Rebekah Simons, Grade 8
Valley Oak Middle School

High School

The alarm goes off, I roll over to turn it off.
I spring to my feet to go to school to meet,
New friends who are really neat.

The bell will ring; and I will go to class.
And there, I will have a blast.

The day is over before I know it,
I have been to class
I've made it through lunch,
It's off to the softball field, where I will have a blast.

We are the black and gold and we are mighty bold.
Just ask around and you will be told,
We will be the team to win the gold.

Whitney Smith, Grade 8
EV Cain Middle School

Mirror Heart

Staring right back at you
Your thoughts and your soul
Holding your past and blind to the future
As you get older it grows too
Slowly dying inside of you
Not staring back anymore
It's a lifeless plain mirror
No longer your life holding heart

Chelsea Fabun, Grade 8
Merryhill Preparatory School

Waterfall

Within the forest there is a waterfall
That creates a thunderous sound

The water falls upon the rapids
And mists of water fill the air

The fall has endless streams of water
As it flows into the raging river below

The water cascades from the cliff
And plunges deeply

It creates a rumbling noise
Echoing among the trees
Throughout the forest

Min Kyun Choi, Grade 8
Madrona Middle School

Flower

Beautiful gentle creation of nature
Made to amaze all eyes
Bringing lovely scents to noses
Sits peacefully
Watching the sky
Rose in hope
Roots to hold to the Earth
Shining happily when water is poured
Listening to the singing wind
Bothered when picked and cut
So lonely at night
When closed for the day
Awaits in excitement
For the next sunrise.

Joanna Sanchez, Grade 7
St Alphonsus School

Colored Canvas

Painting
Many colors
On the canvas they go
Making beautiful creations
Finished

Gavin Ferris, Grade 8
Connecting Waters Charter School

4 Year Tragedy

A lot can happen in 4 years.
A loved one can die
and life becomes insanity
with questions asking "why?"

A lot can happen in 4 years.
Families at war
and kids now in the middle
of the problem more and more.

A lot can happen in 4 years.
Relationships come undone
and are put back together
over and over more than once.

A lot can happen in 4 years.
Kids learn how to talk back
and rebel against life
when things go out of whack.

A lot can happen in 4 years.
But just take it day by day
and eventually…
things will fall in place the right way.

Anyssa Mendoza, Grade 8
La Joya Middle School

Flowers

Friends are like flowers
you can pick and choose them,
until you find the right one

Each flower is perfect in its own way
just like good friends

There are no perfect flowers,
no matter how hard you look
each one is original
and can't be replaced

Although we can,
pick and chose them
we are only drawn to the flowers
who are just like us

Erin Gonzalez, Grade 7
Holy Family Catholic School

Friends

My friends are the best
They are sweet as can be
They will be with me through everything
I love my friends with all my might
They are my friends to eternal life.

Zaida Dominguez, Grade 7
St Vincent Elementary School

Making a Difference

Making a difference
Is what I try to do
I recycle cans
And other stuff too
I brush my teeth
Day and night
Keep up on my homework
And stay out of fights

I clean my room
To make it nice and neat
I might eat candy
But that doesn't mean anything
I get straight A's
And it keeps my mom happy
I'm always nice to her
So she's never crabby

Some people don't think
I'm really making a difference
And that's the way it is
But here's a question
Can you top this

Danielle Thomas, Grade 7
Citrus Hills Intermediate School

Rain

"Rain is God crying,"
a little girl said one day.
He cries because more people
die each and every day.
Some from disease,
some from war,
and what did He make these people for?
Not to argue and to fight,
but to make this world right.
So sadly He weeps,
at his residence above,
wondering where is the love?

McKenna Heath, Grade 7
Las Flores Middle School

Pigment

Yellow sings the sun
Blinding circle above chants,
The Realm of Happiness.
Dark Blue dreams of rain,
Subconscious imaginations
Cry storms on
Depressed feelings.
Black darkens Shadows,
The lurking;
Monster.

Steven C. Bonilla, Grade 8
Nobel Middle School

God's Creation

The ocean and sky
how striking they are
especially at the horizon line
where they meet.
A new baby bird softly chirps
nestled in the tree,
flowers all around
floating, moving with the wind
dressed in bright pink and orange.
The waves sway and rush
to meet the dry sand.
Animals prance through meadows
and graze in the luscious green grass.
Bees buzz through the forest and rest in their hive.
God's creation — sometimes indescribable and so amazing.
Most outstanding of all creations
are you and I, the people that we are.
God has made us all unique.
God's creation — a sight to behold.

Alexandra Gosiengfiao, Grade 7
Linfield Christian School

Just Laugh

Take this moment in little sister
Because before you know it today is long gone.
Don't hold your tongue and speak your mind before
What's done is done.
Have fun and don't stress
Because before you know it you're a mess
Take this advice from someone who has done that
While everyone talked and laughed, just sat.
It seems like you know what to do and where to walk
But always know that I'm here to talk.

Makayla Agueros, Grade 8
Hesperia Jr High School

Waterfalls

Shhh!
The peaceful flow of fresh water is coming
Lazily floating down the river
As if it were clouds in the sky
Unaware of the fate that awaits

The harsh winds blow
The clouds seem stormy
And the river flows gathering speed to its destination
As it sees the fall below it tries to run
But it's too late
And the water falls down, down, down

I can hear it screaming and yelling as it falls
Then a moment of silence comes from down the river
Water is joyful that the perilous plunge is over.

Lindsie Swank, Grade 8
Madrona Middle School

Most Beautiful Girl

This is a story of the most beautiful girl
If I must speak my feelings, she rocks my world.
I try to never fear for the worse,
For who else would flaunt that leopard purse?
She definitely has more than looks.
She's loving, sweet, and even cooks.
She's a godly woman, who knows the devil's a fraud.
Whenever she's been sick or down, she keeps her faith in God
I'm more than thankful for her, and my dad.
They always care for me, especially if I feel bad.
If there was a contest, not one would come close.
But don't worry, she would never boast.
We pray as a family every night
For everyone's health, so we'll be all right.
Every so often, we'll go out to dine.
My brothers, Dad and I, we like to spend time.
I'm just glad, the most beautiful girl, is all mine.

Chase Lombard, Grade 7
Chino Valley Christian Schools

The Time Will Come

I, like many others, live in a gruesome world.
There is fear, death, and prejudice every day.
I have to live through it,
I have to struggle, stumble, and sometimes crawl through it.
If this isn't bad I'm tortured.
I am whipped, punched, and kicked for no reason.
I come home to my shack bleeding, sobbing,
Screaming in the thrashing pain
I live in a dictation.
I have no freedom.
The government cannot hear my cries,
Cannot feel my pain.
Somehow out of all of this I know one thing —
It can be stopped.
One way I can stop bleeding, stop screaming.
There is one way I will no longer bow before my knees
Many have stopped believing, but I have not.
Maybe one day I will be free from these shackles,
Free from behind these iron bars
I know this is true, and so do only a few
But for now I wait — praying, hoping, having faith

Christopher Denson, Grade 7
Holy Family Catholic School

My Brother

I wake up and see my brother
I love him more than any other
We play together and have fun
I'm glad I only have one
He's funny, gentle, caring, and divine
But, he could sometimes drive me out of my mind
Every day I thank the heavens above
Because now I have a young sibling to love

Joanna Herrera, Grade 8
Almond Tree Middle School

Separated

Don't forget the moments
Don't forget the memories
Always try to remember
Though we're separated,
You'll never be alone.

If you are in sorrow
If you are in despair
Always try to smile —
I'll always be there.

This is your final moment.
Close your eyes and think ahead —
Think of your future journey.
And we will be united…

Yet again.

Jason Cura, Grade 7
Corpus Christi School

Fun at the Beach

Rough sand on my skin
With a few mists of water
Ahh, quite relaxing

Justin Estepa, Grade 8
South Tahoe Middle School

Skiing

Soaring down the mountain
With the snow and wind in my face,
It is so cold but so smooth as you
Glide down the mountain.

You can soar through the air
And come down in the powder
With no worries.

It's like flying
But you're still on the ground
It's effortless you feel so free.

No one can hold you back,
Silent but powerful
There are endless possibilities.

Zack Lamb, Grade 8
St Joseph's School of the Sacred Heart

Soccer

S core a goal!
O pen for a pass.
C hip the ball and
C ross it.
E nter near the goal and head it
R ight into the goal!

Ricky Guzman, Grade 8
Our Lady of the Rosary School

My Best Friend

Do you ever wish, just maybe…
You could see an old friend again?
I do.
Traveling back through time in your thoughts,
Seeing an image of your best friend in 5th grade,
Running around freely in the cool shade of trees.

We would share our things together, walk to class together,
And we'd even do everything together.
Sometimes we fight, like dangerous wild cats,
But this fight doesn't separate us completely,
Just maybe a day or two.

Time flies by like the leaves in the wind,
Ripping the air from minutes to seconds,
How I wish for this perfect moment to go on,
How I wish for this to never end,
How I wish for time to slow down.

Three years passed, and the sun slowly creeps behind the mountains,
As I wave good-bye to her.
She stopped waving, and made a kind, heart-warming smile,
I smiled back, and at the same time I knew,
We will both see each other again.

Andrea Vaca, Grade 8
McCabe Elementary School

Losing You

Losing someone you really love hurts
The tears come down your cheeks
You see him talk to other girls and flirt
In my heart I feel really weak

Love is love that's how it is just pain
I always go to the same spot we would be and bring back memories
I miss kissing you in the rain
When you would hug me it would feel cozy

When I see you my heart beats really fast
When you would touch me I would feel butterflies
I knew we were never going to last
All you told me were just lies

When I'm with you, you make me forget about everybody else
Your touch and warmth made me comfortable
Right now you're in love with someone else
I thought you told me I was lovable

Losing someone you love really hurts
The tears come down your cheeks
You see him talk to other girls and flirt
In my heart I feel really weak

Cassandra Casillas, Grade 8
Almond Tree Middle School

To Be Young Again

O to be young once again
The feeling of our heart's content
For our boys will age into strong young men
To the adolescent, growing old is a thought to lament

They know not what blessings have been given
We their elders have long wished for their gift of youth
To sit behind the wheel of the life we've once driven

We who have squandered our years
Are now destined to watch the young grow old
At this our eyes drip tears
When we watch our child's life unfold
We view their life as a mystery
Waiting for strange events untold
Wishing their names to be passed on in history
As our own legacy grows cold

The sorrows that touch my heart
Son, lend this old man your ear
Use your years wisely and continue on without fear

Matthew Draughn, Grade 9
Linfield Christian School

April

April
Playing tricks on you
Look out, they are coming
The time to laugh, joke, and have fun
Gotcha!

Jasmine Lewis-Kates, Grade 7
John Charles Fremont Intermediate School

Why Has This Happened?

A jungle of buildings
Where corruption is rampant
No light emits till dawn
But our hearts are still black
Sirens of police cars only to be drowned
By the screams of people
And the gunshots of gangs
This demonstrates the heart of how cold people can be
Fear strikes through me
Of them coming to end my life.
The smell of thick polluted air
It smells like hell has been on earth since the dawn of time.
The taste of this place
Is beyond imagination
It is like blood and hatred in a glass
Dark as night
Evil as a demon, cold as a blizzard
And as human as we are, this doom was sealed long ago.
But why?
Why has this happened?

Ken Nicolay, Grade 7
Alta Vista Elementary School

Freedom

A dove
white, pure, lovely,
trapped in a cage
it escapes
flies toward the vast sky
far away form chains and broken dreams

Mary Onglatco, Grade 9
St Joseph Notre Dame High School

The Heroes of Then

The heroes of then, the heroes of now,
The heroes of when, the heroes of how.
The heroes go back very far,
And when they came, they left a scar,
A scar on the world that will never go away,
Like the greatness of Jesus that will never lead us astray.
The righteousness of Paul,
And how he answered God's call,
The intrepidness of Moses,
His wisdom goes before us.
The heroes of then, the heroes of now,
The heroes of when, the heroes of how.
The heroes of now are great, I must say,
They are saving people day after day,
Their commitment to this world is great,
They help God control this world's fate.
The heroes of then, the heroes of now,
The heroes of when, the heroes of how.

Brandon Cahill, Grade 7
Linfield Christian School

Good Night Tree

I stand tall in the breeze,
Mighty and strong.
My leaves rustle in the blowing wind.
I am a tree.

The sight from up above is breathless.
I could see the rolling hills,
As green as the dark seaweed below the ocean surface,
The setting sun,
Glowing with colors that are so warm like a campfire,
And the birds flying off,
Gracefully across the sky like ballerinas.

As the sun sets,
It disappears.
Now the sun is gone
And the moon has wakened.
The sky is pitch black,
With bright stars blinking in the dark.
Now it is time to say,
"Good night."

Kimsa Nguyen, Grade 7
Morrill Middle School

Twists and Turns

Two roads, one twisting, one turning, and both were in my sight.
At first glance, neither road looked welcoming, neither road looked bright.

It was hard to see the road to the right. The fog was much too thick.
But as I walked closer to the path, I could see that the fog was just a trick.

I could see that there was fun and excitement. I saw my family and my friends.
But I also noticed a storm coming, and that's where my line of vision ends.

I walked toward the road to the left, and my sight here was clear.
But what I saw was shocking, because nothing would appear.

I thought my eyes were playing tricks on me again, but as I walked closer, there was still nothing there.
I knew I had to choose a path soon, but all I could do was stare.

I thought long and hard about my choice, my choice did not come quick.
I finally decided which road to choose: the road on the left was the one I would pick.

I headed toward the road with nothing there, a surprise was something I was yearning.
I would never forget this day; the day where I picked between two roads, one twisting, one turning.

Andrew Banh, Grade 9
Westview High School

The First Time

The first time I looked into your eyes I was in a trance, but as time went by all the joy and magic started to fade. From day to do day, I started to realize this was all a lie. Your smile, the way you look, I used to shake, but now I just put a fake smile on my face. I wouldn't dare to get too close anymore for fear of rejection and hurt. The first time I made you smile, you sent chills down my spine. But now when you smile, I look away. As I turn back, to get another look at you, I see hurt in your eyes could it be. Now as I walk pass you, through the hall. I look back to see my mistake. I now see my feelings of rejection brought me to this, to see you walk past and not say a word. I don't feel joy, happiness, or bliss. My heart is bleeding, but there is no cure. I don't even bother to look at you anymore. It's a crime because you're not mine. Once in a while, I wish everything was like the first time.

Daniela Martinez, Grade 8
Henry T Gage Middle School

My Childhood Memories

I remember my third birthday party and the park playing hide-and-go-seek
And feeding the cute little ducks
I remember on Halloween when I was four going out as Minnie Mouse
And my brother went as Mickey
I remember on Christmas morning seeing the cookies with bites taken out
And the milk halfway gone
I remember pushing my sister out of our bunk bed
And being so scared that she had died that I hid for hours on end
I remember getting an Easy-Bake Oven for my seventh birthday
And making cookies
I remember when I performed in my first school play as Minnie Mouse in *The Christmas Carol*
I remember going out of state for the first time to California from Oregon
I remember going to Disneyland with my little autograph book going around and getting the characters autographs
I had so much fun
I remember when I got in a huge fight with my best friend
And I did not talk to her for a week
I remember when I went to Disneyland with my school band
And me and my roommates stayed up all night

Amanda Deigan, Grade 8
Daniel Savage Middle School

Time

Time flies by so fast,
Doesn't it?
A day goes by in a second,
And a week goes by in a day.
Tick tock, tick tock.
I always wanted to freeze time,
Like how you can simply press pause on an iPod.
Time flies like an arrow,
And no matter how hard you try, you can't grasp hold of it.
Tick tock, tick tock.
I wish I could rewind back to the early days,
And fast forward to my future.
Nothing seems the same anymore,
As I stand motionless in awe of what is happening around me.
Tick tock, tick tock.
I'm not quite sure if I'm ready for the real world yet,
Where the stakes are high and where time is money.
Time can have several meanings,
But there's only one true meaning: it's a part of life.
Tick tock, tick tock.

Kristin Wong, Grade 8
Madrona Middle School

Waiting for It to End

Day after day I sit and do the same thing;
Read, write, or look out to them.
The Nazis come and take them away,
One after another, and I watch
Knowing I can do nothing.
Dark heavy clouds hover over us
As we wait for the war to end.
Knowing that I can't help
Seems to be saying I have turned my back.
Not knowing when I will be discovered,
Not knowing when my time will come,
Makes time come much faster.
Dark heavy clouds hover over us,
As we wait for the war, to end.

Ambyr Madison, Grade 8
Cucamonga Middle School

Friends for Life

Friends for life is what we are.
Through good times, and bad times you were my friend.
Trusting in you, you gave me support.
The strength to get up, and go again.
If my heart was broken, you'd heal it.
If my heart was happy, yours was too.
You are my best friend
always, and forever.
It's been good,
the best friendship ever.
Never end, now and forever.

Jenna Krantz, Grade 7
St Hilary Elementary School

Hiding Something

I am the thinker
Covering up the sad past
With a fake, Barbie smile
Which no one notices
Dreamer of helping
Someone else in need
Worshiping Lord Jesus
Don't praise the god of greed
I am the Sagittarius
Piercing the evil hearts with love
The kind of person who melts the ice in others
With the fire of Christ burning within
Kristina, Kritina, Silverluna
My identifications
Call me whatever you like
Even the meanest word in the whole world
I'll cherish it forever
Don't mistake me for someone else
I'm unique, I stand out
Not special to you
But to Jesus and God

Kristina Chepak, Grade 7
Grace Lutheran School

Books

Books are red, brown, blue, and black.
Books taste like adventure.
Books sound like another world's sounds.
Books smell like smells from another place.
Books look like a fantasy world, visited in my head.
Books make me feel like I can go anywhere.

Haley Gantt, Grade 7
St Mary of Assumption School

Reset...

The veteran gamer drives past all opposers,
Dodging, weaving, flying around; look at him go!
It's getting close… Wham! He slams into a semi,
Game over.
Yet the gamer presses reset and the game goes on!…
Yet the gamer presses reset and the game…
Yet the gamer presses reset…
The gamer presses reset…
Presses reset…
Reset.
Time stops for no one, not ever for our gamer.
War goes on, life goes on, death goes on, we go on…
The world goes round, round the sun, round the universe…
Like the hands of a clock, round and round…
Timing us until it's maxed, and then…
You know.
So next time you play, when the racer says,
"On your mark, get set…"
Reset.

Brennan Thornton, Grade 7
Joan MaQueen Middle School

Drugs

Drugs
Bad for you
Destroying your inside
Changing who you are
Hurt your body
Causing sickness
You disappear
From your family and friends
The people you love
It's not a good choice
In your life
Don't do drugs!

Kimberly Lopez, Grade 7
St Alphonsus School

Blue

I am the ocean
Deep and blue.
I am a friend,
Always true.
I am like the sky
With rain pouring down.
I'm sometimes bright
Other times, I'm a letdown.
I'm summer and winter.
I'm the speed of a sprinter.
Hush! I am calm, I am sad.
I am depression, and I am never mad.
I am blue.
Oh no, you softly say.
It's blue! How sad!
I'd better stay away!
But remember all the things I am,
Not just blue.
I am not bad, or negative, or sad,
What I am is true blue.

Erin Kelly, Grade 7
St Patrick Parish School

The Love That Hurts

Life is full of hopes and joy
But mine is full of pain
For I had met a darling boy,
Who threw me down the drain.
With all the things he told me so,
He sent me down to hell.
The words whispered made me cold,
My body then began to dwell.
Like any other normal day,
You began to make me bleed.
But on that special normal day,
You began to plead.
That wonderful day finally came
For you to say "I'm tamed!"

Connie Rocha, Grade 8
John Adams Middle School

Your Demise

Look into my eyes,
And what will happen will be explained.
Your quizzical expression shows your confusion clearly,
But as to the source of your confusion, I myself am bewildered.
Have you not paid attention at all?
Have you failed to see what has been happening this whole time?
Of course you haven't.
But your perplexity will soon be gone,
And my mind cleared.
Many will be relieved from your pseudo power.
Oh, I can't wait.
Now it shall be done,
The elimination of the horror and exasperation.
The joy is going to be great.
Good-bye my foe,
May you never rest in peace.

Genevieve Mullins, Grade 9
Shasta High School

Happy Mother's Day

MOM!

Through the years you've taught me the meaning of life,
You've opened the doors to so many possibilities,
And most important you've taught me how to love and be a gentleman.

I just want to give back to you so,
Happy Mother's Day
Mom!!!

Tucker Johnson, Grade 7
Las Flores Middle School

Waterfall

Slowly trickling down the mountaintop like a tear rolling down a young child's face
Sparkling in the sunlight crying tears of happiness in the daylight
Giving nourishment to the many beautiful flowers
Its mist covering the glistening rocks nearby
Moving gracefully past the rocks and trees as though it were a ballerina
Causing the sun to rejoice, kissing the waterfall
Making beautiful colors of red, yellow, and blue to appear.
Giving the life to everything surrounding it
Filling the air with the mist of water
So cold, so refreshing, so full of energy
As the rushing water comes down from the mountaintop
As pretty as a bouquet of wild flowers
Powerful like a charging wild stallion
Lukewarm to the touch but cold to the sweat rolling down your face
As old as the tallest sequoia tree, knowing tales from ancient past
About kings, queens, warriors, and wandering people
Always calm and cool when crushing and shaping the rocks around it
Filled with the hustle and bustle of fish spawning, birds, and other creatures
Puffy clouds of mist coming from its mouth
Roaring shouts of hello and how are you doing
Waterfall, making nature

Erin Lee, Grade 8
Madrona Middle School

Heaven

M an I'm happy, can't you see
Y eah I feel good, I feel so free

S o take me by the hand and let's fly away
O ver the ocean, and leaving today
U nder a tree, breeze swayin' through
L ove and compassion have led me to you

I nner light, shinin' so bright
S ky is my blanket, and I feel so right

C an't stop smiling, I don't know why
O n shine the stars up in the sky
N ight breaks to day, day into night
T oday was tomorrow, tomorrow when light
E verything's perfect
N o one in plight
T he blindness is gone, and clear is my sight

Eugene Alforque, Grade 8
Santa Rosa Technology Magnet School

If

If this heart stopped beating,
Would anyone care?
Would it be all right and finally fair?
If this heart stopped beating,
Would you pay the price?
Of all the guilt held for the end of a life?
If this heart stopped beating,
Would it finally be
A distant thought, a memory?
If this heart stopped beating
Would the world stop too?
Would everything change to gray and blue?
If this heart stopped beating
Would it find relief?
From all the past, find a sense of peace?
If this heart stopped beating
Would it still be alone?
Or dance with angels of worlds unknown?
If this heart stopped beating
What would you do?
Would your heart be still and stop beating too?

Eleni Verveniotis, Grade 8
Tierra Linda Middle School

My Kind of World

I believe in a world of peace
I believe in a world of love
in a world where we are free to fly like the doves
where we can run in the meadows and play
where we can rock in our own cool way
and where we don't have to be brand-conscious
but where we can all be self-conscious.

Duy Le, Grade 7
Sarah McGarvin Intermediate School

The Best Thing About School!

Homework is the best thing ever invented!
Although, I don't understand why it is so, hated
Teachers happily pass 'em out
To each and every student who shout
They whine about all the work
Until, they transform into a hideous berserk!
From math to history
To writing a short, emotional story
Homework is incredibly fun
Especially when you do it under a hot, shining sun!
You can stay after school
And get help from an old lady sitting on a stool
Do it with you best buddy
Or get it done with your old daddy
It doesn't have to be a pain
But there's a ton to gain!
Doctors, lawyers, architects, and teachers, too
Got their jobs by doing theirs every night or two
Kids say it's the worst part about school
But I think, homework is really, really cool!

Akash Salam, Grade 7
Ruth Paulding Middle School

Staci Kaye Barnett

Kind
Caring
Loving
Who wishes of being with her family
Who dreams of working with animals
Who wants to have a dog
Who wonders about her brothers
Who is afraid of not reaching her dreams
Who likes dogs
Who believes in God
Who loves her dad
Who loves her mom
Who loves her brothers
Who loves her sisters
Who plans to be a big sister
Who plans not to screw up her life
Who plans to be successful in life
Whose final destination is home with her family

Staci Kaye Barnett, Grade 8
Almond Tree Middle School

Laughing

Communication,
Hurtful, fun
Talking, laughing, replying
Mom is talking on the moon while ignoring me
Excommunicating, relaxing, unspeaking
Boring, alone
Silent

Erica Hartman, Grade 7
Santa Rosa Technology Magnet School

Hatred

I hate the way you smile,
It sometimes gets me scared.
I hate the way you look at me,
I'm always unprepared.
Can't stand the way you lie to me,
And the fact that you're never there.
Despise the fact that you're never wrong,
And I am never right.
It makes me sick that every day,
There's always another fight.
Hate the way you talk to me,
With such great disrespect,
And the way that whenever we talk,
You have to change the subject.
Hate the way we're different,
And have different points of view.
But most of all, I hate the fact that
I really don't hate you.
Jennifer Perez, Grade 8
Corpus Christi School

Just Friends

You told me we are friends,
That is what we'll always be,
Now should I smile and laugh,
Or cry, because how it is for me?

Your jokes, your poise,
Your laugh, your smile,
Your personality;
Your wit, your voice,
Your faith, your style,
All bring me to reality.

We're just friends,
And not much more,
Yet why do I still wonder,
What the future has in store?

You told me we are friends,
That is what we'll always be.
I hope one day you may see,
More than just a friend in me.
Tricia Lin, Grade 8
Foothills Middle School

He's the One…

He's the one who makes me blush.
He's the one who loves me.
He's the one who cares for me.
He's the one who's special to me.
He's the one who's everything to me.
He's the one who's just for me.
Claudia Alvarenga, Grade 7
Corpus Christi School

What Are Questions?

What are questions,
You always ask?
What are answers?
Are finding them an easy task?

What is truth?
And what are lies?
Who is that?
Is that whom you despise?

Why do you think?
How do you cry?
Why do we sleep?
Why do we count the days that go by?

Who are you?
Who am I?
Who are we in this world?
Why, why, oh why?
Jessica MacCleary, Grade 7
Alta Loma Jr High School

Clock

Fascinating timepiece
Designed to keep us on track
Propelling its hands
Without halting for a second
Hearing the ticking sound of its hands
Depressed when it's not functioning
Delighted when helpful
Keeping you on time
For school or work.
Jorge Luevano, Grade 7
St Alphonsus School

Stalker

The way you eat dinner
So politely
Makes me smile

The way you carefully
Undress for your evening shower
Makes me smile

The way you laugh
When your friends are over
Makes me smile

One day
You will notice me
And when you do
I'm just on the tree
Outside
Gwen Willis, Grade 9
Balboa City School

Mother Nature

The sky is blue
With its light colored hue
You feel so great
When you stand under its weight

The sea is so vast
When you get stuck in it you gasp
Sometimes you get caught in its crash
You might, just get mashed

The sun is so bright
Without it there is no light
Plants thrive on its heat
In its light us people meet.
Christopher Ortega, Grade 7
Almond Tree Middle School

Nature

lions
lions are awesome
the lions are carnivores
lions are graceful

trees
trees are the best plants
the tree gives up oxygen
trees are wonderful

birds
birds are colorful
birds are in different sizes
birds are the coolest
Arjenix Ayala, Grade 8
Almond Tree Middle School

Moonlit Night

Sitting on a mossy log
My face wears a frown
Waiting for the fog to clear
I try to find my way in the forest
But I trip on a tree root
And a startled owl makes a hoot

The foggy mist dissolves
And the moon lights my path
I run down a hill towards the lake
There a family of ducks take a bath
The meadow surrounding the lake
Has but one firefly
A pixie-like glowing ember
That resembles a bright star
Then I realized I found my home
It is close and no longer far.
Ashley Smith, Grade 8
Madrona Middle School

Ode to Baseball

Oh, America's favorite pastime
The roar of the spectators,
The wisp of hotdogs and burgers
The sweet sounds of game day

Oh, the fresh smell of a new, leather ball
The feel of just-cut grass
Oh, how it can just take all your troubles
Just to be part of the game

Oh, the exhilaration of a homerun
Or make a beautiful web-gem
And the sweet sound of bat and ball colliding
Oh, the fun, just to play ball!

Ricchie Gonzales, Grade 7
Santa Rosa Technology Magnet School

Friends

Best friends are good.
They normally give you food.
They're always by your side
when you fall off a slide.

They're never gone
because of their strong bond.
They make you feel good about yourself.
They help you reach something on a high shelf.

They listen to what you have to say.
They never go away.
You and your friends have a lot of things
like small pieces of string.

These are what friends are for —
when you get a good one, you'll want more!

Leah Bishop, Grade 7
South Fork Middle School

The Forest

Here comes the rain
To give the thick forest a shower.
Everything looks fresh, everything looks new.
Everything looks clean, everything looks green.
The water drips from the leaves of the tree
Making a "taap! taap!" sound.
The birds are singing a sweet song.
A small speckled sparrow flies
From tree to tree chirping
Saying "Wake up! Wake up! We have a new day!"
The trail in the forest is clean and soft.
Inviting us wordlessly
"Why do you join us for this new day
As we start?"

Samiksha Waghchaure, Grade 8
Madrona Middle School

Ode to Nature

I sit outside
watching the leaves jump
in the balmy autumn breeze
My back sets against the top step
and the warmth of the sun
gently heats my face
The wind matures
causing everything to come to life
and stillness becomes a thing of the past
A lonely leaf lands on my lap
I make a gesture to move it
but it has already drifted elsewhere
To my left, flowers in the garden sway
like dancers in the rhythmic wind
so free of heart and mind
The weeds aside the applause
in awe of the colorful show
still going on before them
I must now retreat to my own house
for my visit in Mother Nature's mansion is over
but I shall miss her elegance and beauty

Taylor Cifuentez, Grade 8
La Joya Middle School

Cars

C ustom cars are great
A udio systems sound cool
R acing cars is a rush
S peeding is only for fools

Matthew Ordaz, Grade 7
John Charles Fremont Intermediate School

First Love

I remember when I first fell in love
She made me feel so good I could fly in the sky above
I remember when I first told her I love her
I thought I would be with her forever
I remember my first kiss with her
I knew it would be a kiss that I would always miss
I remember her beautiful face and her precious eyes
I remember that when I see her she would leave me out of sight
I remember out first date
When I'm around her I feel so safe
I know she is the best she made me feel so blessed
I remember our first song together
The song is "Always and Forever"
I remember when we broke-up
I felt like I wanted to give up
I remember when she was gone
I felt so alone
I still think of her exact
Because I still want her back
Now I have to live in this cold world called life
Now I'm alone and have no one to love by my side

Jose Rubio, Grade 8
Daniel Savage Middle School

Running Free

The whistle blows
I start running, running, running
Everything around me is a blur
I'm not thinking only breathing
And running, running, running
As fast as I can

I watch my feet, under me
They look so funny going back and forth
Running, running, running
I passed the finish line. Yay!!
Michelle Jimenez, Grade 7
St Vincent Elementary School

Never Last

Throw it down,
Throw it to the blasting music,
Up and down,
'Round and 'round,
Swinging super slow or really fast,
Never last.

Throw the yo-yo,
Around the string,
over your hand,
Under your leg,
Behind your back.

Flying high as world champ,
Yuuki Spencer does the impossible
All stare when Yuuki yo-yos,
He is a young yo-yo Yoda.
Vincent DeZutti, Grade 8
St Joseph's School of the Sacred Heart

Myself

Cool
Funny
Wishes to sing
Dreams of a family
Wants to have a career
Who wonders about the future
Who fears rats
Who is afraid of ghosts
Who likes dancing
Who believes myself
Who loves clothes
Who loves playing
Who loves dancing
Who loves sports
Who plans to be a doctor
Who plans to not fight
Who plans to be in college
Whose final destination is Miami
Maria Diaz, Grade 7
Almond Tree Middle School

The Toaster and the Toast

in a big green house on a kitchen shelf
sat a shiny silver toaster all by himself
until the day he met little miss Lola
the day when a human lay down a loaf of bread and a cola

Lola the toast was the first on the plate
she saw the toaster and knew it was fate
they looked at each other with a love so true
on that beautiful day with a sky so blue

this happy relationship was sadly not meant to last
for the end for Lola came all too fast
morning came with the hunger of the brand new day
Lola was toasted then taken away

before toaster nearly burned her to a crisp
he said, "I love you" with a childish lisp
Lola replied with a Harrison Ford flair
"I know" then left toaster in despair

that day he made a vow to never toast another piece of bread
and he shut himself off and lay down his head
but as the human took Lola away on her funeral plate as white as a dove
he whispered, "I'm sorry. I'm just a hunk of burning love."
Amanda Blazey, Grade 8
Our Lady of Guadalupe School

Wintertime

As the snow silently and swiftly falls upon the ground
The children's faces are compressed against their windows
Gazing out the window with smiles on their faces
Moments later they charge outside into the magical winter wonderland

The snow is soft and fluffy
They begin to make snowmen
And snow angels
As the snowflakes start to fall once again

The children begin to complain now of aching bodies
It's been hours since they've left their warm, heated houses
Their toes are rosy and frosty as their cheeks
So they leave their smiling snowmen and rush inside

They cuddle in front of a toasty warm fire
Where they roast marshmallows,
And warm themselves head to toe
With hot chocolate in hand, of course with mini marshmallows

As they lay in their soft, warm beds
They dream of tomorrow's activities
They rest for a new day
Guaranteed with new adventures
Erin Shields, Grade 8
Tierra Linda Middle School

Stars

S itting on top of the sky
T winkling at midnight
A lways bright as the heavens
R aying with beams of light
S parkling all through the night

Kylie Bohnsack, Grade 7
John Charles Fremont Intermediate School

The Visions of Yosemite

Yosemite's nature so peaceful and calm
Streams that drip and filter slowly through your palm
The crickets that chirp, the bears that roar
The deer that graze, the birds that soar
The mountains so mighty, so massive and tall
The elevated tip tops covered with snow fall
Yosemite's sky night so sparkling and high
Watch the shooting stars drift and fly by
The fresh Yosemite air that blows through the face
So tranquil, so smooth it floats with grace
Sometimes it's freezing sometimes it's not
For during the summer it is blazing hot
The big beautiful waterfalls that flow so fast
Watching the strips of water pound is a blast
In order to make one's trip successful and right
one must take a picture to capture the sight
Nature slowly captures hikers and takes their breath away
As they blissfully gaze at the enormous trees' slowly sway
Yosemite, Yosemite, one of God's fondest creations
Ponder and dream of the next visit with great anticipation

Colin Johnson, Grade 8
Sacred Heart School

Moving On

It's getting close
So I start to wonder
What will it be like?
Am I ready?
These past two years have been great.
I've learned a lot
But now it's time to move on
It's been almost two years now
Since I went through a similar time
Where I had to leave a place I had known well for seven years
and go to a different, unfamiliar place
Here
Like a caterpillar changing
Changing into a beautiful butterfly
We must move on
Even though I am reluctant
I know this is for the better
Better experiences lie ahead
This is an important part of my journey in life
I might be ready
Even if I'm not I must move on

Daniel Larsen, Grade 8
Valley Oak Middle School

Friends Forever

We've been friends for awhile now,
through good and bad times.
We've had those crazy days and those,
"You just had to be there" moments.
We know our friendship would be nothing
without these moments.
All the times we spent together
I will always keep in my heart,
no matter where life takes us.

Tori Duarte, Grade 8
St Hilary Elementary School

My Little Blue Suitcase and I

Together we have circled the globe
My little blue suitcase, and I
We have slept, walked, ran
Across time zones

My little blue suitcase, and I
Its wheels run down on cobblestone and dirt roads
Across time zones
I pull it everywhere

Its wheels run down on cobblestone and dirt roads
Carrying gifts and pieces
I pull it everywhere
Rolling, coming, going

We have slept, walked, ran
Across time zones
Together we have circled the globe
My little blue suitcase, and I

Annakai Geshlider, Grade 7
Synergy School

Midnight Stars

Midnight stars, in our sky, glimmer as we sleep
Every star is winking, every star is blinking
All these stars watch over us, as we count our sheep
We may not ever see them, as we are fast asleep
Midnight lights, in our sky, twinkle as we sleep

Midnight stars, in your sky, are not different than mine
In fact, every star is the same, no matter where it shines
A twinkle here, a glimmer there, they are all the same
All these stars are shining, shining like a flame
Midnight lights, in your sky, twinkle as we sleep

Midnight stars, in my sky, glow like the vibrant sun
Just like us, these stars rise and fall, with the coming of the day
All these stars cannot shine forever, but there's some hope
Just like us, these stars stand tall and glow like the sunset
Midnight lights, in our sky, twinkle as we sleep

Logun Spellacy, Grade 8
Madrona Middle School

Looking Back from Here

As the eighth graders stand up on stage, before parents' proud eyes,
They recall their years at Challenger School, times both good and bad;
They stand up in turn to accept their diplomas, amidst their final good-byes,
And proudly hold them up with a cheer, turning to face mom and dad;
Walking down from the stage, close friends embrace each other,
They cry and stomp and whine, saddened by the fact;
That they only have one summer left together,
And then high school comes rushing, making a sudden impact;
And countless years of memories, come rushing back to all,
They bat away tears of sadness, and try to imagine a world;
Where they can stay with their friends, people who will raise them when they fall,
As high school is an unknown world in which they will all soon be unfurled;
Parents and graduates pose for photos that will be recalled years from this day,
Teachers are happy to share in the joy; there is not a single dry eye in the building;
The choir continues singing its jovial tunes, and louder the musicians play,
After all this, the graduates have surely had one great evening;
From a different perspective, they think of leaving their friends behind,
And they realize they'll make new friends, through academics, or even football;
They now know that high school is just school of another kind,
Thinking about the great adventure that awaits them, high school doesn't seem so scary after all!

Pranav Pradhan, Grade 8
Challenger School – Ardenwood

National War

Heavy bullets rain down, envy full of greed.
Lifeless, longing for power. Over time we grow, naive.
Enough is enough, another man dies.
Relinquished, till we banish. Hearing our cries. Is it over?
Sobs of children somber. Artilleries with no remorse.
Death of many invite a force of, savagery. Enraged.
Against all odds sadness trapped and caged. Establishing a dark age.
So what do we believe in? Is it money? Is it fame?
Is it the power that would drive us insane?
We are all in war, and we didn't know it. Our ignorance led us far, and we never saw it.
We're infected with lies. And it spreads unseen.
Are we really number one? Like it's always been.
One day it could be us. The ones destroyed, then what?
Who would save us all? With this great land beginning to spoil.
But there's a cure. We just need to find it, and the answer is within,
Within our mind and soul. We can get rid of the disease so foul.
We only need to, embark on a quest. Unraveling a test and finding a cure.
Living unsure, inside a cage to release the rage.
You free yourself from, an addicting lie so no one will ever die. People will say equality any day.
And spreading, care for others enforcing peace and love. In this new land of doves.
Soaring the sky corruption will cry. Under God we relinquish the cage to establish a new age.

Patrick Villarosa, Grade 9
Los Angeles School of Global Studies

Because of Me

Are You sad because of me Lord? Because of the decisions I make. Is that why You cast rain from the heavens above? Tears from Your eyes fall from Your face, onto mine and it makes me happy, but it makes me sad. I am happy because I know You care. I am sad because You cry for me. Because Your child is doing wrong and is sent to an institution. Because of me, I am here. Because of me, Jesus is dead. Because of me, I have failed. Everyone, every spirit, every soul. I am not worthy. That's why I'm here. Because of me.

Rondalyn Skramovsky, Grade 9
Crossroads School

Special Night

Drop, drop, drop
Water pouring down from above
Stars shining so bright
On one special night, on the streets of Paris
It is a very special moment
Me and you, looking at the sky
Looking at France's most romantic city sky
Wishing you and I were the only ones alive
Walking on the streets,
Hoping this night will last forever
Hoping this isn't a dream,
And that it'll never end.

Giarelli Chavez, Grade 7
John Adams Middle School

Music

I always start from silence
Like a river never stopped
My tradition is defiance
Always changing never lost

With emotions never ending
I dance like the sun's sweet rays
Swiftly soaring on a wing
A loud, now silent gaze

Making you happy, making you sad
Then BANG, I make you jump
My ups and downs, my accents glad
I make you race then BUMP

Living free am I
A winding road you travel
More colors than the sky
Listen carefully and my secrets you'll unravel

Marie McDonald Hulen, Grade 7
St Patrick Parish School

True Love

I knew from the time I laid eyes on you,
I was meant for you, you were meant for me,
This love, one love, was absolutely true,
I felt, for the first time, that I could see
Your exotic eyes took my breath away,
I had known it when I first saw your smile,
I was so amazed with nothing to say,
Our relationship would last for a while,
Like a Gobstopper, your heart never fades,
We have similar things that we favor,
Our conversations can last for decades,
This love is something to always savor,
To maintain this love there has to be trust,
Anyone can see this love is a must.

Alexa Shafer, Grade 8
Las Flores Middle School

Love Is a Feeling

Love is a feeling, a very special feeling.
Sometimes I can't describe it,
it's sometimes far too strange.
It's a feeling you can't remove,
It's sometimes like a treasure worth keeping.
Believe in it and enjoy it because when the time is right
You won't want to leave it.

Frida Niebla, Grade 7
St Mary's School

Learn to Bloom

Flowers grow in springtime
Leaves die in fall
Snow evolves in winter
I do not bloom in the summer — not once, not twice, not all.
Presents arrive on Christmas
Turkey is served on Thanksgiving
Candy is a treat or a trick on Halloween
I do not know why it is worth living.
Water is scarce in the desert
Fire is yearned for at night
Light is needed for brightness
And I have reached with all my might.
Mother is here to love
Father is there to care
Sibling is here to understand
Yet none know all that I have to bear.
Everyone is gone now
Everything has filled with gloom
It is up to no one
But luckily I have learned how to bloom.

Jennifer Tran, Grade 7
Sarah McGarvin Intermediate School

Rainforest

The rainforest is like a jungle with animals
You can hear the splashing sound of a waterfall
And you can hear the sound of the crunching leaves
You can hear the sound of a beating drum

You can see monkeys swinging from branch to branch
While the birds are singing
The tree's leaves are dancing in the wind
Tigers are acting wild
So vicious, so fierce

Jaguars eyes are like a piercing light
Once it hits night
It is a hunting party
You fight for food

You will kill; you may die
It hits morning
You go to sleep

Bianca Quesada, Grade 8
Madrona Middle School

Ode to Hope

Hope
Is a wondrous thing.

It
Makes life worth living.

Warm
In the winter cold.

Rain
In a dry desert.

Clear
In a sky of clouds.

Light
In the dark of night.

Good
In an evil place.

Sweet
In a sour life.

Love
In a world of hate.

Hope
Makes us find a way.
Allison Daniel, Grade 8
La Joya Middle School

Your Face

Your smiles are fake
Your lies are true
You spread rumors…
That's all you do

You never cared
You turned your back
Whispering to people…
Trustworthiness you lack

Your face brings back memories…
Bad memories, too
There's nothing else I can say but…
I never want to see you!
Ariene Gregorio, Grade 7
Almond Tree Middle School

Rush of Spring

The water rushes
down through the mountain
just in time for spring.
Veronica Charles, Grade 7
South Tahoe Middle School

Just Because I Don't Have Wings

Just because I don't have wings
Doesn't mean my imagination can't take flight
Doesn't mean I can't be in the sky
Doesn't mean I can't live with the clouds

Just because I don't have wings
Doesn't mean I can't follow nature's calling
Doesn't mean I can't rise with the morning sun
Doesn't mean I can't be one with the wind

Just because I don't have wings
Doesn't mean I can't soar through the sky
Doesn't mean I can't follow my dreams
Just because I don't have wings — let me find my own way to freedom
Winston Eng, Grade 8
Dorris-Eaton School

The Beach

The sand feels warm and soft on my feet, the salt water comes in swells
When I think of my favorite place there's no place like the beach
The waves may crash relentlessly against the wooden pier
But as I lie across the sand their sound is silent noise
There are so many memories I have had at the beach —
It's like my second home — to swim, to run, to just relax seems just like a dream
Although I love the beach besides I have one perfect image
Of the place I wish to be in all moments of the day
The beach I visit when I dream where Ruby's Diner is on the pier
Where dolphins play beneath the waves
Where crabs crawl calmly cross the sand and palm trees sway with the breeze
Walk down the street and you will find food, fun, and shopping
But down on the sand right by the water is where I'd rather be
During the summer my favorite thing is to be doing Junior Lifeguards
I'm at the beach and having fun — what's not to love?
The beach is always a great place to spend time with friends
We swim and laugh and all relax 'til the day's end
Everything about the beach makes me so excited
To think of how God made the beach to make His children happy
Mikayla Mager, Grade 9
Fountain Valley High School

Bike Ride

I looked at it sitting there in the road
Gleaming from the reflected sunlight.
There was a sense of glee yet also of fear.
When I sat on the seat, the anxiety built,
Kicked the stand out from under me and off I went.
The wheels rolled and I started to move,
Slowly at first, ever increasing speed. Down, down, down the hill.
Wait!
The bottom of the hill was coming increasingly closer,
And I had no idea how to stop.
I hit the curb at such a speed I flew over the fence into the canyon.
By the time I could stand up straight my dad was already there to help.
I simply looked at him and said…"Let's do that again!"
Austin Hill, Grade 9
Westview High School

Shopping

Shopping is something every girl does and loves,
It takes our mind to a careless world,
Where we don't mind spending every last penny in our account.
Besides, we're not the one paying for anything,
Our parents will take care of the expense eventually.
We say we are leaving in a while,
But shopping pulls us in like a drain pulls in water.
For us there is no stop, we shop 'till we drop.
Our closets are full but we still can't stop,
It's like being addicted to shopping without a stop.
Family problems we can't bear,
Parents think shopping should be rare.
We get to the store in no time,
And run around 'till the fashion stores come to our site.
We beat the other customers for the greatest sales,
Devouring them like biting off our nails.
We leave the store without a trace,
Competing with other shoppers making a race.
We always win with a grin upon our face,
Knowing that we have won the shopping race.

Brisa Velazquez, Grade 8
Martin Murphy Middle School

The Universal Language

Music, one little 5 letter word.
How can such a little word mean so much to the rest of us?
They call this the universal language, but why?
This is something that all people can understand
From the High Priests in Ancient Egypt,
To the man singing to his true love from a balcony,
To the black slaves in early America.
The priests sang to praise their gods.
The lover sings to pronounce his undying love.
The slaves sang 'cause music gave them hope.
One word, many voices that have, are, and will
Be raised over the ages.
One *song* in the universe,
But many hearts harmonizing together
To make it beautiful.

Julianne Rodriguez, Grade 8
St Hilary Elementary School

God

God is so good
God created everything,
even the world.
He gave us life, free will
and gives good things:
food, family, friends, clothes, and shelter.
He gives a choice to follow or not,
He gives patience, miracles,
and tests us to find love in Him.
He is our soul defender.
God is so good.

Miguel Lopez, Grade 7
Renuevo School

The End Is Near

The end is hear
He's full of fear
The tears welled up in her eyes
The destruction and corruption
He caused her pain now he lives in shame

The end is hear
She screams in fear
She can't believe his lies
He laughs, she cries
Her heart slowly dies

Their end is near
The love they shared
It's all over now
Oh now I think
The end is here…

Natalie Anderson, Grade 9
Shadow Hills Intermediate School

Spring Breeze

It's warm and easy
Makes the pages of my notebook turn,
Which makes it hard to write.
The breeze turns to a wind
And messes up my hair.
My neighbors turn on their radio.
I hate the music they're playing.
I think it really sucks.
My hand is cold due to my Starbucks
And the wind isn't helping.
The day starts to get miserable.
The wind is too fast.
The sun is too bright,
And here comes R.J. jumping the fence
But I know it'll be all right.
It's all a cycle.
My neighbors will stop playing that crap
R.J. will go back inside
The wind will calm down
The sun won't be so bright
And the warm and easy spring breeze will start again.

Carrie Gutierrez, Grade 8
Spring Grove Elementary School

The Lion

They call me the king of the wild.
I am the most ferocious of them all.
I am the most beautiful creature you will ever see.
My roarrrr might frighten you
But I am just trying to protect myself and little ones.
Don't get too close or I might just take a bite.
I am the lion.

Elide Vargas, Grade 8
Almond Tree Middle School

Rain

Rain, rain, clear our way
You come at anytime of the day,
Sometimes as mist, sometimes as drops,
Sometimes you never seem to stop.
But when you go,
You leave your rainbow.

Louis Napoles, Grade 7
Chino Valley Christian Schools

Frappes and Lattes Are Your Friends

Friends are like frappes and lattes.
When you are cold and empty,
they will make you warm and lively.
When you feel fiery and dangerous,
they will cool and calm you down.
When life gets harder,
they will stay by your side.
When you want to give up,
they will help you to go on.
When you're stressed to the core,
they will try to make you comfortable.
This is why friends are
like frappes and lattes.

Richard Nguyen, Grade 8
La Joya Middle School

Ode to the Elements

Air, so cool on my face,
Fire, too warm to embrace,
Water, so beautiful and immense,
Earth, so strong and intense,
Spirit, too majestic to conceive,
Oh, elements for me, please never leave!

Sammie Silveira, Grade 7
Santa Rosa Technology Magnet School

Best Friends

My friends are the best.
They are always there.
No need for a test
Good friends are rare.

They will always care
When we go to the mall.
They will always be fair
When we walk down the hall.

My friends are great.
They are more than okay.
There is no hate
If we don't get our way.

We will always spend time together.
They are my best friends forever.

Gisella Diaz, Grade 8
Almond Tree Middle School

Ode to My Small Basketball

I hold you in my hand, and I squeeze.
Gravity doesn't matter now,
For you are safe in my tight grip.

I eye the hoop, and shoot!
The ball slides off my fingers sending chills down my body.
I see a whirlwind of blue, white, and red arching through the air.
Swish!
The net slows you down you roll back to me
Like an obedient dog returning to its owner.

I hold you again in my loving grip and take a deep breath, awwhhh.
I start running, picking up speed quickly.
Then I push all my energy against the ground,
And I'm in the air, gliding, and defying gravity.
Nothing matters now.
As I see the hoop approaching quickly I
Stretch my hand up in the air,
Lengthening me like an accordion.

I bring my hand around from behind my head and push it into the hoop
Like a catapult throwing rocks against a castle wall.

SLAM DUNK

Ben Hoffman, Grade 8
Tierra Linda Middle School

I See Him*

I see him through the eyes of an admiring child,
Though my face smiles for my friend
My heart is aching and crying at the thought of him being gone tomorrow.

I make myself think of right here right now.
Today he holds my hand, even if tomorrow he won't be able to.
He smiles at me, so I capture his beautiful face in my heart and remember him.

"What is the point of all this?" I wonder.
Life is lived only to die.
But I can't help remembering his words of hope after death.

Suddenly I want that hope of a promised eternal future, as never before.
I long for that day, that marvelous glorious day,
When we'll be going home together.

So now that I feel his kiss on my cheek and hear him whisper "I love you,"
I can accept his departure from me.
And I will always be a better person because I see him now and will see him again.

I saw him,
I loved him,
And I will remember him forever!

Jenna Weir, Grade 9
Pathways Charter School
*Written for my Dear Uncle Carl

Me and My Feet

When I hear the music my feet start tapping
Even in preschool my teacher says I need to start napping
I need to stop moving
It's just when I hear the music I can't stop grooving.
When I hear the music I hear it through my ear
I will dance even if you sing a cheer
Some music brings forth a tear
But the music I hear comes from my heart
And that's where it starts
There is some music like Alvin and the Chipmunks
And that kind of funk
But some listen to Rap or Punk
Some people think that's just junk
But the music is in their heart
And this is where it starts

Gabby Frazier, Grade 8
Calvary Chapel of YL

Follow Your Dreams

It can be hard to believe that life is so cold
We had always thought that our life was like gold
But when we spread our wings and fly
We could tell that it was hard but we try

Time to time we look around
To find that we all fall to the ground
But we all get up and try again
So just remember that you can do anything if you try
again and again

Look to the left look to the right
Look for the star that shines so bright
Now flap your wings and start to fly
Reach for the sky and fly real high

Jocelyn De Avila, Grade 8
Madrona Middle School

Music

Music is what flows through my veins,
Music is what pumps my blood.

I always have to hear it playing,
Especially when I have to concentrate.

I love listening to almost any genre,
As long as it gets me going,

Music surrounds me, engages me, engulfs me.
If I'm tired, or blue, or in a preppy mood,
It's what I look forward to.
My music is my medicine,
My music is my soul,
My music is what gets me through life.

Devin McFarland, Grade 8
EV Cain Middle School

Frisky Fall

Summer ends,
Fall begins
With the fresh smell of brisk air floating.
Newly fallen leaves surround me, and
Apple pie invites me to grandma's window sill.
Leaves turn and
Slowly drift sadly from their home.
The leaves lay silent as
I get ready to pounce into a
Pile of Happiness.
Pop,
Crackle.
I jump over a million times that day.
The crisp weather
Shows my breath in the air.
Winter arrives,
The days turn gray and a
Frozen hush covers the ground as
Frisky fall ends, and wishful winter arrives,
Preparing for the rebirth of spring

Stephanie Paulson, Grade 7
Rolling Hills Country Day School

March

Month of spring
Time for celebration
Happy, glorious, joyful, green
Saint Patrick's Day!

Alejandra Vargas, Grade 7
John Charles Fremont Intermediate School

Crinkly, Crunch, Tippity, Thump

"Crinkle, crinkle," moan the leaves,
Under the weight of my new school shoes.
They mourn the loss of their brothers,
The bright colored blotches descending into the grave.

"Crunch, crunch," whispers the white world,
That lies frozen beneath my Christmas boots.
As a geisha paints her skin, to hide her face,
So does the earth hide its shame with a blanket of ice.

"Tippity, tap," sings the formal footwear,
Which assist me to walk to Easter service.
The flowers in bloom are a kind reminder
Of the risen Christ and the new life He brings.

"Thump, thump!" shouts the ground.
As I run barefoot in celebration of vacation.
The warm breeze carries the kites to freedom
And so will my Father carry my spirit where it can truly rest.

All seasons were formed by the Creator,
That we may learn what they have to teach.

Tenney Rizzo, Grade 8
Visalia Christian Academy

He Loves Me, He Loves Me Not

I'm not sure of what he thinks
but he knows how I feel
so I bought a bouquet of flowers
picking each petal one by one
I do all of this just to find an answer
either he loves me or loves me not

Manuela Ramirez, Grade 7
Sarah McGarvin Intermediate School

This Is Where It Will All End

She was my heart, she was my soul.
She was the girl who made me whole.
She made me whole, she made me one.
She made me laugh with a silly pun.

Her puns were cute, she was too.
Now she's gone, what can I do?
What should I do, where should I go?
All these questions, I really don't know.

I do not know but I did care.
We made such a beautiful pair.
This pair is dead, so am I.
Your, "I love you" was just a lie.

All your lies, I did believe.
My heart is broken, you did achieve.
You achieved you also failed.
You're now sad like it just hailed.

It just hailed on your life.
You could have been my lovely wife.
You're not my wife, nor my friend
This is where it will all end.

Jestoni Caban, Grade 7
Almond Tree Middle School

Nerd

Just because I get A's,
It doesn't mean I'm a bookworm.
It doesn't mean I study all day.
It doesn't mean I don't have a life.

Just because I use my brain,
It doesn't mean I was born intelligent.
It doesn't mean I always know.

Just because I'm smart at times,
It doesn't mean I can't blank-out.
It doesn't mean I can't be dumb at times.

Just because you are jealous,
Don't call me a Nerd.

Sze Chieh Chen, Grade 7
Lawson Middle School

Ode to Guitars

Les Pauls, SGS,
Strats, Teles,
Frankensteins,
Lead 1s, Lead 2s,
Warlocks, Flying Vs
Gigmasters,
And don't forget the brands:
Fender, Dean, Gibson,
Epiphone, Martin,
Paul Reed Smith,
And Ibanez.
These guitars,
All shapes and sizes,
Rock my soul,
Propel my heart,
And amp my feelings.
When I turn the volume to 11,
The lights go down,
The dark goes up,
The licks crank out.

Adam Colcord, Grade 8
Crittenden Middle School

Me

My name is Kevin
I remember when I was seven
I used to play ball
At my house in the fall
We would swim in the pool
My sister would act the fool
My dad would barbecue
And play pool with a cue
My mom would read the good book
And give the fools bad looks
And the dogs would play
Sometimes they would play all day
And when the sun went down
And Kevin the clown
Would smile real sad
We know the day was not all that bad.

Kevin Mealey, Grade 7
St Mary's School

babies

little babies
big babies
newborn babies
chubby babies
skinny babies
all different size
but to my eyes
all the same to me
and very annoying at three

Amy Nguyen, Grade 7
Sarah McGarvin Intermediate School

Now There's Light

I was in the dark
I couldn't see
Now I'm found
I can be

In a lifeless life
It's always night
You came in
Now there's light

Christian Burnsed, Grade 8
EV Cain Middle School

Pressure

Like a headache
Keeps coming back again
It sometimes never stops
You feel like
You are going to explode
Teachers keep giving you more work
when you already have too much
I feel like a mouse going through a maze
Just getting to the end to enjoy life
You always have a story to share
You will remember what paid off
Maybe even learn from them
Experience again and again.

Ruby Diaz, Grade 8
St Alphonsus School

The Game

The game starts
in hopes of killing
their hearts
the Porterville Pirates that is.

Our Giants make basket
after basket, free throw
after free throw 'til
the buzzer goes off.

Halftime's over. score:
fifty to ten
we're winning

Again basket
after basket, free throw
after free throw
buzzer goes off
end of game.

score:
101 to 40
WE WON!!!!

Zac Bland, Grade 8
La Joya Middle School

Afraid of the Dark

Through the dark is where my life's been at
Similar to the life of a lonely bat
No one here to share joy with you
Afraid but there's nothing you can do
Pain and sorrow, no way to get it out
So inside you scream and shout
Wish you had a flashlight that's bright
And lead you through this dark long night
I've been broken down and not built back up
I'm on my own, alone and dreadfully stuck
In this world, no one sees you
You're invisible and your nightmares jump into
Reality and come true
It's like a flower without the sun
Like a Catholic school, without a nun
Like a baby without his blanket
Or a child without her train set
I will rise, by myself
I will rise without any help
I will rise to the top
And keep my joy, it will never stop

Bree Peters, Grade 8
Dodson Middle School

Ready. Set. Go.
Ready.

The engine roared to life
as the crowd screamed and cheered.
I sat anxiously.

Adrenaline rushing to the sound of speed,
knowing one wrong turn
could be the end for me.

Heart beating against the echo of screams,
winning this race
would complete my wildest dreams.

Set.

I had the need for speed.
I thrived to win.
But don't we all?

The competition in my eyes
blazing with aggression.
Speed! Win! Success!

Blocking out distractions.
Watching the announcer.
The flag went down.

Go.

Myasandi Aung, Grade 8
La Joya Middle School

My Poetry Assignment

It must be sixteen lines,
But no more than twenty-one.
It's got to have a million literary devices,
If a million equals four.
The first word of each line must be capitalized.
Punctuation goes at the end.
The counting clock is ticking the time,
For I must finish my poem soon.
It must have a very good title and be truthful by line,
And a great magic 3 too.
My mouse goes *click, click, click,*
As I edit this page.
I'm so close to the finish,
Almost done with my poem,
Like finding the solution to an ancient riddle.
So there it is.
This is my poetry assignment.

Nick Entin, Grade 7
Rolling Hills Country Day School

The Magic Book

Look! It's a book!
It is more interesting that it looks.
I was curious to see what it was about.
So I opened it without a doubt.

The title is "Magic."
It is neatly covered in plastic with very interesting graphics.
Now very curious, I wonder.
What magic lies under?

Excited I opened the book.
And to my surprise, I was hooked!
With interesting tricks nicely described.
And magic materials, you can't believe your eyes.

I read and read until it filled up my head.
And suddenly my mother called me…
"It's time for bed!"

Ryan Fong, Grade 7
Holy Family Catholic School

Summers

I love summers, three months is just not
enough time to kick back and relax.

No school, no homework, no more getting up early.
More time with friends and family, that's what I call living.

But if you are like me you are in a basketball league
playing your best just to impress the scouts and coaches.

Summers are the best.

Dorian Walters, Grade 8
Orville Wright Middle School

Butterfly

A butterfly soars
Gently through the sky it goes
Freedom in the air
Xitlali Ramirez, Grade 7
Almond Tree Middle School

Ricardo Cubeiro

Fast
Active
Outgoing

Wishes to play football
Dreams of flying
Want to have a Viper
Who wonders about college
Who fears space
Who is afraid of rides
Who likes pies
Who believes in ghosts
Who loves mom
Who loves dad
Who loves kids
Who loves marriage
Who plans to be a cop
Who plans to not be a hobo
Who plans to be a football player
Whose final destination is a Super Bowl
Ricardo Cubeiro, Grade 7
Almond Tree Middle School

Friends

Friends are…

People who care
Those who are there
Making up dares
Oh the fun that we share!
Eating ice cream
Making each other scream
Lots of indoor jokes
We make while sipping our Cokes
Talking about troubles,
Making lots of bubbles.

Having fun
Sitting in the sun
Not telling lies
Dragging out our "goodbyes!"
Going shopping
Watching popcorn popping
There is none that I like most
And I am not trying to boast
But I am truly blessed
'Cause you guys are the best!!
Melissa Stewart, Grade 8
Citrus Hills Intermediate School

Deadly Innocence

As I walk toward the glistening tide,
I feel the gritty texture working its way between my toes.
A gentle zephyr lifts my hair from my face,
And I can sense the familiar smell of salt and rock.
When I finally reach my destination,
The water splashes against my ankles.
Spraying a faint mist into the air,
I can taste the familiar salty flavor.
As I admire the vastness and clarity of the cerulean tapestry,
The orb of light above shines its rays lovingly onto the sea,
An the sea reflects it back shimmering with an air of elegant simplicity.
The rippling surface seems almost unreal,
Like a fantasy land a child may dream about in a deep slumber.
It is the epitome of tranquility.
The lure of the tide drags me dangerously closer to the heart of the sea.
I remember the previous lives that had been taken by this briny deep,
And realize that deception could be deadly.
Elly Nakahara, Grade 8
Rolling Hills Country Day School

Daddy

I think of you each morning
I dream of you each night
I wonder how you are
If you are all right
I learned the world's toughest lesson and I learned it on that fateful day
It was that our time here is numbered when God took you away
But what we should remember is he's in a better place reunited with his brother
Even though he left his loved ones including his mother
Daddy's little girl a nickname I used to love to be called
Brings back memories like how you were always there to pick me up whenever I'd fall
We must take life for what it's worth
You did that like it was easy and didn't take much work
I will remember all the memories that we made
I'll keep them forever locked up in my heart where no one will ever take
Erika Canchola, Grade 7
St Hilary Elementary School

Beach

Sand tickles my feet, salt glazes my mouth, foam licks my legs, wind rustles my hair
Waves lap at the shore, calm and steady, the repetition of a heartbeat
I watch shimmering fish dart this way and that, tiny silver scales glint in the sunlight
Small fluffy clouds dot the vast sky, like whiffs of cotton candy
Little grains of sand are wedged in between my toes
Sun rays glare on the water, blinding me for a second
Giving the sea the glitter of diamonds
Squishy seaweed brush past my legs, then are left behind on the shore
Abandoned there as if the ocean had thrown it out as a punishment
Previous seaweeds scattered on the beach look more like giant raisins
Wrinkly and basking in the sun
Waves knock me over; I retire to the dry, powdery sand
Closing my eyes, breathing in the salty fresh air, listening to the ocean's heart beat
As the waves roll and smash the shore, I fall asleep
My heart lost out at sea, my pulse in harmony with the ocean.
Maggie Fong, Grade 8
St Joseph's School of the Sacred Heart

The Boy

Deep down in this boy, this young man
Is hope and despair
Wishing to show his other side
A heart that he doesn't get to share
Thirteen years of teasing
Life without those who can accept him
Like a shipped box with no address
A fear of always regretting
Haunts him and taunts him
To look up at someone not so different
And beg not to hurt him another day
With sorrowful eyes
Something no one should have to do
But a day he goes on, is a day he is adored
By someone who sees his brighter future

Keara Reardon, Grade 8
Adaline E Kent Middle School

You Make Me Happy

When I wake up
In the morning
I think of you
Only of you
When I see your eyes
My heart turns pure
Just like my love for you

You make me happy
You make me smile
All day, all night
I think of you

When I am sad
You make me happy
I know you will always be there
To help me out
And by my side you will always stay
You make my day and you make my world
Be filled with colors
The only thing I wish
Is for you to be happy
Just like I am with you

Sulam Fontaine, Grade 8
Palm Desert Middle School

Pencils

When we are two years old we may have our first pencil.
With a pencil we write our feelings, or work.
We also sharpen it.
With pencils we write and erase of writings.
Pencils are many different type of thickness.
But that is fine.
Because with a pencil I write this poem.

Clarissa Arellano, Grade 7
St Mary's School

Lost

Never will he return to me.
My arms can never hold him close.
My heart cries for him.
For my love,
my love,
is Lost.

His eyes I will never see again.
I can never, hear his voice.
Never will I feel his arm wrapped around me.
For my love,
my love,
is lost.

Can anyone hear my cry?
Will I ever feel again?
Can I move on with my life?
Without the love,
from my love.
For my love,
my love,
is lost.

Sarah Giles, Grade 8
Santa Rosa Technology Magnet School

My Great Grandma Mamina

Nothing is more painful than the loss of a loved one.
Not a shot in the arm,
Or a rout in the Super Bowl,
Or even a Stock Market crash.

My Grandma Mamina could make a sick monkey laugh.
She was like the sun.
Always cheerful but could understand if anyone was sad.

On her death day
The plants cried.
Leaving their dew on the grass
As their way of mourning Mamina.

When my mom and I buried her,
I saw the whole of nature surrounding us.
For she was the garden queen
With the green thumb
And the huge heart.

Austin Schoff, Grade 7
Rolling Hills Country Day School

Robby

R iding my bike
O ver the mountains I like
B ecause I like fresh air
B ut sometime I ride my bike out of despair
Y et I ride my bike, and that's what I like.

Robby Cano, Grade 7
St Mary of Assumption School

Chaotic Rhapsody

The world ebbs and throbs, pounding in a consistent beat, booming to the rhythm swaying to the tides.
Every voice, every heart, every thought, moves in sync with the tune.
The whole world connected by music, flowing and escalating, streaming and pouring consistently,
Pounding with the vitality of life.
Suddenly the symphony of life is shattered into chaos,
Falling into a discord of thoughts emotions and feeling, inundating everyone,
Deluging the population swamping and choking them.
Then a bright, clear fluorescent sound of the trumpet piercing the rhapsody and fractioning it forever,
Leading to the slow arrangement of musical instruments following the bold leader.
The eddies and tide pools flow back into to the proper places, swirling with heavy mist.
The musical storm has abated.
The slow tide returns, on the endless sea in the kingdom of melody.

Josiah Godfrey, Grade 9
Mount Everest Academy

Yosemite Valley

The Earth is full of many things
Yosemite Valley is where nature sings
It sings out happiness so that we can smile
It gives us shade so we can rest for a while

Nature makes us feel comfortable so that we can feel free
It gives us a cool, silent place where we can dream
The trickling sound of a rain drop on the ground
Can lead to so much more such as the sound of thunder and sometimes lightning is found

The waterfalls mist cools your skin
As the cold air soothes you when you breathe in
Then at night the stars brighten in dark sky
And sometimes you will see shooting stars vanish by

The wildlife is beautiful
The birds and the deer
The fish in the lakes
The lakes that are a clear as a mirror

Yosemite is there for you when you are dreaming
Dreaming about the stars and the lakes gleaming
The weather is perfect, it is warm and it is calm
I want to stay forever but I have to move on

Travis Woodward, Grade 8
Sacred Heart School

Me and My Heart

My love, my all, you've already dominated my heart what else could you take from me that I hold so dearly to my life? You know that I love you; don't you know that at least? You are worth more to me than any expensive thing I own. And I know I've failed in many ways as being your lover, but believe me I am trying my best to stabilize this love between us. If you ever left me, my world would end up collapsing and I'd see no point in staying alive. My heart would end up dying from losing the lover it holds so dearly to itself, but it would be terribly afraid of perishing because if it did, that means it would end up losing all your love it stored in itself. My heart would not be able to take this pain, this pain would be worse than any incurable disease that has ever been known to mankind. Well, whether or not you find a new and better lover that I never was just remember that I always belonged to you through everything we've been through and whether I keep my constant breath or not my heart will try its best to stay alive so it won't be able to lose the love you gave it and I promise you for as long as I live I will never forget about you nor forget about how much I loved you.

Tiffanie Manopichetwatana, Grade 7
Bethel Christian School

MaryBeth

You've left me, now I am dead
Your absence tears straight through me
Black bleeds through the warmth which once was red
You killed me
I wish you knew how it feels
Take a dagger to my heart
It feels so real
Doesn't she know she's pierced me deep?
Doesn't she care?
Racing tears from my face, they seep
Your reasons are convoluted caused by screaming voices
Throw them out, clear your head
You'll regret those self-hearted choices
Those destructive forces pull us apart
They don't matter; let's leave them behind
For you I'll pour out my heart
Come home, forgiveness waits for you

Courtney Niemeir, Grade 9
University Preparatory School

A Perfect World

The rain came down and washed away all of her troubles,
And the mud,
and the loneliness,
And the dead leaves,
And the sorrow,
And the yellow grass,
And the madness,
And the silt,
And the anger,
And the moldy logs and sticks,
And the bad dreams,
And the starless nights,
And the famine,
And the hate,
And most of everything mean and nasty she knew,
Because life goes on and brings joy to those who
Live it.

Rachel Molina, Grade 7
Round Valley Elementary School

Northern Lights

Lights that are above the sky
Where do you all go?
Do you go to the ends of the Earth?
Or do you just stay at home?
Do you visit your relatives in the North?
Or do you just show off your beauty?
I wonder if you're blue when you're sad
Or if you're yellow when you're happy.
Do you have lots of friends up there in the sky?
Or if you're very lonely and about to cry?
I want to know! I want to know!
But you just won't tell me.

Mavrick Gaunt, Grade 8
Madrona Middle School

Life

What really is life?
Life is a gift from God.
We can love the gift of life.
We can hate the gift of life.
But we all have to live it.

Life is also hope, love, and dreams.
We hope for happiness and lots of other things in life.
We love because it is the only magic we have in life.
We dream about what we want in life.

Life is hard.
Life is never easy.
We all get mad or tired of life.
But we should be mad at ourselves not life.
We have to work to make life happy.
We have to accept the gift of life and live it.

Pauline Nafash, Grade 7
Holy Family Catholic School

School

My last year of middle school
The best and exciting year
8th grade
Graduation screams in my ear

This year was filled with lots of challenges
Then the last day came
I will be moving onto bigger dreams
Yet I will be the same

The hard work has paid off
But the year went by so fast
Looking forward to becoming a freshmen
Graduation will be a blast

Scott Pearce, Grade 8
South Tahoe Middle School

Sports

Sports are great for bringing family and friends together,
Every time you play them you wish they'd last forever.

Everything you do and everything you say,
All you want to do is play, play, play!

I like baseball it's my personal favorite,
When I'm at bat I usually get a good hit.

Now I'm at first,
And ready to burst.

The ball is hit and I start to run,
it's out of the park, now for some fun.

Tyler Johnston, Grade 7
Monte Vista Christian School

I'm Not the One

Why do I sit and wait for you?
I know you will never come.
And yet I sit here every night.
Hoping, praying, and wishing.
That somehow you could love me.
But I know that will never come.
Because I'm not the one.

Kelly Shearing, Grade 9
University Preparatory School

Sea

The blue sea is calm
It bangs against the seashore
Everyone has fun.

Matthew Hernandez, Grade 8
Almond Tree Middle School

Rainstorm

Hit the ground with
gentle grace
and open up your
liquid skin.
Let the sunlight you once stole,
spill over,
erupting into gold,
and breath.
And let the moonlight
glide over the soil
in its sad and silver flesh.
But hold on tightly to
the memories
and take them with you when you sink
deep into this earth,
forever and forgotten.

Ela Banerjee, Grade 9
Roseville High School

From the Altar to the Grave

Been together for so long
And all a sudden
Things just go wrong
We love each other so much
But the older people do not see
That we were meant to be
My heart beats when I am with you
They want me to find someone new
I just don't see why
I just start to cry
And I want to die
We promised each other to never let go
And that is a promise
That I will keep forever
We will be together
From the altar to the grave

Christine Phan, Grade 8
Holy Family Catholic School

My Day Today

Today is the day that we're with our advisory class
Although it started out being fun,
And it slightly got dull towards the middle
I got tired easily, which felt like rocks were on me that weigh about a ton.

This felt like La Vina Middle School,
And it seems like they have tedious classes
I don't like the day today,
And I feel like lying down on grasses

Seventh graders are taking a writing test,
And I'm not having a blast at all
I thought it would be a kick back day
Which appears that my plans started to fall

My day was all right,
Next time it should be tight.

Mary Jane Cabanban, Grade 8
Almond Tree Middle School

Teenager

T here is more to life than increasing its speed
E fforts and sublimation of the ego
E veryone points to the other man
N othing can be achieved without working for it
A ttachments and forgetting to worry over success or failures
G rief is the state of mind
E ntirely eliminated by patience
R estlessness of the mind and unsteadiness of character

Harsimran Gill, Grade 8
Martin Murphy Middle School

An Ode to My Mom and Dad

My mom and dad, as the moon and the sun,
both gave me light, night light and daylight,
nighttime and daytime for me to read and learn;
and they're following all my life,
worrying, caring, catching as the bind,
surround me day and night,
warming and embracing to hope I shine.
My mom and dad, as the river and the mountain,
both gave me the source of life —
River as the source of soft water, breath to my heart when I need it;
Mountain as the might that surrounds my health
as the plain seed.
Day by day, night by night,
over and over, I grow and grow.
My mom and dad, older and older, however and ever,
a puppet under their eyes, a need under their care,
a precious gift under their hands,
a love they could not lose,
a I am, will be their child forever...

Franklin Ngo, Grade 7
Sarah McGarvin Intermediate School

Does He?

I love a guy but does he have feelings for me?
I love a guy but does he know I exist?
I love a guy but does he know my name?
I love a guy but does he think I'm beautiful?
I love a guy but does he love me back?

Jessica Garcia, Grade 7
Richland Jr High School

The Journey

Drip, plop! Drip, plop! Drip, plop!
All my water droplet brothers and sisters
Have gone before me.
Now it's my turn.
Drip…
I fall through empty space
Expecting to plop.
But I don't, so I wait
And wait, and wait.
Plop!
Where have I landed?
Not one of my siblings is in sight!
The landscape here is foreign to me.
It's a desert out here,
Hot and barren.
With the sun glaring at me,
I journey through empty, gray lands; rest on tall, green trees;
And slide down steep, transparent mountains.
Now, I approach a steaming volcano of metal.
No! I'm not gong to make it!
Hiss!

Amber Fong, Grade 7
Rolling Hills Country Day School

I Am Me

I am funny and smart
I wonder if the wars will ever end
I hear people laughing
I see Daniel Radcliffe in front of me
I want to always be happy
I am funny and smart

I pretend to dance in front of the world
I feel like a pink unicorn
I touch the softest bed worldwide.
I worry about my brother's future
I cry about the thoughts of my friends leaving
I am funny and smart

I understand that life is not fair
I say life should be fair
I dream about being an architect
I hope I never need to grow-up
I am funny and sweet

Anu Varshneya, Grade 7
Lawson Middle School

Sonnet for Thee

My heart so painful watches you leave me —
A tear in my soul, a rip in my chest.
In my eyes, tears scream out like a banshee,
My arms reaching to clutch you to my breast.

My legs twitch to move in your direction —
The sun, the stars, the moon and the bright sky,
Blink out, one by one, in my rejection,
As you walk away without a goodbye.

You are always moving up in success —
My cold spirit is frozen black and white.
Unable to move on or make progress,
My tears form lakes and oceans in the night.

My heart is crumbled to dust before thee,
My heart so painful watches you leave me.

Samantha Zhang, Grade 8
Canyon Hills Jr High School

Enemies

When I'm playing my video games
I jump for joy whenever I'm winning,
But when I'm losing
I feel like throwing the controller across the room.

My mom hollers, "Come here!"
I feel so misunderstood,
Because I don't like to lose to just a video game.

Julian Perez, Grade 8
Almond Tree Middle School

When Time Flies By

Days turn into months, months turn into years
The past becomes a memory
Memories slowly fade away
The love soon disappears
Who we used to be
We will never be again
Our lives are a new life
We no longer see another
Because we have taken a separate route
What happened to before?
When we used to be like one
Promises were made then
Always to be kept, never to be broken
That we should always be together forever
But look what happened, to all of us
Who used to be so close, be like one whole
This happened because
Days turn into months, months turn into years
The past becomes a memory
And the memories
Slowly fade away.

Chedva Vojdany, Grade 8
Perutz Etz Jacob Hebrew Academy

The Mask We Wear

The mask covers us all;
The dark covers your face,
And covers your liberal feelings;
What is that?
That is the mask we wear.

Our strange different faces;
Sometimes funny,
And sometimes annoying;
Shows your real face besides
The strongest mask we wear.

Behavior changes everything;
Talking changes everything;
The artificial mask
Which comes out of the blue,
Hides the partial behavior,
Makes the feeling dreadful.

Shreejit Padmanabhan, Grade 7
Thornton Jr High School

Rain

Dripping of tear drops
The sky is weeping
All the flowers enjoy the drinking
The dark clouds fill the sky
Grass tops beneath our feet are sinking
All nature is being garnished
By a light sprinkle
The coolness is like a breath of fresh air

Nicole Garcia, Grade 8
Madrona Middle School

Soar

There is a wish that many have,
To soar.
To fly.
Yes there are planes,
And yes there are jets.
Yet,
There is no thrill
Unless the wind
Beats upon your face.
The clouds,
An ocean beneath you.
The sky above,
Clear and never ending.
The air,
Crisp and clear.
Unstoppable.
Unmovable.
Anything is
Possible...

Elizabeth Sailors, Grade 7
Anthony Traina Elementary School

Stars

Watching over us
Guiding us in the darkness
Providing us light.

Nicole Santiago, Grade 8
Almond Tree Middle School

Sizzle

A family cookout in the summer
In my favorite outfit
Having the ridiculous idea
Trying to eat baby-back ribs

One drip-drop
Missing the plate
Landing on my pants.

What to tell my mom
She'll be furious

Sitting,
Thinking
What to do.

Sauce sprinting down my leg
Into my shoe.

Loren Adams, Grade 7
Southpointe Christian School

Hurtful Love

When I see you pass by
I feel a tear slide down my cheek
I feel my face growing hot
And my heart becoming weak.

On cold, empty nights
I'm unable to sleep
Only thinking of you
Simply makes my heart weep.

My heart awaits for the day
When the sun will shine once more
The day when our love will be
Just as powerful as before.

Days have passed
And years have went
Yet you haven't come
Leaving me in a world full of torment.

Yet I have resigned myself
That we can never be together
We will be like two unknown strangers
Avoiding each other forever.

Mayra Nuñez, Grade 8
Almond Tree Middle School

Alone

As I sit alone
Trying to act tough
I tell myself it's not enough
Trying to smile
But all I can do is frown,
While looking at everyone around
Bursting in tears
Scars on my arms
My face never looks alarmed
I've waited for my death
Ever since I've lost my best friend
Ever since she past away
No happiness comes
Not even a day
Thinking about the past
I finally knew my life is about to last

Lory Pabalate, Grade 7
Almond Tree Middle School

Good Bye

"He died"
Mom recited
All I heard, as hot tears flooded my eyes
I cried
Good bye
I thought
The ocean was rough
Crashing against the shore with anger
Sorrowful gray clouds filled the skies
My siblings began to cry
My uncle was...
Dead
I felt enclosed in wave of despair
Plunged into the depths of the sea
Drowning, gasping for air
It can't be true
It's not my uncle
But how...
Motorcycle accident on my dad's Harley
He rode into our lives on a motorcycle
And rode out on one, without a goodbye

Andre Brasil, Grade 8
La Joya Middle School

The Charmed Love

Rose petals and soporific talk
Filched angel heart and lover's lock
Blood of bird, unicorn tail
Fluff of cloud and bride's old veil
Lover, lover, be there for each other
Kiss me now or forever suffer
When the clock strikes the indefinite one
Beware a caveat that soon will come

Solange Etessami, Grade 7
The Mirman School

My Love My Mom*

Mom you have been there
all my life in the good and the bad,
you have cherished me and set me good examples.
And if it weren't for you I don't know where I would be
And I thank you for all that you've done for me.

Ariana Perez, Grade 8
Shadow Hills Intermediate School
*Dedicated to my mom Rocio Perez

Ode to an Elephant

Walking, walking, walking away
He dreams of plains of Africa,
To be free
And walk with family and friends
Wanting to leave but can't
Alone with the other animals stuck along with him.
Dreaming, dreaming, dreaming of far away
Somewhere to roam in a carefree world
Able to eat anything anytime anywhere,
Daydreaming of somewhere past his sight
A glimpse or two of a watering hole,
Or maybe members of his natural enemy.
Though he doesn't see them here,
He wants that feeling of danger.
Dreaming, dreaming of walking away,
Unable to do anything but dream,
Wanting,
Oh so desperately wanting to leave
The prison cell of my bedroom,
To leave the safety of my bed,
But all he can do is sit and dream.

Allison Dorantes, Grade 7
Joan MacQueen Middle School

I Don't Know What to Write About

I don't know what to write about.
My mind is so blank, I just want to shout.
I don't know how I will figure out,
What I am going to write about.

I can't even think of a rhyming line.
This poem is taking up so much time.
I keep on searching my wandering mind,
Trying to find the perfect rhyming line.

First, I should probably think of a theme.
Maybe I'll write about my softball team,
Or maybe, about my favorite blue jeans.
It's gonna be hard to think of a theme.

Maybe I'll come up with a clever pun.
Then I'll be able to have some fun.
I can go outside and play in the sun.
Hey, look! My poem is done!

Paige Maberry, Grade 8
EV Cain Middle School

Baseball

B aseball is America's pastime.
A udience's screaming as you round the bases.
S melling the hot dogs roasting as you wait for food.
E ating your food as you watch.
B iting your lip as you wait anxiously for the pitch.
A t last the pitch.
L et's see if it has the distance.
L ong gone.

Garrett D'Angelo, Grade 8
Santa Rosa Technology Magnet School

Words…

Words are paper roses and magazine cover skies…
Picture perfect moments, curly hair, blue eyes
Quiet rooms and sewing machines
Electric guitars and ripped up jeans
Train tracks and how the bluebird sings
Hands stained red and violin strings
Blood, sweat and tears stream down
A smile that's returned by a frown
Little yellow flowers and big brown teddy bears
Bright orange balloons and weekend fairs
Neon lights and cardboard butterflies
Coffee mugs and the purple sunrise
Scotch tape and broken hearts
Diamond rings and shopping carts
Magazine cover skies rain on me
Paper roses wilt, crashing waves on the sea
The feeling of a little boy's kisses
The beauty, when a Miss turns into a Mrs.
True love at first sight.
A hug, with all his might
Words are paper roses and magazine cover skies…

Lisa McCroskey, Grade 7
Monte Vista Christian School

Dreams

When you fall asleep what do you do?
Dream.
You dream of places
Beyond the stars where there aren't any cars.
How do you travel? You ask.
By flying of course,
Just like a bird does ever,
So quietly and gently.
Anything is possible when you dream.
You can twirl your hair, scream, shout,
And blurt out loud without
Making a sound.
A mysterious place are dreams.
But if you just believe they just might
Turn into reality.
Just as if it wasn't a dream all along.

Karly Alfaro, Grade 8
Spring Grove Elementary School

The Beach

As we travel to the place,
The place where there is space,
To laugh and giggle and run free,
A place where you can see true beauty,
A place where you can dream,
To be anything you wish,
Who knows maybe you can be a fish,
Or maybe,
A captain at sea
Or a pirate with booty.

Tyler Walker, Grade 9
Valley Christian High School

A Spring Morning

The sun awakened,
Blossoms all the flowers,
With its gentle glow.

Allison Bannar, Grade 7
South Tahoe Middle School

The MP4

The MP4 that sings to me,
The MP4 with a lotus as a background,
The MP4 that gives me company,
The MP4 with great voices,
The MP4 that had fallen to the floor,
The MP4 that had punk songs,
The MP4 that had Chinese songs,
The MP4 that had instrumental songs,
The MP4 that releases me from danger,
The MP4 that I sleep with every night,
The MP4 that can't play with people,
The MP4 that gives me hope.

Tony Ng, Grade 8
Purple Lotus International Institute

Amazing Grace

Amazing grace.
A voice that speaks,
Within my heart,
Eternally.
A cry within,
A cry without.
A shout that echoes,
All about.
Amazing grace.
A place for me,
To reach the lost,
And teach the free.
A hope for all,
A hope for me.
A place that all,
I need to be,
Is ME.

Delanie Shepherd, Grade 8
Home Educator's Resource Center

The Temple

The constant hum vibrates the air.
The sound of cloth scraping the marble floor makes one shiver.
The cold, smooth marble floor sends a chill up your spine.
The intoxicating smell of incense and crushed flower petals glazes the eyes
of everyone in the room and makes your mind drive away.
The chanting makes you drowsy while the sharp clang of cymbals
temporarily awakens everyone from their unearthly slumber.
Men wearing dark robes shuffle around while fingering beads.
The constant, sweet clang of coins as they impact with other coins
in the donation box constantly draws your attention.
The bright auras created by the candles illuminate the surrounding darkness
and its fine flame warms the body and soul.
The golden, intricate statues line the walls while producing an unworldly gleam
from the candlelight.
This is a Buddhist Temple; mysterious, dark, cold.

Justin Wong, Grade 8
St Joseph's School of the Sacred Heart

The Power of Dreams

When giants seem to surround you
Don't be afraid because there are others behind you.
Don't be afraid to stand up for your rights and dreams
Because if you do, you can accomplish anything.
Remember the sacrifices people have made
So you could succeed and live in the freedoms of today.
You know deep inside that the world has not seen
What one person can do when they're in pursuit of their dreams.
Never give up, never give in, never back down.
Give it all you've got, whatever it is, the time is now!
Keep moving forward, don't stop trying, oh no,
Because history will remember what you were fighting for!

Gadiel Lopez, Grade 9
Lucerne Valley Jr/Sr High School

Seasons on the Countryside

The early sun rises high, into the very soft, blue sky.
Flowers don't seem to stop, blossoming in every crop.
The animals come from every direction, from all the meadows, every section.

Then the sun becomes bright and hot. Is the sky soft now? I think not.
The flowers and plants start to grow, from every hedge, from every row.
The animals become very lazy, the bees, the mammals, everything's crazy.

The sun starts dulling; it rises later, the sky is dark; it hangs bitter.
The plants all ripen; the smell so sweet, they are so delicious; ready to eat.
The animals rush, expecting cold, the wind blows down the rabbit's hole.

Then the sun is dark, the wind so cold. The sky is gray, so very bold.
The plants hide in the soil, the vines start to curl and coil.
The animals sleep with tummies full, unaware of the cold winds pull.

Then the early sun rises again,
The plants and animals live once more,
Hoping to do good before spring ends and summer begins.

McKenna Johnson, Grade 8
Almondale Middle School

Ode to the Mall

Baby doll tops and straight leg jeans
Even a dress that looks like green beans.
Wedges, high-heels, and Uggs galore.
Tennis shoes, ballet flats, boots and more.

Teenage girls searching for their prom dress.
Little girls pretending to be a damsel in distress.
A group of women looking for their perfect makeup.
Elderly women drinking coffee from the Dixie cup.

The mall can cater to your every need.
Especially if you want to participate in a stampede.
You can unlock your social and fashionable side
Visit your local mall and join in this hang out worldwide.

Taylor Singleton, Grade 8
La Joya Middle School

Long Lost Dream

I have a dream, a long lost dream
You've probably heard before but not today
Mine is a twist on a long lost dream
Most children dream of becoming
A doctor, an astronaut, a pop star
But not me; I dream of changing the world
Ever since I was four I have danced
I loved it the first time I hit the floor
The music takes me away into my own little world
As soon as my tap shoe hits the floor I am ready to perform
When I dance it looks like I am floating on air
But I don't just want to change the world by dance
But by my attitude, the way I act
I want to set a good example; a good example for my fans
I want the parents to be confident
Confident in what I teach
I won't just teach them about anything
I will teach about Jesus' love; the love for you and me
That's how I am going to change the world
I will work my way to my dream
We all have to start somewhere!

Elyse Anderson, Grade 7
Linfield Christian School

Trees

Trees,
You dance in the wind
When it blows really hard
Your leaves are like clothes on your body
All different, but still matching
You are nature's lungs
Giving air for us to breathe
You dance in the wind
When it blows really hard
Trees

Nicole Wong, Grade 8
Madrona Middle School

A Camper's Senses

The wind rushes
The pine branches twitch in the wind
An owl perched in a tree hoots
A tree sings with the wind

A fire blazes with ashes of light
The sweet smell of marshmallow fills the forest air
A wolf howls in the moon's light
And one tired camper in his tent snores

Eric Nguyen, Grade 7
Sarah McGarvin Intermediate School

Victor

Victor was your name,
I used to think it was beautiful,
It was kind of peaceful,
But peaceful was the total opposite,
Because in life you had to quit,
You never quit anything,
That's why I thought they were kidding,
When they called and said you were gone,
I thought they were wrong,
I mean my cousin kill himself, never,
But nobody was so cleaver,
Nobody saw that something was eating you up inside,
You thought it was something you had to hide,
But if you would have just said,
You wouldn't be dead,
So cousin I hope you rest in peace,
Because my love for you will never cease!!!

Gaby Villa, Grade 8
Almondale Middle School

Spring Reading

On a sunny, cloudless day,
I like to read books as you can see.
The place where I like to stay,
Is underneath the shade of the trees,
The smell of their pages reminds me of spices.
The sound of the wind whistles through the trees.
The firm, leather cover looks so nice,
A book is like a golden key,
That leads us to a whole new place,
A place where mythical beings can live,
Where one can be anything, in many cases.
There's so much books can give!
Their words weave a story, an adventure.
You don't need a car to leave home.
All the places where you can venture,
The stories can take you as far as Rome.
The characters in there give you new points of view.
I don't see how anyone can dislike books.
Books offer information, ideas, all of that's real.
Never judge a book by its looks.

Olivia Nguyen, Grade 9
Fountain Valley High School

I Can Make a Difference by…Being Me

By being me, I am many things, a fundraiser, supporter, and daughter to a "King,"
For the poor in Africa, there is money to be made, while most of us are sitting here as if we have already paid:
Well I will be that difference you see, and I can do this by just being me.
I will come to your door or ask for donations, hopefully people will realize the wealth of this nation;
I'll give you some pictures of comparison between them and us, then you will be convinced that you need not make a fuss;
Just give from your heart the help that you can, it will definitely be an appreciated hand,
I can make this difference you see, and I can do this by just being me.
Our military is stationed throughout the Earth, how hard can it be to show appreciation for what they are worth?
All it takes is dedication that is deep in our hearts, they're out there for you and me so don't even start;
I am just here to help them, that is all I want of your money, so do not slam the door on me, it would not be funny:
Our heroes need this support from the whole nation you see, and I will make a difference to them, by just being me.
With one person's help, then two, three and four, we could all work together, therefore accomplishing more.
All of our citizens in America will see, that the difference between you and me,
Is just our heart, it's what we feel; it's how bad we wish that others could have a meal:
I want these things, for everyone, once I have conquered every minute despair, my work will be done;
I will make a difference in this world you see, and I will make it by just being me.

Amy LaRue, Grade 8
Las Flores Middle School

Growing Up

I remember pulling flowers out of the ground in my grandpa's garden
I remember Dad yelling at me for it
I remember Grandpa telling Dad, "Leave that lil' girl alone"
I remember when Grandpa died
Everyone was sad
Especially Dad
I remember all the kids my parents had
Me, Alyssa, Jacob and Dylan
I remember being always broke and still having the most fun
Playing hide and go seek behind the huge weeping willow tree in front of our house
I remember seeing Dad on the floor with Mom crying by his side
I remember the ambulance coming and taking him away and saying, "Don't worry. He's going to be fine"
I remember those dreadful months when Dad was in the hospital
I remember growing up
It was confusing and very surprising
I remember my first day of junior high school
My hands shaking from being so nervous
I remember my first boyfriend
Dad was NOT happy!

Ashley Owens, Grade 8
Daniel Savage Middle School

My Best Friends

I have a lot of friends.
But even more best friends!
They've been with me through the ups and downs.
We fight here and there but, I love them all to death!
They are special to me in their own ways.
They're funny, they actually listen, give me awesome advice, and well, have been there for me!
I do the same thing for them as well.
They make me laugh, cry, shout all the emotions we have.
But at the end of the day
I love the fact that they are
My best friends!

Tatiana Escalante, Grade 7
St Vincent Elementary School

The Beautiful Butterfly

It starts out in a cocoon
the caterpillar begins to grow and change each day
once it feels it is ready to try out life,
the caterpillar bursts from its secure, safe home
and gives it a try.
It's a beautiful butterfly
feeling safe and now enjoying the things that were
never noticed before, it is scared to lose all of this.
The Butterfly feels as if it is on top of the world,
showing off all its beauty.
but it is still afraid of if it gets held too tight it will be crushed
and held too loose, the beautiful butterfly will fly away.

Summer Steinert, Grade 8
La Joya Middle School

Love

L oves me all the time
O ver every problem we had
V ery close than before
E veryday together

Alexis Rodriguez, Grade 7
John Charles Fremont Intermediate School

My Caring Family

Through the years times get tough.
We always need somebody to be there for us.
I look to my careless friends, they bluff.
I look the other way, I see caring hands tear through the crowd.

It is my family ripping and fighting their way to me.
I run to them in hope of help,
I am glad they are here to comfort me in a time of need.
There is no more sadness or gloominess that I once felt.

They say it will be all right and everything will be fine.
I feel a since of warmth and love.
They opened my eyes when I was blind.
My family is always there, just like a beautiful dove.

Alec Garofalo, Grade 7
Holy Family Catholic School

Glasses

The glasses with a blue-rimmed frame
The glasses that shaded the sun's benevolent rays
The glasses that gave others the impression of a boy
The glasses that left me blind for a day
The glasses that left two very unpleasant red dots on my nose.
The glasses with a bent leg
The glasses that once got smashed by a big bottom
The glasses that attempted suicide
The glasses that made my vision clear
But last of all…
The wonderful glasses that love to go on a date of their own…
Leaving me stranded alone with bruises on my forehead.

Karen Shum, Grade 8
Purple Lotus International Institute

Do You Remember

The things we used to do together
All the fun we had when we were kids
All the games we played

The times we would spend fighting against each other
The contest we had
The games we played

The times you saved me like a hero out of a comic book
The time when we had a staring contest
The time when we both were like stones in a pond

Our first time on a plane
The places we traveled to
The hundreds of people we had met
The things we had learned

The loud roars in the stadium as if it was a lion's roar
The thump thump thump sound when we rolled down the hill

Do you remember…
Do you remember any of that…

Michael Saetern, Grade 8
Valley Oak Middle School

I Am

I am a dog who has food and shelter.
I am a student from the school of fish in the sea.
I am a rabbit hopping with joy.
I am a dolphin in the sea swimming for freedom.
I am a deer running away from a predator.

Martha Chavez, Grade 7
St Mary of Assumption School

What to Do?

What to do? When you're in love?
When he messed up and did dumb stuff.
What to do? When you're fed up?
When you're done and had enough.
What to do? When you're too blind to see
All the bad things that happened to you and me.
What to do if this love doesn't last.
What walk away and put it in your past?
What to do if you can't walk away?
What stay and keep going through pain?
The best thing to do is just let it go.
Wait for the right person to come along.
You only have one life, live it!
Today,
Tomorrow,
The next,
Ain't promised. Life is too short to waste one day.
Don't let any boy get in your way!

Santeea Ralph, Grade 9
Opportunities for Learning Center

Risk

Little boy,
Standing tall,
No one to pick him up as he falls,
No one to see him do his best,
No one to help him take a risk,
He's your heart alone and sad,
Take a risk and make him glad.

Emily Larson, Grade 7
Holy Family Catholic School

Dandelion Dreams

Fragile,
Delicate,
It sways with the breeze.
One touch, one action
Is all it takes
To ruin it.

But then,
Why do so many feel
The need to chase them?

I blow the dandelion
And watch
As the wisps fly away —
And I smile,
As if I could do the same
And soar
Into the welcoming sky.
Lighthearted,
Without doubts,
And carefree.

Lucy Chen, Grade 9
Westview High School

Ice Cream

Ice cream is as
white as snow
when sitting there
in a snow cone

Ice cream colder
than the snow
in Antarctica

There are also
different colors
and flavors too
mmm, mmm, mmm

Tastes like a
sugary wild beast
going in your mouth
mmm, mmm, mmm

Enrique Vargas, Grade 8
Valley Oak Middle School

Shattered Glass

There will always be that one that lingers around forever
Every detail, outlined in my mind.
Your voice haunts me over and over like a skipping record.
We had it all chemistry, love, the works so why did you walk out?
Turn your back you can't leave without a reason can you?
You always knew the right the wrong completely obscene
You knew me down to every blink I knew you I think.
I know I'm young and love is possible I know because I found you.
Did you care?
I cried every night enough to flood the world over like a whirling hurricane
So tell me did you shed one, simple tear?
Do you have regrets, remorse? Bet not. You were always last to own up.
"Don't live in the past" now the past is the only thing clear
You, the only thing I hold dear
Now gone, vanished, without a trace.
The letters you wrote told me a story of you, of me, of us
As if I were a child listening, wishing, waiting.
They spoke don't cry! Too late don't lie! You did don't hate! How can't I?
You shattered me like glass a mirror rejecting a reflection
Rejection?
Now I'm rejecting you!

Alexa Bardsley, Grade 9
Fountain Valley High School

Fireflies

Small specks of light,
Fluttering against the dark night sky,
My heart stops to see the light fixtures up there,
Looking like stars against a big black blanket,
Floating in the sky.
They are different types of constellations,
Twinkling while the mini stars illuminate the space around them.
Their light outshines many things in the evening,
And their gleaming smiles will give you hope,
Showing you the way through the dark,
And back into the light.

Kaela Yonemoto, Grade 8
Madrona Middle School

Zachary

He is my best friend we stick together until the end
I know him like the back of my hand because I won't judge him, but understand
Met him during track said his name was Zach
His favorite colors are white and black he likes goldfish for a snack
His best friend is Nick G. he's as tall as a tree
Loves the Packers works hard, he's never a slacker
So many memories too many to name, not one of them the same.
Yosemite, Disneyland, Knotts, days that will always last because we always have a blast
When we go to Sunview I get filled with glee sitting under the whistling tree
Jake and Ryan never want to leave us alone not even when we talk on the phone
I know it may seem like we always fight but in the end we're always tight
I always know my friendship with Zach is something I will never lack.

Rosa Galvez, Grade 9
Fountain Valley High School

Where I'm From

I am from California
sandy beaches, seashells
and cherry ices.
I am from the four seasons
from lemonade stands
to snowball fights, smelling poppies
and jumping in leaves.
I am from the mall
clearance sales, size 0 tall
and Wetzel Pretzel.
I am from studies, 4.0 average
funny teachers and monkey bars.
I am from my family tucking me in bed
packing lunches, doing hair
and picnics on the beach.
I am from Sundays at church
growing up praying at dinner
and walking with Christ.
I am from all of these things
from what I love
what makes me whole and to long endure.

Taylor Johnson, Grade 7
Linfield Christian School

Dolphins

Dolphins like to hide
In the water flowing free
Water play all day

Cecilia Arevalo, Grade 7
John Charles Fremont Intermediate School

Eternity

A crystal crescent smiling upon me,
A white pearl.
In my hand lay a wilting velvet fabric,
Red and divine.
Diamonds splattered across the black canvas,
Gold mines lie beneath.
The midnight blue glass, breaking every now and then, says,
"Look deeply into me,"
I see an eternity to come,

"What more shall come!"
I say to thee in a soft plea.
Weeping, here I lie.
Tossing and tumbling, round after round,
Spraying my body frozen and numb.
The black horizon gives no reply.
Trying to slash all traces left behind.
Gone you are now,
My heart aches and bleeds.
All fades invisible; no tide, no sand, pale and white.
No longer do I see an eternity to come.

Kristina Zahabi, Grade 8
Hesperia Jr High School

Choices

I sit here thinking,
Debating in my head.
Making choices makes me crazy.
I would much rather be outside.
Yet I'm here choosing,
Choosing important high school classes.
I am swimming in a pool of homework,
And to get this done is also my choice.
Why can't I hire someone
To take care of it for me?
I think not,
My choices determine my fate.
Classes determine where I go in my life.
Who I will be,
What differences I will make.
The rest of my life will be
Filled with making choices.
The choices made now and in the near future,
Will determine what those choices will be.
The choices I make reverberate forever!

Kayla Dawe, Grade 8
Spring Grove Elementary School

Ode to Soccer

Running, dribbling, going for the goal
Whatever it takes soccer is our soul
First to the ball and last to give up
That's what a soccer player is made of
Nutmeg, scissors, rainbow, and snake
Beat your opponent with one great fake
Connections, overlaps, and take overs
Give it our all until the game is over
Proud to put our uniforms on
Ready for battle as we step on the lawn
Championships and rivalries
Bring out the competition in every team
As you win you hold your teammates close
For they're the ones that matter most
The weak hang their heads as they fail
Because only true winners prevail

Cierra Gamble, Grade 8
Citrus Hills Intermediate School

Stars at Night

The colored stars that shone so very bright,
moved as if they were dancing in the night.
They twinkled like nothing ever seen before,
and rose above the wide ocean floor.
Against the black sky they were contrasted,
and were so beautifully color blasted.
The clouds and rain were jealous of their friend
who received much more attention than both of them.
They continued to shine throughout the night,
until morning came, and the sun gave sight.

Anne-Marie Bulone, Grade 8
Oxford Academy

Rain

Dropping from the clouds,
Lightly falling on the earth,
Kisses of water.
Joanna De Anda, Grade 8
Citrus Hills Intermediate School

Spring

Flowers blooming the
Fresh sent of roses
Blooming new buds
In red, pink, and white
Dulce Jimenez, Grade 8
Almond Tree Middle School

Mother

How can I be so blind
that you tore my heart away
and left me behind

How can you be so cruel
you played me for a fool
and I just have to say
I hate you for hating me

How can it be that a mother is so weak
you didn't care for me
and now it's killing me

You're there but not for me
it's devastating that you don't even try
to hide not loving me
and all I can do is cry

I won't even try to win your love
I know I will never win
because all you will ever see is her
Blanca Palacios, Grade 7
Almond Tree Middle School

Fire

Fire is hot
Fire it burns
It heats the pot
and kills the fern

It's red and yellow
and always moves
It makes you bellow
and takes down roofs

It may seem bad
and hurts a lot
But don't get mad
It keeps you hot
Andrew Phan, Grade 7
Sarah McGarvin Intermediate School

Dinner

Silver steam hovers over the plate in front of me.
I sit in my chair, my right leg tucked under my left.
My mother nibbles on a piece of bread.
My father shovels pasta into his open mouth.
My sister slurps her milk and wipes her mouth with the back of her hand.
I drop a sliver of chicken to my left;
The floor below me is a sea of white carpet.
I wait for a familiar cat to come and devour the scrap,
But she does not come,
And she will not come ever again.
Amelia Alvarez, Grade 8
St Joseph's School of the Sacred Heart

Betrayal

You betrayed me with all the trust I had
You put me through anger I have never felt
You call me mad, but it is you
Who put me through so much stress I think I'm going to melt.
You threw me into the jaws of depression.
And it has taken me a lifetime to get out.
And now I have one thing to say to you,

I've tried to give you a warning, but everyone ignores me
I told it too clearly, but you don't want to hear me.
I have a heart full of pain, head full of stress, hand full of anger held to my chest.
I have nothing to gain,
Everything to fear.
Emily Northrup, Grade 8
Valley Oak Middle School

Ode to a Paintbrush

O paintbrush,
Your glistening handle,
Your straight sharp bristles brown,
Are all lost when you dip yourself in a pot and make beauty.

O paintbrush,
Make your fine lines of maroon and moss,
The most inspiring sight my eyes have ever seen.

O paintbrush,
Let your colored tears fall on the work of Post Modernism,
Your delicate splotches a radiance on a dull horizon.

O paintbrush,
Give color to the gray of the pencil,
And life when you highlight and shadow your objects of pure splendor,
Let your tip be thrown about on the canvas.

O paintbrush,
Be the perfection of a page
The light of my life,
For I am an artist,
And I need you.
Walker Livingston, Grade 8
West Marin Elementary School

The Rehearsal

My instrument is poised and ready
The sounds that come can be quick or slow.
The conductor comes, his feet are steady
But until it starts you never know.

His arms alert, his hand just lingers
With a wave the music starts
The notes flow out my excited fingers
The graceful clumsiness of my bow darts.

I can imagine the violas, cellos, and bass
With their vivacious vibrant voices I hear.
The energy I feel is not without grace
The beats and rhythms dance so near.

It's only a rehearsal but I still grin.
This is how I feel when I play my violin.

Darlene Tieu, Grade 9
Fountain Valley High School

The Perfect Accident

A nice warm day in the middle of spring,
She walked out the door and strolled down the road,
Having no clue of what the day would bring,
Something good to come for her karma flowed,
Brown hair moving freely and green eyes too,
Taller than most, he saw above them all,
He ran for a reason that no one knew,
His long legs were there to catch his own fall,
She felt a nudge and looked past her shoulder,
And there he was, she couldn't look away,
His stare was tense, as strong as a boulder,
So perfect he longed the moment to stay,
    They gazed at each other with great delight,
    It then hit both of them, love at first sight.

Kathryn Lim, Grade 8
Las Flores Middle School

Summer

It was a hot summer day in France,
I was warm when I put on my capri pants,
I was excited,
And very delighted,
For it was a hot summer day today.
I looked at my French book by the pool,
And wondered just how can I get cool,
I drank some iced tea,
With Amanda, mes amie,
And tried to get cooled, poor me!
Later I went outside to freeze,
But there was only a little breeze,
I ate une glace,
And got cold fast,
I was finally cool, yippee!

Alexis Olivas, Grade 7
John Adams Middle School

Duck Hunting

It's early October time for hunting!
All summer I was doing nothing

duck hunting is so much fun
you can't wait to see the duck and point your gun

you wait patiently in your blind
then someone shouts watch out it's coming from behind!

as another comes you use your duck calls to lure him in
right before you pull the trigger you show a grin

you watch the sight in front of your eyes
well he's in for a surprise!

Matthew Gamez, Grade 7
Monte Vista Christian School

The Night Ocean

In the night the stars shine bright.
In the night there is a moon in the sky.
In the ocean there are dolphins in the water
and whales, like the killer whales in the ocean.
In the ocean there is you and me in the water.
In the night the owls are hunting in the night sky.
In the night I'm in bed and asleep
and the clock chimes midnight and I'm still asleep.

Marisa Lynch, Grade 7
Sterne School

Friend in the Sky

Friends are there for you
To help you tie your shoe
They comfort you when you are down
They never let you have a frown
Friends are there to encourage you
To do the things you need to do.

But when I needed a friend the most
All of them were off to boast
Of worldly possessions which I declined
The sky is where I resigned
What did I find?
The answer to my prayer;
A different kind of friend who will always be there.

He's three combined in one
Father, Spirit, and Son
He's a special kind of friend who'll feed
And cleanse your soul when you're in need.
He is like a treasure
Who will give you pleasure
You'll surely be awed
Because my special friend in the sky is God

Ryan Buck, Grade 7
Holy Family Catholic School

This Is Just to Say
I'm sorry
   for tormenting
    you
teasing you

I read your diary
   I didn't meant to
   It was just…
    there

You left it open
   for people to see
So you can't really
    blame me

I know your secrets
   the guy you like…
Try to hide it better
    next time

This poem is just to say
   I'm sorry, but
   it was your own
   fault.
    Jahziel Castañeda, Grade 8
    St Sebastian School

Red-tail Meadow
A meadow so calm
'till a hawk breaks the silence
soaring on the wind
    Salome Byrd, Grade 7
    South Tahoe Middle School

Realizing Reality
You cannot be young forever
For one day you mature
To become whoever
A feat you must endure

For me I was nine
Life had been just fine

Until responsibilities were given
And nothing was forgiven

An innocent face was washed away
And replaced by a realistic display

No more excuses understood
My actions were my fault
Even if they were not good
My childhood was at a halt
    Cara de Freitas Bart, Grade 9
    El Segundo High School

The Sun
The sun is God's hand
   reaching out and healing
    all of its creations.
The sun's warmth is like
   the joyous feeling
a child has during his first Christmas.
The sun is a symbol, a sign of hope.
   It is the sign of peace, power
    and happiness.
The sun soars over Earth
   powering over all
   like a father of all stars.
The sun's a young child's pillow
while his mother tells him stories
   under the tree's cool shade.
The sun is the food
   for all plants.
It is the life force for many animals.
The sun is God's hand
   reaching out and healing
   all of his creations.
    Kolini F. T. Coleman, Grade 8
    Madrona Middle School

Ode to Nuts
Inside a bright
   Hard shell
   Or a soft
   Breakable one
   Peanuts, walnuts
   And cashews too
   Nature's fiber source
   A crunchy
   Kernel
   Inside each shell
   Harvest in summer
And ends up as a lunchtime
   Snack
    Bryan Jesberger, Grade 8
   Citrus Hills Intermediate School

Car Crash
Before the world was disfigured,
It was perfect,
Just like my life,
Until the world was damaged,
By natural disasters,
Just like the world got disfigured,
So did my life,
A car crash ruined it all,
It seemed like my life had ended,
Like the world has its damages,
So does my life.
    Nora Botros, Grade 7
    St Cyprian School

Summer
Pretty flowers bloom
Cute children begin to play
Summer just began!
    Jhovana Espinoza, Grade 8
    Almond Tree Middle School

The Reason I Love You
Well there's so many to list
But the #1 reason is,
Because of the way we kissed,
Each night before I go to sleep

I always reminisce.
On those good times we had
Me and you, You and I.
And now that you're gone
I love you even more, after
All that we've been through.

Well after all you put me through
I still have to tell you one thing
And that is I love you!
    Brenda Madrigal, Grade 8
    Almond Tree Middle School

A Summer Day
Summer days are fun
Resting under the sun
Fun in the sun all day long,
Listening to my favorite song
Sitting out by the pool,
Trying to stay cool

Enjoying the sounds of the waterfall,
I hear my mom starting to call
While her voice drones on,
I try not to yawn
Then I hear her ask
For me to complete another task

Now that I am back,
Let's get back on track
I practice my dance
And people start to glance,
To see how hard I try
So now it's time to say good bye!
    Jennifer Wild, Grade 7
    Holy Family Catholic School

Snow
Snow is very cool,
It is white like a cloud,
Fluffy and freezing.
    Juan Martinez, Grade 8
    Almond Tree Middle School

I Am the Spirit Bear

I am big and powerful
I wander around the island
I am not looking for trouble
I am just curious
I do however defend myself when I need to
I am big and powerful

I walk on the beach
I stare at someone coming at me
I don't want to hurt him
I have no other choice
I use the strength of ten men to protect myself
I am big and powerful

I stay at the island
I think I went too hard on the kid
I went to walk I saw him again he looks different now
I don't think he wants to hurt me anymore
I see him a lot more often
I am big and powerful

Gerardo Castellanos, Grade 8
Palm Desert Middle School

Amber

There once was a girl named Amber
Her birthday was in December.
She lacks on her school work.
And acts like a dork.
There was always things she couldn't remember.

Julia Villareal, Grade 8
Almond Tree Middle School

Blanket of Smoke

I was safe from the fire
But the smoke was inescapable
The ground was buried under a blanket of ash
The sun beamed a sickly orange
The sky became a ghastly hue
For days I could not see blue
The smooth sapphire that I saw every day
So magnificent
Was hidden by a layer of soot
It hurt my eyes
I used to look into the sky
And it would captivate my mind
It was never ending
It went on forever
I always knew
That behind the smoke the sky was there
I always knew
That the wind would blow away the filth
And take all of my troubles with it
And it did

Ilima Kung, Grade 8
Madrona Middle School

A Shadow's Many Faces

Your very own twin,
Dark and on the ground.

A person eating up the light,
Leaving nothing but the darkness.

A secret spy,
Following you everywhere during the day.

Home of good shade,
Taking many forms but still very cool.

A way of entertainment in the dark,
Only a flashlight is needed.

Your own personal mime,
Mimicking all your movements.

Patrick Nguyen, Grade 7
St Barbara School

I'm Sorry

I'm sorry, I really am.
I'm sorry for telling you the truth.
I should have known better.
I shouldn't have put you through so much pain.
When I told you, I could have cried.
Your face, once playful, now serious and sad.
Your eyes so confused, so full of questions.
I'm sorry once again.
When I saw your face, I could've hugged you.
I wish I could tell you that I know how you feel,
That I understand what you're going through.
But I can't.
I've never gone through so much pain.
So, I can only try to make you smile and tell you
Everything will be fine.

Alex Quezada, Grade 8
Spring Grove Elementary School

Puppy Love

Beauty itself cannot compare to yours
Like the stars your eyes attract attention
To be with you, I will try to get fours
Heaven clearly looks like your reflection
I try to ask you out but chicken out
Talking to beauty itself makes me shy
Without your presence, I will feel like a lout
If you ever said yes, I could just fly
I have been friends with you for a while
If you say no then let us be good friends
We have ran together several miles
I hope this does not lead to any weird trends
My love for you will always be alive
I will just wait for your love to arrive

Marguin Sanchez, Grade 8
John Adams Middle School

Attention

You never listen
you act like I'm not there
when I do something good
You never seem to care

This hurts me so much
don't you see
when times get hard
I need you there for me

All the games you missed
Every play you skipped
When I look in the crowd
You're no where to be found

My heart calls for you
Will you ever pay attention
I love you so much
Those are words you forget to mention

Nikki Johnson, Grade 8
McCabe Elementary School

Nature's Thoughts

Quiet are the mountains,
Quiet is the stream.
A picture worth a thousand words,
A million in a dream.

Oh nature, quiet nature.

Gentle are the waves,
Crashing on the shore.
Want not, Waste not,
Wish for nothing more.

Oh nature, gentle nature.

Mighty is the night,
Mighty are the stars.
Beauty is only skin deep,
So none see the scars.

Oh nature, mighty nature.

Alison Le, Grade 7
Sarah McGarvin Intermediate School

Angora

A fire is on
Through the thick pine forest
Homes go down in smoke

People lose it all
Pets ran away in fear
The fire still lives on

Cody James Higgins, Grade 7
South Tahoe Middle School

Me Not We

We are boys living a life of danger in chaos
No structure, no discipline, no consequence, no repercussion
But also no praise, no reward, no love, only loneliness
Our life is an empty void of pity and no recognition
We believe we need no one, but it's an illusion
Inside we are scared, inside we want to be clutched and cared for, but by whom?
Losing my mind, the idea of being in mourning and melancholy
For the rest of my existence is terrifying
I can't be forgotten anymore
No More!
I am no longer we, I am now only me
I will be above the influence
I have a loving family, people who love me
I have friends and food and clothes and money
I am living the American dream whether I want to admit it or not
I will be released and free my inner me
I just hope all the we's can find their me

Randall Stovall, Grade 8
Seneca Center

I Cry

You know those tears…
Those tears are like the waterfalls of the earth,
They run down as if daisies in the meadow,
And the crescent of the moon is my only symbol of happiness,
Because I cry in your death,
But I still remember when we used to look at the moon and smile to each other.

Michelle Chavarria, Grade 8
Madrona Middle School

The Missing Key

Locked away under her bed
She never wanted to see it again
It hurt so much so she locked it up
But she was numb too long and she's ready to feel it again
She finds the box only to see a lock
The only thing she was missing was the key
Where did she put it
Did she throw it away
She thought and thought but couldn't remember
And began to feel hopeless
Then these thoughts clouded her head
She wanted to feel his touch again
She wanted to feel his voice send chills to her spine that always made her jump a mile
She wanted to hear his delicate voice whisper I love you
So sweet and pure it sounded so true.
How could she be so stupid
If you taught me how to love
then teach me how to forget how I feel about you she thought
Tears began to well up in her eyes and she felt a throbbing pain in her chest
Suddenly the lock broke open and she wondered why
Then she realized that she found the key to her heart.

Jenny Na, Grade 7
Monte Vista Christian School

Autumn

In autumn,
Traverse an open field
To a glow in the sky before darkness falls.
Just walk leisurely as a breeze.

If darkness comes and the street lights turn on,
At a corner of a shady bench where nobody has come
Yearning and sorrow sink into my mind
As a yellow wave.

When maples paint a mountain red,
My heart beats as reddish as maples,
Then a flutter spreads into my mind
As solitude.

Autumn
Fallen leaves pour down and passage birds leave.
Even if it is the season of feeling empty,
A feeling from you
Is all beauty.

Gina Hong, Grade 8
Madrona Middle School

The Last Dragon

I am a dragon flying high
I wonder if I'm the last dragon in the sky
I hear screaming and crying when I pass by
I see people running and hiding for me
I am a dragon flying high

I pretend to be a human being
I feel sad when I'm alone
I touch my scales when I'm bored
I worry that they are going to kill me
I am a dragon flying high

I understand I am scary
I dream to be a dog
I try to be nice
I hope I can turn into a human being
I am a dragon flying high

Thomas Morfin, Grade 7
Richland Jr High School

Family

Family is there when you need them
They are supportive of whatever you do
They are awesome adults or grumpy grandparents
However they are nice and loving
They defend you in your time of need
But mostly they are funny and fun
They are big goof balls but you have a good time
It even sounds like the soccer ball is having a good time
Family is the best thing a kid could have

Jocelyn Alejo, Grade 8
Almond Tree Middle School

Love Is an Emotion

Love is a great emotion.
It's so powerful you never know when it hits you.
You are the one special person in my life
that I cannot forget no matter how hard I try.
I have this feeling inside me.
I don't know what it is but I think it might be love.
I might be in love with you.

Jennifer Rodriguez, Grade 8
St Vincent Elementary School

Bored in School

I went to school and I was half asleep.
Since I was late I went where I eat lunch.
I was sleepy so I thought I saw sheep.
Since I was hungry I couldn't wait for brunch.
I was so hungry doing work in classes.
I tried so hard not to get distracted
But my teacher began explaining gasses.
Since I was bored in class I remembered
I had some fun with friends in nutrition.
I played soccer with friends and scored two goals.
In History we studied migration.
To study hard and learn things are my goals.
When I go home I am happy to learn
I can't wait to go back to school to learn.

Jose Ambrosio, Grade 8
John Adams Middle School

Bonds of Friendship

The gift of a God who truly cares,
yet the clouds of anger can hinder this view,
but be it a curse or a snare,
it is still a gift indeed.

The moments of utter despair and shame,
is when they come along side,
then there's the hour of fame,
where the brilliance can't be denied.

The laugh of a thousand strangers brings comfort,
but the laugh of a friend brings overwhelming joy,
the memories from good-times past,
involving the imagination of a boy.

From the outer reaches of the galaxies, encouragement,
from the inner regions of the earth, content,
but the uplifting words of a companion mean much,
especially when their expression was meant.

I now speak of a legacy long and lasting,
the true and faithful never cease,
though the body is gone and in the ground,
the gift of a friend remains.

David Wahlman, Grade 9
Redding Christian School

My Friends

My friends are like dogs, as long as they get food they're happy.
When I think of them I think of the parties and bonfires we have at the beach.
When I am with them we usually play sports so we smell like sweat.
We always go to Full Moon sushi to eat, it's the best place around but it's hard to find a seat.
Usually we play football and it gets a little rough.
If you see us all together we are probably at the beach.
Everything for us is a competition.
These are my friends.

Bret Woodley, Grade 9
Fountain Valley High School

The Land of Wonder

Yosemite was an experience that will last a lifetime, setting goals and seeing how far we could climb
Challenging ourselves to make it to the top, looking down with success and seeing the massive drop

Listening to the waterfalls crash against the sturdy rocks, relaxing and meditating on our personal solo walks
The radiant sun beating down on our tired backs, searching for wildlife and following their tracks

Venturing into the mysterious spider cave, in complete darkness you had to be brave
Climbing in, on, and around Dead Fred, being apart of the trust walk you were carefully led

Trees that are so enormous they could touch the sky, silently watching deer, squirrels, and bunnies pass by
Meadows so wide and valleys so vast, trying to sink in the memories and make them last

Sitting by the warm campfire late at night, looking up at the twinkling stars and the magnificent sight
Peace and tranquility surrounding my soul, my mind and body came together as a whole

No pollutants in the air only the small of fresh Sequoia trees, as their rough branches swayed we felt a light breeze
Listening to the quiet flow of the water stream, encouraging and bonding to become a team

I will never forget this marvelous place I went to, it is the kind of memory that is deep within you
Looking around at the beauty and wonder of the lands, it is as though God painted a picture with his magical hands

Jennifer Zanardi, Grade 8
Sacred Heart School

We Are the Soldiers

We are the soldiers who are out there every day, fighting and working the day away.
If one of us falls, another takes his place, but not with a smile on our face.

Our guns loaded and shoes tied, we aren't surprised to know five died.
When we state the pledge do we really know, the difference between friends and foes?

We wonder when it's all going to end, so we can get back to our lives again.
When the sun goes down and the moon rises, we go to sleep and are filled with surprises.

Do we ever wonder if we were going to wake, or what orders we'll have to take?
Can we tell the difference of crime and respect, sometimes it's hard to know what to expect.

There are fifty stars on that flag, and not one of them could have known how bad
The problems were and what they had turned this country into it's really sad.

How many more lives does it have to take, to finally realize what decisions to make?
How many fathers must be taken away, for someone to finally stand up and say
What this country really needs and what it's about, what we really need is someone beyond doubt.

Nicholas Glorioso, Grade 8
St Luke the Evangelist Catholic School

The Light of Hope

A light ray out of nowhere flashed beyond the sea
It awoke the dark sky as if it were morning already
That the light pierced the darkness like a sharp needle

This dazzling light came from a rigid structure
That watches above all waves of oceans seen below
And down at the oceans below
Are sailors hoping to find guidance to the light
To sail safely throughout the night

It seems like an endless night
Searching for guidance like a lost bear looking for its mom
The sailors prayed for mercy hoping to find this guide
But monstrous waves grabbed them like a lion's bite
Until the light has shown them where to come

With the world ever-changing and going
Time itself moved on
You see the lighthouse
But less and less are unaware
That the lighthouse ever stood there

Nathaniel Suarez, Grade 8
Madrona Middle School

Alone

Alone is turning down a million dollars.
Alone is a ring in your ear that won't go away.
Alone is never getting enough money for Halo 3.
Alone is a friend not trusting you.
Alone is the bus coming early.
Alone is no one here.

Alexander Mabe, Grade 8
Citrus Hills Intermediate School

Stewart, I Miss You

I held you in my arms to make sure you didn't die
As a teardrop fell from my eye I started to cry
It's just my luck to have to see you go
I just wanted to tell you that I still love you so
I miss you
I miss you
You really don't know
How much I will miss you when you must go
I loved you as much as a father loves his son
But my time with you has barely begun
You're in a better place now
Far, far away
You don't know how I loved you so
How much I missed you that day
Farewell, for now
You've made me proud
I'll always know that you'll be watching me
From up on that cloud…

Jace Tarbell, Grade 8
Valley Oak Middle School

Moving

My dad is in the Navy.
This means we move a lot.
We go from state to state.
My friends come and go often.
I become afraid to get close to someone,
Because I know I will have to move soon.
Every time we have to move,
I have to start the same thing over.
The first day of school is the worst,
I get butterflies in my stomach,
And they make me too nervous to eat.
On the first day of school, I always have to be very careful,
Of whom to hangout with.
I learn that people judge very easily,
When they do not know you.
After the first week of school, if I have found friends,
Things get better.
Eventually, I get used to the school and people,
And everything turns out fine.

Nicole Mattingly, Grade 8
Coronado Middle School

Rain Drop

Drip Drip Drip Drop.
When the sun starts to hide,
I begin my descending glide.
Drip Drip Drip Drop.
Soaring like a bird through the clouds,
Passing planes are immensely loud.
Drip Drip Drip Drop.
An aerial bird am I, flying high in the sky.
Drip Drip Drip Drop.
Far down I scan the ocean,
Before I jump into the commotion.
Drip Drip Drip Drop.
My flight is almost over,
So I spot my landing clover.
Drip Drip Drip Drop.
Boom!! Splash!!! I hit the ground.
Now I'm in a muddy mound.
Drip Drip Drip Drop.
I am gone, I now cannot run,
My time here on earth is done.
Drip Drip Drip Drop.

Faith Zralka and Lisa Dornisch, Grade 7
St Patrick Parish School

Broken Heart

You left my heart broken in two,
it can't be tape or even glued,
I remember all the time we used to fight,
I lied when I said I was all right,
Now that there is an endless gap within my heart,
my love for you has fallen apart.

Jason Ngo, Grade 7
Sarah McGarvin Intermediate School

The Sun

You hold the earth
Like a mother holding a baby
You watch over us with
Your bright light
You care for nature helping it grow
You light the sky with
All of your might
You are a flaming
Ball of fire which I hope
Never dies.

Liyana Arayata, Grade 8
Madrona Middle School

Cars!

Cars are fast
Cars are slow
Cars from the past
Are ready to go
I like cars with trims
And I like cars with good shiny rims
Cars have good engines
And are really shrill
Some of them are calm
And stay still
Cars have TVs
And very good interiors
With chrome rims and good mirrors

Brandon Divas, Grade 8
St Alphonsus School

A Middle School Ending

We're moving away,
from what feels like home.
Into new places,
and new times.

It's a learning experience,
and a time to take charge.
When our whole future,
is in our hands.

The times we laughed,
and the times we cried.
Even the stupidest things,
we did most of the time.

I'll remember the guys in the hall,
paper fights,
and silent ball.

I'll remember laughing for no reason,
or because we trip and fall.
There's no place I'd rather be,
than here with you all.

Emily DeBoer, Grade 8
Merryhill Preparatory School

Necklace

A bond between us, connected tightly
By a thin yet strong relation.
Grew up together, share the secrets and joy,
Our hands linked, so are our hearts.
The world rotates and varies each second, still
The belief of forever friendship had not changed.
We rely, trust, believe in and support each other's decisions of life.
My heart is always open for you, so are yours for me.
Two stars linking together our dreams and hopes
Will never change from what we started with.
Now here I am on the other side of the globe
Thousands of miles away from you, yet we are not separated.
Our hearts are brought together by this tiny silver chain
Two stars that are meant to shine together, creating a light.
I feel your pain, your smiles your worries and tears.
Fly freely and see the world
Faith in my heart that the necklace will bring me to where you are
A connection so weightless yet holds us together strongly
The linkage of forever friendship, two stars that are always there
Always with each other, next to my heart. Always.

Ying-Le Du, Grade 9
Westview High School

O. J. Mayo

He dribbled up the court
The crowd chanting his name to the rhythm of Ole'
the crowd is bouncing up and down with pictures of Will Ferrell
He has a fierce look on his face, the look that he will change the game
He gets the ball at the top of the key and does just that
OJ Mayo nails the 30-foot jumper to secure the USC Trojans' victory over Oregon

Collin Palmer, Grade 8
St Joseph's School of the Sacred Heart

One Day to Be

Down the stairs she was led to a cart,
Where the real laughter would start.
Dry straw rope bound her hands,
That once led many bands.
Hair once powdered and pinned up high,
Was now cropped and smelled like a pig sty.
Up they made her step;
The bottom of the cart her dress swept,
Once in folds and of many colors,
Now was dressed that made some shutter.
And the beast in front obeyed its master's whip,
Jerked the cart forward under its nip.
Every step the cart was pulled,
Her heart began to rip and fold.
The roars and laughter grew;
Many verbal stones they threw.
Looking down piteously she sighed;
Hoping they might live and not die, from this lie-threaded net.
She hoped and prayed that they'd remember her as once their Queen —
Named Marie Antoinette.

Gabriela Hernandez, Grade 8
Heritage Christian School

Time

We are told to use it wisely,
Yet we waste it.
We wish it would go faster,
Yet we say it went too fast.
We keep track of it,
But we lose it.
We see it everywhere,
But we can't see it.
It keeps our life in order,
It tells us when to sleep and when to wake up.
Some regret how they used it,
Some are happy about it.
We don't think deeply about it,
Instead we sometimes take it lightly.
It started our life,
And it will end our life.
It is very important,
But we don't see the importance of
Time

Cassie Landis, Grade 7
Monte Vista Christian School

Without You

I used to wish I'd be a super star,
The one that will always have the hottest car,
But even if those wishes come true,
They will be meaningless without you.

Quynh Tran, Grade 7
Sarah McGarvin Intermediate School

Jimmy

My dog Jimmy is a Cavachon.
He is half Cavalier and half Bichon.
And he is just right for me.

His mommy is a Cavalier.
His daddy is a Bichon dear.
And Jimmy was the cutest of their litter.

His daddy has short, curly hair,
Unlike mommy's long, silky and fair.
But Jimmy's hair is both long and fluffy.

His daddy has a short fluffy tail.
His mommy's tail points like a sail.
And Jimmy's tail is beautiful and flowing.

His mommy is white with markings of black and brown.
His daddy is white all around.
My Jimmy has a coat of peach and cream.

Jimmy has the best of his mom and dad.
And he's the greatest dog I've ever had.
I will always love my Cavachon, Jimmy!

Katrina Mendez, Grade 7
Monte Vista Christian School

Shining Eyes

His eyes were always shining
With truth and love for all
Even behind the shades of death
His eyes were always shining

He fought and killed for all of us
He rescued and saved many of us
But he could never save himself
He died a never ending sleep

And when I saw him there in the open casket
And everyone else in tears
I knew he'd always be watching us
Up in the golden sky
With those same shining eyes

Jason Desanto, Grade 8
Parkside Intermediate School

Happy Birthday

Roses are red, violets are blue,
I'm just stoppin' to say happy birthday to you!
You know I'm 15 and today you are too,
I can't tease you anymore so I'm crying Boo-hoo!
This short little poem took me ages to write,
So don't be too harsh and tell me it's all right.
So now that I have told you what I wanted to say,
I wish you the best on your special day.
Now it's time for me to say good-bye.
But remember this: we'll be best friends for life!

Erika Peña, Grade 9
Santiago High School

The Paralyzed Man

I, this paralyzed man am trapped
on this bed, this prison, this cage.
Looking back at my pitiful life,
I am filled with sorrow, with guilt, with rage.

Who am I, but a paralyzed man,
with this I worry and fret.
Would people still remember me, still love me,
or would they forget?

Oh, I bellow at my carelessness,
"Look what you've done, you fiend!"
Now my time is so desolate,
so meaningless, so routine.

I miss the adventures of my life,
and this is why I cry,
who am I but a paralyzed man,
a useless man, a forgotten man,
left on this bed to die.

Lyn Dang, Grade 7
Sarah McGarvin Intermediate School

Rain of Tears

Day by day, they come and go,
Flitting shadows, tears and pain.
They pass before a girl of stone,
Amid the storm, amid the rain.
When each glowing ember disappears,
When howling gales begin to blow,
When no prying eyes are there to see,
Then her tears begin to flow.
In a rain of tears, the torrents flow,
For to stone feelings are not unknown.
When life turns cold, stone will weep,
For stone is ever flesh and bone.

Julia Wang, Grade 7
Pleasanton Middle School

The Way I Feel

The way I feel for you
Can't be explained
Even though sometimes
It causes me pain
To think what might happen in the future
But not to think in the past
About how much you mean to me
Hopefully it lasts.

Marisa Perrault, Grade 8
Santa Rosa Technology Magnet School

Fire

I am fire hear me roar
For I catch to anything I come before
I am hotter than you can imagine
Quicker than you can fathom
Brighter than you can truly comprehend
and I never really end
You may think I'm gone
But I travel through my sparks
Onto new things to set ablaze
Like forests, mountains, and parks
I can make structures burn to the floor
Set them in a red hot inferno
For I am fire and you will hear my roar

Hunter Taylor, Grade 7
Santa Rosa Technology Magnet School

Ode to My Shoe

An ode to how I love my shoe
It is so colorful and new
It is so pretty and pink
With hearts and stars
It keeps my feet comfy and warm
Even if I'm eating corn
An ode to my shoe
What a wonderful shoe it is

Kaitlyn Boyle, Grade 7
Santa Rosa Technology Magnet School

Hurricanes

Hateful hurricanes
Destroy everything in sight
Homes and hope are lost

Kimberly Lipayon, Grade 8
Almond Tree Middle School

Valentine

Happy Valentine's Day,
For I am in love,
Please do not mind who I am today,
My little, beautiful dove.

You may not know
Who I am today
But when you know
That would be a day.

Please, forever, wait
For I will come
I won't be late
Please stay at home.

When we're together
I am glad.
When we're not with each other
I become sad.

Linda Nguyen, Grade 7
Citrus Hills Intermediate School

Ode to Joe

Light brown with a black tail.
Eats chicken like a wolf.
Crazy like an elephant!
Saved from a shelter.
Frightened at first,
and territorial later.
He makes me think,
He makes me ballistic!
Barks like a bull dog.
But is as small as a mouse.
He is not afraid,
Of what is ahead of him,
Except vaccines — and muzzles.
He is my dog, and I love him.
He may never be replaced!
He is mine, to keep forever.

Shayan Veissi, Grade 8
South Lake Middle School

Uniqueness

Stand out from the crowd
God made us all different
Dare to be unique

Christine Sharp, Grade 7
St Cyprian School

My Family

My family is my life
Filling my heart
My family is my everything
Filling my world
My family is my soul filling everything

Andrea Gutierrez, Grade 9
Academic/Vocational Institute

Who I Am

Adventurous, cool, hilarious
Wishes to be a psychologist
Dreams of everything
Who wants to go to Italy
Who wonders about partying
Who fears bees
Who likes guys
Who believes in God
Who loves her parents
Who loves her whole family
Who loves her friends
Who loves life
Who plans to be successful
Who plans to have a big family
Who plans to travel the world
Whose final destination is to die

Andrea Rabago, Grade 7
Almond Tree Middle School

And Yes

Did you ever wonder if we,
and yes it may sound weird,
all have a reason on this Earth?
Even that hobo with the beard?

Don't you ever question why,
and yes it may sound crazy,
we feel all these emotions,
being sad, being mad, being lazy?

Don't you wish that some people,
and yes it may sound hateful,
would find their gifts that lie within
and be a bit more grateful?

Haven't you ever looked in a mirror,
and yes it may sound strange,
and felt like someone else was your
reflection for a change?

Sometimes, when asked, "Who are you?"
and yes it may sound silly,
I may just ponder to myself:
who are we, really?

Angel Montano, Grade 8
Walter F Dexter Middle School

Global Warming

Global warming
Is a warning
To control our pollution
And find a solution
To care about Earth
And realize we have a dearth
It's time to conserve and preserve
And give back Earth what it really deserves
We should start hurrying
And stop worrying
For it is time to take action
For we are a mere fraction
The world needs to be cared for
For whom else is this world going to be there for
This is a warning
We are upon global warming

Jujhar Bedi, Grade 8
Moreland Middle School

What Happened to Him

He had a choice
We all do

Say yes for a life in the trash
Say no for a life of cash

His friends said no let's just go
But he said wait and that's when he started to hate

He thought the others were cool
Little did he know all they did was drool

When they see him now they remember the genius he was
And now the failure he is because

DRUGS; they changed him; they put him in a hole
They are the reason for all his pain, agony, and lifeless soul

Yasmeen El-Farra, Grade 9
Clovis West High School

Ode to the American Soldier

You wake up to the sound of a bell
And remember the day the Twin Towers fell.
Side by side they stand for freedom
Remembering the army, knowing we all need them;
Memorial Day.
Loving families await
Even though you're in Kuwait.
You're doing a great job, by the way,
Pride, glory, flames, and fury.
Everybody wishes you were here
For your baby's first words
Or the cry of your children's fears.

Chanda Kaloki, Grade 9
Clovis West High School

Trees

I am the happiest tree you've ever seen

I am green
But some other trees are yellow
Some are brown and mellow

My branches are fingers, touching the sky
Soaring high, high, high
But in the fall
My leaves fall like a ball

Some humans are friendly
Recycling and reusing
But some are mean, OUCH!
Destroying and refusing

I am the saddest tree you've ever seen

Ryan Badilla and Sean Plotkin, Grade 8
St Patrick Parish School

Grandma Oh Grandma

My grandma my mother
The light to my life
The hope to my dreams

Grandma oh Grandma
You took care of me
You teach me the way to follow my dreams

You pick me up when I fall tells me to be strong
Even with your illness you showed me faith and strength

Grandma oh Grandma
Always there for me
Happy to see me
You rocking your chair
Slowly singing happy songs

Grandma oh Grandma
You're here with me forever
I sing your song
Rocking your chair
Grandma oh Grandma

Cesar Pena, Grade 8
St Sebastian School

Paintball

Paintball is cool
If you get shot in the face you look like a fool
Under the bunker
Around the maze
I have a shot to get my opponent
I bring my fingers closer to the trigger, shoot and he's out
Puts up his gun and walks on out

Vince Flores, Grade 7
St Vincent Elementary School

Spring

The river rushing
As the snow melts in the sun
So spring starts again
Maddie Bowman, Grade 8
South Tahoe Middle School

Stuck Forever

Like a ship in a bottle
Forever trapped for eternity.
No way to get out,
Staying in the bottle,
Wondering if anyone got
Your message and
Will respond back.
Alone in the bottle,
Safe from danger,
Safe forever in
Your own very space.
Alone at last.
Forever and ever.
With boredom and silent,
Stuck in a bottle.
Phong Nguyen, Grade 9
Gunderson High School

Discrimination

People may not realize it,
But racial discrimination
Is still a big part
Of our great nation.

Does it really matter
If we're black or white?
We should all get along,
We shouldn't fight.

So many gangs,
Too much violence.
They cause people's lives
To turn to silence.

It's just too bad
This world can't see
If we change our ways,
How much better things would be.
Victoria Montgomery, Grade 8
Shadow Hills Intermediate School

Love

Love
Is a puzzle
Confusing
without the right
person
Allee Lattin, Grade 9
Lucerne Valley Jr/Sr High School

Friends

Friends are like blossoms on a tree.
They bloom beautifully, as do friends;
Blossoms branch out, as do friends;
And they fall to the ground to greet other pedals, as do friends;
And to us, friends are also living bonds that are never to be broken.

Friends are like the keys on a piano.
A piano is complete with its keys, as do friends;
The piano can't make sound without its keys, as do friends;
The keys on a piano play across joyfully to make music, as do friends;
And to us, friends are also living bonds that are never to be broken.

Friends are like seasons greeting each other.
Spring helps winter to be young and playful again, as do friends;
Summer dances joyfully into spring's place, as do friends;
Autumn then calms the playful summer down, as do friends;
And to us, friends are also living bonds that are never to be broken.

Friends are like the stars on a dark night.
The little specks of light illuminate the night, as do friends;
As night stretches, stars try to prevent night from ruling, as do friends;
The stars and night, in the end, work together, as do friends;
And to us, friends are also living bonds that are never to be broken.
Christopher Lin, Grade 7
Foothills Middle School

Looking Back with Friends and No Regrets

Growing up, I was a shy and quiet girl
I tried my best to fit in and please everyone around me
When I was able to smile with everyone it filled me up with glee
But inside I still felt distant and alone
No matter what I did I felt almost as if I didn't belong

Until that one fateful day I saw another girl
She was new to our class and seemed quite the same as myself
When she introduced herself to the class I felt like we could become best friends
I took a risk and that first step toward our path together
We spoke with each other when recess had come to an end

Afterwards we got to know each other more and more
I noticed that I shouldn't be scared for I have friends who care about my would be self

This wasn't a dream for my own eyes were my witness
I was not alone my hand has finally reached out to what I was scared of
And I realized it was just the soft light of friendship

Now I have no regrets of what I did for now we still go to the same school
We enjoy each other's company and share our friendship with many others

So as I looked upon the divided roads of my fate
I chose the one that was calling me and that has made all the difference
Stefanie Yenchi Hoang, Grade 9
Westview High School

Still Missing You!

You left without saying goodbye.
Because you were taken.
You were my grandma, but also a friend.
I wish you could be here 'til the end.
You were very important to me.
And I really hope you can see.
All the good things happening to me.

I miss you more every day and night.
I can't wait 'til I can see you again.
I will never forget the times we had.
The good and the bad.
I knew how much you loved me.
I knew how much you cared
There will never be a day I don't think about you
Meme, I LOVE YOU.

Riccie McGruder, Grade 8
EV Cain Middle School

Treasure of My Life

Black, protective, quick, mighty, playful, treasured
His black, shiny coat I could brush all day
Furry and soft like a teddy bear
He would stand tall to block anyone in my way
He guarded me
With such speed he desired to run all day
I recall cheering at the top of my lungs
As he outran the grasp of a pitbull
Attached to a log, down the beach he tried to run into the bay
In amazement I fell to the sand
Marveling at his strength
In my backyard we spent our days in play
Playing fetch with him, I learned how to throw far
He came to me Christmas Day
Immediately we became best friends
But he had only 4 years with me to stay
I will never forget his life with me
My friend departed from me Thanksgiving Day
I know he watches me from heaven
Waiting for the day when we will again play
My dog, my Simba, my treasure!

Julia Rodriguez, Grade 7
St Cyprian School

Ode to Poetry

Rhyming, scheming, wording,
Imagining, feeling, describing
Is all you need to do.
To write a poem in your own point of view
Expressing your own soul
To state your own goal
Confessions of the heart
A written piece of art
Making yourself, you

Myra Cheah, Grade 8
La Joya Middle School

Kids and Their Ways

The sky is blue
The birds are out
Kids playing all about
Parents working all day and night
When they come home they all just fight
Their rooms are a mess
But they do not guess
That their dad is on his way home
They try to run and hide from him
But all they do is find a grin
Now they're in trouble
So they're cleaning on the double
Next time they will know when to clean
Before being lean, mean, fighting machines.

Brionna Harris, Grade 8
Madrona Middle School

The Poem Problem

What is my problem? Is that what you ask?
I can't write a poem, it's as simple as that.
I don't know what to write about
It makes me so angry, I want to shout!
It's not easy, as it turned out to be
Harder than spelling in the Spelling Bee.
Do I make it rhyme or not at all?
Do I write a long poem or keep it small?
Wait just one minute, just look and see!
I wrote a poem, oh yah! Yay me!

Sarah Dervartanian, Grade 8
Calvary Chapel of YL

Cannon Balls

Up and out
Water weighs me down
My arms struggle to lift me
Up and out
I shiver as I leave the warmth of the pool
And the cool breeze grazes my shoulders
Puddles collect at my feet
The scent of grilling hamburgers
Floats in the air
I breathe in
My mouth waters
My stomach grumbles
Bracing for my big splash
I taste the chlorinated water dripping from my brow
I take a running start and jump
The air cracks past as I fly
My feet cut the water's surface
I open my eyes and in a split second
I see water spray above me
And I hear my friends gasp
My famous cannon ball crashes once again

Allison Rogers, Grade 8
Tierra Linda Middle School

The Fight in Me

We are killing each other's sisters and brothers all day, every day and just to get paid
We over there killing people and they want more, sometimes I even forget what we're fighting for.
They say it's for freedom, well guess what we're free.
They try to lie but they can't stop the truth in me.
But before we stop fighting each other we've got to stop fighting ourselves.
Sometimes I wish we could just put our feelings on shelves.
Sometimes I think we need to stop, drop, sit, think, and slow the roll,
Just chill for a minute and take control.
They try to shut me up; they tell me I'm wrong.
But that's why I'm chilling here singing this song.
I'm wrong they say, they don't see how we see,
But until then, man…they'll never stop the fight in me

Noor Abasi, Grade 7
Holy Family Catholic School

Listen to Life

Listen, the first sound is heard,
The baby has just arrived and has been brought into this world
Listen, the first word has been said as tears glisten and cheeks go red
Listen, the child has taken its first step, then down it falls and pride is kept
Listen, hear the arguing and complaints about wanting this and that,
But how when there isn't enough money to spend on a hat
Listen, to screams of rage and stress while trying to pass school with success
Listen, to the parties that are going on as graduation has just ended
Listen, to all the confusion and worries to get into college oh wouldn't that be splendid?
Listen, adulthood has reached and soon they have left, and I am here to weep
Listen, I am old, but I am happy that my children have grown and now my life has been known

Kimberly Le, Grade 8
Martin Murphy Middle School

September Was My Birthday

I don't understand. Why did Daddy have to leave?
I don't understand. Why don't the pictures show him smile instead of bleed?
Mommy, I don't understand. Why are you crying and clutching me so tight?
You promised me my Daddy would be holding me tonight.

Daddy, where have you been all my life? We were supposed to meet for the very first time today.
You were a brave and fearless soldier that fell for his country is what they say.
Yet I stood with flowers in my hand until the thorns began to prick and burn.
War is bad, but you were a good guy — that's what I've learned,
So how come, Mommy, isn't Daddy coming home?

Daddy, I'm real confused. Mommy tells me you were a hero, a man who left to help.
But Daddy, if you were helping, why did they torture you to death?
Mommy tells me I have your smile, identical dimples and similar teeth.
Is it wrong of me to smile when our gazes have never even met?

I was an infant when you left me, I was five when you died.
Years have passed; nevertheless when darkness takes over sunlight, I still cry.
I wonder if you thought of me, that night you passed away.
I didn't want to believe them, but the truth prevailed to my dismay.

September is why you've left me.
September is what I became.

Vered Hazanchuk, Grade 9
Fremont High School

Stars

Stars are like bright glowing lights.
Glowing and flashing all through the night.
No chance of a hello or a simple good-bye.

Flickering and flashing all through the night.
Next thing you know they're no longer in sight.
Like light bulbs bursting in mid-air
Or shiny like glowing blonde hair.

Stars are like flashing spotlights scoping the sky
And like wild kids on a playground
Jumping and hopping in all directions
Or like Peri's eyes
Twinkling in the midnight sky.

Byron Davila, Grade 8
Madrona Middle School

The Mall

I went to the mall feeling happy
Starting out my fun shopping spree
My mom got a frown on her face
"Money please nothing is free…"

We started walking, I ran in the store
I went crazy looking at all the cute shirts
I couldn't decide what pretty thing to buy
I really liked a pair of pants and a colorful skirt.

I didn't buy anything, but my mom sure did
She bought a lot of clothes but nothing for me
I couldn't believe it I wanted to cry!
I sighed and said "So much for my shopping spree!"

Melissa Ramos, Grade 8
South Tahoe Middle School

Out in Flames

You come to the point
where the road crosses
to a street you've never walked down before
and you stop to think
where am I going?
I've cut corner
taken shortcuts
but all for nothing
just an empty, barren wasteland
turning around is so hard
when you've lost control of the wheel
gripping onto that little thread
so weak, so hard
then you find the Light
the past turns to ash
as you find change
and go out in flames

Lance Sutherland, Grade 8
Grace Lutheran School

The Dream

Imagine a family in a foreign country
A mom, dad, sister, brother, and a baby
They live in poverty, barely making in through the day
Their one dream is to live in America
They have no future in their country
In America they can go to school
Get a job, and live a fulfilling life
It is their only chance to have a rewarding life
It is…
The dream

Jasmin Camarena, Grade 7
Sarah McGarvin Intermediate School

Flight

I fly through the air,
I fly over the oceans,
over the mountains,
I feel free
nature and life is what I can see
when I am flying my life takes flight,
not only during the day but also during night,
the stars twinkle in the sky,
and I realize I am very small
but wonders like these are in us all
I can soar any time
all I have to do is close my eyes
my dreams always take flight
one day I wish to soar
with people both rich and poor,
with diverse people unlike me,
I just hope this could be a reality.

Mark Shyba, Grade 8
Palm Desert Middle School

Ode to Hands

Everyone has their very own pair
Each are different but they are yours to wear
Used as a tool to perform many tasks
They're at your command, do whatever you ask

They can be smooth or rough
Show if you are dainty or tough
Sometimes they are big, other times small
They can draw a picture or throw a baseball

Hands are a bird's big and feathered wings
She needs them to do various things
To fly through the endless skies above
Every bird has them pigeon and dove

Some people though do not get a set
Of hands it's sad but do not fret
For we can live without them but don't you see
Because of them life is much easier for you and me

Allison Yasuda, Grade 8
La Joya Middle School

After School

I have no time for play nor laughter.
Instead, I sit at my quiet desk,
Decorated with hundreds of paper,
Doing laborious homework,
While feeling
Miserably lonely, frazzled and fatigued.
I munch on my sizzling spaghetti dinner,
Savoring the home cooked meal
Until I accidentally spill a little sauce
On my clean match text book.
I can't help but think back
To my happy preschool times
When a day was still long and carefree.
Oh, how I miss those days!
Now, I am a controlled robot,
Spitting out homework,
Meeting dead-lines
And listening to enthusiastic teachers,
Who forget that even robots have to rest.

Tiffanie Hassanally, Grade 7
Rolling Hills Country Day School

What Is Music?

What is music?
Is it a melody?
Or is it just a bunch of lyrics?
It penetrates the mind.

Is it a way
to express
Feeling for something
or just a song?

Is it a bond
like a father and
a son or is it
a way of life?

Whatever it is
it must be good,
because it brings joy
to people's hearts.

Ryan Dill, Grade 8
Madrona Middle School

The Lake

I love to walk to yonder lake
To watch the fishes swim
And the frogs, their mouths agape
Catch flies on a moment's whim
Beneath the water, cool and green
Crayfish, snails, and tadpoles gleam
The wind stirs in the swaying grass
As I sit and watch the gray clouds pass

Tobin Holcomb, Grade 8
South Lake Middle School

Shattered Hearts

I don't mind pain it's something I can always endure.
The physical pain no longer makes me content or empty.
It's the emotional.
The emotional pain is what severs the arteries and destroys the heart.
And eventually when the heart is filled with so much pain and sorrow it gives up
Instead of a heart filled with warmth and love.
It becomes stone cold and desolate
Denying itself the sympathy or love for others.

Connie Chong, Grade 9
Diamond Bar High School

Unfathomable Reality

The wind whispers your name and you could've sworn it was me
All those lonely nights spent crying
And all you wished was to be free
Of the pain of loneliness that vows to haunt you

Your eyes are the stars that sparkle in the dark, night sky
You wish upon a shooting star
Then tears form, but you refuse to cry
But one by one, they end up falling anyway, like a river on your face

A tear for every time I looked away
A tear for every day I refused to see
A tear because of that little voice that says to just give up
And let it be

You choose to remain in the darkness
Not wanting to be found
Because one simple kindness
Just wasn't lying around

Jennifer Anaya, Grade 8
Valley Oak Middle School

No Address, Return to Sender

In life trickery and lunacy are always abound and afoot,
Always finding way to put people in a sweat and avoid staying put.
In fact, most people think that seeing is truly believing,
But really, the truth is, looks can actually be deceiving.
In simple geometric means, a sinkhole hidden from view endangers,
But one you change the angle view, noticing it can be a lifesaver.
What may be one man's garbage could be another man's treasure,
So a cardboard box to an adult might serve a child's imaginative pleasures.
Returning to the point, a mountain range, the odds can shift your way.
And is one man in power if he is the one left standing?
If he's the only one left, who will come to his crowning?
Is "life" just a transition period from one death to another?
Or is it supposed to be a time of redemption, where we forgive each other?
Is Earth the only one of its kind here in the universe?
Or are there other kinds like it that have either better ecosystems or worse?
I know that I am asking more questions than saying answers,
But I strongly believe that knowledge IS the major power.
Some say, "It all depends what you think in retrospective,"
But I say it all depends on an individual's perspective.

Victor Dang, Grade 8
Challenger School – Ardenwood

Thank You

The way the years fly by
And I am so very grateful.
Grateful for all the blessings you've given me.
So I just want to say thank you.
Thank you for the birds in the sky,
The love from my family
And for just waking me up every morning.
To find a new journey that you set for me.
Every day is a true blessing.
Everything that happens to me,
Everything I own, love, and care for are from you.
I know there are days where
I'm not so thankful.
So I made this poem for you, my savior.
So thank you, Lord, for everything you've done.
Thank you.

Brittney Buccat, Grade 7
Thornton Jr High School

Wish Upon a Star

A shooting star could be my lucky charm
And make my wish come true
In the darkness of night
If there is a shooting star
I would wish that my life would turn to perfect
That it would make no difference who I am

A shooting star is always alone
Something I understand too well
No matter where it is
It always falls to a far off place
Somewhere all alone
I guess a shooting star wants a friend.

It may never appear again
To make my wish come true.

Sue Lim, Grade 8
Madrona Middle School

Clouds

The clouds pass in a blue sky too white to be true
In different shapes scattered like white Elmer's glue

They move like graceful birds in the sky
When it rains we watch them cry

They are a shield over our head
When the sun is blazing red

Tweet, tweet, tweet the birds go
As they pass they entertain us with a show

We watch the clouds as we lay down in the grass
They slowly crash

Bella Vidaña and Haley Rutan, Grade 8
St Patrick Parish School

Adrenaline

Opalescent glass stained with winter breath.
Chest rising with each erratic heartbeat
at the sight of a landscape painted with snow.
Eyes stray to a side glance
gazing at a silhouette framed by stars gone astrew.
And then strides turn into miles a minute runs,
as limbs guide the mind
and the mind guides the muscle
that motioned faster than their erratic heartbeat.
A miscalculated tilt drives them over edge
and they are drowning — suffocating, in navy blue.
The lights go out, and the cost of adrenaline
becomes an evanescent clear
and the stars glitter for the last time.

Rene Bell, Grade 8
Thurgood Marshall Middle School

These Noises

Stop and hear all the noise within my head,
All these stupid voices scream in protest.
"Let me out, let me free, to see you dead."
"Pull the trigger!," they all make the request.
To prolong this infinite futile life,
I stand alone in this endless black hole,
And walk through the notions of endless strife.
Slowly sweeping me as they take control.
I try to imagine a clearer day,
I ponder, these voices are not a curse.
For they have helped me find another way,
Inside of me they give me strength to nurse.
A fight within me for eternity,
To rid myself of insecurity.

Tanya Sandoval, Grade 9
Orthopaedic Hospital Medical Magnet High School

Freedom

Freedom is like a voice,
So listen for the call,
So get your head out of gossip, the mall too.
You live in the USA
that means nothing is impossible.
Do you know what that means?
You're unstoppable,
follow your dreams until you get it
Never give up until you win it.
You have unlimited potential
it's all in you.
Don't let somebody bring you down,
or you'll be handing someone a menu,
be a star no matter what you are.
And no matter where you're from
I'm giving you inspiration,
now my poem is done!

Sam Washington, Grade 8
Madrona Middle School

Treacherous Funnel

Turning raging winds
Twisting vortex of chaos
Twirling destruction
Juan Hernandez, Grade 8
Almond Tree Middle School

Who Am I?

Funny
Sad
Cool
Wishes to dream
Dreams to hope
Wants to have a life
Who wonders about earth
Who fears happiness
Who is afraid of life
Who likes sodas
Who believes in family
Who loves mom
Who loves brother
Who loves homies
Who loves sister
Who plans to be a teacher
Who plans not to fail
Who plans to be a winner
Whose final destination is joy
Lidia Acosta, Grade 7
Almond Tree Middle School

A Snowman's Bane

Spring, spring go away
come again another day
for, surely, if you come again
it will transpire to my disdain
my buttons for eyes will droop
my carrot nose will go to poop
and my top hat will be befuddled
in the puddle of my former self
Vincent Dinh, Grade 7
Sarah McGarvin Intermediate School

Shooting Star

I think of you like
You are a shooting star
You are who you are
You help me believe
You help me to live
Without you I would be no one
I am who I am only because I have you
I am tired of saying I love you
I really want to say baby I need you
Now I say to myself
You aren't like a shooting star
Baby you are my shooting star
Melissa Mathai, Grade 7
Thornton Jr High School

Star

You cuddle in the corner,
And the darkness drowns your room,
Until you see that star shining bright in the midnight sky,
It stands alone,
No others to be found,
This one is different from others you've seen,
This star shines with radiance lasting forever,
It's as if it's calling to you saying you're not alone,
I'm here with you,
Then the darkness fades away,
The sun comes out with blue skies,
But you know you're not alone because you still see that star shining bright!
Juliann Coronado, Grade 7
Holy Family Catholic School

Raindrops

Pitter-patter, pitter-patter, raining on my head.
Raindrops keep falling, covering the land,
Fertilizing fruits, furnishing forests, falling freely.
The raindrops are a sign for everyone to see.

Drip, drop, drip, drop, raindrops landing on the roof.
The roof of the chapel where the funeral of my mom takes place.
We know her love surrounds us because the rain is coming down.
She is crying because she hates seeing us so sad.

Lost family members now looking down from above,
Shedding tears as they watch little children grow up.
Happy for those succeeding in life,
Raindrops are a sign of everlasting love.

The sky clears up after the long storm.
Sparrows sing songs of satisfaction.
The world is a garden once more,
Waiting for new things to live and love, grow and die.

Alison Knysh, Grade 8
Sacred Heart School

What St. Vincent Means

St. Vincent's school means so much to me
When I am at school I'm as happy as can be
Although things in life are not always fair
St. Vincent's teachers and staff always seem to care

No matter what it is or situation I'm going through
My teachers encourage me and tell me, "There's nothing I can't do."

I have friends and teachers who love me very much
Through the help of St. Vincent's my life has been touched
I have love in my heart that won't go away
St. Vincent's school is in my heart and forever it will stay

Erick Celis, Grade 7
St Vincent Elementary School

Ballet Class

The room is filled with dancers
With their shiny satin Pointe shoes,
Dirty canvas flat shoes,
And bright waist elastics.
There are black leotards
And pink tights,
And hair twisted into perfect buns.
Music floats through the air
As we dance swiftly.
Our artistry expresses the music.
Each step is different,
From tendu to grande jeté.
We dance at the barré,
Doing a million painful temps levés
And glide across the floor into the center;
We walk as if on air.
Feet get blistered, muscles become sore,
But we dance on anyway.

Kaitlin McGillivray, Grade 8
Rolling Hills Country Day School

Swinging

In a town there is a school,
At that school there is a school yard,
And in that school yard there is a swing set,
And on the swing set there is a girl.

She doesn't swing but smiles,
At the memory of a person,
Swinging next to her.

Melissa Treseler, Grade 8
St Joseph's School of the Sacred Heart

It's Our Friendship

Me and my friends are crazy
So many memories it becomes hazy
Movie nights with junk food
Pick Up Stix forces us to be in a good mood
Nights spent with endless laughter
No one ever wants to go home after
Meaningful conversations with tears
All trying to help with each other's biggest life fears
Countless pointless videos and random pictures
All of my friends feel like my brothers and sisters
Hundreds of prank phone calls
Several trips and falls
Joking fun fights
Even a broken light
Some of these days we may regret
But the best ones we will never forget
And through it all we will make it
For all the memories I'll never trade it
It's our friendship

Ondrea Ortega, Grade 9
Fountain Valley High School

The Game

On Saturday I lost a soccer game,
We were beaten by more than seven goals,
The other team thought we were very lame,
The game we lost was locked up in our souls,
We found out that we were not the best team,
We cried and wept at our latest defeat,
We knew that we had lost our playoff dream,
In our next game we expected a beat,
But maybe we're not the worst in the league,
If we work hard we can become the best,
Even in losses we will not fatigue,
Will try our best to defeat all the rest,
On Saturday we played a game again,
We won the game, it was very insane.

Paolo Reyes, Grade 8
John Adams Middle School

I Am

I am a drama queen and I am spoiled
I wonder why humans have 2 eyes instead of a million
I hear flying cars beep their horns
I see weird things
I want to be a veterinarian
I am a drama queen and I am spoiled
I pretend I'm a rock star
I feel happy when I'm with my friends
I touch the cars wings
I worry I won't make it to college
I cry when I'm alone
I am a drama queen and I am spoiled
I understand why kids can't be adults
I say "one day I'll be successful"
I dream that one day I'll see my Nae Nae again
I try to be as less dramatic as possible
I hope to graduate, some day
I am a drama queen and I am spoiled

Jannetta Jackson, Grade 7
California Virtual Academy

Lone Wolf

The lone wolf knows not what he hopes to find
He will travel alone for days on end
Forgetting not his brethren long behind
Alone he's weak, this he cannot pretend
Surviving with no home no mate no friends
Day and night he'll go on he'll never cease
His hunger weakness and sorrow won't end
He'll keep living, the chance that he'll find peace
A new home, new land he can call his own
The hope to start again with a new pack
The day he will no longer be alone
Although a dream has not a scent to track
The cold is bitter and the hunt is tough
But a dream, to the lone wolf is enough.

Raymond Elwell, Grade 9
Gunderson High School

Risk It Don't Think It

Afraid of rejection
And failure,
Always need protection,
Can't leave your comfort zone

Dare to cross the line
Embrace the risks,
Surprised at what you'll find
No more "what ifs…"

Don't regret, remember
When you took that extra step
You'll never forget, it's forever,
You made it last today.

You'll love what you've gained
after pushing the limit
You made it through the pain,
And it's worth what you're receiving
Miguel Flores, Grade 7
Sarah McGarvin Intermediate School

Hollywood

Hollywood
Shiny, sparkly
Shopping, acting, dancing
Stars, stores — Rain, clouds
Raining, walking, boring
Dark, freezing
Santa Maria
Emily Garcia, Grade 7
St Mary of Assumption School

i am

i am a small fish in the sea.
i am the chocolate in the cookie.
i am a bear in the wild.
i am a star in the sky.
i am a flower in a field.
i am a bird with dreams.
Jennifer Marie Avalos, Grade 7
St Mary of Assumption School

Growing Up

I wonder if I am ever
Going to stay
The same
Or if I will ever
Grow taller
And have longer hair
Or if I get shorter
I just want to
stay the same
Sandra Merino, Grade 7
Richland Jr High School

The Place of My Dreams

France is the place of my dreams
It has so many rivers and streams
France is the place I would like to be
For the first time I would travel
I would go on an airplane and see
I would not have to go by camel
France is the place of my dreams
I would like to taste the French cream
I would like to speak their language
And try their cheesy sandwich
Selene Perez, Grade 7
John Adams Middle School

Money Doesn't Grow on Trees

Money doesn't grow on trees
Even though it's paper

A rich man takes it
Even though it isn't there

It's dark inside the house
Even though there's light

There's starvation everywhere
Even though there's food

Cars drive along
Even though they're out of gas

The coats are warm
Even though it's not cold

A rich man takes for granted
What he knows others don't have
Rachel Demers, Grade 7
Monte Vista Christian School

Anger

Anger is fire,
Anger is a volcano,
It is a facade,
Anger dwells in your body.
Joshua Camit, Grade 7
Almond Tree Middle School

Up in the Sky

At the top of the hill we lay
looking up into the sky
darkness surrounds us
dots twinkling in our eyes
up high in the evening sky
thousands, no millions,
stars in the sky…
Tracy Vu, Grade 7
Sarah McGarvin Intermediate School

Without You

Hearts red all turn to pink.
Forever on my mind, making me think.
Thoughts fill my head,
like a pencil without lead.
No one can fill the emptiness within,
like a thread without a pin.
Like a book without words,
like a morning without birds.
When you're gone I have no meaning.
Without you I cannot live.
Alecia Lewis, Grade 7
California Virtual Academy

Separation

Fall comes,
It's time to go.
She says goodbye
To who she knows.

Wish she had stayed,
'Cause I'll never know
How far away
She'll truly go.

Will she come back,
To stay with me?
Well, until then,
Waiting, I will be.
Jackie Chisholm, Grade 7
St Cyprian School

Silence, the Double Edged Sword

Hushed whispers
Whispered tones
To those I know
I only speak to
I have been branded
With several names
Smart
Quiet
Geek
I don't care what they say
But at the same time I do
My shield is weak
Many get through
I would rather use
My painter's hand
Than talk the current talk
I have learned to be strong
To deal with today's
Awful talk and ways
Until the barrier of silence falls
Silence shall be my double edged sword
Taylor Kruger, Grade 8
La Joya Middle School

Ode to Air

You may seem invisible, but I know you're there
You're sun kissed and crisp
You are air,
You help me breathe and cool me down,
Thank you air for being around.

Carissa Alforque, Grade 7
Santa Rosa Technology Magnet School

Tell Me if You Love Me or Not

I love
and I want you to love
Do you love me or not?
I just need to know
I really need to be with you
but I have to face the fact that it might not happen
I really love you
My love is a fire that can't be put out
As time flies by so fast
I long to say "I love you"
But whenever I try
My heart tells me not to tell you
Because of the fear that you will not love me back
Although I could get hurt
I'll continue to love you
But I really want you to say yes
So we can be together
So do you love me or not?!

Ryan Chang, Grade 7
Sarah McGarvin Intermediate School

Can I Tell You Something

Whenever you talk to me
I see your beautiful smile
You always look lovely
Why can't we hang out for awhile?

I treasure the moments we had
It felt like it would never end
Do you remember the things we said?
We'll weather the storm and will not bend
I'm tired of all your excuses
I tried so many things so you'd notice
Girl, what we had is special
Has our divine love ever been true?
What can I do now…
Now that you don't want to be mine?
Did I let you down?
On that one special night…?

Should I tell you everything I know?
Because I don't want to lose you
I thought that you would be mine
Looks like I have to tell you:
I want you till the end of time.

Allen A. Lucas, Grade 7
Corpus Christi School

Jesus, the Light of My World

Jesus is a child of God, just like us.
Jesus is a teacher who teaches us to follow.
Jesus is the light that makes morning come.
Jesus is the judge who will judge in the end.
Jesus is the love that opens our hearts.
Jesus is the step that shows us the way.
Jesus is infinite; He is as big as you want.

Sadie Miller, Grade 7
St Mary of Assumption School

Dedicated

You smile like the dazzling stars at night
Eyes sparkle like the light from the moonlight
When you're short dreamy hair passes through tight,
Fingers feel like feathers out of sight
When I hear your voice it feels like I'm lost,
Navigating the deep ocean below
Dancing is what you do at any cost.
You move like Chris Brown in the video
Caring for me is what you do best like,
A mother caring for her newborn kid
I love it when words come out of your mic,
And you make me laugh nonstop, love you kid
When you speak to me I love it when you,
Make me feel I'm the only one with you.

Desiree Fuentes, Grade 8
Henry T Gage Middle School

Piles of Books

Piles upon piles of books were lying in her room.
They told stories: some of victory, some of doom.
Some of the books were fantasy and science fiction,
Others told of fights between people which caused friction.

Some of the books taught how to cook a delicious meal,
A few showed how to clean a boo-boo so it would heal.
Quite a few books were about traveling the world;
Some told of wild winds that swirled and twirled.

Some were picture books with pretty illustrations,
Others told of mountains with tall elevations.
One was a book that told of many arts and crafts;
Another instructed how to make wooden rafts.

All of the books were of different colors and sizes.
Some of them were so beautiful they could have been prizes.
On top of a little green hardback book there tottered another,
One that was larger and heavier and had a darker cover.

Some of the pages in some of the books had darkened with age;
Others were younger, and inside their covers new was the page.
Because of their differences, each book is a tapestry,
And in each one the author writes for us a truth or story.

Sara Kipps, Grade 8
Challenger School – Ardenwood

America

The land of the free
And the home of the brave

This means America

The land of the free

To be as free as an eagle
Soaring in the breeze

A land where everyone
Is as free as you and me

To be as free as a flowing river
As free as the gentle wind

This means America

The home of the brave

To lay down your life
To save your country

To say goodbye
And not cry

To fight through impossible odds
For the one you love

This means America

The land of the free
And the home of the brave.
Daniel O'Connor, Grade 8
Ysmael Villegas Middle School

Winter

Winter is windy
It is really cold and breezing
It is really fun
Isabel Covarrubias Romero, Grade 8
Almond Tree Middle School

My Valentine

My valentine
Is my true love
He is not very tough
As I gaze
Into his eyes
I see love, joy,
And happiness
My valentine is
Just the right guy
For me.
Mercedes Miller, Grade 7
Richland Jr High School

A Simple Gesture

One can only imagine the misery and despair
Felt by all the poor little kids who don't have a true home.
Never having been loved. No one ever seems to care about them
As they see it through their sad neglected eyes.
To them all hope seems to have vanished before them.
However, that can be changed with a small effort.
Make a donation, give them a toy, give clothes to charity.
Do anything that you can do to make those poor kids happy.
When you do so, you will know, deep down in your heart,
That you had done the right thing; you had made a difference.
You had improved the lives of some depressed child.
You had helped to revive the hope of a young, shattered soul.
A soul that had been crushed by the fatigue of their lives
Lives, oh, such lonely lives, punctuated by grief and remorse.
Their lives had truly been miserable, but you had helped that to change:
Through a simple gesture, you had given them hope.
For when they realize what you had done for them,
They will know that they are not alone, that someone truly cared.
Morgan Zachary Brubaker, Grade 7
Citrus Hills Intermediate School

My Brother

My brother is a pain in the rear end.
He's always bugging for something he wants.

Everything I get, he wants.
Everything I do, he does.

There is no reasoning with my little bro,
He always wants and gets.

And when I want something he has,
I am not to touch because it's his.

Now that he's a little older he got a little better,
But still a little annoying.

Since he's older his punishments are like mine,
So when we get in trouble we get the same punishment.

but I think that he was just annoying because he didn't understand.
Now that he does, it's my turn to get him in trouble.
Valeria Estrada, Grade 7
Almond Tree Middle School

Learning French

I never thought that I'd learn a new language.
Specially French, before I took that language I thought it would be hard.
My first year wasn't that hard.
Neither was my second year.
It makes me wonder if I will take another year.
The third year is really special.
It is special because maybe I can go to France.
Going to France will be awesome.

Mary Rivas, Grade 7
John Adams Middle School

Let It Go

Now I know this has all been true,
Time to take out the old and bring in the new.
So now it's time to give it a rest,
Trying to show out all of my best.
Knowing the hurtful truth, has been hard for me to know.
I can't hide this feeling anymore, so now it's got to show.
You've been going through my mind like a movie in my head.
Here another tear for me to shed.
This seemed so long, but ended so soon,
Guess I've been acting like a ridiculous goon.
In the end, I feel this emotional depression.
Seems like this feeling is starting to be an obsession.
Never knew that the day of sadness will ever come clear,
Knowing the truth wasn't ever going to disappear.
The feeling will stay as it's supposed to be made,
Nothing, not anything at all will make it fade.
This mood isn't what I expected it to be,
Guess you haven't figured out it was all about me.
So until this day forward, I'll be forgetting this ever started,
But for now, my heart will be parted.
So all I have to do now is just let it go.

Kimberly Reyes, Grade 9
Great Oak High School

The Sound of Music

Music comes in many ways.
I just like the way it plays.
When I listen to the beat,
It makes me just want to tap my feet.
Wherever I go; whatever I do,
Music just makes me want to yell woo-hoo!
Too bad nothing lasts forever…
But should I ever deny the sound of music? Never.

Michael Tran, Grade 7
Sarah McGarvin Intermediate School

The Sanity Corner

You can take your castles
And your statuettes of power
(They chip and crumble in the light)
You can take life's majesty in all
Tall things, my friend.
But leave me my corner.
Leave me my closets of grace,
Of embezzled wealth and burned-out matches.
Leave me my cheating husbands,
And the poor who sleep under bridges.
I will need it some day —
A featherbed to take my rest on.
And my children, they'll be few
And be children of a lesser God
But still, I will cradle them close come dawn,
Come the shining of your people.

Lana Frankle, Grade 9
Los Gatos High School

Walk with Me

Will you walk onto the future with me?
Our hearts happy and light
With our faces towards the sun,
We'll be as one
We'll walk hand in hand,
The steps we take will be slow
You and I are the only ones,
At this moment, here, now
The rocky path laid out before us,
Hand in hand, we go as one
You shiver with the cold,
I wrap you in the fold
Our hands reach out to touch one another,
The warmth of our hearts is felt in that touch
We know we will get through the storm,
The storm around us breaks
But we bravely walk on,
Towards the sun seen through the clouds
Walking towards the future,
Hand in hand, we are one.

Stefan Hollinger, Grade 8
Palm Desert Middle School

William's Toy

There was a boy
Who had an awesome toy.
His name was William
Who fell in plutonium.
It wasn't the finest hour
As he took a long shower,
To wash the radiation away.
They think he is insane to this day.
He has long hair,
Be careful not to stare.
He has a big grin,
That is not a sin.
Now he is in a padded cell
Waiting to escape his personal Hell.
I have his toy and I am the one grinning now!!!

Lorenzo Leibig, Grade 7
St Linus School

Memories

Another year flies by once more
Flies by fast until it flies nevermore.
Years are full of memories, some old others new
Good memories are cherished, they're only a few.
And those that are remembered are filled with you
Of the good old times you and I had in the past,
Unfortunately those years have flown by oh so fast.
They flew by quickly, faster than light
Until the years slowed down to see the magnificent sight
And make new memories to cherish once more,
To remember until you and I are no more.

Ian Esparza, Grade 8
Walter F Dexter Middle School

A Kid and His Bike

Every day I see this kid riding his bike down the street. He goes, but he never comes back. I wait, and I wait for him to come back. But he never comes back. But the next day he always comes back at the same time every day. So one day I stop him and ask him, "Where do you go to?" and all he does is shrug his shoulders and keeps on riding and riding.

Sutter T. Choisser, Grade 7
Holy Family Catholic School

Purple and White Tulips Forever

The ride was now over, "time to go," she said
as I gather my possessions I think to myself, "Is this the last?"
Is this the last time to say? "Hello, good-bye, good morning, good night," or even "I love you?"

I stand as straight as a soldier, ready for anything but still terrified
she says it's time to go, I go
I look and see the beautiful yellow house, with its fresh cut green lawn
and bright purple and white tulips

I walk closer and closer to the door, but with each step I get further and further
as I walk I think, but dare not say, "will I ever see you again?"

For so long now I have been the son of a murdered father,
but now, for the first time I'll become the song of an abandoning mother
I do not want to go! I hate you!

Arguments put to side, because now I'm here
the door bell rings, door opens she says, "It's about time"
I look around and see the green lawn,
and the purple and white tulips, and the yellow house

No longer shall I have a mother today I disown her
I'm on my own now
Purple and White Tulips Forever!

Adrian Lee Vannorsdall, Grade 8
La Joya Middle School

A Life Changing Moment

BAM, I open my eyes as I hit the windshield and fall back into my seat
I look at my mom as she moans in pain
I try to get out of the car and get help and my mom says no, stay in your seat and be still
As I sit and listen I feel a wet sensation on my face
I go to wipe my face and look at my hand and I see blood and glass
Crying just won't take the pain away
As I ask my mom if I'm going to die my door opens
An off duty firefighter tells me that he just saw the whole thing, then tells me his name
When I hear the ambulance I just didn't really think
After I was out of the car on the stretcher they told me that they were going to take the hair out of my wounds
As they peeled the hair off my face one by one I think to myself
Crying just won't take the pain away
As they are putting an intravenous tube in my arm
I try to look around but I can't see any facial expressions
My eyes were taped closed
And I think to myself, Crying just won't take the pain away
As I'm getting my last stitches I start to cry and now they are done
I think to myself,
Crying just won't take the pain away

Ashley Wangenheim, Grade 8
EV Cain Middle School

Ideas of the Unknown

I look into the sky
And I hear the flyers bellow of the untried
I look into the ocean
And I hear the waters shout of the broken
I look into the Earth
And I hear it yell of unknown worth
I look into the forest
And I hear the trees wail of the drowning of the greatest
Ideas of the unknown men

I hear them all cry out
Of how all the unknown fade-out
Bringing the greatest of everyone
To be shot by the gun
Of the judging who want
To be the ones who flaunt

Why the unknown never can be heard
Maybe they are all marked as a nerd
Maybe they are all marked as a crackpot
Maybe they are thought to never have a way to the jackpot
Maybe they will have the new idea

Alex Bertsch, Grade 7
Holy Family Catholic School

High School

Today is the lucky day,
I'm going to be a freshman
The nail-biting choices I will have to make,
The teachers will be harder
And will get on my nerves,
But, hey, it's high school,
The drama will get crazier and more twisted,
Crushes will be crushed and others will happen,
Some friendships will be broken
Some will be renewed,
But, hey, it's high school,
You have to remember to be yourself
And don't give into pressure,
There will be some struggles here and there,
But, hey, it's high school.

Christian Flores, Grade 7
St Alphonsus School

I Never Promised You a Rose Garden

I never promised you a rose garden
so why are you telling me I did?
I never promised you a rose garden
so why are you telling me so?

I never told you not to go
so why are you saying it was me?
I never told you not to go
so why are you saying that I did?

Jennifer Le, Grade 7
Sarah McGarvin Intermediate School

Mother of Mine

Mother of mine why don't you listen to me
I call your name but, you're still not listening
You're hardly home so when you're here it's a dream
I love feeling your beautiful hair
Run through my fingers like crystal clear streams
Mother of mine your presence is dear
So please come home and let me know that you're near

Priscilla La Salle, Grade 8
McCabe Elementary School

Family Reunions

Summer is coming, together we'll be
Traveling the distance
Playing games with family

Hugging everyone we see
Getting together with uncles and aunts
Summer is coming, together we'll be

Singing and dancing Karaoke
Grandma teaching cousins the chicken dance
Playing games with family

Telling stories of family history
To be the first in the shower you have a slim chance
Summer is coming, together we'll be

Cardboard cutouts of our missionaries
Taking pictures with cousins, grandparents, uncles, and aunts
Playing games with family

Building up the family tree
With love that's deeper than a passing glance
Summer is coming together we'll be
Playing games with family

Hannah Nelson, Grade 7
CORE Butte Charter School

Summer Days

Summer seems hot, but it's never ending.
Every day seems like an endless torment.
Flowers grow but everything is pending.
Too bad for those who miss it.
The sun shines brighter than the silver moon.
Yet we are blinded by its gorgeous view.
Even the small creatures make a nice tune.
Beautiful places could be just a few.
Mountains, forests; endless skies are great art.
It seems unreal but there is more to it.
Nothing can be compared but we can try.
At least there are places to go visit.
The world should be full of serenity.
Day and night, we should admirer beauty.

Ana Choc, Grade 8
John Adams Middle School

So Much Left to Say

So much left to say,
as you leave the stage.
Once a friendship is lost,
you get locked in a cage.
People become friends,
but then they follow the trends.
So they come and go,
to your final goodbye
Then you realize,
there was so much left
to say…

Raquel Balboa, Grade 7
Stephens Middle School

I Am Lost

I am lost with no where to go.
    Do you know how I flow?
    Please tell me where to go!

I am away from my family —
    Away from my friends —
    And away from the people that I love.

I am hungry and cold,
    Scared and dazed,
    I am lost.

Cynthia Romero, Grade 8
Santa Rosa Technology Magnet School

Friends But Lovers

I saw her
I saw him
best friends in love
but they don't tell
how they feel

I want to tell him
but don't know how
I want to tell her
but ashamed to tell.
What if she doesn't feel the same
I'll feel embarrassed
what if he doesn't like me
I'll turn red and be ashamed

This is how I felt before I knew
this is what I said before I found out
this was tough we should have told
each other sooner

Our friends think its weird
but we don't care because
we are two best friends in love
and that's why we care!

Leslee Martinez, Grade 7
Sarah McGarvin Intermediate School

Thinking of You

I think about you each and every day
Every second, every minute, every hour
I think about you in my sleep, and in my dreams
Hoping you feel the same way

I miss your kisses and your hug
And the way you used to hold me and look at me
I miss your sweet, kind words

I miss the days when I ran up to you
With tears running down my face
And all you did was hold me
And tell me everything will be ok

I miss the days when we just walked hand in hand across the beach
When my hair was flying all over the place from the wind
And you moved it with your gentle hand

Even though you left me, I will never forget you
A million words won't bring you back
Neither will a million tears
R.I.P. to my closest friend: Jay
You're gone but never forgotten

Diana Abdelmalak, Grade 8
Madrona Middle School

The Ember

My internal fire forever burns. Tiny embers started it a while back.
It's eternal, unique, everlasting; It brightens what was once pitch black.

My internal fire forever burns. It defines everything I wish to be.
Carrying my emotions, my thoughts and wit, this fire burns on gracefully.

This internal fire that forever burns strengthens as I gain more sense.
My parents, friends, family, and others all added to my fire an influence.

My internal fire forever burns. It has given me a goal:
That one day I can be the ember that lights the fire in another's soul.

My internal fire forever burns, but I hope that in ten years
That the person's fire that I lit can light another's with no fears.

And if more internal fires are lit…and more and more and more,
They will illuminate and always burn; brightening what was dark before.

So the internal fires that will burn will be because of me
Because I made the difference by being an ember allowing more fires to be.

My internal fire forever burns, and this it does no less.
My internal fire cannot be extinguished, even when I lay lifeless.

Saraiyah Hatter, Grade 8
Citrus Hills Intermediate School

Utah, I Love Thee

I'd rather be a Utahn, than be a Georgia peach
I'd rather be in Salt Lake than on a California beach
I'd rather hear the buzzing of a lovely honey bee
And sing out loud our state hymn, "Utah We Love Thee"
I'd rather not admire pine when I can have blue spruce
I favor rocky mountain elk over the lowly moose
I will refuse to cha cha, for me it's just square dance
I'll help myself to cherries, whenever there's a chance
I'd rather wear a topaz than diamonds or a pearl
It seems to me, I'll always be, a true blue Utah girl

Rachael Cohen, Grade 7
Kadima Heschel West Middle School

The Clock

On your wrist or on your wall
One foot high or three feet tall
I am your help I am your guide
When on your wrist, always by your side

I tell the time 12 numbers in total
Just like a year a dozen full
I make you early and make you late
My presence is vital, there's no debate

Hours, minutes, seconds, too
This my service, I give to you
The hour strikes ten my bell goes DONG
For Mr. A's smart clock my time is wrong

It doesn't matter my design
I do one thing, I tell the time
On your wrist or on your wall
Anytime I tell them all

Brian Kobayashi and Billy Slane, Grade 8
St Patrick Parish School

Love

Pink candy hearts line the hugs and kisses of everyone
While red roses touch the hearts of romantics.
Chocolates cause chaos among crowds
And
Purple bears stuff the hearts of children everywhere.
What day is today?
It is the day of kisses and hugs,
The day of love.
The one day when cupid is able to run free.
Today is Valentine's Day.
Love fills the air with a sweet aroma.
The sky is filled with chocolates and roses.
I think to myself,
"Love shouldn't just be celebrated one day out of the year,
But every day."
Love is boundless.

Alexia Martin, Grade 8
Rolling Hills Country Day School

Flag of the Free

The flag of our nation, the flag of our past
Its power and honor will always last
Waving, pulsing and tugging away
Lies the stripes of red and the stars of grey

For all the soldiers who have died to protect
You have shown your flag ultimate respect
She welcomes people who want to be free
She is the symbol of being all you can be.

What do you see up there so high?
That we bow our heads as we pass it by
I see that flag that represents you and me
The flag of the brave, the flag of the free

Carl Otto, Grade 7
St Hilary School

The Freedom of Life

America is full with freedom
The soft green grass
The wonderful animals on the strong terrain
The rivers and streams running through our states
The beautiful trees in our natural parks
The bees obtaining pollen in our colorful flowers
The ocean waves crashing on our shoreline
People enjoying the American Dream
Our presidents leading our country
We are free
The freedom of life is in our hearts

Ariel Gootnick, Grade 8
Kadima Heschel West Middle School

Miss Spring

As Miss Spring comes along,
All flowers open up to show what they've got.
They want to impress Miss Spring,
For she is the boss of them all.
As Miss Spring comes along,
The leaves from the trees come out to show their greenery.
They race each other to see who is the newest,
And the winds rush, to see who is the coolest.
As Miss Spring comes along,
She pours her charm into the garden,
She makes people sing,
And out come the magical colors of spring.
As Miss Spring comes along,
Every plant and creature sings a song,
To greet Miss Spring,
For she loves them all.
As Miss Spring comes along,
She gets them ready for the next season,
Everyone is full of joy,
For Miss Spring has come for one and only one reason.
Miss Spring has come to wake them all.

Luciane Lee, Grade 8
Madrona Middle School

Life

Life is about wondering and discovering
What is happening to you
And everyone around you
Life is the way of freedom
And how we live in our environment
It's the way we act, learn, play, work,
And figure out who we are
We hope that life
Won't let us down
But you have to remember
Life is full of surprises and wonders
Natasha Pimentel, Grade 8
Madrona Middle School

Sound

Sound is like a whispering ghost
It can be soft, cheerful
bleak, terrifying
Sound is like a symphony
It is forever
joyful
Sound is my life
for without it
I won't live
Sound is my world
for without it
I would not exist
Sean Mahamongkol, Grade 7
Lawson Middle School

Nature

I'm walking down a path
The trees seem to whisper to me
I laugh in spite of myself
The trees look like Christmas trees
As the morning mist gleams on them
The sun is smiling down at me
And I feel like a brand new person
As everything around me comes to life
Kristin Whaley, Grade 8
Citrus Hills Intermediate School

Ode to My Best Friend

My friend, my friend
What can I say?
She's my source of laughter
All night and day

On picnics and hiking
Big smiles while biking
Watching our favorite movie
Man, we together are just…
GROOVY!!!
Vanessa Zin, Grade 8
Citrus Hills Intermediate School

Success with Friends

Success with friends,
Always the hardest,
Why?
Because trusting people.
You hardly met,
Is pretty hard,
You know it's true,
The only people you can trust
Are the friends you've,
Known your whole life,
These people aren't just friends,
They are best friends.
Salem Valdez, Grade 8
Hesperia Jr High School

Wonder

Why did you leave?
Was it because of me?
I was an inconvenience.
I completely agree.

You were just a teen.
I was a bit unexpected.
A child of your own?
Your sanity had been infected.

I often sit and wonder,
how life would now be.
Would it just be you,
And mommy, and me?

Don't you get it?
I want you to come and see.
That girl that you left behind.
The woman yet to be.
Jasmine Balderas, Grade 8
La Joya Middle School

Metamorphosis

I used to be a slow, slimy caterpillar
But now I'm a beautiful, swift butterfly.

I used to be a boring snow white egg
But now I'm a cute little chick.

I used to be wet slimy paint
And now I'm a masterpiece painting.

I used to be a puffy cloud
But now I'm clear rain.

I used to be at the beginning
And now I'm at the end.
Lauren Wittkopf, Grade 8
Citrus Hills Intermediate School

Soccer

Soccer is a lot of fun
You must run, run, run
You try to score a goal
Do not get the ball stole

You can have 12 players on the field
When it starts, do not yield
Every player needs to pass

This is a game of teamwork
At practice you must work
At the game just have fun

This is a sport I love to play
If I had time I would do it every day
That is my favorite sport, soccer.
Liam Crotty, Grade 7
Joan MacQueen Middle School

Seasons Change

Watching the day pass
From day to night.
Colors changing leaves and grass
With the sun out of sight.
The light of day
Covers the painted blue sky.
Only if we could all stay
Me wishing with a sad sigh.
Seasons change
When we don't even know it.
This action may be strange
But, we shouldn't just quit
To find a way
That leads us all
To one place
At one time
Where it isn't blocked by a wall.
From white to brown
Yellow to red.
Trees and bushes cover the town
But, it's already time for bed
Kirsten Vega, Grade 7
St Dominic Elementary School

Spell to Cure Lies and Gullibility

Word of truth and mind of gold
Wipe away the grime and mold
Salutary judgment, too
Get rid of lies, through and though
Sight of owl and ear of bat
Cure fractious trust just like that
Make a person smart and wise
Scourge the false, darkening lies
Sage Miller, Grade 7
The Mirman School

Mournful Love

You know you love someone but you don't show it,
You regret what you say but you just don't know it,
You can see the pain in their eyes,
But all you hear are jokes and lies,
You want to tell them how you feel,
But you can't because your love is so real,
The fiery passion within your soul,
Has died out and now is coal,
You think they like you back,
But you don't know for a fact,
You try to play it cool,
But you act like a fool,
So let me remind you why you never lie,
So don't let your feelings die
Because the person you love will pass right by,

Andrew Carrillo, Grade 8
Valley Oak Middle School

A Poem Is Not So Easy

I am just sitting here trying to think of a ballad,
About science, math, music, or even about fruit salad.
However, I cannot seem to get a single good thought.
Just about any will do, whether I like it or not.
I can write a long documentary all about life,
Describing in vivid detail, the happiness and strife.
I have an idea now, alas, it is not so good.
I will not write senselessly about anything I could.
As I cycle though my list, from each idea to the next,
Maybe I will come back to that one, or I will find the best.
Unfortunately, nothing I think of seems to be the right one.
What else is there to think of, everything seems to be done?
I have a wide variety of topics in my head.
I can do sports, school, my friends, or even my life instead.
As I discard each fleeting thought or idea in turn,
It becomes harder to think, but much easier to learn.
I am nearing the end of the line, my thought will come soon.
Any idea right now would seem like a mystic boon.
An idea is forming; I really hope I am not wrong.
Aha, I have got it, I will write on how to write a song!

Arun Pingali, Grade 8
Challenger School – Ardenwood

Love

Love is sweet, love is romantic.
Love can hurt you as love can kill you.
As we look down on each other,
love is in the air and in our hearts
That we soon combine as a pair.
Our passion together will result in eternity,
forever in our souls, as we open our hearts to ourselves and
Look within the true meaning of love.
We look down in a deep dark hole
Where we soon find the light of passion forevermore.
Love is all you need to live.

David Contreras, Grade 8
Spring Grove Elementary School

Reality

Decisions on what to do
Disappointment on what he said
Angry at myself
For being so patient for him
To change his attitude

His decision making
Ashamed that he didn't even notice
That my heart was damaged
Through the pain
To feel neglected is more than enough
Why can't he notice what is happening to us
The pain is almost over

Now to tell my true love
That there is no chemistry between us
Although one heart was broken
Our lives are still the same

Norian Valencia, Grade 7
Monte Vista Christian School

One Day

The shrieks of horror faded,
An unsuspecting silence came,
One final deep breath before the plunge,
The eyes of evil open,
And in an instant our loved are stolen.

A home of safety invaded,
Two towers that once touched the sky,
Fell to the ground in which they so elegantly stood,
Five sides turns to four,
And a green field turns to fire and ash.

An evil bent on its rise,
Out of malice, hatred, and cruelty,
It will not stop,
Until all bend the knee.

It reached out to murder the good of this world,
On a day that will never be forgotten.

Connor Park, Grade 8
Tierra Linda Middle School

Our Home, Earth

A place with green trees and clear streams.
Blue skies with puffy clouds…
The way people live starts changing,
Caring for the environment is a rare action…
Waters turn black and the skies go dark…
The weather starts changing and frozen giants collapse…
The only chance left is to make a change,
Before there is nothing left.

Francelia Acosta, Grade 7
St Mary's School

Television

The television is a
God made machine.
Lighting up like the sun
Shining on a ravine.

The television talks to anyone
Who wishes to see,
For the television is a friend
To everybody.

When I turn it on,
There's no turning back.
I'll keep on watching
Until my eyes crack.

I'd organize my room,
Clean the dishes to precision,
And go to bed early
Just to be with the television.
MacKenzie Menthen, Grade 8
Rolling Hills Country Day School

The Snow

Snow is purely white
People make rounded snowballs
Snowmen stare ahead
Liana Novak, Grade 7
South Tahoe Middle School

Ants in My Pants

Do you know that feeling
When you feel a slight tickle
Something is crawling up your leg
You find you're in a fickle

You're stuck there in a chair
Your legs and arms squirm
Hope everyone doesn't see you
You start to feel like a worm

Your leg gives a shake
Your hand gives a scratch
Keep yourself hidden
Let that ant get snatched

Your uneasiness draws attention
You are very uncomfortable now
Running to the restroom
Ridding yourself of the ant somehow

You hope no one will remember
That weird little dance
Next time make sure you know to
Beware of ants in your pants
Jeni Pinson, Grade 7
Calvary Chapel of YL

Frozen

You flip the page, and what do you see?
A small little baby frozen in time,
Being held by Grandpa, smiling away,
The baby so small, Grandpa's hand like sandpaper
But with the gentlest touch he rubs the cheek
That's softer than new leather, baby sleeps,
Knowing Grandpa is at her side, never wafting here or there
His love undying, undying, for he cares too much for his newborn granddaughter,
Soon baby awakens, pacifier runs to her, but does no good,
Grandpa, who is always near, picks her up and soothes her,
She quiets hearing Grandpa's voice so tender,
Yet it booms like more than ten storms
He smiles at her, for her cry is so cute, knowing she loves him a lot,
He is so into her, not even food, for he is a big man, can pull him away,
He is asked to stand up and smile real big
A flash is seen, it has been said a picture holds a thousand words,
But it wouldn't fit into twenty-one lines,
Who is that baby you ask? Why, it's me, now fourteen,
Back then I was not even a year, but Grandpa is gone, now up in Heaven,
But he still loves me and I still love him,
I flip the page and know he is mine.
Korina R. Ruelas, Grade 8
Valley Oak Middle School

The Nation's Dove

She is remembered with great respect.
One known to be brave and courageous,
Eleanor Roosevelt definitely portrayed her kindness.
Civil rights was her main project.
She will never be forgotten, I expect
Because if that were so, it would be outrageous.
It would also diminish her greatness.
When her husband was stricken with polio, her goal was to protect.
Eleanor was a woman with power;
She stood alone because she was not part of a herd.
She was, what you would say, a beautiful flower
A white dove, a free bird.
All her accomplishments cannot be described in only one hour
With great impact, she spoke her words.
Divya Gowthaman, Grade 9
Irvington High School

War

War is very devastating,
Deaths are caused, lives are ruined, and horror is about.
Tears are shed and blood is, too,
Tears come from the ones who lost someone very dear to them.
While tears from the soldiers are replaced with their blood,
But, their deaths do not go in vain, for they are
honored on Veteran's Day.
Violence explodes on the battlefield and carnage is everywhere,
But, everything will be a distant memory and all shall be forgotten.
The soldiers' bravery though will not be forgotten,
All shall lean towards peace as war is just a memory now.
James Lozano, Grade 7
Tenaya Middle School

All Around Me

All around me, people claim to care.
All around me, nothing but concerned faces.
The only one missing is the one I want the most.
My mind tells me to forget him,
My hearts says give him a chance.
All around me, I'm finding out the truth.
All around me, every lie he ever told is slowly unfolding.
Every word he ever said was nothing but deceit.
My mind tells me to let it go,
My heart say to find out how he feels.
All around me, confusion rules.
All around me, but I'm still missing that one face.

Chelsea Quick, Grade 9
Orange Glen High School

God's Promise!

God's promise gives us hope today
To live our life in his own way
His love his grace and mercy too
Create new light with the morning's dew
As flowers bloom and green grass grows
God's promise shows through pretty rainbows
God's promise gives us hope today
That those who are lost
Will come to be saved

Alexis Washington, Grade 7
Chino Valley Christian Schools

I Am a Phoenix…

I don't fly like a bird,
I don't soar like a plane,
As I swish silently past the sky,
There's a path of flame.

I am a Phoenix,
Watch me flyyyyyy
Whoosh!!!!!!
I'm flying through the sky!!!

As I roll on the fairway,
Nothing is heard,
Waiting for the dramatic finish,
No one hears a word.

Hole in one!
Hooray! Huzzah!
Look what I have done!
Everyone is left in awe!

I'm not a bird,
I'm not a plane,
As I swish through the sky,
There's a path of flame.

Michelle Hickethier and Katie Sullivan, Grade 8
St Patrick Parish School

One

Never underestimate the power of one.
One tiny thing can turn into something big.
One argument can start a war.
One agreement can create peace.
One handshake starts a friendship.
One spark can destroy a forest.
One seed can create a forest.
One weapon can kill a person.
One doctor can save a person.
One book can educate a person.
One use of a drug can ruin a person.
One storm can destroy a ship.
One compass can guide a ship.
One victory can create happiness.
One loss can create sadness.
One president can lead a country.
One dictator can ruin a country.
One tree can provide oxygen.
One ax can cut down a tree.
One cry must start a life.
One last breath will end it forever.

Youjin Kwak, Grade 8
South Lake Middle School

What's Imagination

What's imagination
Is it think you're someplace magical
Is it going on an adventure
Is it doing something you never thought possible
Or is it hoping that one day something
out of the ordinary happens and takes you on a wild ride
Well I guess we'll have to leave it to your imagination

Esteban Rodriguez, Grade 8
Almond Tree Middle School

Rumors

Those words said that are not true
They cut like a knife
and spread fast too

Once these stories are said they go
on, and on
They spare no one
and pierce the heart
These stories kill friendships
That's the saddest part

Rumors are whispered through the treetops in the wind
Sometimes ruin things that will never mend
Who they hurt they do not care
Everywhere they go and share

So the next time an awful rumor passes by
Think once or twice before you share that hurtful lie

Katelyn Dunn, Grade 8
Valley Oak Middle School

A Rainy Day

"Splish…Splash…Drip…Drop…" the penetrating sound of raindrops is heard as they bounce off her pink polka-dotted umbrella. The wind whips her blond pigtails, plastering them against her rosy little chubby cheeks. Dropping her umbrella the young girl tilts her head back and catches, 1…2…3…4…raindrops on her outstretched tongue. Icy droplets of water splash from a puddle, into her pink rain boots as she twirls about. A voice is heard from inside the house, calling the little girl out of the downpour. Dripping wet, she splashes all the way into the warm and cozy house. Met by a blanket and a bear hug, the raindrops are wiped from her face. The little girl then cozies herself by the fire, and begins to watch the raindrops fall on the windowpane…"Splish…Splash…Drip…Drop."

Emily Sept, Grade 8
Camerado Springs Middle School

Jack and the Beanstalk

Jack sold a cow for beans, he didn't have anything to eat or drink
His mom got mad and made a scream, planted the bean and beanstalk he had seen

Jack had an idea or dream, he decided to climb if he went extreme
Jack got up and saw a castle with a giant inside, Jack went inside so quiet as a mouse to hide

Jack saw a goose and a harp in gold, he heard the giant saying FE-FI-FO
As quiet as Jack was nobody could hear a peep, the giant was eating and he fell asleep

Jack got ready for action, the giant woke up and thought he needed distraction
He threw the pan and then he ran, grabbed the goose and harp in hand

Swoosh! Jack raced across the castle's teeth, he made it down the stalk and hardly could breathe
He saw the giant sliding down, Jack went and got a hatchet and holds it with a frown

As you can see Jack defeated the giant, he was so happy he didn't even remember his name
Jack finally had money for his family, and now they live so happily

Marithza Soto, Grade 8
Almond Tree Middle School

My Colossal Adventure

Hello
People from the Earth
How are you this fine day?
Me I'm scared (of the Earth)!
What do you do in this planet?
I've been to all the other planets
It's fun it took me about 6 months to
Get here from Pluto I have 7 rockets
If you want to come look at them today
Then let's go!! The other planets don't have
Any people there. But this planet has lots and lots
Of scary looking things (Like you!) When I got here I
Landed in New York!! There are lots of scary looking things
There walking around. I traveled here to California and I got to this
Place it had lots of ride kind of things and I went on this ride and it was
Scary it flipped and turned so many times I got sick and I didn't know what to do
I didn't have any of that green stuff you call —*I think it's called mon-ee* so I asked
Some creatures if they had any of the green stuff then they said, "Get out of my face, freak!"
What are those rock looking things — *I think they're called aeroplanes*! I said I want to
Go home!!! To planet Arieana 29695 in Valencia galaxy!!

Thank you for your time in your weird life

Arieana Valencia, Grade 8
Hesperia Jr High School

Today When She Left

Today when she left
My heart was pounding faster and faster
My heart wanted to say "don't go"
Even though my heart was shouting
My mouth didn't say a word
It was like living a nightmare
A nightmare where I was speechless
My heart is saying why, why today
For the rest of the day I won't be able to see that pretty face
The beautiful girl who walked out the door
Won't be here for the rest of the day
My heart is broken and I won't have another girl like Yazmin
To be with me for the rest of the day
Now you see what happens when you leave
I get a sickness
And the person with the cure is Yazmin.

Mohamad Sakr, Grade 8
Almond Tree Middle School

Coldstone

My dull day turning bright
Indulging in this frozen delight
We seem stuck, still sitting against the wall
Our favorite worker will always be Paul
Tuesdays, Thursdays, any day
Like an oasis, we're just taken away
Anyone, anytime, anywhere
We enjoy our ice cream without a care
With her graceful clumsiness, she didn't fall down
But all the ice cream is now on the ground
Their store signs are on my mirror, they stick so well
How they got there? I shouldn't tell
To you this is just ice cream, what a bore
For my friends and me, it's so much more

Carrie Ly, Grade 9
Fountain Valley High School

The Game I Love

Basketball is the sport I love
The game that I must play
I can't stop playing
I practice every day
The ball runs with me down the court
This truly is my favorite sport
When I'm bored
I have basketball at my side
No one will stop me from playing
A game they have probably never tried
Basketball is like an endless sensation
Within every game there is a large amount of fascination
Even if you're small or tall
Or don't have any skills at all
Just never give up
A sport you will always love.

Zachary Matar, Grade 9
Fountain Valley High School

I Love You

Loving you is oh so very simple.
I love you in the night and in the day.
A shy smile between your two cute dimples.
You are my cold water on a hot day.
Softly your hand touches mind as we walk.
Your gleaming eyes remind me of the beach.
I can never escape your love headlock.
Love so deep no scuba diver could reach.
Sweet words like honey from a honey bee.
Your eyelashes really long and curly.
Your cologne always paralyzes me.
To see you I would wake up real early.
With a heart so big, your love overflows,
When I'm with you rain turns into rainbows.

Gabriela Papias, Grade 8
Henry T Gage Middle School

Music

music is my passion
music is my life
without music, it would cut like a knife

what would I do without such a thing
it's like a bird trying to fly with one wing

you got yours
I got mine
we all have a different kind

the lyrics with such effect on me
with music it's a whole different world I see

Jessica Mai, Grade 7
Sarah McGarvin Intermediate School

Monkeys

Monkeys, monkeys everywhere!
Monkeys, monkeys in your hair!
Like tiny little toddlers, they follow you all over
They'll follow you to work,
and do your dirty work
like little toddlers hard at work

Monkeys, monkeys everywhere!
In your house
skittering like a mouse
Destroying everything there,
like little toddlers, here and there

Monkeys, monkeys everywhere!
You tell them to stop
but they won't listen
they just do what they've been doing
like little toddlers, they will be everywhere!

Eric Cuyle, Grade 7
Lawson Middle School

Splash!!

You purposely pushed me in first
It wasn't really right
I know you didn't want to go in
But I always have to win

So I purposely pushed you in
I know you did not like it
Since you were crying
I sat aside of the pool sighing

I guess I am sorry
You did deserve it though
Sorry, the pool was cold
As you were told

Sara Cejka, Grade 8
Madrona Middle School

Expression

Expressive thoughts
Un-timed
Through words aligned.
Verse
After
Verse
Of the best
And
Of the worst.

Katarina Jarvis, Grade 7
Tenaya Middle School

The Freedom of the Sea

To sit and watch the ocean.
To sit and watch the sea,
Oh, how the sea makes me feel free!

If I could swim like a fish,
If I could feel the ocean breeze,
Oh, how the sea makes me feel free!

If a dolphin walked out of the sea,
And said, "Why don't you play with me?"
Oh, how the sea makes me feel free!

The waves crash softly on the rocks,
As fish jump up and down with a plop,
Oh, how the sea makes me feel free!

I can hear the waves through my door,
I can also hear children on the shore,
Oh, how the sea makes me feel free!

To sit and watch the ocean,
To sit and watch the sea,
Oh, the freedom of the sea!

Hannah Patrico, Grade 7
Joan MacQueen Middle School

Expressions of Yosemite

The cool, crisp air whips across your face,
The warm sun illuminates the scenery in this lovely place.
Extremely tall sequoia trees seem to tough the sky,
Exhausted hikers walking the trails continuously pass by.

Beneath the serene bridges, lies a calm river or stream,
A vast array of constellations surround the moon's glowing beam.
Pounding waterfalls become a gentle flow,
Plants and wildlife continue to thrive and grow.

Cozy cabins keep you dry and warm,
They relieve you every worry during a cold, windy storm.
Atop the terrain, sit rough and smooth rocks,
Visitors usually enjoy the tranquil nature walks.

Sit around a campfire to enjoy the rising flames,
Sing campfire songs and play enjoyable games.
There is a smorgasbord of food to eat,
A good meal after a long day is a terrific treat.

Dark, cold caves welcome you if you dare,
Hopefully you won't run into a large, hungry bear.
Winds begin to stir on a high elevation,
Yosemite is quite a glorious creation.

Rachel Budenholzer, Grade 8
Sacred Heart School

Broken Heart

You gave my heart a reason to live
you watched me cry
you watched me laugh
you made my life take one more step.
But it only takes one day
for you to break my heart
I loved you more than you could ever love one person
but at the end love is just a word
and you were just another one who broke my heart.
All the things you said were a lie
you broke my heart and there's no one in the other side
to put it back into one piece.
But I miss you.
I miss your face, your laugh, your touch, your everything.
Everything I see reminds me of you because I love you.
I miss you come back to me
I am just counting the days you're not next to me but I just have to give up now
because I have tried too much and I finally gave up.
I know you and I will never be back together
even though it hurts me more than it hurts you
I just have one last word for you. Good-bye

Andrea Pérez, Grade 7
St Mary's School

Tree

A tree is an aged elder
Hovering above our innocence
Standing wisely
With so much knowledge

A tree is a perfect portrait
Its leaves glisten in the sun's reflection
While its gentle arms
Sway in the breeze

A tree is a dedicated warrior
Towering proudly
As children scream and play
Around its mighty trunk

A tree is a loving parent
Watching as we come and go
Both of us changing over time
But still the same person we once knew

A tree is pure and natural
So many words to describe such simplicity
Speechlessly beautiful
It will always and forever be a tree

Adrienne Aladen, Grade 8
Madrona Middle School

Deadline

My depression is deep
like a cut on my wrist,
I want to fit in
before my time is up
I'll do anything to be one of them,
For piercing pressure is nothing to
Death.

Will I betray who I am?
I know not what lies before me,
It is just a matter of time before
Death.
My soul is empty like my heart,
My eyes have a lonely look — like me,
My life is almost at an end
My Death is meaningless
And so is my life.

We cannot see what is crystal clear,
For we are blinded by our judgments.
Do we have to prove ourselves?
I want to choose my path to destruction.

Life has a meaning but man does not know.

Ismael Noel Ramirez, Grade 7
McCabe Elementary School

My Dog

You do not know how important you are;
You're my companion and keep me happy,
I will always be with you near and far
With you, I'll never feel way too sappy;
You run ever so gracefully around,
That it makes you look like you are royal;
You are ever so thoughtful and profound,
How I love to stroke your warm golden hair,
It is always soft like a new pillow;
Your beautiful hair is always so fair,
Unlike the branches that of a willow;
Your face will never be shrouded in fog,
Because you'll always be my friend and dog.

Lichi Dong, Grade 8
Las Flores Middle School

Peering Eyes

You're walking down the street
Trying to be discreet
But you're wearing purple shoes
And singing off key blues
Your bus is passing by
Looking to see what's going on in that mutated mind

You get a glimpse of the others running away
And you feel happy and dazed to see them scared
If they walked up to you it would be a dare
Thinking so hard about those tiny specs down the street
You drift up to the sky
Only to escape those peering eyes

Katy Scheck, Grade 8
Santa Rosa Technology Magnet School

The Trees All Around

Walking through the woods
On a lovely fall morning,
The leaves are falling gracefully
From every treetop,
The wind is whistling,
The stream's water is calmly flowing.

As I look up all I see are trees,
The sky is completely covered by the branches,
I deeply intake a breath,
Then slowly breathe out the good fresh air,
I hold my hands out, praising God for His beauty,
And a leaf of brown falls into my hands.

Walking through the woods
On a lovely fall morning,
The leaves are falling gracefully
From every treetop,
As I start heading home I take one last look
At the trees all around.

Chanel Nye, Grade 7
Chino Valley Christian Schools

The Sun and the Moon

Once upon a time
High above in the sky
Sat the Sun so sublime
He could only sigh
As he sat all alone

Then he saw from afar
A beauty so fair
That he thought she was a star
But the Sun's heart would tear
For their love could not be

For the Moon was she
Only at night did she appear
At day he could never see
She was never near
So their love could not live

But every so often
There was one glimpse of hope
Their hearts they would soften
That would let their love cope
As they joined together
The eclipse brought them together
Tori Maraga, Grade 8
Our Lady of Guadalupe School

Leaves

Leaves fall off of trees
They fall in many places
All around the world
Yajaira Beltran, Grade 8
Almond Tree Middle School

Changes in Friends

Best friends, we were
Inseparable
Then all of a sudden,
It all changed.
You weren't the person
You used to be,
You were always there
When I needed you,
I was always there
When you needed me.
What happened
To the trust we had?
We were like Romeo and Juliet
Now we are like one
Mouse trying to catch cheese
You're different now
That's all I can say…
Now all I have is
Memories of you and me
Cynthia Castaneda, Grade 8
St Alphonsus School

The Power of You

Most people unconsciously have the power to change the world
Establish a new order for all boys and girls
Mankind would not succeed without people such as these
Always remember difference is key
Don't always believe the hype on TV
Remain unique secure your own identity
You have the power to change your own destiny
I sense the end of this crazy, crazy world as a closing door
But always remember in the words of Scarface the world is yours
Ryan Ramirez, Grade 8
Robert E Peary Middle School

A Jewel in the City

There was a small girl named Jewel. Her mother had given her one rule:
Always stay near and you will have no fear.
So here they lived in L.A. It was a delightful, dazzling day.
Her mother was going to see her boss, so she said, "Don't get lost."
Five-year-old Jewel was a curious girl. Her golden hair bounced in curls.
A cheetah, she rushed out of the room, and got in a taxi; zoom!
But what she found was that she couldn't get around.
But Jewel was smart, she almost knew the city by heart.
She could find her way by the end of the day.
Her mother would never know if she could only get back home.
She thought about what to do. Her house stood near the zoo!
If only she could get there, she would be very near!
But she had no way to dash. She had run out of cash.
Quickly she began to think before the sun began to sink.
So she took a chance and like a tornado, she began to dance.
People threw in money. They said, "Look at that little honey!"
So she made her way back on the subway track.
She raced inside, finally by her mother's side.
Therese Ackman and Megan Miller, Grade 7
St Patrick Parish School

What If…*

I was sitting on an airplane and wondering…

What if we fall and hit the ground what if it does not make a sound
What if the sky turns gray what if I find I have nothing to say
What if I am forced to pay what if this flight gets a delay

What if I get a new pup what if I never get to Mulluk
What if I turn blue what if I get covered in glue
What if I eat too much cream what if I release a girlie scream

What if I get covered in ink what if I start to shrink
What if I get stuck in a sink what if I turn pink

What if I'm forced to dance what if I rip my underpants
What if I move to France
What if I forget how to swim what if I get renamed Pim

The pilot says, "we will be landing shortly, please buckle your seat belts."
Andrew Burgess, Grade 8
St Raphael School
*Patterned after Shel Silverstein's "What If"

Christmas

it is a special holiday
comes once a year
families get together
families sing songs about God
families give hugs and kisses
celebrate the holiday with lots of joy
Christmas is a legal holiday
families open presents
also make different types of food
Christmas colors and blue and white
this holiday is like Thanksgiving
Christmas Day is God's birthday
Christmas is a day of happiness
everybody eats
everybody talks
the Christmas ornaments are like bouncing balls
the Christmas tree is as pokey as a porcupine
best of all
Christmas Day is an awesome holiday

Martha Ceja, Grade 8
Almond Tree Middle School

United 93

Courage,
Heroism, will,
Unifying, fighting, undaunting,
Common people, fighting for the future of our country —
Defending, daring, unwavering,
Bravery, patriotism
United 93

Daniel Brumby, Grade 8
Santa Rosa Technology Magnet School

Death

Death is everywhere
Nobody knows
When, where, who or even why
But everyone has an end and a beginning.

Death takes us
Anywhere, anytime
No discrimination
No consideration of any sort.

Death cannot judge
Or even criticize
It takes without warning
From families, friends and loved ones.

Death leaves us with
The bittersweet memories
Of the good and the bad
It ends life for some
And starts it for others.

Paige Lino, Grade 9
William Finch Charter School

Success

Success as a journey goes up and down,
That one will follow through without a frown.
Those who take the path of success are winners,
And never quite because they are believers.

With perseverance and determination,
One becomes closer to their destination.
While their hard work and willpower becomes substantial.
Those willing to succeed go beyond their potential.

Each road to success is chosen by the heart,
That guides every person from the very start.
Winners have the willpower to take chances,
And they control several circumstances.

One rides this bumpy journey with pride and passion,
With their choices set, they show strong ambition.
When one's desire reaches the extreme,
The world around will help fulfill their dream.

The seed to true success is within you,
Believe in your dreams and they will come true.
Achievement does not go to the fastest or strongest man,
But it always turns over to the one who thinks he can!

Kavitha Arulmozhi, Grade 8
Challenger School – Ardenwood

You Are My Light

There was a time
When I was down
Feeling hopeless and in the darkness
Thinking I was nothing but a darkened soul

Then you came along
Like a bright light shining
That took me out of the darkness
Enkindling life pure-hearted

It was then that I found out
You are the one I expected
To make me happy, confident, full of life —
No longer in darkness that dwells within the soul

You have a smile that shines so brightly
That brings happiness and life all around you
Your smile and touch make my day
I'm wishing you'll be with me every inch of the way

I was worried that you'd go away —
Then be gone my bright light and smile
But you promised you'll never leave me,
Now I'm happy, inspired and alive!

Neil Capulong, Grade 8
Corpus Christi School

Light

In the forest,
After dark,
The light dances.

They hover, float, and shine,
Until the sun rises.
In the trees,
And the tall grasses,
The light dances.

Though the stars above glisten,
Though the moon is full and bright
The light below dances.

Every summer I wait
For the dancing lights,
The lights flicker and hover in the air
The lights dance just for me.

Morgan Martinez, Grade 8
Madrona Middle School

Through the Looking Glass

There once was a man
who longed for another
and here's what he said
when he found his lover

"We're perfect for each other
we see eye to eye
I trust you completely
'cause you never lie

I love your brown eyes
they look just like my mother's
and oddly enough
your smile is my brother's

We'll be together
till we're old and gray
'cause you'll never leave
unless I walk away

I've never felt
such a connection,"
said the man
to his reflection.

Mandy Leon, Grade 8
Our Lady of Guadalupe School

Pouring Rain

Rain started to pour
Thunder started to come in
You could hear the roar!

Michelle Diana, Grade 8
Almond Tree Middle School

The Winds

Can you hear the winds?
Like howling voices; captured!
With the vicious gusts of wind,
Their spirits are released.
They fly around the world.
Destruction!
But when the spirits settle in,
And are restrained once more,
We start to build again.

Aidan Shockley, Grade 7
Beacon Day School

Light Years

The time passes by throughout space
So fast you can't even see it
Like a big blue
It zooms past your eyes

It is moving as if
It is a shooting star
In a firey outburst
It shoots across the galaxy
Creating fireworks among the stars
Barely visible from earth and its oceans
Until it vanishes from sight
Into the deep dark depths of space

J.J. Costanzo, Grade 8
Madrona Middle School

Fall

The leaves turn orange
There are no leaves on the trees
School starts at this time.

Julie Ann Marie Cariaso, Grade 8
Almond Tree Middle School

The Faulty Microwave

Put the food in,
Put it in for five,
It will never survive,
Beep, ding, dong,
Big or small,
Sweet or bitter,
The microwave will destroy them all,
Crackle, fizz, gurgle,
Don't grab that pot,
It's flaming hot,
It'll burn your hands,
Blurp, cling, fizz,
It is as safe as sticking
A match in a gunpowder room,
Boom!
The faulty microwave

Sam Burba, Grade 7
South Tahoe Middle School

As the Waves Crash

As the waves crash,
I hear the seagulls calling,
For they are hungry and have no food.
As the waves crash,
I wonder how the ocean can be so blue
And how it's almost see-through.
As the waves crash,
I look in the tide pools,
And see all the wonderful creatures.
As the waves crash,
I look for seashells,
Trying to find the prettiest one.
As the waves crash,
I fall asleep
And dream that I am in the sea.
As the waves crash,
I see the people playing in the water
And hope they don't step on a crab.
As the waves crash,
I see the beautiful world around me,
And thank God for putting me here.

Tess Mattimore, Grade 8
St Hilary School

The Beach

The beach is pretty
with animals and fine sand
all merry with life

Ria Dosanjh, Grade 7
Carden Academy of Santa Clara

Our Dream

What was your dream?
what was mine?
I can't believe
that I was so blind
it's right
in front of me,
but I could never see
so you tell me
what to believe.
I see a comedian
I see a doctor,
far away
in my future,
a few years later
you'll see me
follow my dreams
and spread my wings,
a few minutes later
I'll see you
go to your calling
and away you'll fly.

Cindy Tran, Grade 7
Sarah McGarvin Intermediate School

The Best Time of the Year
Spring is here
The best time of the year
Flowers will blossom all around
Buds will pop up from the ground
The weather changes before your eyes
First the rain, then the rain dies
Sometimes, you could take a swim
No need to go to the gym
Some fruit is ready, to be picked
Watch your fingers, they might get pricked
It's worth the hard work of collecting
So you can eat, after the inspecting
In spring, there is a little everything
From hot and cold, wet and dry, and in between
There is no better time of year
For, spring is here!

Elaina R. Lewis, Grade 7
EV Cain Middle School

The Moon
I look to the sky and see the moon.
You can see it at midnight, but not at noon.
In it, I can see a face,
Constantly staring at the human race;
Studying our behavior, day after day,
Watching all the children play.
He's watched us for thousands of year's,
Shining up high, without a fear.

Christopher Carlson, Grade 7
Carden School of Sacramento

No Words
A situation
A span of time

Not knowing what to say
Not knowing the right way

Not knowing the response
Not knowing the reaction

He looks at her
She nods her head
What a relief he thought he was dead

They look to the future
They say that it's bright
But in the end they find that they are never always right

Everything begins to crumble
Their children's hearts begin to break
No beautiful words can describe what has just taken place.

LeAnne Kubiak, Grade 9
Arcadia High School

Apologize
You always do something wrong;
That makes me feel weak.
You always say you were sorry and it is okay,
But you broke my heart and I turned away,
When you think it couldn't get any worse,
Everything starts to hurt.
It was incomplete and it wasn't unique,
If you would just apologize,
I wouldn't weep.
But forget it you are not that kind,
And you will always make me, Cry.

Barbara Aguirre, Grade 7
St Mary's School

Bear
A heart of ice awaits you.
Every winter its calendar stays true.
It's a sleeping Goliath,
Quick before he striketh!
He still is hibernating.
And yet is still waiting,
Waiting, waiting, waiting.

Crash! The monster has awakened.
All love has been taken.
A hunter respects its beauty,
But fears its mighty strength.
It's like a graceful ballerina you see,
But also like a monster, never backing down.
He's a bear.
And I'm the hunter.

Michael Schoen, Grade 7
St Patrick Parish School

Circus Club Granitas
The warmth of the sun
The soft rustle of leaves in the breeze
My favorite shade of cloudless sky blue
A scene you could find on a painter's canvas

Swim bags by the edge of the pool
Goggles, flippers, and towels too
A tall splash of someone jumping in to the water
Helps them relieve from getting hotter

The smell of the grill
The fragrance of flowers
And the scent of fresh cut grass
Leave you cheerful for hours

And Circus Club granitas
That taste so sweet
And make you smile
On a perfect summer day

Natalie Krikorian, Grade 8
St Joseph's School of the Sacred Heart

Deceived*

The dust is thick.
People are getting sick.

The thoughts of California's
wonderful harvest
always on our minds;
Tart oranges,
crimson tomatoes,
and sweet golden corn.

We pack our things,
and everyone sings,
"California, here we come!"

The road is long,
but now we're here.
It feels all wrong
and we shed many a tear.
There is no food.
All the people
are very rude.

We want to go home,
so just leave us alone!
Kara Stallings, Grade 8
Visalia Christian Academy
*In response to "Children of the
Dustbowl" by Jerry Stanley

Mountain Bikes

M ountain
O ff road
U p hill and down hill
N ice and easy
T wice as fun as anything else
A ll out
I n it to win it
N ow go!

B ikes
I n bushes and dirt
K ind of hard
E asy too
S o so fast
Kyle Williams, Grade 7
Joan MacQueen Middle School

The Thief

That thief,
the one in the shadows.
She will linger with me,
in the passages of my mind,
and in the labyrinth that is my heart.
Forever.
César San Miguel, Grade 9
St Joseph Notre Dame High School

Vacation at the River

Listen, my children, and you shall hear
Why the family of five wanted to cheer
The closer we got to our vacation house
The excitement grew as we got near

I said to my brother, "I just can't wait!"
The inner tubing, the wakeboarding so much fun,
Finally we arrived at the beautiful gate
Let's get out of the car and into the sun
Jump on the quads and dirt bikes and cruise on down to Uncle Mikes

Then I said, "Let's take the boat to the river"
Hopefully it won't be so cold that we'll shiver
Once the boat was in the water it seemed as though it was getting hotter
So before we jumped in, I did a 360 spin
And we just sat there peacefully floating
It was time to get back in and go boating

We sped down the river and reached the casino
Where someone was drinking Sprite and maraschino
Above us was the treacherous water slide where you lay on your side
Then plummet down into a dome
But as much fun the family of 5 was having
It was time to return back to their vacation home

Austin Welby, Grade 8
Norman Sullivan Middle School

Listen My Children and You Shall Hear

Listen my children and you shall hear
Of the one crazy day we spent by the pier.
We gathered our things and headed for the beach;
We arrived in a rush and the brakes made a screech
We were all so excited; we jumped into the waters
And danced in the ocean like little soggy otters.

We swam 'till our feet were wrinkled like prunes;
Then got out, dried off and listened to some tunes.
We ate our lunches of "PB and J;"
Then got back in the water ready to play.
We waded and dove in the deep frothy sea
Almost as if we were mermaids to be.
We swam and we swam almost so deep
That we could see Atlantis, where King Triton sleeps!
There was a school of fish ready to learn;
They were all so bright, we almost made a wrong turn.
So we headed to shore where we said good bye once more,
Then packed up our stuff, and got to the car.
I then made a wish on the single first star
That soon we would be back and for the fish not to travel too far!
Nicole Bell, Grade 8
Norman Sullivan Middle School

Kittens

Cute, cuddly, fuzzy.
Lots of people have them,
Lots of people love them,
But some do not,
And I can't live without.
I love their cute little faces,
Their soft fuzzy fur,
And their funny little purrs.
It makes me laugh to see them play.
They bring me so much joy,
Especially when they play with toys.
I love it when they snuggle up,
Like when they get to the size of a teacup.
I don't understand,
How people can live without,
These cute, cuddly, fuzzy kittens.
Because I don't know,
If I would be able to.

Madison Lopez, Grade 8
EV Cain Middle School

Nature

The river is flowing
While the birds are chirping
And the wind is blowing
While the baby birds are on the windowsill

Jose Campos, Grade 7
Richland Jr High School

Hallelujah God Is Here

Hallelujah! For God is here!
Hurry! Accept Him now,
Before it's too late.
Before God has closed Heaven's Gate.

Once dead, you can't go back,
For that is an easy fact.
It's either Heaven or Hell,
You decide, before the final bell.

Live life the Christian way,
Before you die, on that cold winter's day.
Heaven's the beacon that we all should seek,
Our souls will leave our body, our earthly physique.

Now Heaven is a sight to behold.
An unknown place with streets of gold.
It's an unimaginable place of peace and serenity.
Only for Christians who have accepted God.

Now I have warned you,
There is a chance.
You might be saved,
If you choose Him, Christ Jesus!

Shawn Robertson, Grade 7
Linfield Christian School

No One Like You

I know that you don't even notice me…
But I stay strong and move on.
I've tried to get you back…
But nothing I did every worked.
Isn't my love enough for you?
I cannot get you out of my mind.
I've tried clearing my mind…
But all I see is you.
Haven't I worked hard enough?
But you still don't notice me
I see you around every day.
But one day came, when we met face to face.
As I gazed upon your eyes I saw a
Beautiful
Unique
Independent
Person
Only now do I know there is no one like you
Only Now…

Sir Lorenz Cruz, Grade 7
Corpus Christi School

The Footsteps I Follow

The footsteps I follow
Lead from danger
They keep me from bad
They lead to good
And keep me from the world

The footsteps I follow
Get harder as I go
And sometimes I stray
It's hard to find my way

When I get to the end
I imagine it will be fine
When I get there I'll meet the one
That led me through the footsteps I follow.

Quinton Musselwhite, Grade 7
Linfield Christian School

Metamorphosis

I used to be a little seed,
Now I'm a big strong tree.
I used to be bare, snowy ground,
Now there's a snowman to be found.
I used to be confined to my nest,
Now I'm a bird flying like the rest.
I used to be a grape on a vine,
Now I'm sweet crisp wine.
I used to be an immature kid, running and at fault,
Now I'm a mature, young adult.

Kathleen Mitchell, Grade 8
Citrus Hills Intermediate School

My Grandfather's Rock

It was a beautiful day, but it was sad,
It was my grandfather's funeral.
I tried to remember my grandfather during the service,
His snow white hair and round belly.
"Grandpops" is what I called him.
"Here," My grandmother said at the funeral.
"It was one of your grandfather's favorite rocks I painted."
I took it without saying anything
And watched my Grandmother walk away on the verge of crying.
A lot of people came up to me and my family at the funeral and said,
"He was a good man," or "I am sorry about Bruce," and "He is in a better place now."
But I didn't listen to them.
I looked at the rock.
One of my grandfather's favorite rocks,
And now it's mine.
With its bright colors:
Red, white, and blue like our flag.
With its intricate designs,
And as smooth as silk edges.
My grandfather's favorite rock,
And now my favorite rock as well.

Mallory Thompson, Grade 7
Rolling Hills Country Day School

Humpback Whales

Swimming through the great, blue seas as if lost in a reverie,
Dreaming of the wondrous noises ingrained in a memory.
The humpback whales wallow wildly with poise, like great, triumphant viceroys,
As if strumming their new guitars like little girls and boys.
They sing their song to legions afar, to sovereigns and noble grognards,
Awaiting a response of a multitude with great praise from kings and czars.

Projecting their voices like a beatitude, with the sound of persistent fortitude.
The notes are like a chorus of euphoric violins, followed by a concluding vicissitude…
The water darkens; the creatures go in, back to their homes, resisting their fins,
The whales stop their singing, their voices go down. Only water flows like the pitter patter of a corinne.
Nighttime ambles in just about now. The moon goes up, the sun goes down.
The whales are owls, ready to burrow up, as no sounds are heard in the sea and around.

John McCready and Jackson Rodewald, Grade 7
St. Patrick Parish School

Christs

C hrist has everlasting love like the trickling stream or laughing brook
    His love has no end.
H is protection showers upon us like the rain upon the petals of a gentle rose
    He will never harm us.
R esurrection is when Jesus died and rose again
    He died to save us from our sins of past, present, and future.
I have faith in Christ
    I have devoted my life to Him, so that when I die, I will be in God's kingdom forever.
S tudy the Bible! I read it every day.
    The Bible is where all the answers lay.
T rust in God with all your soul, all your heart, and all your mind
    And you will receive peace and prosperity.

Victoria Alexandra-Lugo Traudt, Grade 7
Linfield Christian School

Out of the Dark, into the Light

Unpredictable in spirit, it never comes as expected.
I await the day, stuck at the point of no return.

Hiding in emotions, I search for the light.
Trying to get myself out of this endless hole.
Seasons pass, and yet I am still in the dark.

Which way to go? Which road to choose?
Trying to please everyone, yet pleasing no one.
Avoiding mixed passions, yet feeling forevermore confused.
Causing countless regrets.

Many moons pass, I still debate between the paths.
Never looking back, I choose the forbidden one.

Behold! The light! What a place to be!
Exquisite in delicacy, pure in essence.

Living beyond potential, chosen from the garden of life.
The light shines through me, making all the difference.
Victoria Wu, Grade 9
Westview High School

What We Can Do

We are weak
We took care of the wounded in the Crimean War
And earned the Noble Peace Prize

We are feeble
We fought in the Hundred Year's War
And found polonium and radium

We are fragile
We gave birth to new lives
And raised those souls

They call us weak
But we call ourselves

"Woman"

Janet Lee, Grade 8
Lakeside Middle School

Veronica Martinez; a Very Beautiful Girl

Veronica Martinez was my cousin, yes she was.
And the reason that I loved her was just because.
She was so friendly, innocent, and very sweet.
She was as close to me as much as my heart beat.
On that tragic night when I found out you died,
For two full weeks, I just cried, cried, cried.
You left me alone with nothing but memories;
Forever in my heart will you be there for centuries.
Stephanie Mendoza, Grade 8
Almondale Middle School

Depression

Depression can make you mad.
Depression might make you sad.
Depression might make you say,
"Please make life go away!"
Depression can make you cold,
Depression can make you old.

But when there is a friend,
On which you can depend
Then life doesn't get so sad.
Well, you might even say "I'm really glad!"
Mark Auyoung, Grade 7
Sarah McGarvin Intermediate School

The Love of Springtime

My gloomy days fade away
When I'm with you
The leaves are falling
The flowers are growing
Everything seems perfect
Like nothing can go wrong
A moment of silence creeps by
As I'm breathing in the fresh spring air
So nice and so refreshing
When I think of you I think of a growing flower
Our love just keeps growing
When a pedal falls over time it grows back
Our love can live forever
Or just fall apart when it's not taken care of
So take care of Mother Nature
Let the flowers bloom
Let the trees grow
And let your spirit roam free
Adriana Moreno, Grade 8
UHS Schools Hemet

Flowers of the Spring

How I compare you to the deep blue sea,
As beautiful as can be,
Like the wind moving free.
Some may say that you are small and weak,
But to me you are as powerful as a tree.

5 petals, 4 petals, 3 petals, 2,
I don't think you realize the special things you do,
But you make all of my dreams come true.
With roses, carnations, and beautiful tulips,
Don't forget daisies, irises, and cherry blossoms too.

The way you rise up on your incredible wings,
It makes my heart sing, sing, and sing.
Ladies and gentlemen, queens and kings,
Please let me introduce to you,
The wonderful flowers of the spring.
Alexis Moore, Grade 8
Madrona Middle School

Leaving

it's so hard to face the days
knowing I chose it to be this way
i'll make you regret
every word you never said
every lie that passed your lips
you'll know how i feel; when i'm dead
constantly longing. for. your. voice.
constantly regretting. this. choice.
to spend the days i had with you
with my head down, eyes to the ground
i should have enjoyed every second
and held you tight for my life
now you walk away and i'd say
please come back to me
don't break my heart this time
the second i thought
i got you back
you leave
me
behind.

Jessica Adams, Grade 9
Fred C Beyer High School

Freedom Fighters

It was hard times then,
In the early 1940's.
Determined by the heart
And forced by circumstances,
With a voice louder
Than a lion's roar.
How they would do anything
And everything
For independence.
How they held their heads
High of pride,
Never bowing down to injustice,
To discover even more injustice
And even more strictness,
And knowing that they were going to die
But still fighting for freedom.
Caring for family
While being hanged,
Holding their heads high.

Kritee Sekhon, Grade 7
Chino Valley Christian Schools

Poetry

Poetry
expressive, imaginative
loving, hating, sharing
expresses your inner feelings
caring, hearing, thinking
creative, appreciate
masterpiece

Jordan Odle, Grade 8
Santa Rosa Technology Magnet School

Show Master

I had a friend who liked to dance
Of course with shorts or pants!!!

I wish he was still here so that we can all give a great big cheer!!!

We all miss him very much and wish
We could give him a great big hug!!!

Keith I miss you and I will always remember you and love you!!

I know that God and Jesus wanted you more
And they knew that it was time for you to go home with them.

But just remember to give them a great big show
on the big open floor!!!

Deseree Lona, Grade 7
St Hilary Elementary School

There Is a World

There is a world out there for me.
A world without war
A world with peace
A world that can be something beautiful
Won't this chaos ever cease?
There is a world out there for you
A world without hatred
A world filled with love
A world that we can all share
Sometimes I wonder, what is this wonderful world you speak of?
There is a world out there for them
A world without wars between nations
A world with colorful creations
A world that has a good foundation
But is that world only vivid in our imaginations?
There is a world out there for us.

Danica Nguyen, Grade 7
Sarah McGarvin Intermediate School

Shades

Those who don't know her think she's open and truthful.
They think she tells her best friend everything on her mind.
They think there's nothing untold about her.

But I can see the darker shades in her eyes that she tries to keep to herself.
I know the secrets have a chaotic outcome, if ever revealed. And I won't reveal them.
And I feel her pain, even if she wants no one else to bear it.

All have secrets; it's what makes your eyes different shades.
All have a pupil that's as black as the secret they hold.
We are blinded from other's shades because our own can only hold our own.
But one only needs to accept the darken parts to see.

Yeah. That is.
Shades

Rachel Shields, Grade 9
Westview High School

Water in a Bottle

During the morning you drink water.
During noon you drink water.
During the evening you drink water.
Everyone takes water for granted.
No one gives a care in the world about water.
Water is being renewed over and over again.
People bathe in water and people drink water.
But no one ever thanks the water.
They believe, really believe
That water is here to stay
Without an effort to try to save it.
The next time you want to drink some water,
Too bad! It's all gone!

Derek Tat, Grade 8
Martin Murphy Middle School

The Best Classmates Ever

The small class of '09
holds the greatest people ever.
So much potential
stored in every last one of them.
Ideas waiting to be thought,
hidden talents waiting to be exposed,
have already leaked out.
Amazing feats were performed by accident,
and stylish tricks were thought out in a snap.
The quiet and timid have their talents.
The loud and outgoing have their ideas.
And almost everything is fun.
The ideas and talents make things easier,
things more fun —
and somehow, make the whole class feel
like a family.

Jomari Geronimo, Grade 7
Corpus Christi School

Just Because…

Just because I go to a private school,
It doesn't mean homework is all I do.
It doesn't mean I am a nerd or geek.
It doesn't mean good grades are my only desire.

Just because I go to a private school,
It doesn't mean I never have fun.
It doesn't mean I don't play sports.
It doesn't mean I don't have a life.

Just because I go to a private school,
It doesn't mean I don't have a sense of humor.
It doesn't mean I'm spoiled and rich.

Just because I go to a private school —
Don't start judging me.
Get to know me first.

Rahul Batra, Grade 8
Dorris-Eaton School

Watching a Sunset

The sun is just starting to go down,
And I am sitting in the sand
With the waves hitting my feet every two times.
It's about 82 degrees outside
With a little breeze.
My brown hair barely touches the sand,
As my brown eyes reflect off the sun.
I can't see the sun that well now,
So I start to head to my house
About 40 yards away from the beach.
It feels good on my feet
Touching the warm sand on my way back home.
When I get home, I look back,
And it's dark.

Tyson Tavalero, Grade 7
Marina Village Intermediate School

Football

Some people think football is a game
Some people think if you lose it is a crying shame
Some people take the game too seriously
Some people just don't care
but everyone agrees that football is a sport
and only the opinions of the players matter
People don't listen to them
they are unheard and paid no attention
Which fills them full of aggression
If we just pay attention everyone will win

Ricky Page, Grade 9
Lucerne Valley Jr/Sr High School

Free Throw

Players lined up
Bleachers dead silent
He is at the free throw line
Sweat dripping
His heart beating faster
He closes his eyes
Visualizes making the shot
Dribbles once
Wipes the sweat off his forehead with his jersey
Dribbles again
Then one last hard dribble
His eyes now fiercely concentrated on the rim
Bends his knees
Snaps up
And releases the ball
It's a swish
The bleachers go crazy
He tries to hold in his happiness
And smiles
And continues to play the game…

Reginald Tanega, Grade 7
Corpus Christi School

Special Dream

The world is cruel
Just like I say,
But every time you look at me,
It becomes a better place.

Sometimes I wish
You were there for me,
With a tear to share
And a long time to live.

You've may not notice,
But I have a dream,
It is special
And very sweet.

I'm longing and longing
For the time to come
When our worlds would meet
And our love to be just one.

Maria Rico, Grade 8
Martin Murphy Middle School

Redwoods

A beautiful sight
As they stand tall and bold
The mighty Redwoods

Rosalie Annand, Grade 8
South Tahoe Middle School

Cancer Hurt

Cancer means hurt,
Cancer means my mom,
Cancer means I'm sick,
sick of life the way it is,
Cancer, it hurts,
it really does,
and I'm sick of it,
I wish it was done,
done forever.

Kayla Weinreich, Grade 9
Malaga Cove Academy

The Dodger Game

The game has begun.
Let's all have some fun.
There's a big crowd,
and they're pretty loud.
The Dodgers come about,
ready to strike someone out.
As the game went on,
the batter made contact and it was gone.
The game was done,
and the Dodgers had won.

Jonathon Corona, Grade 7
St Hilary Elementary School

Woes

Why Delilah?
You broke my heart.
Once you left my heart
I had great woes
With the smell of lilac
And a slight hint of rose.

'Twas a warm summer's day
when we first met,
It was love at first sight
I had to bet.
From that moment on
It was blue cloudless skies.
I thought we'd always be together,
Or until one of us died.

But still I'll never forget
How on that dark stormy night,
You called me up on my phone,
And said forever, goodbye.

Byron Perez, Grade 7
St Vincent Elementary School

Best Friend

I have a friend
I call the best
Because I love her
more than the rest
People think I
don't have any
But I know I
have plenty
There may be good times
There may be bad
But in the bad time
I won't turn sad
We can play with
or without toys
We don't fight
over boys
We will always
stick together
forever and
forever.

Mariah Wallace, Grade 8
Our Lady of the Rosary School

Sadness

Sadness
Feeling depressed
Losing someone dearly
Is opposite of happiness
Sorrow

Jenella Julian, Grade 8
Almond Tree Middle School

Hope

H olding
O n
P atiently for the
E nd

Clay Krowpman, Grade 8
Santa Rosa Technology Magnet School

West of the City

Far from the city
Far from the smoke
Lies the great land
Right on the coast
The green hill and the blue sea
Tell us of the land that should be.

Green bushes, short trees
Golden flowers, and yellow bees
The rocky shore and the sandy beach
Should remind us of what land is.

As the city tramples the original land
The forest is now our lawn
The desert is now our home.

Stop and think!
Do we still want the beauty?
Do we still want the song?

Alejandro Perez, Grade 8
Madrona Middle School

My Great-Grandpa Ernesto*

My Great-Grandpa, Ernesto
He may be old, but very smart
He's a wise, wonderful man
Though I don't know him well
I still love and care about him
He's my great-grandpa
I met him three years ago
With the rest of my family
I saw him during the summer
Then in August we came home
But two weeks later we got a call
He was very ill
My dad returned to Mexico
But sadly he didn't make it
We all got the tragic news
I had lost a loved one
But he's in a better place now
Now I had a great-grandpa
But in my heart he is still here

Adilene Velazquez-Mancilla, Grade 9
San Benito High School
*Dedicated to my
great-grandpa, Ernesto
May he rest in peace.

Life's Lessons

We fall and then we get back up,
We get up and then we fall back down.
We frown and then we cry,
We cry and then we frown.

We make mistakes,
And we learn.
Sometimes we crash,
While other moments we burn.

But no matter how many times we're lost,
We always are somehow found.
And no matter how far we fall behind,
We always seem to recover our ground.

I know now that life is never complete,
Unless we are able to make use of life's lessons.
And if we never get back up when we fall,
We will never reach life's destinations.

Brooke Knight Webb, Grade 8
Mountain Creek Middle School

Shoe

S he slips on one, then the other,
H olding each lace as she hovered,
O ver and under, then pull together,
E ventually each bow is discovered.

Sierra Howard, Grade 7
John Charles Fremont Intermediate School

War

War is no man's game.
There isn't victory,
but only periods of rest,
only because destruction is all you see.
Past blistering winds,
fiery blows,
whistling bullets,
and cannons in rows.
Soldiers in pain,
for they have no guidance.
Families in mind,
and friends dead in silence.
What is our problem?
What is our motivation?
We are only human,
but we are against another nation.
However, we blame ourselves.
Agony, suffer is made and more,
is all caused by us,
for where there is man, there will be war.
Ask yourself, why is there war?

Victor Le, Grade 7
Sarah McGarvin Intermediate School

Night and Day

The wind races through the night,
so swiftly, so cowardly and shy.
As the thunder roars in my ears
as a lion at night with glistening eyes.
As the lightning flashes sent from above,
brightening the midnight sky.
The rain darts to the ground,
such as a missile shooting from an enemy in the sky.

Then a sudden silence in the air,
because the sun has risen
in the sky once more.
Ending such a frightening war
letting hopes and dreams soar
starting a new day once more.

Cameron Smith, Grade 7
Bancroft Middle School

We Live

I feel the cool breeze from the ocean,
It engulfs me in its arms with a swift motion.
I melt from head to toe,
Why does it happen, do you know?

I see the forest green and dense,
No beginning or end marked by a fence.
Its calm and serene environment,
Is great for people in retirement.

I wonder why people sit at home,
When they could be out exploring Rome.
I hear people talking trash,
Stop and think, why burn and crash?

I help them choose right from wrong,
Keep them on track with a happy song.
In the end I believe we should dream,
About what we can do to be a better team.

Lisa Xu, Grade 9
Westview High School

Leaves

Waking in the dawn of spring
Stretching out to the rising sun
Taking April showers
During midday they show their colors of green
Rustling to the songs of birds on their wing
Dancing with the wind
Taking off their vibrant colors of green
Into their nightgowns of red, orange, and yellow
Changing into colorless dusk
Falling down gently to a peaceful sleep
Floating quietly in the cold winter night
Resting on the ground

Benjamin Lee, Grade 8
Madrona Middle School

Not Gonna Give Up

Until the day I die,
I'm not gonna give up.
Until it's you and I,
I'm not gonna shut up,
I'll do whatever I have to do,
Just to have you.
I want you in my arms,
I want you next to me.
You are the best of my
Good luck charms,
And my only VIP.
I'm not gonna stop,
Whatever it takes,
I'll do it till I drop.
Now I just hope,
That one day,
You will stay.

Gustavo De Hoyos, Grade 7
St Mary's School

Grammar

So many new things
Nouns, Verbs, Adjectives, Adverbs.
So many things
So little time
Too much grammar
So many different kinds!

Grammar is boring and dull
I know it's important
But what is the point?

So many new things
Infinities, Interjections, Prepositions
So many things
So little time
So much grammar
Too many different kinds!

Michael Murphy, Grade 7
Carden School of Sacramento

Life Is Like Work

Life is like work
you stick to the same route
you do one thing wrong
then you have to do it over
Life is so hard
you do so many things
but you get nothing in return
you give but you don't get
Life is like work
you struggle so hard
then when you get what you want
you don't want it at all

Jaime Avelar Jr., Grade 8
Almond Tree Middle School

The Life You Show

Each person manifests a different personality,
Which varies from acting shy to always wanting to look pretty.
Some get angry way too fast, while some stay cool all the time.
Some are so greedy that they will not even spare a single dime.

Some choose to stay in the corner and watch from the inside of the tent,
While some choose to get out and be part of all the excitement.
Some people enjoy talking and chatting and will not even stop for a diamond ring,
And some just sometimes, while other would even stop for a puppet on a string.

Stage fright settles into a lot of adults and children,
While some do not mind standing on a stage again and again.
There are words such as kind, cooperative, and even nice.
But, there are also words such as mean, rude, and as cold as ice.

These words describe personalties and the types of personalities friends will hold.
If a person's personality is good, a friendship can be as good as gold.
There are also people who quickly get afraid and will refuse being blindfold,
And there are those who will go out and try any stunt and are daring and bold.

Some people often get away with everything since they are sneaky,
And some people get in trouble if they do something the slightest bit freaky.
Each person's own personality is worth more than a priceless antique.
No one person has the same, and in its own way each is unique.

Japjot Bal, Grade 7
Challenger School – Ardenwood

I'd Rather

I'd rather feel pain than nothing at all
I'd rather feel depression than anger
I'd rather be miserable than outspoken
For nothing is worse than being ignored while speaking your mind
To be isolated from everything else
I'd rather stand out and be myself
Than be a conformist and not know myself at all
I'd rather be hated for who I am
Than loved for who I'm not
I'd rather be mute than blind or deaf
For I'm soft-spoken and barely heard
So my words wouldn't really matter much at all
Nobody knows who I really am
Nobody knows how I really feel
The pain inside is just too real
I'll need someone to come along
Just to come and keep me strong
Not letting these feelings make me feel so void and empty
So why run away
When people really want to say
I'd rather be me

Samantha Kong, Grade 7
Bancroft Middle School

Crossroads of Life

Life
With many decisions to make
Sitting there debating on which path to take.

Sometimes you get lost, there are no signs
Blocking you from trouble and hurt are the lines.

As different things pass you by
At times you want to break down and cry.

When you make a mistake
All you want to find is that one sign that says break.

No people behind you waiting for you to turn
Is simpler for you to grow and learn.

With many different paths to take
You hope your decision was the right one to make.

Kasi Gonzalez, Grade 8
La Joya Middle School

Angel/Demon

Angel
Singing, protecting
Hope, strength, love
Heavenly, peacefully; wickedly, powerfully
Harmful, evil, mischievous
Sinning, tempting
Demon

Barbara Melo, Grade 7
St Cyprian School

Life

Life passes.
Each year we grow.
Life is a candle
And each time the wind blows, a flame disappears.

Life is like a radiant rainbow
Showing unique color.
Life may be unfair — and unfair may be life,
But this helps us learn.
Nothing is perfect.

I feel the whistling wind
Blow my face
And Taste the crunchy sweetness of the air,
As a child, I played.

My parents tell me a zillion times
"I Love You!"
In return I try my best, but

Where did my childhood go?

Chiharu Grace Yagasaki, Grade 7
Rolling Hills Country Day School

The Flag of Liberty and Justice

The colors of the flag are red, white, and blue.
Our soldiers fought for me and for you.
On the battlefield, they stand faithful and true.
With guns in their hands, they march like a caravan.
To guard our seas, and protect our lands.
Because of their courage we can be free,
to truly celebrate our liberty.

Eric Wayne Browne II, Grade 7
Grace Christian Academy

Snow

You fall from the sky
So white, so pure
Each flake with a unique crystallized design
Only to fall to the ground
A divine yet unnoticed phenomenon
And to help envelope one town to the next
In a thick blanket of white
Your simple beauty and natural elegance
To be wasted on humans
Who shape you into spheres for pleasure
Or simply shovel you away
As if a burden on their imperfect souls
And eventually pristine white will mix with the dull hue of mud
Something so innocent
To be soiled by the impurities of Earth
Why has the sky abandoned you so?

Nancy Nguyen, Grade 7
Sarah McGarvin Intermediate School

We, the Youth

We are young only once.
Only once do we get the ability to live carelessly,
Like a dog in the wild,
Free, untamed, and full of joy.

Nothing can stop
This sense of childhood and adventure.
Only once are we able to explore,
Able to roam free from blame,
Everything we do is innocence.

Anything and everything is precious,
As precious as a zillion stars in a clear sky.
Only once can we experience the lifetime of youth,
A life time of memories.

We are today's generation.
We shape the world.
Only once do we have this chance,
A chance to make a difference.
We are the youth of today.

Suriya Patel, Grade 8
Rolling Hills Country Day School

At the Beach

I like to walk on the beach in the sand and listen to a really good band
I go on the beach and talk or have a very good walk
The waves are like mountains going into the ground
I like to listen to the soothing crashing sound
When I go in the water it is very very cold but when I look at the ocean it is ever so bold
When I smell the beach it smells like salt but to me the beach tastes like a malt
I love all the shells and how they feel and when we have family parties we have a good meal
I also like to ride my bike on the beach, that is what I really like
We sit around the campfires and watch the wires
Of the kites that fly like birds in the sky
Then when I hit the waves there are marshmallows that I crave
Then the sand tickles my feet and by the end I am beat

Megan Chism, Grade 9
Fountain Valley High School

The Deciding Path

As I continue to embark upon my long forsaken journey, a fork in the road has confronted me and brought me worry.
Which route is best? How will I know? Inside this densely populated forest, the trees have become my foes.
For they have disrupted my sense of sight, by the sun's descent I could see it would rapidly be night.

One path seemed old, worn-out, and yet mysterious, another more bright, new, and provokes me to become curious.
I turn to my left, I point to my right, deciding which way to go, which path would make my future seem bright?
At last I realized my path, all new and green, patched with grass,
It seemed so open, so welcoming, as if by taking it, I could erase my past mistakes and have a new beginning.

I took one fateful step towards that seemingly open road, turning my back upon that other so worn-out and old.
I did not turn back for I did not have a choice, so excited was I that gone was my voice.
That fateful decision has decided my future, writing out my fate as if it written on paper.

I sit here now, telling this story having no regrets, no doubts, no worries.
All because I had chosen that bright, open road, instead of the one so mysterious and old.

Kevin Chen, Grade 9
Westview High School

The Trains

You can hear the immense trains coming from afar
Tears dropping down people's faces
You can see the tired suitcases crying with despair
For they are too scared

The look upon people's faces is hard to bare
Their beautiful faces are pale white like a porcelain doll
You can hear the rough soldiers march towards you
The musty trains are coming closer to you

The violent soldiers push and shove the Jews inside
And you can hear the frightened people moan and cry
Again the suitcases cry out with despair
But they are too weak and no one seems to care

They reach the concentration camp in a few days
As they get out of the musty train you can hear their stomachs growl loud as a lions roar
The suitcases cry out with despair
But they are too weak and the violent Nazis don't help or care

Ivka Stimach, Grade 8
Sacred Heart School

Looking for a Friend

A friend is someone that everyone needs,
Is someone that is always there for you,
Someone you could tell your deepest and darkest secrets,
A friend is someone you can't lie to,
A friend is like your own sister or brother,
A friend is someone that listens to what you have to say,
A friend is someone who will never let you down,
A friend will always stand up for you,
A friend is someone special to you,
Who will never leave your side,
Will I ever find a friend like this?

Erika Crispin, Grade 8
St Joan of Arc School

Fear

I'm in the back of your head
I live under your bed
Hidden in the closet
I'm the answer to your posit
In the form of many scares
I live under your stairs
I make you teary your body feels weary
I come in the night filling you with fright
When I come from the hills,
Like a fever I make you feel chills
Every night I start my flight
I arrive in your room BOOM!
Then fill you with doom
It always seems I'm the reason for your screams
Filled with belief
Overcoming with grief
It makes you feel that I am real
There's nothing to fear but fear itself
I am fear

Karly Loberg and Katie Fogelstrom, Grade 8
St Patrick Parish School

The Human Heart

The *human heart* is a counting organ
Like a clock counts minutes the heart counts life
Each beats a sin and a sin forgiven
And these miracles which aren't rare but rife
A rhythmic remind of the tears we cry
A declaration that we've lost control
Each day our strengths not enough to get by
Each beat is a prayer that's said of the soul
When irregularity kindly invades
The heart can't adapt so it skips a beat
And for sincere love rhythm makes fair trade
And the old pattern admits its defeat
Each beat in value is unrestricted
Each beat is a beat we take for granted

Sarah Jo Ramsey, Grade 9
Moorpark High School

The Wind

Sitting on the grass,
Playing in the playground,
Every time I do these things,
I could feel this everywhere.

Having fun with friends,
Eating lunch under a tree,
Every time I feel this thing,
It feels like I am free.

Running around the field,
Jumping way up high,
Feeling the wind against my face,
Makes me feel free and ask why.
And that is the happiest feeling in the world.

Jennifer Shyong, Grade 7
Thornton Jr High School

Leprechauns

Of all of the world's mysteries
There is one that stands above all,
It takes its place in the land of Ireland.
Near where the leaves slowly fall.

Leprechauns are what they are called,
Living near groves of thick trees standing tall.
Many reports tell of their great skills
Like their ability and concealment from sight.
Hiding at all times, from morning to evening, from day to night.

Though recognized for their great stealth,
They are also known for their immense wealth.
Even though they are quick and witty,
You will be rewarded if one is caught.
Hidden at the very end of a rainbow
Is your prize, a large pot of gold?
Though none have ever been seen,
Their stories and legends are continued to be known
As myths and a great tale of old.

Gerome M. Sunga, Grade 8
Our Lady of the Rosary School

Bruises of Love

Bruises of love, hidden under your smiles
Your sweet innocence, like that of a child's
You were an angel — No! A saint!
Your deep, endless eyes, that no artist's brush could paint
I remember your laugh, your smile, your voice,
I'd bring you back, if I had a choice.
But…you know…
I remember that day.
The day that I held you as you slipped away…
If you can hear me, I hope you hear this:
I've cried at your grave, Every Night Since…

Amy E. Johnson, Grade 8
McCabe Elementary School

What Is Poetry?

Poetry is your soul
Sharing it with the world
Pouring love into a bowl
Letting them keep hold

Always seeming to be bright
Never letting people down
Always making sure it's right
Never letting people frown

Making sure it's never plain
Send a poem to a friend
Never talking in vain
Making sure it'll never end

So what's a poem to you?
Write it down on paper
Don't let it go off into the blue
Give it to a neighbor

Lauren Green, Grade 8
Madrona Middle School

Thinking Thoughts

Have you ever felt like
you couldn't get
that one thought stuck
in your head, out?

People tell you not
to think about it,
but that makes you
think think think
more about it

It could be a sad
thought or even
a happy one
the more you
think think think
about it, anxiously

Until it really hits
you, that thought
inside your head
that you've been
think think thinking
about forever and ever

Kim Nguyen, Grade 7
Sarah McGarvin Intermediate School

One Last Time

Your eyes watering,
Like the sad clouds crying out,
One last hug, goodbye.

Mitchell Kendig, Grade 9
Oak Knoll Alternative School

I Am the Totem Pole

I am vibrant and full of beauty
I wonder what it would be like to have legs
I hear the wind howling from high above
I see the water crashing onto the shore
I want people to see my carvings in me as beauty
I am vibrant and full of beauty

I pretend I am a never ending beanstalk that can see the whole world
I feel the coldness and warmth every night and day
I touch the tool that is carving more beauty into me
I worry that I will fall over onto the ground
I cry when people carve into me without thinking of the beauty
I am vibrant and full of beauty

I understand when people show their feelings
I say that true beauty is what comes from the heart
I dream that one day the whole world will be elegant and pleasant
I try to help make the world beautiful from the inside and out
I hope that one day everyone's dreams will come true
I am vibrant and full of beauty

Ashley Josephson, Grade 8
Palm Desert Middle School

The Diverging Path

Walking down the hallway, chatting continuously with my friends,
Getting scolded by my teachers for talking with no ends.
Going to each class, listening to teachers, and preparing to learn,
All for that one day, the end of the road, and the diploma to earn.
These fond memories of middle school are ones that I shall always keep,
Especially as graduation and separation times slowly seem to creep.
Whether it be reading classic novels or playing basketball,
Through these experiences, I can say that I have done it all.
For all of the tough tests and challenges that together we have faced,
There has never been on quite like this for which we have ourselves braced.
For as the end of a journey and all of our struggles comes near,
We must remember our lessons and values and live life without fear.
As we cling onto yesterday and avoid seeing tomorrow come,
We wish time would just freeze and leave us endlessly numb.
For what we are leaving behind may be more than we can ever gain,
Great teachers, best friends, beloved school, more than one can explain.
The path is diverging, here and now, further apart as we speak,
The countdown is edging closer to an end, week by week.
Before we know it, our accustomed lives will soon be part of a past,
Our memories will live on in our hearts, and the experiences shall last.

Nicole Dalal, Grade 8
Challenger School – Ardenwood

2 of Them

I have two of them
Just two
Two brothers who love me and care for me
Two brothers who I can trust and talk to every minute of my life
Sometimes we annoy each other but that happens once in a lifetime
Nothing in the world will separate the love and friendship we share

Yarley Martinez, Grade 7
St Vincent Elementary School

Gary

When someone dies
we all cry.
It is hard to move on with our lives.
We miss the people that go.
We miss the going out together.

What is life without them?
It is love that we should have for them.
One thing is for sure: God.
He will help us go through hard problems,
like someone's death.

Desiree Zuniga, Grade 7
Renuevo School

Where I Am From

I am from
going to school in a different country,
from crying on the first day
because I didn't understand.
I'm from a dad
who worked as a school bus driver.
From eating chorizo on a Saturday morning.
I'm from walking with Grandpa,
and watching novelas with Grandma.
I am from the warm smell of Jiffy,
to narrating a play.
I'm from Jazzy, my Lhasa
to reading to my heart's content.
I am from the smell of the rain,
to the smell of clean fresh air.
I am from my parents working hard
to get me the best education.
All of these things make me who I am.
I am from the hard work of my family.

Sienna Lujan, Grade 7
Linfield Christian School

Normal?

what is normal?
with anger and frustration,
hatred and confusion.
with war and fighting,
racism and dirty looks
at those not the same color as you.
how can anyone be normal?
why is life so miserable?
are we living in an everlasting dream
we just can't get out of?
are we gong back in time to what was?
are we living in it right now?
look around,
look at what our world has become!
are we living in what they thought could've been…
the dream

Hope Marie Walton, Grade 7
MIT Academy

Aging

We are aging not every minute,
But every second.
We are aging even if we don't feel it,
And that's the bad part about it.
When we age it means we are growing up,
And growing up means more responsibility.
Growing up also means we are no longer little kids,
We are young adults that are starting the hardest part of life.

Adrian Jimenez, Grade 7
St Hilary Elementary School

Only in My Dreams

Take away the pain
Maybe we could live forever
In place that's not insane
'Cause I can never remember that day in December
When you finally walked away

And I laugh at myself every day
To cover up this feeling of shame
And I'm sorry I love you
It's not like I want to, maybe one day it will fade

And if I never wake up
At least I know now that it's not what it seems
'Cause I will always love you
And you will always love me
But only in my dreams

Tejah Fortino, Grade 8
Holy Family Catholic School

Hey There Boy

Hey there boy
so whatcha been up to
I've been busy and I
really haven't met you
I've been waiting for a guy
like you…so true
for years and years seems like
we've been together through and through
you know me inside and out
my thoughts and fears, my frown and pout
your arms are like a protective shield
you protect me with your words you yield
your eyes are like their own person
speak your mind much more and
wide and wonderful is your touch
tender and thoughtful your love is much
you carry me past my tears
you carry me throughout my fears
hey there boy
I miss you

Lauren Porton-Ayala, Grade 8
Valley Oak Middle School

Sudden Death

The young flower wilts
Its small roots bank no moisture
Its life ends today

Haley Henson, Grade 7
St Cyprian School

Wallpaper

And there goes everyone
All happy
All smiling
Eyes glimmering with tears of joy.
As I sit in the corner
Watching and observing
Looking deep into their souls,
I see
The sadness
The confusion.
Feeling out of place
Out of words to say
I sit in the shadows
Wishing I could feel it all too.
Every laugh
Every cry
Every spear of anger
I'd like to know how to have it all.
And even if it means gaining nothing
I'd just
Like to know.

Irene Shih, Grade 8
South Lake Middle School

My Dog Pongo

When we found you
Tears ran down my face
I wanted to be there
So I could have helped you
But I wasn't
So I had to trust
In God that
You were safe
Up in Heaven
Where someday
We will stay together

You are still
In my heart
Wherever I go
I love you and miss you

Every day I think of you
Not a day goes by without
You in my heart and mind
I love you and miss you
Pongo

Paige Brandt, Grade 7
Linfield Christian School

Home

Home, the place I always dream of
Non-stopped, the place I focus and have fun without end and without thought,
Time passes by five times fold
And good times will always last, and always be remembered eternally.
Home, the place where memories that go back
To when I was nearly three years old and will be remembered until I leave this Earth.
Every time I go back, I take in a memory,
And enjoy the time with family, and friends that friendships have been saved
And locked in my heart until doomsday.
Weather there is never good,
Never perfect, never just right
So parting is always happening.
It can be rainy, cold, humid, too hot, misty,
Foggy, freezing,
Snowing, or hailing,
But no matter what,
Nobody in my family is going to be affected even the slightest bit,
Not by the largest casualty.
This place I call home is, and always will be,
My first pick, this place is New Jersey,
My heart's true home.

Nicholas Pizzuti, Grade 8
St Joseph's School of the Sacred Heart

Home Sweet Home

There is one dwelling more impressive than any other,
where love and happiness are in accord with one another.
A place where vivid sunshine and astonishing beauty happily dwell,
an unimaginable area where everything seems harmoniously swell.

A dreamy garden full of comforting warmth and undying peace,
where joyous moments and everlasting glory never ever cease.
With jingle bells, that ring all day, and cockle shells,
to tiny, magical fairies casting wondrous and amazing spells.

A lush, lively forest where every heart longs to beat,
with elves singing their merry songs that are ever so sweet.
Like a soft, savory ice cream castle in the air,
with silk feather canyons scattered around everywhere.

A breathtaking place where almighty gods come to bless us all,
to gladly help us up when we have a heartbreaking fall.
Where pleasant laughter hosts the great and extravagant refuge,
and red, exquisite roses blossom in grand and festive deluge.

When encompassing greatness and merriment never have to lose,
and picturesque rainbows show their vibrant and luminous hues.
And of all the wonderful places where you would love to roam,
not even one is as magnificent as the one called home.

Ajay Krish, Grade 7
Challenger School – Ardenwood

The Clock

Upon the wall where I see all
Is where I stand telling time with my hands.

Breakfast is here time to yell in their ear.
As they eat I see their treats.

Time for school I'm only doing my job
Get going you fool.

Here is lunch it's time to munch
TICK, TICK, TICK.

Once again it is time to chime at least, while the sun still shines.
Now it is dinner they eat like kings and will never get thinner.

They go to bed with dreams in their head,
But, I chime instead.

Leah Walsh, Grade 7
St Patrick Parish School

Tryout Day

Listen my children and you shall hear
Of the stressful Friday of this year
When hundreds of girls tried out for cheer
Tons of girls in red shorts and white shirts
All with hair up, all are huge flirts
April eleventh, the day we tryout
Girls looking frightened all full of doubt
Off to the gym, scared out of my mind
Remember the moves, the judges aren't blind
Arlene and Kayla are the first they call
Hands stop shaking, don't trip and fall
The cheers went smoothly I'm surprised about that
Jumps are next, oh where's my spring mat
I have to focus, my tumbling is bad
My round-offs are good, my handsprings are sad
The dance is next, it's the final key
If I do well I might make JV
Make sure you smile all the way through
Try to have fun, do the best you can do
Please post the teams I await my cheer fate
This stressful Friday turned out to be great

Kayla Shires, Grade 8
Norman Sullivan Middle School

My Big Heart

I have a big heart,
I'm filled with love;
I'll do anything because you're my best friend.
I know you so well, so I thank you
for being there for me.
Friends are there 'til the end and forever.

Beatriz Uribe, Grade 7
Renuevo School

The Beach

The beach is where memories are made,
It's where we have fun and even sunbathe.
The beach reminds me of summertime
When everything is perfectly fine.
I love watching the dancing waves
While I soak up the sun's blazing hot rays.
As much as I love the beach
I'm not a big fan
Of the seagulls and the sand.
But I look past those things
And enjoy this great place
Because there is nowhere else I'd rather be.

Breanna O'Neil, Grade 9
Fountain Valley High School

They Said

They said, I wouldn't make it to the basketball team
They said, I wouldn't be starter on the team
They said, my team wouldn't make it to the playoffs
They said, I'm not going to become an All-Star
They said, I'm too short or weak to be on the team
They said, they said, they said
You keep talking,
I keep shooting.
Now they said, I would make it to the basketball team
They said, I would be starter in the team
They said, my team would make it to the playoffs
They said, I'm going to become an All-Star!
They said, I'm quick and strong enough to be on the team
You keep cheering,
I keep shooting.
Finally they said, I'll be on a varsity team
They then said, I will be drafted to the NBA
And they said, I will be on an All-Star team
For the All-Stars, in the starting lineups!

Ernest Lardizabal, Grade 8
Corpus Christi School

Secret Admirer*

It was months ago on the beach
That I met her, my secret admirer.
We kissed on the sand,
Me and my secret admirer.

She looked as beautiful as a new puppy.
We went to my house.
We went to my room and hung out,
Me and my beautiful secret admirer.

We passed out on the floor of my room.
The next morning when we woke up,
We could not remember what happened.
Me and my secret admirer.

Rowen Kamfiroozie, Grade 9
The Winston School
*Inspired by "Annabel Lee" by Edgar Allan Poe

Ode to America

from countryside sun
pounds the beaten hills
city, with vast buildings that never sleep
with floods of yellow
sweep you away to your destination
with forest like an umbrella
catches the sun
desert eaten by water,
sun baked
an oven
America
unique
my climate
Austin Navarro, Grade 8
Santa Rosa Technology Magnet School

Cherry Blossoms

swish swish side to side
ride the breeze until midnight
floating flowing on the breeze
the beauty brings you to your knees
then i see the one i love
dancing swaying up above
i twist and turn so small and frail
dancing through the gates of jail
tiptoe through the skies of black
never ever looking back
glowing in the pale moonlight
the stars will guide my way tonight
sneak through whispers never heard
secrets never trusted words
never caring not at all
and when the breeze fails i should fall
flipping through the frosted air
find the sidewalk landing there
from here is where i watch my love
still off drifting far above
Ophelia Morreale, Grade 8
Bancroft Middle School

One Single Night

One single night,
So little time,
I need these last few moments,
In case something happens,
My family is all I have left,
The prisoners say;
I only have one single night,
What does that mean?
Do I try to escape?
Do I sacrifice myself for my loved ones?
One single night,
We might die this next day.
Luke DeNuccio, Grade 8
St Joseph's School of the Sacred Heart

The Little Cottage

As I walk down the hillside,
On a narrow, worn path,
I hear the gentle waves on the shore,
See the friendly cattle, and
Admire the huge, fatherly mountains.
The grass, wind-torn and brown,
Waves to me.
Halfway down the trail,
A small rock juts out,
Surrounded by dandelions and weeds.
I perch myself atop
And gaze over
The lazy, lapping sea.
Far in the distance
White cotton balls
Graze the ocean.
I leap off the rock, and
Hike back up the slope,
Back to the little cottage on the hill
Where I feel safe surrounded
By the comfort and love of home.
Annaliese Miller, Grade 7
Rolling Hills Country Day School

Time

The time in the hourglass
Is running short
My time is about to end
All I remembered was when
I was writing a letter to my friend

Oh how lovely it was to see her
Eyes light up with joy
I thank her for the memories
But now my time is short
All I can say is goodbye
Charles Molina, Grade 7
St Cyprian School

A Colorful Rainbow

There was a rainbow.
It had a lot of
colors.
With a shiny
sun.
Miriam Osorio, Grade 7
Richland Jr High School

The Mountain

The mountains so near so white
But so cold I wonder will I get
A cold though the snow just piles up
Just to create an avalanche
Jesse Ferrer, Grade 7
Richland Jr High School

Perfect Flavors

Look at the triangle-shaped goodness
Its flavors perfect
It tastes like a little slice of heaven
If you listen closely
You can hear your taste buds applauding
As they prepare to chow down
The fragrance of the cheese
Before every bite
Is a satisfier
The mixes of the flavors
Cheese, sauce, bread, and pepperoni
Go down your throat smooth
As your mouth requests for more
You give it what it wants
And your stomach cries for more
Though it is full
It still has chronic cravings for more
As the last bite is taken
The taste is savored
The amazing taste of pizza
Ernie Montano, Grade 8
Our Lady of Guadalupe School

Love

Love is the reason to a broken heart
Why did we even fall from the start?

Love is sometimes not returned
This heartache is a lesson learned

Love is love, it can't be stopped
Your love, it can't be topped
Shantel Dang, Grade 7
Sarah McGarvin Intermediate School

Nature

Birds sing
Flowers bloom
sounds ring
with power and gloom
Colors change
to and fro
Animals climb high and low
All things large and all things small
are important to us all
Trees give air
that we can bear
Air whistles in the sky
up above birds fly high
Leaves falling orange and brown
slowly floating to the ground
The sun shines bright
just like a candlelight
Demi Lomeli, Grade 7
St Hilary Elementary School

Karma

Behind your back talking
Floating among the air
Voices all around mocking
Dirty looks and crude stares

Tapping on your shoulder
Tap! Tap! Tap!
The weight like a boulder

Judgmental thinking
Firing awful feelings

Your future is determined by your past
Karma will come at last

What goes around comes around
What goes up must come down

Karma is your friend
Karma is your enemy
Karma is the end
Karma is everything

Karma

Gabriella Gabos and Maddie Relator, Grade 8
St Patrick Parish School

Autumn

The autumn leaves fall to the ground
Painting the Earth orange, red and brown.
The subtle wind makes a pleasant sound.
The trees are shedding their crown.

It's the season of Thanksgiving and Halloween
Families gather together
An autumn day is a beautiful scene
Surrounded by peaceful weather.

The branches are stripped bare
To prepare for winter's cold air.

Holly Limm, Grade 8
Madrona Middle School

Lightning

Thunder always comes after lightning,
And sometimes it could be very frightening
It looks as if it was a threatening sword,
Electricity is kind of like it except it is inside an electric cord
Sometimes it can look like fireworks in the air
Like the flashing lights from a county fair
It doesn't need rain to form,
Sometimes it can be a thunderstorm
It might look like flashing lights,
Remember not to fly your kites

Chris Kim, Grade 8
Madrona Middle School

Colors

Blue is the cool water we play in for fun
Yellow is the big, bright, warm yellow sun

Orange is something in the fall
Brown is something very tall

White is the soft fluffy snow
Gray are big clouds that flow

Red is a juicy treat that I eat
Pink is what I wear to look sweet

Blue, yellow, orange, brown, white, gray, red and pink…
These are the best colors, don't you think?

Brianna Murphy, Grade 8
Martin Murphy Middle School

An Ode to My iPhone

My iPhone is in a way,
The most amazing thing I've seen in days,
The way it's such a fine device,
Makes you feel you're very precise,
I love all of the things it can do,
I honestly think it can't receive a boo!
So many people think it doesn't deserve this so much,
But I cannot figure the meaning of such,
It is wonderful, splendid, and a lovely thing to touch,
I never though I could enjoy it this much.

Jake Penta, Grade 7
Santa Rosa Technology Magnet School

Ode to Cars

An ode to cars
Cars are so cool
They make you travel faster
Big or small, wide or skinny
They are the things that help the world
They can be dusty and old
They can be new and bright
But they have the same function
(Though I would prefer the cool new car)
I don't care if you are costly
It takes a lot of work to care for you
I don't care if I have to wash and dry you
Feed you with gas
Give you a drink of oil
I would like to drive you
Giggity giggity, giggity goo
I want you if you are young
I want you if you are old
Ferrari or Porsche, Lamborghini or BMW
I would live to drive you

Ian Sherman, Grade 7
Santa Rosa Technology Magnet School

The Story of Life

You open your eyes,
And see for the first time.
You become aware of sounds,
And hear for the first time.
You move your fingers,
And feel for the first time.

Where one life must end,
Another begins.
The end of one story,
Is the beginning of another…

Now you close your eyes,
And see for the last time.
You become unaware of sounds,
And hear for the last time.
Your fingers stop moving,
And you feel for the last time.

Now as your life ends,
Somewhere another is beginning.
Now your story has reached its end,
While another has just begun…

Alex Michels, Grade 8
Shadow Hills Intermediate School

Nature

Black, dark
Scare, comforts, haunts
Puts people to sleep
Darkness

Bobby Elliot, Grade 8
Citrus Hills Intermediate School

No Matter

No matter how many times,
when we close our eyes,
the mistakes will still haunt us.

No matter how many times,
we wish away consequences,
they all come back to us in our sleep.

No matter how many times,
the decisions are wrong,
God is there to tuck us in at night
and assure us that we are all right.

Renée Brisson, Grade 8
Visalia Christian Academy

Night

The moon shines brightly
The sky is dark like the soil
The animals sleep.

Donnell delaPena, Grade 8
South Tahoe Middle School

night

the sun and the moon
the light that you get
the light that you don't
i won't forget
for the time it is here
i don't want to forget all the fun that we have had
we will wake up with the light and sleep with the night
we will never know how long we will get
we cannot know for the fate that we will have
you can look at a clock and think you know but do you really know
we will sleep at night and ponder it but it will not help one bit
so the sun and the moon will come together
at night forever
so good bye and good night

Maddie Peck, Grade 8
Palm Desert Middle School

World Peace

W ith much equality,
O ur world will become fair.
R eal people will help make this happen.
L oving, caring, and enjoying every part of life,
D oing it all with many others.

P eople worry about when the war will end.
E ven with all the conflicts we have it is possible to be tranquil.
A nd when this happens we will truly be united.
C ausing all people to be just with one another.
E nding all conflicts and creating World Peace.

Cristina Aviña, Grade 8
Martin Murphy Middle School

A Wish

There I sit waiting in my car for something to happen
I twist and turn and dream sweet dreams and count my way up to ten
And then, when I close my eyes a bright light shines onto my eyelids
I squint my eyes a little bit and when I did open them, the light hid
As I move towards the window to wonder what I saw, a shooting star I see
Up in the blue black night going right above me reflecting down on the Greenland Sea
Coming down in a small spark of light glittering high above in the sky
I make a long lasting wish until the shooting star was seen no more by my little eyes
As we got home at about half past ten, I walk inside the house as if I am in dreamland
There I see my dad with a big smile on his face holding the cutest puppy in his hand
I stand there in such a shock as a smile slowly appears on my face
I run and hug my daddy as he looks at my pale face
The puppy's eyes were a sparkly color of brown and his paw was the size of my thumb
Oh, what a delight, I laughed a little and my cheeks turned red and he was gleesome
Kuppy was the perfect name for him and I told everybody he was my lucky charm
I carried him everywhere I went and it wasn't so hard since he fit in my arm
When my days were bad at school Kuppy would cheer me up so fast
Everybody loved him and thought he was the cutest puppy because he never harassed
I sit on the deck dreaming looking at the fire which was so warmish
I thank that lucky shooting star and I love my daddy for fulfilling, a wish

Nishi Saksena, Grade 7
Challenger School – Ardenwood

My Perfect World

The sunlight glimmers on my skin,
I run around, and feel the breeze on my cheeks.
My bare feet are damp and velvety.
My arms spread apart to feel the morning air.
I am dazzled by the lights and the wind,
Being able to feel, and touch the world.
I feel as if I could be lifted up to the sky,
Able to understand all aspects of nature,
Smiling while the breeze brushes through my hair.
The sound of rustling leaves gives a feeling of security —
The sunlight starting to stroke my bare skin,
The birds talking to me, telling me to be wild and free.
I am free to be whoever or whatever I want.
No one is there to talk about me, or to judge me.
I can just be myself — simply who I am.
I can fly, I can soar, I can run, I can be…
Anything can be possible in this Perfect World of mine.
This world may understand me, while no other can…
A world where just being myself is accepted.

Jennalyn Kabiling, Grade 8
Corpus Christi School

Little Children

Little children have big imaginations
They are pirates sailing the seas looking for their treasure,
x marks the spot; they found it!
They open their eyes and their pirate ship is a sandbox,
their treasure a pile of rocks,
and their sea is grass.
They close their eyes again,
Now they are astronauts blasting off to the moon.
five, four, three, two, one
Blast off!
They open their eyes and their rocket ship is a swing set
And their moon is a huge tree in the backyard.
For little children imagination is always possible not impossible
At times, they open and close their eyes and it's the same.

Ashley Gudgel, Grade 7
Monte Vista Christian School

The Thrill of Flying

Zipping down the mountain
Cutting through the snow with my skis
I spot out a jump
And head for it
As I approach it I slowly crouch down
Then pop off
I feel like I am soaring like an eagle
And I am invincible
As I watch the skiers move slower
Then touch back down
And crouch to absorb the shock and ski away.

Max McKelvy, Grade 8
St Joseph's School of the Sacred Heart

An Ode to Pie

It tastes delectable
It's the fruit of the gods
There are many tasty types
Sweet cherry, delicious blueberry, and awesome apple
It's steaming hot
The aroma calls your name
It calls you like a siren's song
Like a flaky flavored cloud
Rain of flavor on your tongue
Whirling colors flavors smell
What's your favorite?
Mine is all
I like any of the tasteful flavors
This heaven's fruit is pie

Mitch Tanaka, Grade 7
Santa Rosa Technology Magnet School

A Light, Fluffy Treat

A blueberry muffin lies on the table ready to eat,
Tempting all those who see it to consume the lovely treat.
Emitting puffs of steam from its surface that's piping hot,
Freshly baked is the muffin that from the oven is brought.
Shaped like a mushroom and baked into blueberries in bread,
A sugary confection that delights whom it is fed,
Being chewy, light, and fluffy make it appetizing food,
And to top it all off, with blueberries is the treat strewed.
With numerous ingredients is this delicacy made;
These are mixed together and in the oven are neatly laid.
My mouth starts to water when on the muffin I set my eyes,
For a deep longing for this confection soon starts to arise.
Just with the first bite my taste buds overflow with delight
At the delicious taste of the treat so fluffy and light;
One bite after another, I shall savor each single one
'Cause after several more bites, one muffin becomes none.
Lingering on in my mouth is the blueberry muffin's taste,
Yet I stay somewhat depressed for eating it with too much haste.
As I recall the great taste of the treat I just ate before,
I look forward to the day when I can eat it once more.

Meghana Bhat, Grade 7
Challenger School – Ardenwood

Metamorphosis

I used be the bark on a tree
Now I am a poem on paper.
I used to be a cotton ball
Now I am Hanes comfort soft underwear.
I used to wear Huggies
But I'm a big kid now.
I used to be just a cub
Now I am a big bear.
I used to be a little calf
Now I am a whole leg.
I used to be a Colt
Now I am better, a Patriot.

Tyler Moreno, Grade 8
Citrus Hills Intermediate School

I Believe

Magic is sorcery where you're not quite sure how the trickster performed his tricks
One moment his palms are empty with air, dancing with a laughing smile
And the next, when he opens them there is a bee sitting on a pollen filled flower
I know I believe that that was magic
Everyone knows the classical bamboozle in which the rabbit is pulled out of the hat
At first his hat is displayed as empty, but after the trickster says his magical twisters,
Behold! A rabbit has been pulled out of his hat
I know that I believe that that was magic
Magic is portraying that your hands can run a race and your eyes may watch,
Even if your eyes may not see your hands run by
The enchanting thaumaturgy can take you from sawing someone in two
And from simply doing a card trick for someone you know, or someone unknown to you
I believe a simple deed as that is magic
However, when day's glory has ended with a red hazel brown sky
And a fragile, new and weak baby has been born
One who is attenuated with rarefied heartbeats, one who is predicted not to live long
Dwindling life, and at death's door, unarmored and innocent
A sweep of mercy that none can explain, surges life within its minute body
Magic? No. But a miracle of God's kind

Calene Morris, Grade 8
Madrona Middle School

Shame

The sun slowly fades into the glossy sky, leaving an amber shade on the land below. The street lamps ignite, and they illuminate the streets. Now all that is left is the eerie orange glow from the lamps as dim as could be. Over a hill and far away, there stands a lone house. The rickety rocker, which I remember so well, now sits empty on the house porch. The home so vivid, now lays abandoned, an eye sore on the countryside.

The house was the color of the sky, a beautiful blue. Now it is the color of mold, a gruesome grey. Looking at my past life is looking into an elder's face. The life was sucked out, and left was its cracked face. That was my father's face I saw in this house. His breathing slows, and his eyes close. The structure he built from scratch lay in my worthless hands. And I shamefully sold the shack, and now I live in shame.

Nathan Steinberg, Grade 9
Balboa City School

Control

With every bruise there's a memory
With every scrape there's a scar
Without a parent there's pain
With life there's suffering
You can't feel you don't have control
You can't laugh you don't have control
But you can ache that's their control
Every memory in your life every smile every cry means nothing eventually you die
You can always have faith but who's there to hold you?
You always have family but you'll leave
You always have friends but they'll leave
In the end you're alone independence isn't easy
It's the closest thing to loneliness
When you're young you're the world but you probably won't make a difference in it
When you're old you're wasted and life goes on without you
Are you living life to the fullest? Do you cry over things that matter?
Do you laugh just because you can? Do you work to get somewhere?
You only get to live once even through your scrapes, your bruises, the problems your parents caused.
You live your life…and that's the only thing you control

Chelsea Montville, Grade 9
Fountain Valley High School

Group Home Life

I am from a foosball loud and proud.
Basketball being thrown around.
Air hockey clinging in my ears.
While people on the couch throw up cheers.
I am from a room where the car should be,
but now is a playroom for everyone and me.

I am from TV in the background.
To kids running around, the smell of cooking in the air,
as I'm eating a delicious pear.
I am from a place that is supposed to be home,
but feels like a place for eternity I must roam.

I am from 42 presidents in my country,
to where is the Statue of Liberty.
On a horrible day of September 11th,
some of my fellow Americans went up to heaven.
We are more than the colors of the flag,
All mixed up in one cultural bag.

Garrett Von-Flue, Grade 8
Milhous School

Softball

In the box, ready like a fox
You never know what will happen when I step in the box
My knees shaking and butterflies racing
I am a bomb ready to explode
I hit that ball and everyone knows
I run toward third and go, go, go
I think I am going to cross home plate, or am I too late
I slide into home and what do you know
I am safe, safe, safe

Priscilla Hernandez, Grade 7
St Hilary Elementary School

High Up in This Tree

In a universe made for myself and me
I'd sit here alone
High up in this tree

No worries, no trouble
It's all gone away
I'd sit on this branch just daydreaming all day.

I would dream about things like nothing before,
Bright orange elephants would show up at my door.

Oh the things you can find when you open your mind.

Sitting on this branch high up in this tree
Has brought many things to my mind you see.

So, no matter how big, how short or how tall,
In my world you count, no matter how small.

Jacqueline Vallera, Grade 7
The Winston School

Sparrow

As it soars through the deep, blue sky,
The wind whispers quietly to it.
As it lands on a pink blossom tree branch,
The flowers bloom to welcome it.
As it pecks the ground for food,
The little specks of grass say hello to it.
Then when it flies away to its nest to rest,
The sunset glows upon it —
A tiny sparrow that inspires nature,
A sparrow that is a symbol of life within itself;
What an amazing creature that sparrow is!

Jennifer Phan, Grade 7
Sarah McGarvin Intermediate School

The Sea

Always calling to me, smooth and steady
Your deep azure expanse hides untold mysteries and riches
Amazing creatures soar through your depths
No one can control you
You are untamed
Your anger is your raging cyclones
Your beauty is your tropical expanse
Your kindness is your calm seas
Humble fishermen make use of your riches you give up willingly
You have a constant battle with the land,
As you batter it wave after wave
The remains of your inhabitants call for you, and me
You are mine
Your beauty
Your anger
Your kindness
You are always mine
My sea

Logan H. Bleeg, Grade 8
Martin Murphy Middle School

Waterfalls

Water rushing down,
Rushing down to hit the ground,
Like a child jumping into a pool.

Making a loud roar,
As it hits the bottom,
Like a lion showing off to a mate.

All around its surface,
Everything is simply quiet,
Like a classroom taking a test.

The smell of mist surrounds the falling water,
Freshness fills the air,
Like a pine-scented forest.

Courtney Shibuya, Grade 8
Madrona Middle School

Baseball

The sounds of them
The smells of them too
All the roaring fans
Waiting for a hit
They yell and yell
All day long
Just waiting for
That 7th inning song
Hope the home team wins
Or I'll be mad
The noise of them
The aroma of them too
I love ball games
Hey don't you

Lukas Wade, Grade 7
Linfield Christian School

Winter Sun

I peer out the frosty window
And glimpse what life
Has become for me today
Tender innocence
Sheltered from the world
By layers of bulky cushioning
Lumber out the door
Lift up a shielding hand
From the bright, blinding
Winter sun
Run, run, run, and scream
Fall, roll, laugh, and lay
I wave my arms and legs
And leap up to see
A white, shining angel
I turn, and a small flash of green
Startles me
A lone minuscule weed
Fighting all odds
In the barren landscape in which
It resides

Cherry Mullaguru, Grade 9
Westview High School

Hurricanes

Hurricanes are destructive
and dangerous for the people
that's why people don't like them.
Hurricanes
Hurricanes look tight
but they are very very dangerous
Some people like them some don't.
Hurricanes
All the hurricanes are dangerous
they look like scary monsters
I wish there is none.

Wilifer Cervantes, Grade 8
Almond Tree Middle School

Glowing in the Night

I found my eyes looking up to the sky at night
My eyes resting on a cool glowing sight.
It seems to call to some.
It always rises within the nights that will finally come.

The pale glow sometimes shows its face
Although it might not even leave a trace.
Some always seem to howl to its glow
which makes quite a beautiful show.

Eyes shining bright
in the darkness of the night.
Calling to their equals.
Each song creates another sequel.

Beautiful howls float through the air.
Sometimes even made by more than just one pair.
Usually showing their feelings to their friends.
Their friend's and their conversation finally ends.

A lot of the time these creatures will find themselves looking up at night.
Their beautiful glowing eyes resting on the cool bluish looking sight.

Ashley Fortin, Grade 7
Monte Vista Christian School

The Castle in the Sky

A Holy Land in the sky up above
Where angels soar, no cease in love.

God will sit on His golden throne with His son by His side,
His glory shone, what will He decide?

He will open the gates to the Castle in the Sky,
Glory awaits, on Him you must rely.

Your sins forgiven; bad memories washed away.
An eternal life forever, it is here where you shall stay.

The beauty of the Heavens, lingers at your grave.
When your soul has left you will no longer be enslaved.

Much farther than the stars, is the place you soon shall be.
Much farther than the planet Mars, much higher than the sea.

The glory of the Lord, you too shall see it true.
Your time will come to live eternally, you'll have time to think it through.

So join your only Father in the Castle up above,
Where there is never a shortage of everlasting love.

Alexa Taylor, Grade 8
Santa Rosa Technology Magnet School

Ode to Bed

Ode to the palace of slumber
With your gracious nights of dozing.
A palace so full of dreamy riches
Help me sleep through starry nights.

Ode to the kingdom of snoozing
Where the owner is a king.
A king wrapped in a cottony sheet
Holding the king like a mother holding her baby.

King of rest protects me from much.
The cold of Arctics and stressful pressure,
Man-eating monsters and soul-taking reapers
Don't stand a chance against the king.

Night, Bed spends fighting evil.
Morning, Bed spends recharging its sheets.
Evening, Bed prepares for another fight.
Many battles won but an endless war.

Bed, my leader,
my prince,
my hero,
Ode to Bed.

Mindy Chen, Grade 8
Presidio Middle School

A Moment in Time

Time is the mystery of the world that makes things go round.
This puzzle is the key of live as it controls everything around.
Imagine a tedious boring life without time
The sun would never rise and the moon never climb.

Never underestimate time or think it it worthless
It will haunt you down and cause a big mess.
Good or bad, times is never in your hands as it never stays
Time never takes a break and never has any delays.

When you are having lots of fun, time flies like an arrow.
But the clock ticks on and on when you are bored and sorrow.
Whether it's someone in Russia or a Brazilian broker
Time is different around the world from one side to another.

A man in Mexico will be sleeping peacefully in his bed
While a guy in Japan is busy on a hot day eating cornbread.
There is a time to cry, a time to laugh, a time to act
A time to learn, a time to play, and time to react.

Even though sometimes we never really know how to use it
There is always a time to do something and never quit.
Time is a precious object that is beyond our control
So use it wisely to always achieve your goal.

Aniket Saoji, Grade 7
Challenger School – Ardenwood

What Loud Is

Loud is the sound of my cousins shouting,
Running, and playing
Sliding down a slide and swinging on swings
They scream so loud it's like a blow horn
Blowing by my ear.

Loud is the sound of a train when it
Blows its horn
Going down the train track as slow as a sloth
But longer than a football field
It's a very noisy vehicle that travels
Throughout the world with no destination

But the loudest of all things is the sound of
Christmas joy when families are brought together
With the sound of music sharing with each other
The sound of loud

Byron Hernandez, Grade 8
St Sebastian School

I Would Do Anything for You

I would sing you a lullaby,
if you can't sleep at night.
I would cuddle you in my arms,
if you have had a fright.
I would stay with you forever,
even until the day I die.
I would walk a hundred miles,
just to see you smile.

Lisa Khuat, Grade 7
Sarah McGarvin Intermediate School

Perfection Is All

How the world tilts
And we tilt with it
But when one tilts
The rest bow to disbelief
And the one becomes an outsider
Loneliness is despair —
— the odds have it
(But then again, don't we all have it?)
No, there is a constant and forever
The stars are seemingly every expanding
Us as imperfect
At first thought we consider ultimate power
(But) Roman rule comes crashing down
Would not the stars implode?
Since there lingers imperfection in societies
Yet, think to aid!
There is reason for every matter
So doesn't all have sense of perfection?
Must it be contradiction…paradox
Tell me no more
Perfection is all

Victoria Lang, Grade 8
San Elijo Middle School

Anonymous

I thought we were clicking,
I swear we were meant to be.
But when I saw you with her,
I knew you weren't for me.

I don't know how I thought that,
I'm nothing close to her.
She's so perfect and beautiful,
And the opposite of me!

She makes me feel so dumb,
I thought I had a chance.
It was just a game!
And I'll never get that chance.

Why didn't you tell me,
If you knew how I felt.
You did it on purpose,
Now you've made my heart melt!

Diana Ayala, Grade 8
St Linus School

Poetry Is...

Poetry is love
The love for doves
Not told but written
Not said but read
Poetry shows emotion
For or against someone
The way you tell
How your heart swells

Angel Revolinski, Grade 8
Madrona Middle School

9/11

Two twin giants
fall in two quick blows.
Like a baby bird
falling out of its nest, helpless.
Thousands of lives
lost in two shots.
Two metal birds
break thousands of hearts.
Two metal birds
create nothing but chaos.
This chaos
is causing more death.
Over many years,
the fight is still raging.
They cannot see the end,
for they are blinded by death.
But it all started with two twin giants
falling in two quick blows.

Brophy Hiatt, Grade 8
Valley Oak Middle School

To Exist

fading
into the eerie depths of time
into some forgotten world
the soft glow of candles
the calm hum of voices
the comfort of love
call me to another place and time
a place of tranquility
peace

seeing
when we at last become free
when we know how to exist
we begin to understand
love

Claire Connacher, Grade 9
St Joseph Notre Dame High School

Soccer

Soccer
Early morning, late nights
Kicking, pushing, scoring
Letting out your inner anger
Passing, sweating, running
Black, white
Soccer

Riley O'Connell, Grade 8
Santa Rosa Technology Magnet School

Wide Sky

Sky is like ocean
That has everything
The fish cloud is swimming
The cotton candy cloud is flowing
The cat cloud is walking
The face cloud is smiling
Or there is nothing
It is just like clear water

Sky is like ocean.
You can go anywhere
If you are aware of that place
By crossing the big sky
Like you cross the ocean

Sky is like the whole entire world!

Naomi Mori, Grade 8
Madrona Middle School

Beautiful Penguins

I see a penguin!
With his black and white feathers,
Then he swims away.

Jensen Green, Grade 7
South Tahoe Middle School

The Complex Desire

Over the past five years
And countless tears,
Its you who keeps me in line
Even through all this time.
Its you who will be here on a dime
To tell me it's now all behind us;
It cannot restart.
And it's you who watches me in the dark,
Although your consumed in only light;
You're catching me when I fall, despite
That I am running away
Hiding in the furthest cave.
And yet every day
It's you who finds me where I lay.

Rebekuh Martin, Grade 8
Nobel Middle School

Mother Nature!!!

Among the trees
and flowers,
I saw a bug
black and yellow,
on the top of a
purple petal,
Moving around so
it can find its
perfect spot,
All you hear is the
wind blowing the
bee away.

Breanna Plasencia, Grade 8
St Sebastian School

Rainbows

After rain
Beautiful rainbows
From the sky
Appears before our eyes

Rain and sun
Combined together
Making rainbows
For clouds and skies

With many colors
R.O.Y. G. B.I.V.
Shines the sky
Very bright

A good sight for us to see
A magical thing that nature's made
Such a nice feeling to see
A rainbow tonight

Danica Ruiz, Grade 8
Almond Tree Middle School

My World

My world
Is all I need
My friends and family
My house and clothes and everything
That's me

Sabrina Aguilera, Grade 7
John Charles Fremont Intermediate School

Scarred for Life

Racism spreading like a deadly disease,
Felt in the head, chest, shoulders, and knees.
No hope for those poor, suffering souls.
Nazis reaching out for their tainted goals.

Jews reaching out for a helping hand.
Running out of supplies; no more contraband.
Fear all around, could be smelled in the air.
They screamed out for help, but nobody cared.

Trapped in a small room and a candle burns brightly.
Someone shifts their position, just a little, just slightly.
But the tiny move was too much, and somebody heard.
The police burst in, and words were slurred.

Tears flowed like wine from a cracked oak barrel.
In far away safety, someone sings a Christmas carol.
Back in the basement there's pain, bloodshed, and strife.
They're brought in, branded, tattooed, and scarred for life.

Tony Mingrone, Grade 8
Sacred Heart School

Ode to My Family

I've been with them since the beginning.
I've grown with their love.
They are always there for me,
they support me all the way through.
No matter what they always love me,
and no matter what I will always love them.

A blank piece of paper would never live
if crayons were never there to give color.

A light bulb would never turn on
if electricity was never there to give it power.

They give me the wings to fly,
they give me the strength to stay strong.
Without them I couldn't live,
Without them I could never survive.
I love them as much as the depth of the ocean.
I love them as far as the sky can reach.;
They are,
my
Family.

Clara Chun, Grade 8
La Joya Middle School

Unheard Voices

There are the voices that speak out loudly —
The voices whose opinions are heard,
The voices which stand up for beliefs,
And never back down.

But what of the other voices?
Those in the dark,
In the shadows,
The whispers in the silence.

These millions of unheard voices,
Passed from generation to generation,
Quietly, discreetly,
In the background.
Never voiced out loud.

Until one day someone will stand up for that voice.
That one unheard voice.
In the background,
That can make all the difference.

So speak up.
Raise your voice.
Don't let your voice go unheard.

Lillian Wang, Grade 9
Westview High School

Falling Dreams

Gorgeous hazel eyes,
Make me wanna die.

Only if he knew how I felt,
And all the pain that I've dealt.

You are my one and only dream,
Do you think we will ever be?

You like me I like you,
Do you think my fantasy will ever come true?

I hope one of these days you will finally see,
How much you hypnotized me.

I wish you were mine.
Because you make my world shine.

Slower and slower I'm fading and dying,
You really don't see how hard I am trying.

I'm so full dreams, I'm finished too,
And I just want to say that
I love you.

Lauren Clesi, Grade 7
Holy Family Catholic School

9/11

On September 11th
The sky went black with sorrow
Yet then the world was silenced
As the day got mournful
Once the day was done
Many lives were lost
Every year on that day
The world is silent and still

Kara Lomax, Grade 8
Citrus Hills Intermediate School

I Am

I am sad
I wonder if I get mad
I hear laughter
I see happiness
I want good
I am lonely.

I pretend to be evil
I feel bad
I touch my hands
I worry about death
I am lonely.

I understand feelings
I dream happy
I try to understand
I hope no one dies
I am light.

Jesus Martinez, Grade 7
Richland Jr High School

Fruit Punch

Hawaiian girls dancing in hula skirts,
Tropical, fruity drinks,
Nobody knows what's in them,
Sunbathing on the warm, sunny beach,
With the glistening sand,
Almost as sparkly as snow,
Radiant blue waves crash on the beach,
Even though they are only three feet tall,
Once you fly back on that airplane,
You miss the sand,
The clear, blue water,
And the most important thing of all,
The fruit punch.

Katherine Armstrong, Grade 8
St Joseph's School of the Sacred Heart

Shooting Star

Oh! A bright flicker of hope!
Soaring through the galaxy,
Shooting star, you made my day!

Rebecca Nguyen, Grade 7
Sarah McGarvin Intermediate School

Ode to Annie

How your stubby little legs run toward me as I stop into the room
Your baby fat flies all over the place
Your ears flap up and down as you run
Your tongue hangs out of your small mouth

You jump on me
Your dirty paws get all over my new shirt
Dirty prints of love
Your warm tongue gives me lots of kisses
Beef-jerky flavored kisses

I sit down at the table waiting for breakfast
You plop down next to me and place your head on my lap
And you just looked at me
With your beautiful eyes
Eyes the color of the sky at midnight

Danielle Bergen, Grade 8
Tierra Linda Middle School

Ticking Clock

Two hands moving around and around
Circle after circle
Always the same routine
Change by the seconds
Minutes
Hours
Days
Tick on and on as we grow and grow
Hour after hour
Day after day
Waiting for the end

So suddenly did the clock stop
We were waving our goodbyes from the back seat
Tears dripping down his face like a waterfall as we back away
The tan house slowly growing farther and farther away through the rearview mirror
A happy house cracking, crumbling before our eyes
Never again would we be a family
Two young girls
So close with parents so far.

Kennedy Shields, Grade 8
St Joseph's School of the Sacred Heart

Holocaust*

No child cried a single sound that first night, for he was gone.
No elder settled down to sleep that first night,
for she had been fiercely laid to rest forever.
No mother or daughter had embraced each other that first night,
for they were torn apart and slain by the beast that had risen from hell.
Even those who lived, their souls, their faiths, their dreams,
had been thrown in a vast abyss, never to be seen again.
Even then, that first night.

Brooke Hobbs, Grade 8
St Joseph's School of the Sacred Heart
Inspired by Elie Wiesel's "Night"

Take Time to Appreciate

I STAND and appreciate all the treasures
in the world, and through all bliss and contentment;
I HEAR laughter, carefree and blissful,
echoing from elated lips
I SEE gleaming brass, reflecting shiny white teeth
like pearls in cobalt sea.
I SEE amorous hearts,
laced together with passion.
I MARK the days I spend
in this paradise without you.
I SEE the line of the city
drift off into the sunset.
I OBSERVE music notes,
coming to life in a world of gray.
I OBSERVE silhouettes
creating shapes in the pavement.
ALL THESE — All this harmony and artistry in bloom,
I standing, appreciate, see, hear, and am grateful.

Kaelyn Gima, Grade 9
Westview High School

Poor Cat

The big fat cat
Ate a huge rat
The cat wouldn't budge
So we gave him a nudge
But the rat that he ate was too fat poor cat.

Amber Fain, Grade 7
Richland Jr High School

Papa

"Papa, can you hear me?"
"Papa, can you see my candle?"
Sizzle goes the burning flames in the night.

"Papa, can you hear me?
Your soul, a star in the night,
My soul down on Earth."

"Papa, can you hear me?
Praying in the night,
Counting every second of the day."

"Papa, can you hear me?"
The day you left, the day I cried,
The thunder screamed, the day you died.

"Papa, can you hear me?"
"Can you see me?"
"Will you hug me?"

"Papa, Can you hear me?"

Brian Liebson, Grade 8
Rolling Hills Country Day School

Is It Love?

Every day I wake up with you on my mind
Since I met you everything changed in my life
Girl I want you to know you were hard to find
I want you close and please be my wife
When I'm alone I just sit and think of you
I want to call you and hear your voice on the other side
I try harder to get closer but don't know what to do
Whenever you feel bad my heart is open wide
I need to get this out of my chest
'Cause I don't know what to do
I know I got to 'cause it's best
To let you know that I love you

Sergio Sarabia, Grade 8
Henry T Gage Middle School

French Trip

I really want to go to France,
This may be my only chance.

If I save up for the trip,
I might be able to go on it.

To do so, I must raise money,
Because to go to France, it costs money.

I hope that I get enough money,
If not, I'll have to beg for money.

I hope that I get a chance to get a ticket,
Because it would be my paradise ticket.

When I leave, I'll say "Au Revoir,"
But when I get to France, I'll say "Bonjour!"

Wendy Morales, Grade 7
John Adams Middle School

I Love Spring

I love spring,
A seasons of fresh start

I love spring,
When flowers cry for happiness

I love spring,
When the temperature becomes warm to us

I love spring,
When students begin to relax from the fear of Science Fair

I love spring,
When a wind is as fresh as a raspberry

I love spring,
A season for spring break

Hiroki Kaifu, Grade 8
Madrona Middle School

The Changes

There will be many changes as you grow older each day.
When you are young you don't need to be responsible for anything.
You will always have everything your way.
You can eat, sleep, dance, sing, hop, swim, and play whatever, whenever.
Lucky!
There will be many changes as you grow older each day.
As you grow older you have more responsibility for everything you do including small and big things.
You have to work to get pay.
And nothing will always be your way.
So you have to lay your head on your pillow and think of what you would like to be one day.

Helen Tran, Grade 7
Sarah McGarvin Intermediate School

Social Circles

I walk the halls and look upon the peers who pass
I hear snatches of gossip and scandalous retellings of last night's party
I see, at the high end of the social ladder, the closely grouped and exclusive cliques,
huddled together in circles, united by their supercilious superiority
I see, at the lower strata, the bashfully meek and awkward,
not as pretty as the cliques but with a certain beauty still;
I note the subtle separation of the typical castes, divided by closed minds and limited hearts
I witness the impetuous ones so eager to be classified; to appear as their high-class idols
I observe the willingness to cast out those who are not like them;
the nearly unconscious ignorance or snide condescension of the ones who don't fit
I sight the eagerness to judge, the nonexistent motivation to look beyond the screen,
And I wonder —

Am I like them, too?

Aleyni Cerezo, Grade 9
Westview High School

Surrounded by Memories

I sit in my room surrounded by myself, ghosts of my childhood hang on my walls,
Pictures of my mom, dad and me, the world seemed brighter then,
Our faces smile back from a frame, never to be the same again,
Everyone must change, everyone must grow old,
If only we could trap those moments of happiness in a jar,
To be opened later when our hearts are filled with sorrow, acting as lights to brighten our darkened worlds.
I see my teddy bear and blanket, how many times have they helped me?
Acting as my support, wiping my tears when I cried, lifting me up with smiles and familiar faces,
It seems they were always the same no matter how much the world changed.
Souvenirs from all my vacations, little reminders that there are breaks in life,
Bringing smiles to my face as they jog my memories, of summers at the beach and winters in the snow,
Like living memories they gaze down from my walls.
Paintings and pictures of the moon fill my room, with a smiling face and a white glow,
It is a reminder that even the darkest of nights, has a bright light to guide and protect us.
Other things, newer things, fill my room as well, a paper-scattered desk, full of homework and poetry,
Gifts of dolls and small jars filled with stones, light catchers decorate my walls with rainbows,
Small, seemingly useless objects, that make my room mine.
Looking at all of these things gathered through the years, helps me to remember that childhood never leaves us,
We grow more mature, leaving people and things behind, but in our hearts we still live as children,
And though life may never be the same as it was
If we look back on it with happiness we can relive it, again, and again.

Rebekah Nolan, Grade 7
Old Mission Elementary School

My Grandpa

My grandpa was the best,
Until one day he was laid down to rest.
God has taken him to be with Him,
And of this I don't know why.
I just want everybody to know I love my grandpa,
Until one day we will meet again.

Tyler Hill, Grade 8
Chino Valley Christian Schools

Maroon

Maroon to me represents
the heart of the Eastside.
It's not just the color.
Maroon stands for
heart, soul, love
peace, culture, music.
Maroon is the cause, the pain, the struggle.
Maroon is going to the park
having conversations with friends, the ones you care about
getting the grill going
playing dominoes not so serious.
Maroon is living day to day
paycheck to paycheck
staying afloat,
keeping a smile on your face
when inside it's not how you feel.
Maroon trees and the handball courts where we play.
People we talk to and the get-togethers we have.
This is what Maroon means to me.
Maroon is a way of life.

Michael Garcia, Grade 9
Gunderson High School

Ode to the Pianist

her hands are strong but thin
great for scampering across
her Ebony and Ivory keys

she majestically connects
the sharp and flat
she makes them one
musical fusion is a result of that

that was then
this is now and
the black keys are out of tune

the sound now completely new
but the music is still moving
the memory of the old, still powerful
that will have to do

one day the ebony keys will be in tune
and the sound we know and loved will return.

Auzzie Sheard IV, Grade 8
La Joya Middle School

I Dare You

I dare you to live life, with no sadness or sorrow.
I dare you to strive, and live like there's no tomorrow.
I dare you to try, to pass every test.
I dare you to aspire, and to always be your best.
I dare you to be strong, and try hard at all that you do.
I dare you to be smart, and think all of your actions through.
I dare you to dream, to never give up hope.
I dare you to want, but never want dope.
I dare you to evaluate, every task and decision.
I dare you to vacation, to thrive like you have always envisioned.
I dare you to hunger, to always follow your heart.
I dare you to have teamwork, and to always do your part.
I dare you to be kind, to your family and friends too.
I dare you to think, what will drugs ever do for you?

Alexandria Evans, Grade 8
Coronado Middle School

Deserted

When we touched my heart fluttered anxiously,
I could never see us not together,
You always assumed I would want to flee,
I knew I could stay with you forever.
One day I could see your feelings changing,
I could see that something had distressed you,
Your smile gone your features rearranging,
You told me that you longed for something new.
My world was you and you left me alone,
I only hope you never see my pain,
If you come back I know that I won't moan,
With you gone I have nothing I could gain.
I am nothing now but an empty shell,
I still hear you but I will never tell.

Megan Baker, Grade 8
Las Flores Middle School

Reminisce

Looking at the past
when present is more important
thinking of all the trouble you collected
with all the pain you felt along the way
examining all the mistakes you made
knowing you should have changed from it
that's a lesson only you learned
you can't give it to someone else
there aren't just pains, troubles, and mistakes
but also happy thoughts contained therein
don't just live by past experiences
when you can go out and find some more
because the past won't change anything
what is important is the now
go make the world a better place
so stop sitting around and help the world!

Htet Wai, Grade 8
Juan Cabrillo Middle School

Dog and Cats

Dog
small, big
biting, eating, playing
hunger, full — little, fat
scratching, licking, purring
furry, mean
Cat

Joey Romero, Grade 7
St Mary of Assumption School

Colorful

Bubble gum
snickers
sour skittles
rolos
a thousand grand
butterfingers
crunch
kit-kats

Appointments
dentists
drills
cold finger tips
and the sounds
giving me chills
silver crowns
round tootsie pop
with chocolate cavities
in the middle.

Guadalupe Hernandez, Grade 9
Gunderson High School

Lights in the Sky

Lying in the frozen tundra
Awakened by the drums of thunder
Sitting there as I wonder
What is beyond this icy land

Staring up at the sky
I put my hand up high
To reach for a star
But I don't get too far

The lights begin to slither
Like a snake
Showing me their beautiful pageant
Of all the colors you can imagine

Sitting…in amazement
I wish to be up there
So I can be without a care
Rippling, swirling, glowing
By and by

Jesse Armas, Grade 8
Madrona Middle School

The Answer

As I looked out in the starry night
I saw something that was quite a sight
An eagle cut the sky like an armored knight
He took me away, and I chose not to fight
We soared over lands never seen before
Places of old memories and forgotten lore
My eyes were closed nevermore
And still across the heavens we tore
The bird was the spirit of all things good
He wanted us to act, and act we should
The world has a cloak, and we shall remove the hood
I thought of this as I saw the hope in the wood.
I saw an immense battle, a fight, a war
Between men who had forgotten what they were fighting for
Eventually all reasons are lost, there is no base, no core
If not stopped, the war would rage on forevermore
And so the eagle turned to bring me back home
While hope bubbled inside me like ocean foam
Because now happiness and cheer are free to roam
The earth would no longer be covered in its dark dome
I knew there was no longer any wall keeping me from answering the eagle's call

Ryan Brown, Grade 7
Lindero Canyon Middle School

It's Just a Test…

"It's just a test; it's just a test,"
At least that's what everyone tells me.
They say, "Don't worry," but when it comes by,
My happiness dissipates as fast as the current of the sea.

No matter if I studied, no matter if I crammed,
A certain feeling of worry always drops by.
I say, "It's just a test; it's just a test," but still,
My hopes are the bleak and empty night sky.

I assure myself, "It's just a test; it's just a test," but
It's like my calm nature has been stolen by thieves.
Every noise distracts me, it's like everyone's staring;
All while I listen to the trees outside; laughing through their leaves.

Even after the test is over, I still persist to freak myself out,
And even when I say, "It's just a test; it's just a test," I'm still not calm.
But then the test results come in, and I'm ecstatic;
"I did well!" I tell myself, and the nervous sweat leaves my palm.

You may have questions, like, "What's the point of this story?"
And before I depart I tell you this: No matter what feelings that distractions send,
And no matter the size of your worries, always remember that,
"It's just a test; it's just a test," and you will be fine in the end.

Justin Tonooka, Grade 8
Valley Oak Middle School

For All of Time

Your eyes are the twinkling stars of midnight,
Looking in your eyes, my heart beats faster,
When I notice your smile, my head feels light,
Seeing your smile, I feel mightier.
Your personality is perfection,
Your hair is the golden waves of the sea,
Spending my time with you is always fun,
You need to spend the rest of time with me.
Your voice will guide me through the darkest times,
Your kindness is superior to all,
Hopefully I will charm you with these rhymes,
But if they don't, maybe you will still call.
I plan on spending all of time with you,
I just hope you feel the same way I do.

Andrew Warren, Grade 8
Las Flores Middle School

My Friends

My friends that are always beside me
My friends that make me happy, sad, and angry
My friends that make me laugh like crazy
My friends that make me cry like a baby
My friends that play with me
My friends that teach me many things
My friends that help me when I have trouble
My friends that are very important
My friends that I have
My good friends.

Shinn Pek, Grade 8
Purple Lotus International Institute

Destinatus

In the dim light of dusk,
Through the hissing, turbulent wind,
Past the obstacles looming before him,
A solitary figure walks.

He pushes ever forward,
Not stopping to hear the rattle of leaves in the wind,
Not for a drink at the water fountain,
Not even to look around —
He must move on.

His body is battered,
His mind weary from use,
But his will is a mountain,
And still, he walks ahead.

No matter what pains he faces,
No matter where life takes him,
As long a the sun shines,
This man will walk on.

Brandon Yi, Grade 8
Rolling Hills Country Day School

Clouds

Colored white and
Clutched together like
Faces in them,
Cotton balls in the sky,
You see them everywhere
No matter what country sky is above you,
Puffy shapes high up through the stratosphere.

Keena Desai, Grade 7
Thornton Jr High School

That's Real Love

Those who don't know God haven't experienced true mercy.
They think Heaven is a state of mind,
They think praying is a waste of time and words.
They are completely LOST.

But we Christians are saved,
We know God sent His only son
And we understand that He was crucified to redeem our sins.
And we believe in Him completely.

All devout,
All cared for
We are children of God.

Yeah. That is real love.

Heather Hatfield, Grade 9
Westview High School

Dreams

When you close your eyes,
    the dreams come fast.
When you close your eyes,
    time flies past.

Once you lay
your head down,
all the dreams
come around.

Some are good
and some are bad.
Sometimes happy
and sometimes sad.

Another world
you have gone into,
where anything
can happen to you.

But once you wake up, you're back again.
Everything is real, the dream was just pretend.
Or was it really all a dream?
…Did everything happen the way it seemed?

Linn Diep, Grade 7
Sarah McGarvin Intermediate School

Summer Is Soon

Summer is only a day away
Meaning school is almost out
The best time for outdoor play
Having fun without a doubt

The land is covered with lots of green
Blooming flowers and growing trees
An extraordinary place that must be seen
Something that we can agree

While skies are bright and blue
Lakes and rivers are nice and clear
Keeping water lovers spirit true
Meaning summer is almost here

Mark Nations, Grade 8
Coronado Middle School

My Heart

My heart doesn't just pump my blood
It gives me the feeling of love
Inside
When I see you, my heart pumps
Faster, faster, and faster
I can't control it
You were there for me from
The beginning to the end
Ever since you've been gone,
My heart has been completely
Blank
You were my one true love
Now my heart is silent, silent,
Even more silent
Than ever
Sometimes I fear I may never feel
My heart
Pump
Again…

Michael Saidawi, Grade 7
Corpus Christi School

Schooltime

Schooltime
Students, homework
Teaching, correction, learning
Happy, hyper, excited, kind
Smarter

Maricarmen Chàvez, Grade 8
Almond Tree Middle School

Basketball

Basketball is fun for me.
I get to shoot and go for three.
I like to steal and run away.
When I grow up, I'll dunk one day.

Jasmine Mercado, Grade 7
Thornton Jr High School

Spring

I adore the freshness and newness of longed-awaited spring
Everything so filled with blossom and sparkle
Witness what wonderful gifts the sun will bring
As benevolent spring smiles with its affectionate warmth and twinkle

Spring's peaceful green hills delight me
The smell of the grass is so clean
Spring's colorful flowers bring glee
After a cruel winter so lean

The joyful robust golden-haired sun is enchanting
As it warms my wintry and worn spirit
Watching the cheerful butterflies dancing
I thank amazing spring for its marvel and merit.

Steven Philipoff, Grade 7
St John of San Francisco Orthodox Academy

The Soaring Eagle

A majestic eagle with silken wings soars over the gleaming valley.
Nobility is shining throughout the eagle like a powerful king.

It cries to me without words, but the message is clear.
Join me in the magnificent sky, and gaze down at the beautiful valley with me.

Giant redwoods guarding their saplings and the shining-scaled salmon
Gracefully gliding up the roaring river bring the forest to live.

I join the king of the skies, observing the endless valley of trees.
Glazed with mist of fog and the rising crimson sun.

I feel renewed and exalted, soaring with the spirit of the eagle.
Now I know what it means to soar.

Max Fefer, Grade 8
EV Cain Middle School

Who Am I

Basketball is what I love and play
I want to be in the NBA someday
I pretend that I am king of the world
Feeling lightning bolts run through my body
I hope that I can make my dreams come true

I am a brother of five and son of three
An uncle, nephew, and grandson is me
I have a niece whose name is Sidney
Time spent with them is my favorite
They are my family and I will always love them

I understand that the world was created by God and God only
I tell people and know that I am a Christian
I worry about one of my family members dying without knowing Jesus
I thank God for every breath I take
And will count my blessings till my time ends

Eddie Coyle, Grade 8
Linfield Christian School

The Ocean of Me

The ocean of me, it can be still it can be calm,
Sometimes it can have powerful waves hit the shore;
It could be stiff or silent, but it could have a roar,
For if at sea in a storm, it could be knocking at your door.
For when it is silent, it is tame,
But with emotion, it shall be tame no more.

If I am angry, I feel it roar,
But I am glad I feel this no more.
I may be ashamed, I may be glad,
But when I turn for help
I don't deal with the roar anymore, no no, not the roar
For you see, this sea shall be tame once more.

Anthony Colvard, Grade 7
Holy Family Catholic School

Remember

Do you remember the day I met you?
The day I talked to you
And when I would talk to you
I would feel you were mine
Forever
And no one else
Till the day I thought different
My heart was broken
I was crying inside
The day I don't want to remember again
But all I can think of is that awful day
Sometimes I wish I would never have met you
But I want to remember the day I met you
And how I felt inside of me
But now you are gone
All I can do is dream
And wish
And maybe my wish will come true
Just got to keep on dreaming.

Emily Garrett, Grade 7
Santa Rosa Technology Magnet School

Dreamer

In the year 1993
A kid was born into this world with a lot of hope
That maybe one day he'll be famous
Trying to climb the rope

People said he couldn't do it
So he tried to prove them wrong
He trained very hard
His hard training wouldn't take very long

He one day realized
He didn't have a clue what to do
So he became a skier
And knew that dreams do come true

Marshall Curtzwiler, Grade 8
South Tahoe Middle School

Spring

Hooray! Hooray!
Spring has come today
There is no more coldness only warmth
From the beautiful, scorching sun shining down

The flowers wake up from their long dream
The bare trees begin to bring out green leaves
Birds soar in the sky singing in excitement
The bugs crawl everywhere not knowing what to do
Everyone is awake and nothing is still
The Earth even shakes to tell spring is here

Michelle Park, Grade 8
Madrona Middle School

Basketball

I feel sweat running down my face
Extremely confident about my pace
Only five seconds till the end of this race
If I shoot and miss what a disgrace
I have only my basketball to embrace
Oh I hope I don't misplace
The spotlight is on me and no other place
I run, I shoot, the ball and hoop embrace
Finally a happy ending to this race
We won the game without a trace
Playing ball for me is like tying a shoelace
I glide through the air like I'm in outer space
Play against me, but prepare to be disgraced
I make you return to your crawlspace
Don't even think that I could be replaced
Because this court is my birthplace

Haider A. Sheikh, Grade 8
Nobel Middle School

Broken and Unwanted

As they were watching the sun rise and set,
He would turn away as the sun would dim.
And she hoped that somehow their eyes had met,
But her hopes had strayed much farther than him.

She searches for emptiness in his eyes,
Her heart and mind just repeating his name.
She finally realizes it's been lies,
But she can't stop playing his tricky game.

Although she was only loved in her dreams,
Her pounding heartbeat seems unstoppable.
Her deathly silence is broken by screams,
His passion for love is impossible.

And even if heartbreak comes of all this,
She will always remember their first kiss.

Danielle R. Lee, Grade 8
Las Flores Middle School

Face

I see people every day
hiding their true self.
Why don't you show everyone
what's behind your mask?
Show your true face.
Let me see your face.
Don't hide yourself from everyone.
Show everyone who you are,
what you want to do,
and let me see your face.

Jose Rodriguez, Grade 7
Renuevo School

World

Flowers bud in the spring
Children run, grow up
Life goes on.
Blind to reality
Venture into the world
Life goes on.
Color changes
Do they see the truth?
Wars are fought
Darkness
Children and mothers
Suffer
Starvation
Eating away
Physically, emotionally
Disease spreads.
Does life go on?
Hope is a small light
In this world of darkness.
Is there hope?
What can I do?

Ariam Alvarado, Grade 8
Our Lady of Guadalupe School

The Ride

A tree branch broke.
Down it fell,
Into the pond —
Splash!
The current pulled it
Past a little wooden bridge,
Then over a ridge
Of a waterfall!
A roller coaster ride
Over shiny wet rocks,
Past blooming honey suckle
Swish, gurgle, whoosh
Down it goes!

Alicia Lamas, Grade 7
Chemawa Middle School

Music

Music
Loud, different
Dancing, bumping, singing
Tells a life story
Melody

Aliana Fernandez, Grade 7
St Mary of Assumption School

Life

Life is life
Life is happy
Life is sad
Life is merry
Life is bad

Life isn't fair
Life is all right
Life is good
For some it is bright

Isn't life wonderful? Someone would say
My answer to you is for me it's okay

Life is a test for you and for me
Which road to take?
Which one's right for me?

When life gives you lemons
What do you do?
Pray to God and He'll help you

With life you need faith
Life is life…

Justin Co, Grade 7
Calvary Chapel of YL

A Rainbow

A rainbow
Is the sun's beautiful reflection

The sun's rays bounce
And make the most glamorous colors

Gleaming red, orange yellow,
Green, blue and purple

A rainbow
Is a message of hope to all
You can only see one after it rains

A rainbow
Has no beginning and no end

Ashley Flanigan, Grade 8
Madrona Middle School

Ode to Friends

the world is a
difficult place to be
without best friends
they are presents
each one special
and different
they are the bright sunshine
after a big rainstorm
which brings blossoms to us
they are fireworks
that brighten life
when downhearted
they are not birds that fly away
when the weather changes
but are there through the storms
they are there for
every season
the world
is a difficult place to be
without best friends

Nicole Zalewski, Grade 8
La Joya Middle School

Left Alone, Left Behind

Walking a path with three friends.
We walked a journey.
We walked beside each other.
Never left alone, never left behind.
Calling for help, once lost
Calling because they've been,
Left alone, left behind.
The two friends walked away.
Two others calling for them…
Never left alone, never left behind?
And one cries out, "Come back!"
Never left alone, never left behind.
That's a lie!
You've left alone.
You've left behind.
But why?
I shall never come back to thee,
Because you've left alone
You've left behind.

Alondra Fortin, Grade 8
Thomas Jefferson Middle School

Home Is Heaven

Your home is a
Place called heaven.
Where you're loved,
And have everything
You need!

Daisy Perea, Grade 7
South Tahoe Middle School

A Day on the Beach

The soft blue water
Crashes on the rocks
Rolls up to the warm sand.

Small creatures swim with the current
Small children splash in the water
Small castles are defeated by the mighty waves.

The soothing sound of waves running over the rocks
The loud roar of the boat motors as they go zipping by
The sound of laughter coming from everyone.

Alexa Bokman, Grade 8
St Joseph's School of the Sacred Heart

The Day We Spent by the Ocean Pier

Listen my children and you shall hear
of the day we spent by the ocean's pier.
It was a pretty day, so warm and sunny,
who would think it would end not so funny?

McKenna and I had just arrived
when over the sound of the waves she cried,
"Let's go climb the jetty rocks!"
and she smiled and shook her curly brown locks.

So as we walked, we talked and talked,
and at last we arrived at the big tall rocks.
The waves came down like a tumbling tower,
we scrambled from rock to rock so as not to be devoured.

Then one came crashing over us and swept us away,
We thought we would not live to see another day!
But somehow we managed to get upright
The land in front of us was such a beautiful sight!

So as long as we live and wherever we go,
McKenna and I will always know
that long ago was a treacherous day
when the ocean waves almost swept us away.

Christina Bosch, Grade 8
Norman Sullivan Middle School

My Country and Its Flag

I love my country, I love my flag
it's the best thing an American can ever have
I love my nation for it was founded upon God.
But as you look at America today,
you would never have a clue,
that God was the one they looked up to.
All I can do is pray that God would do something
mighty great someday,
that would turn this nation back to him.

Kaprianna Smith, Grade 7
West Valley Baptist School

After the Rain

Outside, there is freshness in the air.
The wind blows its scent through my long hair,
And colorful flowers come alive.
Busy bees emerge from their moist hive.

The sun shines on the world, big and bright.
All the birds sing their song of delight.
Chipmunks scurry upon the damp earth.
The world is greener in its rebirth.

The Earth is smooth, there's not one furrow.
Rabbits venture out of their burrow.
The face of the planet is renewed.
Animals are in a joyous mood.

All these things can come from just one rain.
These sights, sounds, and smells can crush your pain,
And eliminate all of life's stress,
With one taste of nature's loveliness.

Zabrena La Crue, Grade 7
St Luke the Evangelist Catholic School

Why Are Poems So Hard to Write?

Why are poems so hard to write?
I can't believe they take all night.
Though I try and try,
All I can do is cry.

I spend hours and hours waiting for an idea,
Watching time fly,
And wanting to die.

Why are poems so hard to write?
My teacher says that I am very bright.
I sure don't think she's right.

Maybe I'll lie,
Just to get by,
Or tell her a tale,
To save mine.

Why are poems so hard to write?
Math is a hundred times easier.
Aren't I right?

Avery Durko, Grade 7
Rolling Hills Country Day School

Love

L is for the laughter you have in love
O is for the openness you give me when we're in love
V is for you being very special to me
E is for the excitement I have when I'm with you.

I LOVE YOU

Laura Vargas, Grade 8
St Vincent Elementary School

Clouds

Grey and white clouds on
blue and orange skies with light
are changing their shape
Christy Chung, Grade 7
Sarah McGarvin Intermediate School

Linger

If one day
I was to find
Something to confide in
If someday
You were to find
One thing to abide in
Hindrance — I will not be
Cannot settle, you shall see
No.
Do not push me away
I've done enough of that
For today
Morals losing, and like a rat
I figure and abuse your simple kindness
Buzzing, bugging like a gnat
Hear my horrid, uninvited madness
So, do I feel obliged to step away —
One day I wish to contently lay
If I could just...linger
Candice Crilly, Grade 8
Santa Rosa Technology Magnet School

Eternal

I won't give up
Until the sun falls down
I'll lock you in my heart
Following your dazzling sound

Searching my way
Looking for you
Through night and day
Until I do

Even though my heart's turning blue
My hands turning cold
I'll look for you
Until I'm told

You've suffered the night
And left this world
Moving towards the light
My life has finally uncurled

You've shattered my heart
I'm turning to ice
And now I must stop
For we shall reunite
Tiffany Pham, Grade 7
Sarah McGarvin Intermediate School

Musical Story

Music is an art form and you are the artist
Write it anyway you want, because it's yours
Don't let others ruin or tarnish your thoughts and feelings
Add dynamics where you feel is right.
Make up funky rhythms
Listen to other genres every now and then
But remember, it is up to you to make the big decisions
Your music is how you feel
Sometimes it's good, sometimes it's bad,
But don't give up. Just be yourself
If you make a mistake, learn from it. Nobody said it was easy.
But you must remember, every note is written in ink
Some things can't be erased or changed
But enjoy it while it lasts
Before you know it, your song will be written and published,
And you won't be able to change a beat
Don't look back and regret what you've done
Instead, look back and smile at the melody. Look at the beginning,
And then the end, and see how much the musical line has progressed
Appreciate the opportunities and chances you took,
And your last note will not end in vain.
Michelle Kazmier, Grade 8
La Joya Middle School

The Hill Before High School

As you may know, our time together is about almost over,
And there is still so much we have not done together.
Graduating may be hard and our biggest strife,
But we all know well it is a part of life.

Although we may have a scene feeling sad and heavyhearted,
Our minds also wonder what would happened on the road ahead.
As we look back, old memories come back to us, one by one,
Each remembered thought filled with craziness, laughter, and fun.

When we have left this school their memories should not be lost,
Remembering the days before this school's memory may be crossed.
When leaving our beloved school, the place we cherished through our youth,
The place where we learned the alphabets or even lost our first tooth.

It may be hard for us to leave the place; it will be painful when we are apart,
All the friends and teachers we have met will never leave our heart.
There is not much time left before we will say good-bye to each other,
We would be so close as if we were brother and sister.

There might be a chance that we might meet together again in the time forthcoming,
But what would the small chance of that becoming.
As you may know, our time together is almost over,
but in our hearts, we will always have each other.
Jeffrey Zheng, Grade 8
Challenger School – Ardenwood

Dedicated to Yankees

The pitcher spits sticky pink gum,
he sweats like hot sizzle
bases loaded, two outs, full counts, the game tied
no way the pitcher gets out of this mess,
The pitcher positions to throw the tiny stitched ball
nasty fast ball cuts through the air
here it comes
Wham!
The ball flies to the 300 yard mark
crowds go crazy
it's still going.

Shawn Cho, Grade 8
St Joseph's School of the Sacred Heart

When We Don't Do Anything

When I see this piece of artwork
I think of how sad they are
I think that they don't have everything that we do
And all we do is waste it and never look back
We never think about those people who don't have what we do
They look like they're going to go eat
They look like they want to go back home with their families
They just want to be in a comfortable bed when they get home
They look like they don't know what's going on
While we know everything about why they are there
They wish they can go home

Megan Pereira, Grade 8
Buchser Middle School

Election Day

November 4th is a very special day indeed,
On this day people set a new political creed.
The citizens rush to their booths to cast their vote,
They will choose the candidate whom they wish to promote.

The news stations cover the day from inside to out,
They try to conduct polls as people bustle about.
Voting is a process which is easy to do,
But the counters must do an analytical review.

You may go to the station or cast your vote by mail,
There are even provisions for voters who need Braille!
Exit polls and news reviews give you an idea of the race,
Many Americans cheer for the person whom they embrace.

As the day grows old and booths being to close,
Everybody turns their eyes to the TV shows.
The ballots get counted and the votes are tallied,
Most people can see which candidate has rallied.

Recounts and miscounts may happen as mistakes,
Some of them may even hold some high stakes.
Before the day is out a leader will be chosen,
And a new part of our history will be written.

Aditya Limaye, Grade 8
Challenger School – Ardenwood

The War

After three years of working it is done.
The program I've constructed has done well.
When the inscription is read I'll have won.
And over my enemies they shall dwell.
And the grants from the state need to be mine.
But only one person stands before me.
I can just wish our paths don't intertwine.
No, he has broken into my sweet home.
This bad man shall not get hold of my work.
For if we must fight I shall fight 'til death.
I've wasted my life searching for my perk.
I'll know that I've wasted my time in depth.
You'll have to take my work from my cold hand.
For I'll not release my grip to demands.

Jessie Laines, Grade 8
John Adams Middle School

Run Away

Home cannot be here.
An animal instinct lives within
Blistering feet and,
Twitching fingers.
My mind pounds my skull.
I flee through a forest of shadows, into a foggy future,
Away from a quickening heart beat
The crisp air tickles the nape of my neck.
Dew of the early morning fingers through my hair,
And tranquility seems far.
My aching legs, throbbing head, and heaving chest continue to
Tramp, tramp, tramp.
My boots slap hard ground,
No longer galloping to pass the time,
But fighting for survival.
Home is away from here.

Alex Kovary, Grade 7
Rolling Hills Country Day School

The Surface

water, water, water, unfortunately my fear
I swim well, but with each deep swim there is a tear
a worry deep inside, which I cannot control
it lurks beneath the surface, I scream within my soul
for every crashing wave, my heart skips a beat
subtle on the outside, but indefinite in the deep
gather up the courage, set my hopes up high
cool, calm, collective, only when I die
dive off the rocks, feel the waves yank
the cry beneath shrieks, leaking is the air tank
as I come above, the sun shines intense
a gasp for air, very appreciative of this
a conquered fear, achievement, succeeded
the surface where I belong, never forgetting the deep

Phoebe Rivas, Grade 9
Clovis East High School

The Sounds of Nature
When I can't go to sleep at night, I open the window to hear the beautiful sounds of nature.
I love hearing frogs croaking, the coyotes howling, and hearing the crickets wonderful songs.
All these sounds mixed together are so soothing that they make me fall asleep instantly.

Edith Velasquez-Mancilla, Grade 7
Willow Grove Elementary School

What About Dreams?
My mother taught me never to leave, never to deceive, never to lie, and never to try so hard I'd cry.
I won't lie, I won't pry, I won't cheat, and I won't eat until the Earth is right again.
The earth isn't straight or crooked, it's round.
The sun doesn't frown, it smiles.
No while do we speak, do we cheat, do we pray, do we play do we see,
That all the earth needs is to be free.
Whatever they said, whatever they read, were complete and total lies.
It's just people trying to get by with misdemeanors,
Just those interveners, who don't care about who or where.
It's like a grizzly bear, it has no personality. But it has that one technicality.
Where we've got to follow the rules, and not be fools, but go to school.
And learn that sacred song, to stay strong.
For your mom, dad, and that sad sad old man, who never had a plan, to read or succeed,
But to beg and drink from that keg he found on the street.
So go have fun, go life, go laugh, go love, and be free of the pain of losing that one person.
Holding onto them is just going to worsen the act, when a matter of fact,
You just contract, diffract, and distract those nerve tracts.
But all you need to do, is get a clue
Not about who…but about what we're going to do.
To make our Dreams Come True.

Dalena La, Grade 9
Gunderson High School

Comfort on a Rainy Day
The pounding rain plummeted towards their drenched forms
Like cold, glittering needles from the warm grey-wool blanket that was the sky.
He offered her his soft, thick jacket.
Then her shivering body melted in his warm, black coat.
She took it without complaining,
Knowing that he no longer felt the icy blasts of frigid air
Or the stinging stabs of each individual crystal droplet.

The glacial air around them felt so misty and dense, it was nearly suffocating.
She reached out to touch his enchanting shape to confirm he still wasn't only a beautiful mirage.
He clasped her freezing hand in his pale palm reassuringly
And led her toward the colossal, white house.
Once the couple sped inside, he shook his head and twinkling,
crystalline droplets of rainbow water cascaded down onto the beige, hardwood floor.

She stared and took in his radiance for a single, heart-stopping moment.
She adored his liquid gold eyes, worshipped his mystic smile,
And obsessed over his flawless features.
She looked into the not-so-harmless gold of his eyes;
He bent down slightly, and she stood on her toes.
In her eyes, he saw a diamond mirror; in her eyes, he saw what he used to be.
Warm lips greeted cold ones and the cycle continued once more.

Candace Corrales, Grade 8
Rolling Hills Country Day School

Our World Today

Our world is changing, yes, indeed,
More crime and violence in the streets.

More people doing bad and being thrown in jail,
So why does crime seem to prevail?

We must work hard to make the world a better place,
So there's much less violent disgrace.

Much less case of violent activity,
So people in our world will have greater longevity.

To live in a better world, oh, how that would be,
To be sure and confident while we walk the streets.

A better world, a better place,
With less war and less disgrace.

Peace to the Earth,
A new world shall give birth.

A better world...
Oh how that would be.

Anthony Pedersen, Grade 7
Holy Family Catholic School

Mr. Geer

You're happy all the time,
The most organized person I'll ever meet,
You're unique and creative,
When you do your headstands,
And Bullwinkle with both hands.

You love U.S. History,
And your colorful markers,
That make your classroom so bright,
And all the tick-tocks,
Of your cool clocks.

You've been through so much,
From jazz to rap, from hippies, to preps.
From typewriters to computers,
From Central to Tierra Linda,
From hairstyles high to low,
Now straight, then fro.

You've graded so much,
Stressful condition,
Creative Lewis and Clark,
Interesting Great Depression,
You are a great impression.

Malak El-Khatib, Grade 8
Tierra Linda Middle School

Just Like Them

The gray, uniform blob walked down the hall, to the left,
And into room 201.
No one questioned why there was a crowd, but as for me,
I separated from the hypnotic spell.
I was red like an apple,
Nervous like a prey fleeing from the predator,
And hotter than a sidewalk on the Fourth of July.
People question why I was different,
But I kept walking briskly by,
Down the hall, to the left,
And into room 201.
A hush fell over the crowd.
The crowd questioned carefully.
Soon, people copied me.
The gray turned into a rainbow.
What was I to do?
I was an adventurer
Choosing his path carefully.
I was then gray,
And walked down the hall, to the left,
And into room 201.

Jason Liebson, Grade 8
Rolling Hills Country Day School

The Last Years

I look outside and watch the rain,
asking myself why I'm in this kind of pain.
It kills me to see that you're not here,
by my side watching as I near,
near the end of these great years.

Alicia Trinh, Grade 7
Sarah McGarvin Intermediate School

Books: Are They Adventures?

I don't know about you
But I think they are

You could be conquering the seas
Or racing in a car

Flying a spaceship
Or bombarding pirates

Fighting for an island
Or fighting for a princess

Having super powers
And saving the world

I don't care how you look at it
But while you're reading a story, I'm off on an adventure

Because books are like doors, imagination is the key
Can you get in?

Nick Gonzales, Grade 7
Holy Family Catholic School

Poetry

P oetry means…
c **O** mmunication
E xpressing my feelings
wri **T** ing a message
hea **R** t and imagination
poetr **Y** means…*truth*

Delilah Useda, Grade 7
Corpus Christi School

Andres Ayala

Friendly
Nice
Happy
Wishes to be a teacher.
Dreams of famous people.
Wants to have a car.
Who wonders about people.
Who fears about the devil.
Who is afraid of monsters.
Who likes girls.
Who believes in God.
Who loves his mother.
Who loves his family.
Who loves bikes.
Who loves food.
Who plans to be a doctor.
To plans not to be a principal.
To plans to be a teacher.
Whose final destination is to become
A good teacher.

Andres Ayala, Grade 8
Almond Tree Middle School

power turned

crucial yet black
there's no going back
only one way out
and that's down
we look up to the clouds
for solutions to our problems
but all i got was a crowd
free for all mankind to observe
spoke softly made sure not to be heard
stare down avoid confrontation
till a slip was made
a forgotten nation had to pay
innocence was lost
feelings uprooted
for that there was a cost
emotions erupted
many actions not accounted for
the nation was alive
power was turned on each other
and the nation died.

Brianna Thompson, Grade 9
Fortuna Union High School

San Francisco

San Francisco
You might know it as
The city that of
The Golden Gate Bridge, Twin Peaks, the cable cars,
The sports teams, too
San Francisco Giants, San Francisco 49ers, Golden State Warriors
But I know it as
My hometown
Where I've lived all my life,
Where I was born and raised,
Where I first dreamed of being
A Major League Baseball player,
Where I first went to school and found friends
That could be friends for life
And the girl who changed
My life
And
Showed me love
For the first time in my life

Ralsy Sabater, Grade 8
Corpus Christi School

The Difference Between Wanting and Needing

I drive past tall buildings and city lights
Large mansions and houses stare down at me
I go past shops with things I want, but can't afford
I realize most of the world is just like me
People win a million dollars, and want a million more
Never satisfied
I often forget, as well as others that it's not having what you want
It's wanting what you have
I as well as any other teenager want the latest phone, iPod, or computer
But why is it that sometimes people cherish things and use others
Instead of the other way around?
I hope for me as well as the rest of the world
That we can open our eyes and not take what we have for granted

Corinne Moeller, Grade 9
Westview High School

My Valentine

Valentine's is time for romance and love
Giving chocolate in heart-shaped boxes, and giving out some hugs
Showing your mate how much you love her, and how much you care
Showing her that when she's hurt, you will always be there
Every Valentine's I try to be the sweetest guy I can ever be
I want to make her feel like she's the most special girl to me.
This Valentine's, I'm alone.
Why does this gap between us have to be so far and long?
Why does this happen, when I just wanted to move on — live peacefully?
And tell me, where will you find another guy to dedicate a Valentine's poem to you,
Who'd be as sweet as me?
To me, you're everything, you're heaven, you're divine.
And I need to ask you one more question: Will you please be mine?

Emmanuel Vergara, Grade 8
Corpus Christi School

Ode to My Mommy

I love you to pieces
You are so sweet
Even your feet are kind of neat
You love to dance, and you wear cute pants
And you even want to visit France
Your smile is so bright, it lights up the night
And I hate to admit it, but you're always right
But most of all
I love you through up and down the mall
And nobody can take that because you're my doll.

Kailey Warren, Grade 7
Santa Rosa Technology Magnet School

Redemption

Bottled up, the tears of experience,
Poured out onto the pavement.
Ending struggles.
Feet drag along,
Wasting time away.
Wasting time away.
Grasping for a chance,
Praying for forgiveness.
Head under water.
Head under water.
Almost gone.
Asking, hoping, wishing, to survive this time.
To survive this time.
The end can be bright.
Will it open her arms to me?
The fear of being alone closes in — one last breath.
One last glance behind, to stare the past down.
Diving in, all in.
Diving in, all in.
Victory has welcomed me, with his open arms.
Being free is bliss.

Madisen Keavy, Grade 8
Green Acres Middle School

Dance Recital

Girls dressed in leotards and tutus of all colors
Nervousness fills everyone like a plague
Quickly and quietly,
Down to the stage to perform
As we stand to the side,
The spotlights beckon us forward
To stare into the dark sea of people
The music begins and we tell a story
A million words in one arabesque
We become confident as the dance finishes
Thunder and lightning begin as we smile proudly
Swiftly, silently, and satisfied,
We exit the stage
Able to breathe again,
The feeling of triumph in our hearts.

Emily Wood, Grade 8
Valley Oak Middle School

H.B. Surfing

wake up to the morning fog
check the surf report
see some excellent waves
decide to go, call the guys
pile into the truck
step onto the moist sand
wrap in a towel, put my wetsuit on
look to see where the break is
hop into the brisk water, numbing sting of cold water
paddle, push up, play on the wave
step out of the water, sun shining
baking the sand, making it crisp
drop our boards at Chuck Dent
grab a burger and a shake
bands playing in parking lots
all along main street
chicks in bikinis, walkin' up and down
better days than this
simply, don't exist.

Austin Griggs, Grade 9
Fountain Valley High School

Levi

Levi was my brother and my friend,
He said he'd always be there for me until the end.
Levi usually liked everything to be his way,
He was like the sun, brightening my day.

All the times we shared together, he'd make me laugh,
His eyes were as dark as the spots on a calf.
I miss Levi dearly, but I know he'll be in my heart,
But my heart is still empty because we're apart.

Family bonding, and being together,
Now, every day, is like stormy weather.
Life is like a house, with a special crack,
Once it is gone, you can't get it back.

Some days I can't take it, I just have to scream,
To have Levi here, I would do *anything*.
I know I'll get better in the day,
Because, in my heart, he will always stay.

Stefani Castorena, Grade 7
Joan MacQueen Middle School

Life Cycle

A bird sings a song in the morning,
it sings a song in the eve,
and one day it sings no more,
it seems as if the world was hushed forever,
but another bird was born.

Isabel Miranda, Grade 7
St Cyprian School

Heartbreak

You think
You have the worst family —
Think again,
We're the same,
We're all the same…
Your parents —
Divorce hurts
Forever and ever…
I cry, I'm sad…
I need help!
"Choices" is the word
Hard choices,
Sad choices,
They're all alike.
Family and friends
You love
Then say Goodbye.

Christine Sonco, Grade 7
St Alphonsus School

Advent of Spring

The days are short
The sun a spark
Silence deafening
Doused by dark
Lakes of white
Without the shimmer
Coldness like wolves
Anxious for dinner
Sleeping, snoring silently
Furry shadows in a den
Hidden from the world
Coming to winter's end
Breaking dawn
The whoosh of naked branches
Chasing away the darkness
Daylight slowly prances

Jenna Harris and Caitlin Krol, Grade 8
St Patrick Parish School

Ode to Chocolate

Enveloped in a silver wrapper
It was made fresh
Sweet
Much like a
Hershey's Kiss
Caressing
On one's tongue
The taste dripping down
My throat
Crunchy, soft, and tasty too
Chocolate, oh, how I love you!

Audrey Alvarez, Grade 8
Citrus Hills Intermediate School

Spring, Summer, Fall, Winter

Flowers everywhere
Little girls in pretty gowns
Spring is in the air

Splashing and laughing
There's a lot to do
Have some fun and relax

Leaves fall off the trees
In the fallen leaves, children play
Red, yellow, orange

The sound of laughter
Christmas carols in the air
Kids' favorite time

Raina Poria, Grade 8
Martin Murphy Middle School

Tree

Hollow, unique,
Willowing, gigantic,
Beauty of nature
Pondering
Overshadowing
The blazing beam of light
Bringing peaceful shade
To the humongous land
Fluttering, glorious butterflies
Love to perch
upon its leafy green birchwood
Birds find warmth and lodging
Between stout arms
While leaves sprout
Conveying radiant brightness

Shalom Medina, Grade 7
St Alphonsus School

Trapped

Trapped in a life
Trapped in a world
Trapped in a style
Trapped
Trapped in a smile
Trapped in a friendship
Trapped in a stereotype
Trapped
Trapped in a time
Trapped in a place
Trapped in today
Trapped
Everlastingly trapped
In the cage of destiny

Katie Fridlund, Grade 8
Rafer Johnson Jr High School

Baseball Is Fun

B aseball
A drenaline
S tealing
E xcitement
B ases
A ll around fun
L osing is fun too
L ong time play

I s baseball fun, you ask?
S urely it is.

F ans
U mpires
N obody plays and
doesn't make friends

Chris Caldwell, Grade 7
Joan MacQueen Middle School

Nothing

What is nothing?
Something.
How can something be nothing?
Everything is something.
How is everything something
if everything includes nothing
which is something?

Matthew Zaragoza, Grade 7
Renuevo School

The Fool

One that never has to think
He sweeps around the others
Trying to make himself known
Thinking of ways to trick
No one comes around him
All who know him hate him
Thoughts are kept inside
And he is set to prowl again
Forever is his torment
Seeing as he glares around
Beating bloodshot eyes
Forced in his direction
And yet he moves on
Looking for prey
To make him known
To feed his pleasure
The fool will never see
He will never look
He will never find
That is inside him
Dignity

Sam Schaefer, Grade 8
St Hilary School

Tennis Ball
I am bouncy and furry.
But I am never in a hurry.
I am yellow or green.
Obviously, I can always be seen.
It's scary to be hit with a racquet.
When the players look at me, they want to "smack it."
I am used every day,
So everyone can use me to play.

Amanda Nguyen, Grade 7
St Barbara School

The Sound of the Doorbell
Ding! Ding! The sound of the doorbell echoes through the hall,
Its piercing screeching noise shatters through the wall.
It whistles like a bullet propelling through the air,
Disrupting every single thing without the slightest care.
The sound is an alarm, waking me from sleep,
I slowly emerge from my bed for ringing it does keep.
Excitement surges up me as I run to get the door,
But the doorbell rings a second time and then even some more.
I quickly open and look through the small yet clear peek hole,
Surprised I see only the sky, which appears extremely dull.
The door glides open easily, closing in on its own hinge,
Screeching, creaking, squeaking, my face forms a cringe.
I throw the door open, using all of my might,
There is no person at the door, at least not within my sight.

Casey Rebmann and Corey King, Grade 7
St Patrick Parish School

The "Used to Be" Theme Song
Can you hear this song I sing?
This bloody anthem that I scream?
Can you hear these words I cry?
Or is it your choice to let me die?
You know, I wonder if you see
This still healing heart that's wandering
Do you comprehend my language?
Or are my tongues much too foreign?
I want you to watch
Every tear drop from my eye
And I want you to see
That my dreams all fail, do you know why?
I think you do, because I know you
Did you know that I am stronger?
I'm not the ash you left long ago
I have built my own soul's fortress
The healing you thought I'd never accomplish
So watch every tear drop from my eye
And see all my dreams fail, do you know why?
I think you do, because I know you
At least I used to.

Selena Gonzalez, Grade 9
Bullard High School

Flowers
Flowers
Smell wonderful
Pink, green, purple, blue, red
Can be romantic in some ways
Perfect

Arianna Cervantes, Grade 7
John Charles Fremont Intermediate School

A Blood-red Ruby, Strung Up in the Sky
A blood-red ruby, strung up in the sky
A golden mass of magma boiling hot
Like to a flaming furnace, hung so high
The sky's a perfect blue save this one blot

At night, a crystal pearl-like orb glints bright
And bathes the world below in radiance
Aglow with rays of gentle, soothing light
And casts its shadow o'er lands of silence

Beside her twinkle diamonds nicely shined
Illuminating earth with silver gleam
They far outstrip those stones in deep pits mined
However fine might earthly jewels seem

Despite the value of these bijoux fair
While my love lives, for riches I'll not care

Cindy Tay, Grade 8
The Harker School - Middle Campus

The Ocean
The ocean is big, wide and blue.
I love to swim in it too.
There are many creatures that live in it,
But if trash we keep throwing,
Bad things will happen without knowing,
And soon the fishes and eels will slowly disappear.

Melissa Rivera, Grade 8
St Vincent Elementary School

Her
Her eyes are as beautiful as the stars
When I see stars I always think of her
At her window there are a lot of bars
The bars don't allow any one to see her
Her voice is like hearing morning birds sing
Her lips are like the ones of a model
When she cries it hurts you like a big sting
Her body also looks like the one of a model
When you talk to her she says she feels bad
When she leaves you don't see her in some time
When she is gone it makes you very sad
When she comes back it's a different time
But yet ever since the very start
I've been in love with her with all my heart

Franco Leon, Grade 8
John Adams Middle School

A Perfect Kid

1 cup of knowledge,
1/2 cup of adventure,
Combine 2 cups of fun,
Bake at 400 degrees,
Let it cool,
While cooling sprinkle
Some love on,
Then let cool and
A perfect kid.

Pamela Myles, Grade 7
St Barbara School

Water

It is wet and wild
Playful and enjoyable
Cold, fresh, wet and wild

Paola López, Grade 8
Almond Tree Middle School

Appreciate What You Have

To become a saint,
Appreciated by everyone
To feel like God
To know who really loves or hates you
To appreciate what you have
Try to make more friends
Than enemies
To make a difference, even
By giving others what
They need;
More than you do
To feel that life is different
Because of you.

Anayeli Gomez, Grade 8
Valley Oak Middle School

Wonder

I wonder
Will I ace today's test?
If I do, I'll have a fest.

I wonder
Why is the sky blue?
I'm not a genius,
I have no clue.

I wonder
When will the flowers bloom again?
Until then,
I'll wait in vain.

I wonder about many things
Everything
That this world brings to me.

Emiko Nakayama, Grade 7
Lawson Middle School

My Favorite Things

The undulating melody of French whispered in my ear
My mother's dazzling smile that could light a city for a year
Cracking the spine of an anticipated read
The routine morning scramble in my closet for the outfit I need

The enigma of fall
Simply the best season of all
The labyrinth of curls on father's head
My Saturday morning croissant in bed

Cambridge's long-whiskered professors walking down the street
Brilliance on every cobblestone and an abundance of tea and scones to eat
The musk of my godmother's gold and crystal Shalimar
The hours lost on the 405 in my mother's car

The grooves of watercolor paper dripping with paint
The blaring orange of my boyfriend's shirts that show no restraint
The clacking of computers from all corners of the house
Buttoning every last button on a crisp, white blouse

A roaring fire at Halloween time
Writing the last line of a poem in rhyme

Zoey Poll, Grade 8
The Mirman School

The Box of Stone

I hold my soul in a box of stone, it's contents mostly unknown
Though some things I have shown
To other souls that hold the same

I search for wisdom, but find wit and the grades that come with it
And oftentimes, I admit
I find my wit quite funny

My soul holds music and laughter and several talents sought after
And a wish to soar to the rafters
Of some celestial roof

In my stone box I hide tears and anger inside
Though my heart has cried
My eyes don't

But thought it's dark sometimes, I can join the chimes
At least most times
Of my friends' happy laughter

And though my soul is held in a box of stone, and its contents mostly unknown
Many things I have shown
And some souls hold the same

Darcy Thompson, Grade 8
La Joya Middle School

The Orphan

In a world that's so dark and cold I wait for my life to unfold
A roof over my head and a warm soft bed
Is all that I need to hold
The depths of the night fill me with fright
Of this horrible life that I live, yearning for love
And a warm friendly hug, for my family left me alone
Now I must work on my own
Living in the streets with my cold bare feet
I have no clothes or blankets to keep me asleep
I must bare my life to keep me alive
The earth shakes almost as to keep me awake
Boom, splat, bang
The dark streets, as cold as sleet
The wind runs past, my life turns so fast
The night is a hungry bird taking flight it gives me fright
One old, okay orphan I am
For I just found a dinner ham

Taylor Johnson and Ashleigh Sampson, Grade 7
St Patrick Parish School

Words

Words aren't just a series of letters,
They contain thoughts and feelings
Mix them all together and they form a potion
A potion full of different emotions
A simple way to express and share
Whether through music or writing,
they can be hatred or thoughtful
But no matter what
All words are powerful

Yvette Tran, Grade 7
Sarah McGarvin Intermediate School

How Blue Is the Ocean

How blue is the ocean, how deep does it go?
How great is my heart, how fragile I am
Longing for you to hold me again
An ocean between us
No more no less
If I could swim to you
Would you meet me half way?
How blue is the ocean where you are my love?
I'll paint you a garden
Filled with flowers and love
Together we'll stroll
Through roses and lilies
We'll laugh like children
No troubles no worries
How blue is the ocean, salt water tears
We only have this distance
Between us this year
Forever together, our love is true
How blue is the ocean
So blue so blue

Baby Elaine Hernandez, Grade 8
Buchser Middle School

Sacrifice

I opened the door
everyone is as quiet as a mouse
they looked at me as if somebody just died
I ask, "What's wrong?"
my dad sighs
he says, "Sit down"
"I'm going away for 2 years"
I cry out, "WHY?"
he says
he has to do our country right
my heart pounding
my head feeling like it's going to explode
Tears fall down my face
as I think of all the terrible things that can go wrong
I look up with a frown
I say daddy don't worry
you will be okay

Adriana Gomez, Grade 8
La Joya Middle School

Beach

Sitting on the ground
I wait for the sun to go down
Toes buried in the sand
Seeing children with no frowns

The sea crests the land
Like a baby and a mother's hand
Breaking on the shore
Smashing sounds like a drummer in a band

Kids happy to do no chores
While they can lay, snooze, and snore
Some I see run and play
None with a face of bore

Rocks are doors in the way
Shells gently on the ground lay
Hearing many say
WOW! What a day

Akasha Vigo, Grade 7
St Patrick Parish School

I Am

I am a bird flying in the sky.
I am the sun brightly shining.
I am a rubber band very flexible.
I am a frog hopping on lily pads.
I am a monkey swinging from vine to vine.
I am a cloud floating in the heavens.
I am.

Megan Cruz, Grade 7
St Mary of Assumption School

The Unknown

Can we see it all?   Or are we limited
Is there a certain color, naked to the human eye?
Is there life on unreachable destination?
Or unseen life before our eyes?
Is there a smell never smelt before?
Or a feeling we have never felt?
Are there canyons and mountains at the tips of our fingers?
Or forests and jungles at the ends of our hairs?
Is there a door that opens to nowhere or a closet that will take us to different dimensions?
Will unveiling the answers destroy our minds — like a city underwater?
Or will knowing ease the minds in depression — like a mother reuniting with her child?
Will the universe congratulate us for discovering the unknown?
Or will it become angry at us for digging deep into its soul?
Are these questions unknown for a reason?
But what reason?
Is the unknown, unknown to protect us?
Or is it unknown because the universe wants us to search, find, and think?

Sheehan Al-Rabie, Grade 8
Madrona Middle School

Music

Music resonates through me.
There is no way to know the deep connection between it and me.
To some it is just sound, but to others it resides in their very soul.
Such a place can only be touched by sound that carries emotions.
Expressionless emotions that can be understood only by those who understand the wavelengths.
Music can be heard everywhere and found in everything, but sometimes we have to look beyond the varnish.
Music can be a friend, saying things I can't.
Music is me and I am music.
It is in everyone, everywhere, all I have to do is listen.

Shannon Hearney, Grade 9
University Preparatory School

What It's Becoming

We are crashing. A serious end of the clearness;
An end of the pure zone, as far as we can see. This is what it's becoming.
Holes in our blanket of protection, our ozone layer.
The smog is becoming thick, covering Earth's true beauty.
No more hills of green, or skies of blue, and the singing of birds cannot be heard.
This is what it's becoming. The vast seas have now become an ocean of tears that nature has cried.
No, not tears of joy, but cries of pain that absorb the rainforests of the world.
This is what it's becoming. Eyes of innocent creatures, even the eyes of a lion,
Or the bravest soul are crying because of us.
This is what Earth's becoming. Our cars and technology, highways and stadiums
Have been destructive to the environment.
We can only fall, or fall further, without the help of you.
No one seems to care, because all continue this behavior.
And you can change this. It only takes one, one to make a difference.
Conserving water, and catching litter bugs and creating new laws are the changes you can make.
Planting green once again, and making these hills places to support life.
Helping wildlife and the environment will make a difference.
We can see clear skies again, and hear the frogs' croaks.
Together, we can do it. You could be the one. This is what Earth could become.

Kaylee Pierson, Grade 7
Citrus Hills Intermediate School

Where I'm From

Emotions, my thoughts,
I remember my mom telling me I'm not from America.
I'm puzzled.
If I'm not from America, then from where?

Adoption may be just a word to some people,
But it means a lot to me.
I am sad, it makes me wonder,
Is there something wrong with me?
Why did my birthparents put me up for adoption?
Was it for my benefit because they couldn't support me?
Was it because they wanted a boy?
But don't people say boys and girls are equal?

Ernie, a stuffed owl that traveled to China with my parents,
And waited for me in a rickety metal crib.
To me he's a best friend, a member of the family,
One of my prized possessions.

Another prized possession, a little blankie,
Once, a velvet-backed, handmade creation.
Now it's old and threadbare, almost in tatters.
What happens when there's nothing left
And I'm not ready?

Amy Nicosia, Grade 7
Chinese American International School

Friends

I love my friends today
Tomorrow forever and ever
Never forgotten!

Stephanie Tejeda, Grade 7
John Charles Fremont Intermediate School

In His Footsteps

In His footsteps I walk, trying to keep up
Even if I fall down, I know He'll pick me up
In His arms I trust and lay my life
I know He will deliver me and save me from strife
In His shadow I worship and stand
Knowing that He is the Master and He is in command
In His grace I am living today
Going His, instead of my way
In His blood I shall be covered
I know that He is greater and like no other
In His house I shall give Him honor and praise
Doing this for the rest of my days
In His heaven I shall be one day
As long as I stay faithful and do not stray
In His footsteps I shall walk
Giving Him praise and spreading the Word and I will never stop.

Amber Villasenor, Grade 7
Chino Valley Christian Schools

Private Puzzle

God must love puzzles
The way He scatters our pieces
Across the table of the Earth
Squares alike in shadows
Appear to be the same
Though each piece goes to a different lane.
It's only alike on closer examination.
I learn that they are both the same.
Is it for a reason?
For arguments and confrontation?
To just talk or what?
So I ask what do I do?
But I am told
"Just move along to the rest of the puzzle."
So I force through the other pieces.
I finally get through to the front.
I hear a little voice.
They point me to a podium.
And all I hear is the puzzle is complete!!
Now I have fixed the troubled puzzle.

Adam Aguirre, Grade 8
St Hilary Elementary School

Feeling Blue

I'm feeling blue because I miss you.
I'm bluer than the sky because
I don't have you in my arms all the time.
I can't forget you on that summer day
As I stand and think every day.
I still wait for you in that exact same spot,
Even when it's really hot.
Oh how I long to see you in real life,
Instead of the many pictures inside of my mind.
I still have a little hope to see you again.
So just like that day that you went away,
I stay here feeling blue every single day.

Raymund Hernandez, Grade 7
St Hilary Elementary School

I Saw God Today

I was just walking around,
when I tripped over a rock and fell to the ground.
It was then I saw God.
I learned he tried not to make himself that obvious,
but I see him in everything that's on the Earth.
It's true, I know I do.
People think I'm crazy but I know what I see.
He was right there on the ground just staring at me.
I see him as a flower, I see him as a cloud,
I see him in heaven as I pray aloud.
So next time you're on your daily walk,
look around for the white flock.
You can see him in any different way,
but I saw God today.

Stephanie Hanson, Grade 7
Holy Family Catholic School

To the Beat of Nature's Music
Two magnificent trees sit as friends,
along an orange river that glows
from the setting sun
Sudden silence…the wind picks up,
the branches sway back and forth
to the beat of nature's music.

Lucia Michel, Grade 7
Corpus Christi School

A Scourge for You
Tons of essays, school applications,
Fractious work, profuse complications.
Scathing migraines, schisms are a must,
Loads of pressure, though this is unjust.
Tension, difficulty, stress galore,
Not transient, but forevermore.
Causing you anxiety and strain,
Trouble for you and yet me to blame!

Arielle Maxner, Grade 7
The Mirman School

Life vs Death
Life
Blooming, shining
Bright, warm, happy
Lively, lovely; frightfully, ugly
Dark, cold, sad
Wilting, depressing
Death

Jessica Campos, Grade 7
St Cyprian School

Little Kids in Love
Can't sleep?
Please try not to weep
Why are you crying anyway little kid?
Is it something he did?
Did he leave?
Just have faith and believe.
He will come back.
Just keep track.
It's bad he left.
Just don't fret.
Because you know he will regret.
Just look up at the moon,
And he's probably looking at it, too,
And he will be there soon.
Now stop crying,
And wipe those tears,
And just listen to me dear,
That he also has fears.
Now he's here,
Happiness is near,
And he will wipe away those tears.

Marissa Dumlao, Grade 8
Holy Family Catholic School

The Dance
The curtains slowly open
Her anxiety at its highest point as she turns and faces the audience
Legs shoulder width apart; hands linked above her head signal the beginning
The first counts of music are played slowly as she stays in place
Suddenly the music becomes a whimsical melody
And she moves her body as swiftly and gracefully as a bird taking flight
The music is beating faster while she manages to never slow down
Lights flash with wild colors as the fog machine is started
Her movements are so definitive, strong, and powerful
She's in complete control and has captured her audience
Her feet point, her legs stretch, her arms float
Dazzling
The music slows again while she slowly makes her way back to center stage
She takes her original pose and the curtains close for the last time
As the fog still rolls in and the lights are dim

Colleen Reidy, Grade 8
St Joseph's School of the Sacred Heart

The Leap
Behind the closed door, she walks, darkness all around her.
Should she stay or should she go should she turn the knob and walk right through.
Or should she sit there just wondering what to do?
These these are the questions that fill her mind.
Why would she walk into somewhere, somewhere she doesn't even know.
It could be dark, it could be cold.
She could have obstacles, obstacles before her.
"Help, help!" she screams in fear.
"Can anyone get me out of here?"
Why must I be in here in this place all alone?
"It's a leap," she hears someone say
"A leap of faith, a leap of faith that you must take."
"But will it help?" she asks that voice.
"But will it set me free?"
"The leap," it said, "The leap of faith can help you do anything!"

Lydia Redleaf-Barlese, Grade 7
Southpointe Christian School

Ode to My Imaginary Friend
You are the weirdest
Loopiest, doopiest person
That I may ever meet
You are so understanding
And never underestimate me
Always by my side
You always take your time
With my every day stupidity
You have a new name every week
And never sneak up on me with your feet
You never get smelly
Even if you haven't washed since you were in your mommy's belly
You are always invisible and make me look crazy
You are like my antique toy
From the 19th century

Smarlea Scheck, Grade 8
Santa Rosa Technology Magnet School

Broken Bond

You're one of the friends that I treasured the most
One of the few that I truly cared about
You're one of the ones I never thought I'd let go
But things change…
I saw a side of you that I couldn't accept
One that no one would have ever thought existed
But I was a witness to this harsh reality…
I saw the you that was insensitive,
Inconsiderate of other people's emotions.
I would not have minded so much
Had two of your victims not been people I care for deeply.
The haunting thought of the pain they suffered
Visits me every hour of every day,
And I can't bear it anymore…
Dear friend, I'm sorry for what I'm about to do,
But I can't take this any longer.
I've already been pulled into this deep state of depression,
And I don't wish to be like this.
I'm sorry…but…
With these words spoken… — SNAP!
I cut the bond holding us together: our friendship…

Christelle San Juan, Grade 8
Almond Tree Middle School

Class of 2009

Class of 2009 so bold and sweet
listen to us as we speak
be so strong, be so tough.
One thing we say, just never give up.
If we are faced with defeat,
we will just jump back on our feet.
We go one day to the next
not knowing what lies ahead.
So we say don't give up or bend your knees
just shoot for your hopes
and your dreams.

Jasmine Arce, Grade 7
St Hilary Elementary School

Our Love

He seemed to have a stare that could provoke.
Somehow I found a way to look away.
At first I thought it was all a big joke.
But my mind and eyes were going astray.
Could he really feel this way about me?
Could I also feel the same way for him?
It was as if I had the need to flee.
Somehow I believed our chances were slim.
One day I realized our love was true.
I had to do something to make it work,
Even if it meant to start something new.
I could no longer continue to lurk.
I am now happy to be by his side.
Never again will I have to be put aside.

Vianca Munoz, Grade 8
John Adams Middle School

Is It Wrong…

Is it wrong to watch the world show its fear?
Is it wrong to watch and never shed a tear?
Is it wrong to watch the beauty in your sight,
While the people cry with fear in the night?
Is it wrong to feel the wind and feel alive,
As the weak lose the will to survive?
Is it wrong to see the rooftops capped with snow,
And ignore the chaos one can't know?
Is it wrong to hate a foe, one you'll never know,
Or is it wrong to see the world through his eyes?
Is it wrong to plant a seed near a great oak,
Or is it wrong to never let it truly grow?
Is it wrong to watch the children laugh and play,
And not tell them to cherish each sweet day? And yet…
Is it so wrong to support a dying cause,
So long as your heart has human flaws?
Is it wrong to love your life as others hold the knife?
Is it wrong to wish others happiness,
While hiding emotions from the rest?
Is it wrong to hold love dear
As long as you help those near?

Heather Razook, Grade 9
Patriot High School

The Start

The start of saying yes to life
The start of saying yes to success, and a head start
The start of a race from the shot of the pistol
The start is anywhere
From your house to school or a diary
So where is the start for you?

Rafael Morales, Grade 7
Round Valley Elementary School

Friendship

Everybody needs a friend.
A friend to care and understand.
A friend who is loyal, like a dog.
A friend is someone who will stay up to talk
About your problems.
A friend will help you when you are down.
A friend is a treasure box, filled with many jewels.
Friendship is a one in a lifetime chance.
A friend doesn't leave you without saying good-bye.
A friend doesn't make fun of you.
A friend helps you in your darkest times.
A friend will keep your secret to the grave.
Friendship travels among many routes.
Friendship teaches you the meaning of life.
A friend is the best thing in a person's life.
Everybody needs a friend.

AnnMarie Blackburn, Grade 8
Valley Oak Middle School

Stars in the Sky

Lights painted in the sky
Shining so bright
Oh, candles of the sky
Burning with all your might
I plead to you from down below
To never stop shining,
To never let go
Spots of wonder
Burn forever more

Adriana Segura, Grade 8
Madrona Middle School

Sun

What is that so bright and strong?
Is it a planet?
I must be wrong
It's bright and yellow
Filled with fire
It's one of those things
You just admire
When you look up, up so high
You're blinded by the light in the sky
The bright yellow thing
That is so strong
Must be the SUN!
What took me so long?

Jessica Guerrero, Grade 8
Madrona Middle School

Soldiers

You talk to a friend
Laughing and teasing
While they want to end
The dying and screaming

You spread rumors
And you tell lies
While they search for bombers
To end the cries

While you could be sleeping
Soft and sound
They could be weeping
Taking last breaths on the ground

War is real
And war is here
We try to heal
And try not to fear

Soldiers die every day
For you and me
So we can say,
"We are free"

Allison Vidor, Grade 7
Holy Family Catholic School

School

In school, academics is the key to your future path,
You take many classes like history, grammar, and math.
Math is more than just numbers and equations going through your head,
When it comes to hard questions you should not dread and have fun instead.

Those who do not learn from history are doomed to repeat,
When they play jeopardy, they are sure to suffer defeat.
Grammar is a class where everyone must be precise,
You must write properly, be clear to the point, and concise.

In literature, we learn to not use the cover to judge books,
Because what is written inside is more important than its looks.
Vocabulary is a class where you should not be nonchalant,
Because this is where you will learn the words to become au courant.

You know, science is a class in which they teach you how things work,
Watching the teacher blow things up is an unexpected perk.
In computer class, on our extra time, we program faces,
It is difficult to do because you must count the spaces.

Although we work hard in school, man should not live by work alone,
In art, we draw, sketch, and paint and in music, we study tone.
By the end of June after nine long years, when we graduate,
The level of knowledge crammed in our brains will be saturate.

Jennifer Xu, Grade 8
Challenger School – Ardenwood

Katie

Memories flew by her window
The time she was stung by a bee, of course,
The year her puppy was brought home,
And all the moments when her brother and her fought.
Yet, so many little things she had not lived
Where there are elders that live to be 100
There are children that live to be 9
Life isn't fair, life isn't just
For the child's body was cursed with cancer.
And it took over her body day by day
Like darkness consumes a lit room
During the winter.
Hospitals seem like the devil's quarters, so cold, so depressing
And she can hear the slightest voice calling
His voice calls to her, Come to me child, come.
No one wishes, or wants to be gone or forgotten
But she won't,
Because she was some person, someone, not just another human being
Because her smile could change the world, melt the snow.
Then her final breath departs, like a bird leaving the nest,
I knew her once that girl named Katie.

Taylor Tanton, Grade 9
Valley Christian High School

Nature

I'm walking down the path and I see a tree swaying,
In the soft morning breeze
I see a lake that is as cold and as soft as a warm fuzzy blanket
The moss on the trees is,
As warm as a hot summer afternoon.

Lucas Pruitt, Grade 8
Citrus Hills Intermediate School

Beauty Comes at a Price

Drip, drip
Rain falls, making puddles all around
Shh! Listen, do you hear that sound?
The rain is singing, singing his song
He's telling us it won't be long
She will come after he's gone
She'll be here at about dawn

Waiting, waiting
Look, look, the rain is gone
She's here, she's here and it's right about dawn
Purple, blue, green, yellow, orange, red
Hurry and get out of bed
I want to see her and all of her wonder
We have to go past the mountain and yonder
Wow, I can finally see the rainbow
Flowing with all its beauty from high to low

Renee Wright, Grade 8
Madrona Middle School

Saved by Love

With the flowers growing over her
And the scars her body beholds;
He can't help but think of her before she left this Earth.
The pungent smell of regret mixed with
The faint memories of her intoxicating perfume.

The way the flowers sneered at him
Evoked a sick hatred within his soul.
He longed to endure the pain; bring back the passion
He longed to control his inner contempt toward
The being who took her joyful, innocent spirit.

He remembers the taste of her lips
And longs for one last kiss.
He gently touches her face
But startled, retracts.
The warmth and bliss course through him;
He realizes that her blood still flows,
Quietly dripping off his fingers.

Behold, her silent heartbeat, revived by love's sweet touch!

Elizabeth White, Grade 9
Capistrano Valley Christian School

My House

I am from a shelf filled with books
To a night stand that has a TV, PS2 and games.
To a radio full of CD's and music too.
I am from my room — Loud and obnoxious.

I am from people arguing,
To music in the background,
The frustration brewing all the time.
I play sports every day.

Cody Tienken, Grade 9
Milhous School

Anti Ode to an Ode

Odes are ridiculous
They are completely pointless
I gain no useful information
and I do not enjoy reading them
They are exaggerated but very boring pieces of poetry
that the teachers makes you read and write

Odes bore me until my eyes sink into my sockets
my head pops off and rolls away
the color of the world is sucked out
the sun flickers and dies
the whole universe collapses
and everything is halted to an eternal stop

Odes are horrifyingly inaccurate
They are exaggerated so much that
they become messes of unexplainable information
Ode are obnoxious poems
and another useless annoying subject taught in school

Yuzo Makitani, Grade 8
Tierra Linda Middle School

I Am an Eagle

I am an eagle.
I wonder when the next big storm comes.
I hear whales from above.
I see a bay from a distance.
I want a challenge.
I am an eagle.
I pretend to be as weak as a rat to catch prey.
I feel the fish, as I go fishing.
I touch my prey as if it were in a tray.
I worry about nothing.
I cry when I lose a meal, though I barely fail.
I am an eagle.
I understand the circle of life.
I sing about my life in my beautiful screeches.
I dream that my beak is a sharp as a knife.
I try to live my life to its fullest, so I go searching for beaches.
I hope to catch a meal today.
I am an eagle.

Sina Torabi, Grade 8
Palm Desert Middle School

Beautiful Eyes

Beautiful eyes
speak a thousand words.
They are the windows to your soul
and the passage
to your heart.

Beautiful eyes
always
have a story to tell.
Or is it
a story to hide?

Beautiful eyes
are like a jungle —
easy to get lost in.
If only,
I had a map.

Nicole Reichenberger, Grade 7
Lawson Middle School

morning

sunlight hugs your face
walking to the sidewalk

no white winter trace

dried up leaves
in a breeze
Madel Roldan, Grade 9
Balboa City School

A Bad Day

You stub your toe
You fail a test
You cry and no one cares
You don't feel your best
You're havin' a bad day
Nothing could be worse
You think
And then it starts to rain
You get home
And tell your mom
She says ever so gently
Without a bad day
How could you recognize what's good?
That's true, you think
You look outside
The sun comes out
One bad day
To see the good
Is a price worth paying
To me

Samantha Moss, Grade 8
Crittenden Middle School

Clear Mistakes

Pleading and wishing,
For miracles to happen,
Turning to hope,
My heart beats with a passion.

Mistakes become visible,
Almost way too clear,
Like a useless rumor,
I forget certain peers.

Life comes to a stop,
Including everything around,
The obstacles got me,
I stroll with a frown.

Questions are asked,
But answers never appear,
No reply to my apology,
Is everything I fear.

Nicole Bravo, Grade 8
Madrona Middle School

Tiger

My brother, my brother
Is just like a tiger
Strong and honorable.
Nice and protective
Just the way to be.

My brother with a job
And responsibility,
I'm so proud
That he finally got so far.

Shaunta Fellows, Grade 8
Hesperia Jr High School

Choices

In life
People always have choices
usually they are difficult
Especially adults who
Have to pay the rent,
Gas, light and many bills
Being on a team
To work with my teammates
Having communication skills
Follow my coach's rules
To not get into trouble
Having a job to have to be on time
Do your job correctly
Most importantly
To have a good attitude

Jasmin Macias, Grade 7
St Alphonsus School

Welcome to Heaven

I lay in the bed, cold as ice
I hear the tick, tick, ticking in my head
Telling me how soon I'll be dead
Then it hits me, and all goes black
I open my eyes, and see the light
It says, "Now you're dead."
A mysterious figure pops up,
his arms are eagle's wings,
spread open, ready to embrace me,
he asks in a lovely voice,
"Did you love others like I have loved?"
I say to him "Yes, my father,
lift me up to be with you
your love is unending."
He lifts me up,
we walk towards the light,
and to my delight,
He says,
"Welcome to heaven,
you're no longer dead."

Seth Borges, Grade 8
Valley Oak Middle School

Perfect

My life was that way once.
Perfect.
So simple.
So serene.
It happened suddenly.
I did not realize at first —
My life had been destroyed forever.
My friends tried to comfort me,
But they did not understand.
Who can heal a shattered heart?
Why?
I would scream when alone.
Did it have to be me?
Why?
It's no use now.
I guess I'll be scarred for life.
Why did he do it?
He did not have to do anything so cruel.
He did not have to leave us.
It used to be that way [my life] —
Perfect.
Amber Winans, Grade 9
A and A Home School

The Shark

A graceful creature
Vicious yet calm and gentle
Vulture of the sea
Aaron De Santiago, Grade 8
Almond Tree Middle School

The Gecko

Not mighty but meek,
The lumps on its back all aligned in a streak.

Searching, stalking, devouring its prey,
It repeats this cycle day after day.

The nutrients are stored in its tail;
The wastes are deposited along each trail.

To the family of reptiles, this creature belongs.
With a large, plump tail the gecko will live long.

Katie Houser, Grade 8
Chino Valley Christian Schools

Dead or Alive

I have heard wise words from wise men.
I have heard compliments,
And I have heard insults.
I have experienced loneliness and rejection.
I have seen admiration in a staring face.
But where is it now?

The goal in life is happiness, I have heard.
But from who? From weak men, I say.
Happiness is only one sensation, one feeling, one entity.
What does happiness have to offer? To me, to anyone?
Would you dare to agree?
It can only give you so little, and so much it can take,
Would you dare?

So young and naive, you would think.
You are too corrupted inside to let yourself see,
To challenge your own standards, your own code.
Do you see some meaning? If you don't, you are lost,
And that's how you will die, or in this case,
That's why you are dead.

Alejandro Sifuentes, Grade 9
Sweetwater High School

Looks

When I look at myself in the mirror
I see no precious looking like creature
I only see my ugliness clearer
And upset I am about my feature
How can you ever fall in love with me
When there are others way better looking
I can never compare with such beauty
My ugliness makes you look like a king
Yet, you prove to me that your love is true
You do say together we are the best
For all your love I did not have a clue
A couple that is better than the rest
Together, everything we can be
The love you have towards me I believe

Lisset May, Grade 8
John Adams Middle School

Ever Feel Like Dying

Do you ever feel like dying
That you just don't matter
That your world came down
That you just don't care about life
But then you think back and realize
What you've done and what you've been through
You think, and think, and think
and finally realize that you are blessed to be alive.
You are blessed to have a family that loves you.
That you have friends that care about you.
So if you ever feel like dying,
Just think back and realize you are blessed to be alive.

Dalia Aranda, Grade 8
St Vincent Elementary School

Secret Love

You want me to tell her that you love her.
And as a friend you ask for my advice.
Tell her you love her and stay forever.
Give her compliments that are sweet and nice.

Confess to her you love her more than me.
I see that glow when you look in her eyes.
I'll admit that, with her, you look happy.
I hope the best as I keep my eyes dry.

I know she loves you like I do, too.
For my friend's heart I will leave you alone.
I know she will be happier with you
And I can't do anything else but moan.

Now a story ends as a broken dream.
A heart that'll never be the same in me.

Viviana Gonzalez, Grade 8
John Adams Middle School

I Don't Understand

I don't understand
Why people are so different, yet so similar
Why people get sick
Why there is still slavery

But most of all
Why there is hate
Why there is suffering
Why some people want to kill others

What I understand most is
Why most people are good
Why justice usually prevails
Why good triumphs over evil

Bobby Huffaker, Grade 8
Dorris-Eaton School

Pressure

Tired of being
What you want me to be
Feeling so faithless,
Lost under this pressure.
Don't know what you're expecting of me.
Under the pressure
To choose from things I love.
Every step that I take is another mistake.
All I want is to be more like me
And less like you.
Everything that I worked for
Is falling apart.
I know I may end up failing.
I know you were just like me
With someone disappointed in you.

Mary V. Smith, Grade 7
St Alphonsus School

Tubing

all happens too fast,
sparkling water rushing by,
looking soft and warm
but the landing
feels like concrete.

water, dark and green,
and the bottom…endless,
polluted, grimy,
but that won't stop me.

muscles tighten,
gripping for dear life,
eyes squinting against mist,
all for the thrill.

Vincent Shields, Grade 8
St Joseph's School of the Sacred Heart

The Dawn

how is the pain gone?
the noise? the dark?
where is my platoon,
carrying red, white, blue?
where am i? how did i get here?
one minute i am there, the next i am not
the light is coming, coming to take me
so bright, barely i can see.
The guns, the fight
was the last i remembered
maybe i've moved on,
maybe a better time will dawn.
My sons, the heirs,
i hope they'll be proud
the legacy carries on,
the family will stay strong.

Josh Adams, Grade 8
La Joya Middle School

The Steelers

The Steelers are such a great football team
If you call them mean, they will break your spleen
But it was a heart breaking, eye tearing, backbreaking, chin cracking,
Brain hurting, fan zone lowering, tragic whimpering,
Face slapping, down right hair pulling, neck breaking, gut hurting,
Rashes stinging, nose bleeding, loss of the Pittsburgh Steelers,
Loss to the Jacksonville Jaguars at the score of 29-32 in the playoffs
To see who will go to the Super Bowl.

Tanner Reinhart, Grade 7
Santa Rosa Technology Magnet School

Where I Am From

I am from America
From the land of the free and the home of the brave
From fireworks on the Fourth of July to parades on Veteran's Day
I am from a country town
From the land between the mountains and the sea
God's country

I am from a small town
Free cookies at the grocery store
And dry cleaner knowing all my brothers' names
I am from a school where you know each family
And a school where we pray for each other
And go to church every Sunday

I am from a place I call home
From family gatherings every weekend
And always having someone to play with
I am from a place of love
From a place of laughter
And from a home full of family

Logan Wakefield, Grade 7
Linfield Christian School

As Time Goes On

Make the rain fall down,
Just to take away that frown.
Taking pictures in the rain,
It drives us insane.
Hanging out with that group of friends,
Always setting new trends.
But this year is really coming to an end.
We're all prepared for that time,
But I'll still have those memories in my mind.
I'll keep in touch and remember your faces,
I'll keep you tight just like my shoelaces.
I've been with you all for years and years,
Our graduation night will bring some tears.
The time we still have, we should spend with each other,
We're just like a family to care for one another.
When we're gone, we'll be at a different position, a different place,
But these memories will never ever be erased.

Sydney Chiong, Grade 8
Corpus Christi School

A Symphony, an Art, a Poem

To itself is an art abstract
Not to be read for what it is.
Though limited to the words of few
The black river meanders the unwritten plane
And mends a riddle from rationality.

From the myths of time
To the lore of faith
A force expressed in few lines
Defines a story, an emotion, the times untold
Unfathomed in the mind of reality.

A piece written with letters less used
Save by the artists, with their eyes
See the true value of their stand.
Composed with rhythm and rhyme,
The Symphony played with pencils and pens

A Bogart to the imagination,
'Tis conceived in the mind of diversity.
Be it the Abyss below or the Heavens above
The song is heard from the universe afar
Or in the dreams of restful sleep.

Edward Lim, Grade 9
St. Michael's College Preparatory School

War

You leave far from here
No one knows what will happen to you
You might just even disappear
Yet you take that risk

You hear bombs everywhere
You hear them here and there
You know you're alive
Yet you can't feel that inside

People are getting hit
But what can you do?

It's like a nightmare out of your head
You wish you could just be in bed
Close to your family
Away from it all

All you hear is your heart beating
Slower and slower it goes
And all you see before your eyes is your foes
It's over you're gone…

Now to make that phone call…that dreadful phone call
Brenda Lejes, Grade 8
Almond Tree Middle School

March

M onth of spring
A round time of planting
R ich fields
C rops growing
H ouse cleaning

Kolbein Matson, Grade 7
John Charles Fremont Intermediate School

My Personal Smackdown

Wrestling is a sport
A job, a business
Not a game
You wrestle, you don't play wrestling
I prepare myself before a match
I stare at my opponent like a hawk
I stand tall with my hands on my hips
I listen to the mat calling my name
I warm up, jump, jog in place
My eyes never leave my opponent's face
When it's my turn to wrestle
I'm ready to win
1…2…3…RJ, the team sends me out
I wait at the center of the mat
My opponent arrives and I tell him with my eyes,
That he's going to lose the match
Ready…WRESTLE!
Takedown, reversal, escape, takedown
Spectacular throw, pin
It's all over
And I win.

RJ Weinheimer, Grade 9
Fountain Valley High School

True Beauty

A gentle sigh in the whispering breeze,
Traveling far, among the trees,
Causing all listeners to reminisce,
True beauty is revealed through actions like this.
A sound of an enchanting melody,
Produced from an unexpected remedy
Of waves and rock creating oceanic bliss.
True beauty is revealed through actions like this.

Although the sights and sounds of earth
Can create such beauty beyond our own worth,
We mustn't forget our own fathomless abyss,
Found deep in our souls is where our elegance exists.
When released it reaches as far as the eye can see,
To try to help all humanity,
To strive and strive to make things right,
So peace can bless the oncoming night.
Then dream that evil will not resist,
Your fight to dispatch its sinister mist.
True beauty is revealed through actions like this.

Whitney Hansen, Grade 7
St Hilary School

Like a Sister

People look and turn their heads as laughter fills the room.
They see two girls bent over, clutching at their stomachs.
Their laughter is no deafening silence, but instead a deafening noise.
They appear to be oblivious of the staring strangers' faces.
One of them is me, the louder laugher of the two, the other one is Ella, a softer laugh yet just as amused as I.

She is the only friend I can laugh like this with, and act so immature too.
We'll laugh and talk about those "unsaid" things, that no one dares to say,
She'll make comments about the people we see, that cause a fit of giggles.
But she's even there in the serious times, when I have nowhere left to turn.
Not just a caring shoulder to cry on, but a mentor and advisor as well.

Everywhere we go, we have adventures and make fun memories.
Like our road trips to unknown places, going tubing, and the rapids.
We don't just have a good time when we're out on the go,
We'll spend Friday nights watching old movies and telling secrets under the covers,
And laugh until we begin to cry and are silenced by her mother.

I've never met a person quite like Ella. She's my blonde beach bum, best bud.
The one who keeps me accountable, when no one else could care less,
She tells me when I'm screwing up and how I better make it right.
But most importantly, she's the person I can lean on cause I know she's always strong.
In our lifetimes it's important to have one close friend to be there when you're low.
Well I've already found mine — my best friend Ella, and this friend I'm not letting go. Ella is and will always be a part of me.

Brie Roche-Lilliott, Grade 9
Fountain Valley High School

Unwanted Definition

You want a definition, many people can say
That that one definition wanted may not be the same the next day.
How it feels, the connection that is bestowed upon you two,
But once again, it may not be the feeling felt about you.
Oh, how you long and think that they day would come.
When he walks up to you and says something romantic under the setting sun.
Maybe it was not meant to be, just thinking about the happiness between him and me,
When you soon found out that the person he wants to share his love with is someone else.

Lauren M. Sutherlin, Grade 7
St Bernard Elementary School

Best Friend

We've got way too many inside jokes to count, and no one understands them.
We always get in trouble, then get out, I guess that's why we're best friends.
We're way too loud and we know it, we laugh at people, but they laugh at us,
When we scream in public we don't notice, and that's why we're best friends.
When I feel like the world's gonna end, when there's too much in my head,
I know there's always someone there to calm me down, making me laugh, BFF, the same to you, till the end, my best friend.
We fight over boys cause we think it's funny, we'd never let them come between us because that's crazy.
No boy could make up for losing my best friend, he couldn't even pretend.
If you can't love her too, you better walk away, cause my best friends here to stay.
When I feel like the world's gonna end, you pull me down from the clouds instead.
When there's too much in my head, you make me smile again.
I know there's always someone there to calm me down, being without the world would stop spinning round.
Making me laugh, BFF, the same to you, till the end, Nicolette's my best friend.

Aliya Stalone, Grade 9
Mater Dei High School

Her Eyes

Her big blue eyes do haunt me day and night.
They seem to seek inside my very soul,
And when I think of her eyes, round and bright,
They turn my heart pure gold instead of coal.
Insanity makes me long for her love,
For when her cheery eyes stare into mine,
I always hear the wedding bells above,
But only does her death cause her decline,
And yet I feel her soul inside of me;
Her wondrous eyes still haunt inside my head.
As I recall her love for me with glee,
I soon forget that she was ever dead.
I know that we will reunite again,
So wait will I, through snow or hail or rain.

Angela Jong, Grade 8
John Adams Middle School

White

White. The color of a clean shirt
Swaying with the wind
Hanging from a clothes line.

White. Fresh snow falling slowly
Delicately landing on the solid ground.

White. The sheets that comfort my grandfather
Stiff, yet warm.

He lays in bed with needles attacking his arm
He cannot move
He is too weak and too tired.

Christina Colunga, Grade 8
St Joseph's School of the Sacred Heart

School Day

First, is the annoying alarm waking me up
My mother coming and yelling at me
Then the choice of what to wear
My sister crying trying not to wake
Then the strong taste of mint toothpaste
And that sticky feeling of gel in my hands
The sour taste of orange juice in the morning
Almost going to sleep in the car
Getting to school late to first period
Trying to understand math so early in the morning
After that class I was awake
Then the other classes made me sleepy
Then so happy that school is over
Waiting for my sister at her cheerleading
Having no decision at dinner
Cleaning up for bed
Saying my prayers and giving thanks on the day
Then reading and going to bed
My school day is done

Kyle Austin, Grade 7
Linfield Christian School

Get Out Alive

I must run.
I must run for survival.
If I don't, the monster, LIFE, will catch up with me.
I'm still running.
With my lungs protesting and my heart pounding.
My body begging me to stop.
But I can't.
I need to be free.
I need to get out alive.
I reach the edge of the cliff, knowing I can't look back.
Death is waiting for me back there.
If I look back I'm his.
I look down.
I see the endless drop.
I close my eyes and jump.
I spread my wings and a smile creeps across my face.
I am free.
I got out alive.

Megan Mann, Grade 8
Lloyd G Johnson Jr High School

The Lion

Once upon a time
In a kingdom far away
There was a boy with a lion
That would never ever stray
The cat was but a faithful one
He would prey upon his stalks
His weight is about one thousand tons
Of courage and heart they talk
But one there was an incident
A long and as far away
A wizard with special powers and had magic say;
"Boom! Red, yellow, green, white
Make a dragon gold and bright!"
The next day was a fateful one
The dragon came to town
He burned the houses and stomped the fields
With the lion he dragged down

Daniel Nofal, Grade 7
St Patrick Parish School

Life

Life is like a plant,
You are planted into this world.
You are given water and nurtured by the sun;
You try to get the highest point.
You are at the top and you are a big beautiful flower,
But whatever goes up must come down.
You whither and turn yellow,
Then you crumble into dust.

Mohammad Zalal, Grade 8
Santa Rosa Technology Magnet School

Your World

The setting sun,
the rising moon.
The fun is about to begin.

You enter your world,
Where you see teachers
as pets, and dancing pencils.

Cars that fly, guns that
Shoot flowers that
hop, jump, and scatter.

There is a war.
A war between math books
and students.

The charging starts,
there is no way out.
It is starting,
but who will win?

Wake up, it is
time for school.

Marsha Thomas, Grade 8
William Finch Charter School

The First Time

The first time I looked at you
I knew it was love at first sight
The first thing I noticed of you
Were your beautiful eyes in the light

The first time I looked at you
I knew that I would care
The first time I hugged you
I could smell your golden blonde hair

The first time I held your hand
I knew you were kind of nervous
The first time our hands touched
They were a cold icy surface

The first time I kissed you
I knew my lips could dance
The first time we met
My heart was like a lance
For you

Isaac Robinson, Grade 8
Valley Oak Middle School

Cherry Blossom Trees

They are beautiful
They are pink, some can be red
They are in Japan

Demoree Martinez, Grade 8
Almond Tree Middle School

Absence

True happiness is a feeling that is so scarce and rare,
When everything is perfect and all is right and fair.
The world around you melts away, your troubles disappear.
Everything that was strange to you turns bright and crystal clear.

And hope gives you something to work for and a reason to life.
It fuels your every action and thought, no matter how much the strife.
But these, however, are only two feelings, and to others you will succumb.
The others are much more harsh and are what we must overcome.

When sadness overwhelms you, you drift into despair.
Good things are forgotten, and life seems so unfair.
Anger and hatred are hard to withstand.
What makes it worse, they come hand in hand.

Then fears can start to come alive in a horrible nightmare.
Fear makes dread creep up your spine and becomes what you can't bear.
Uncertainty clouds your thoughts and you question what lies ahead.
Hesitating and doubting every move and wondering if you've been misled.

Regret of something you have done spreads guilt across your soul.
Then it starts to feel even worse when you know you have no control.
True happiness is a feeling that is so scarce and rare,
So rare that it is barely found, and hardly ever there.

Mingjiang Yue, Grade 7
Challenger School – Ardenwood

Snow

Softness swallow, soles sink seemingly.
Each step against the roaring winds, is closer home.
Homesickness fills my heavy heart.
A trail of footsteps stalks me.
The cold heat of the sun barely seeps through these clouds of grief.
Surrounded by a white blanket that masks the terrain, I am.
My memory has left me
A haze is what I merely recollect.
Nothing is found.
For this eternity of white has separated my family.
All hope is lost.
Being lost is a silent disaster.
I wander in circles still.
Icy tears roll down my face.
Snowflakes dance gracefully, falling to their deaths.
All is wet and cold.
The ice bites with malice.
Numbness sweeps over my senses.
I long for my family's return.
Their presence still lingers.
This is their silky graver, evermore.

Sally Corvacho, Grade 9
Fountain Valley High School

Bob the Pumpkin

'Twas the twenty-ninth of October, and without a doubt,
This was the best pumpkin I've ever picked out.

This'll be great, I thought with a smile.
If I don't carve him out, he'll last for a while!

Then I considered adding facial expressions.
All the possibilities…Too many to mention.

Bob, for that was his name now, looked good. Then I chose
to glue on some eyes and a cotton ball nose.

And then after pouring out my blood, sweat, and tears,
The pumpkin looked great! He had smiles, not sneers.

And so I kept him, but by week sixteen,
He didn't look good. He was moldy and green.

Then the garbage man came and took Bob away,
Down to the dump where he'd surely stay.

In conclusion, Bob was the best pumpkin I've seen.
I can only just wait 'til the next Halloween!

Nathaniel Skillman, Grade 7
Ruth Paulding Middle School

My Driving Force

Beauty is not on the surface
But hidden beneath the skin
Where the heart lies to the face
And deceives its own kin

The kin is very upset
Because it knows of a noble fact
That may save the mind from fret
But cannot seem to control its act

There is something about this kin —
It lays greedily within
Just as a half is a whole,
It is surely out of control
(It can also destroy your soul)

Just as I wonder what it is that I hear?
My heart whispers to my ear,
"Do not care what others think of you.
Don't be afraid to do something new."

My kin is my knowledge, my power, my strength.
It is my driving force.
My kin is what I need to achieve great lengths.

Vanessa Lam, Grade 7
Sussman Middle School

Their Shadow

Black tears run down the faces of our once lost.
Knees give out and heart stops beating.
Love's last touch brought us together.
And black winds sorrow tore us apart.
They grieve the loss of their families.
But mourn the loss of their lovers.
Shaded behind the shadow
Of one-hundred people who don't approve.
I loved you
I missed you
I held you in my arms so they wouldn't take you away.
To my sorrow they slipped you out.
Now I'm alone.
I'll always love you.
Forget me not.

Jimmy French, Grade 8
Holy Family Catholic School

An Onlook of the Heart

Oh, how fickle is the heart?
At times it can be so very sweet and very tart,
But from this tartness comes the side of us
That brings order to the chaos and fuss.
As to the sweet which is naught but kind,
That helps even the blind
See with clarity.
Of course, such a balanced heart is seen rarely.
Many have hearts dark and cold,
Which can cause even a newborn to grow old
At a glance.
In the odd chance
That a heart is not filled with eternal black,
The good must overwhelm and shove it in the back.
Then the heart shines and makes an angelic song
So that all lonely things may see, hear, and know
What is right and what is wrong.

Graham Frazier, Grade 8
Valley Oak Middle School

The Space Between

The space between us fills, as we get closer
But there is something still missing.
We laugh and smile and have fun together

But what can still be missing?

Ah! I know what it is, the three words
I want you to say, "I love you,"
But say them before the day is over
Because I want you more than ever.
Everyone likes you except a few
But you're always sweet to me and that's all that matters
So say those three words that are so dear to me
Before we got our separate ways and scatter.

Gracie Garcia, Grade 9
Foothill Technology High School

Second Chances

The very first time
I saw you, I missed you.
Your face and your smile,
And your words, through and through.

And bounded by love,
I sought no other.
Because with love and war,
Man fights their brother.

With heart in heart,
And hand in hand;
And heart-set lovers,
So pure like sand.

But when you leave
Which I know will be soon,
Promise to remember me
Like I'll remember you.

So now that you're gone,
Let God see you through,
And don't you worry,
'Cause I'll be there soon.
Erin Jarvis, Grade 7
Holy Family Catholic School

Sun-Star

Up she rises
shining bright
Golden capes
with rays alight

Hot and yellow
that is she
Scorching the land
for all to see

She is the light
that roosters turn on
by croaking
her favorite song

She is the star
biggest of all
She causes fires
and climbs the wall

She falls
at the horizon
Morning tomorrow
then she rises
Miranda Poltorak, Grade 7
Lewis Middle School

Believing Lies

Funny when things never change
even when you say they will
But while you're off pursuing her
my life is standin' still

You tell me that you love me
when I go to leave
You tell me I'm your only one
and I let myself believe

I know that you are using me
but you'll never let me go
I know that you don't love me
I know I'm just for show

I don't know if I can stand
to see you love another girl
You know that you broke my heart
you know that you're my world

But while you're standing by my side
I'll believe your lies forever
'Cause everything seems so perfect
when we are together
Ashley Imel, Grade 8
Holy Family Catholic School

Football (or Soccer)

Here is the game,
The game of fashion,
The sport that's fun,
Played with passion.

Played on a field,
Artificial or real,
Or even indoors,
It's all the same deal.

A game played with feet,
Not with the hands.
Strategy and style,
It's not even planned!

There is a sport
Played all year 'round.
Also played in the streets
To amaze and astound.

It is the sport
To pass, shoot, or lob (err),
It is the sport known
As football (or soccer).
Anthony Ynami, Grade 8
Corpus Christi School

In My Sister's Hair

I have put gum
In my sister's hair.

Gum you would
Want to chew on all day long.

Sorry I put it there
While you were sleeping.

I don't know it's like
It just got up and walked there.

I know that was mean,
But now I feel sad,
Though it's payback from
When you got me mad.

I had to put it there,
Because it was pay back from the heart.
David Garcia, Grade 8
Madrona Middle School

Regrets

Learn from your regrets
but never forget
once you've made that mistake
you can't go back and fix it
Kassandra Mayer, Grade 7
Sarah McGarvin Intermediate School

Song of Nature

Morning dew awakes the rising sun,
Stretching along the sky.
Drip drop drip.

The earliest bird awakes sleepily.
As it lets out its hunger cry.
Eek eep eek.

Wind yawns from tiredness,
Rustling the grass and trees.
Whew phew whew.

Rolling hills rise and mountain tops,
Sitting on their knees.
Crack shake crack.

Sounds of earth,
Noise of sky.
Every morning,
As they try
Singing the songs of nature.
Emily Beauchamp, Grade 8
Chino Valley Christian Schools

Me and You

Remember me and you?
Those years were definitely true.
For only your words can make me blue.
So this is my ode for you.
You are not dead but only our friendship is.
If I can have one more thing from you would be your soft kiss.
It is only you who can put me into my own bliss.
But now our friendship is done.
And I feel all so dumb.
And not being with you makes me so numb.
So follow the beat of the drum.
And maybe we'll be together again.
Maybe we'll be together in the end.
Oh maybe oh maybe
Oh you were as beautiful as life.
Oh I wish you could be my wife.
Maybe when books fly they say.
Will our friendship be good enough to stay.
Oh maybe oh maybe.

Rafael Salazar, Grade 8
Valley Oak Middle School

A Stranger at My Door

Who is knocking at my door?
A stranger on my doorstep
So loud and boisterous the knocker sounds
I can't bear it anymore.

A stranger on my doorstep
At this time of night
I can't bear it anymore
Slipping and stumbling I run to the door.

At this time of night
Who can it be?
Slipping and stumbling I run to the door
Finally reaching that front door I open.

Who is knocking at my door?
So loud and boisterous the knocker sounds
Who can it be?
Finally reaching that front door I open.

Shirley Qi, Grade 9
Monta Vista High School

Spring

The pure blue sky right above my head
The smell of summer is already near
Yellow dandelions in a clay vase near my bed
The sound of sizzling heat and nature, the silence of the forest,
Splashes of icy cool water on my tanned skin
Rough sand between my toes
All that has blossomed in my heart and been
Spring leads to summer, and summer is over in a moment…

Anya Jackovich, Grade 8
St John of San Francisco Orthodox Academy

Dirt Covered Diamonds

You wake to the sound of gunfire
Wonder whose turn it was to die.
It's become like background noise,
No longer gives you reason to cry.

You wander through the streets,
No littered with broken dreams.
For now all is peaceful,
Or so it only seems…

For you know not to believe,
That things will be okay,
Soon clouds of smoke will invade the sky,
Blocking out the sun's meager rays.

This is what your life would be,
If you were a child of war.
You'd see explosions through your window,
Destruction at your door.

You'd be abandoned potential,
Roaming the streets.
A diamond in the rough,
With dirt at your feet.

Nida Aslam, Grade 9
Fountain Valley High School

Sorrow

Have you ever felt sorrow?
I mean you really felt it
The pain closing in on you
The hurt and agony is too much to bear

You think all hope is lost.
You feel down and out
You don't feel important
You feel depressed and afflicted

Be honest.
Have you every truly felt miserable?
You felt like no one knew the true you.
You were carrying the weight of the world.
It's a horrid feeling.

If you've been there, I know what you want.
You want a peaceful way out.
You want a friend to be there for you.

Now let me tell you what you need.
You need prayer.
You need God.

Simone Taylor, Grade 7
Southpointe Christian School

Moon

The moon is like a single woman
Always alone without a partner
Envies all the stars,
Who have each other

The moon has no one to love,
Even with the bright light that it has,
No one wants to dance with her.

The moon is like a single woman
It travels every day
Around Earth to find someone,
But is always as lonely as ever

Julia Choi, Grade 8
Madrona Middle School

Learning Is a Pain

French is a pain,
But there's a lot to gain,
For, it won't be in vain
It's pretty much the same,
So there is nothing left to blame,
Much is to be proud of
Because really, it's not that rough
It takes time and dedication,
And dedication takes time
Learning another language
Is not a crime.

Maria Alonzo, Grade 7
John Adams Middle School

The World

In the world there's many things.
There's trees and colors
and rainbows and animals.
Now slowly and slowly
one thing is happening
I guess nobody knows
our trees are disappearing
while our wilderness goes
we have to help it survive
if you want to stay alive.

Antonio Montes, Grade 7
St Vincent Elementary School

Honey

I have a dog
Her name is Honey.
She enjoys long naps
Under the warm sun.
Honey barks a lot
And annoys me so much.
But at the end of the day
She is my little sister.

Anitzel Montes, Grade 7
St Vincent Elementary School

Springfield

Welcome to Springfield!
I know it looks a little weird but there's no need to frown,
Here we have a power plant, a video arcade, and a very famous clown.
Oh, I see you've noticed that everyone who lives here is yellow.
Don't worry about that though; most people who live here are pretty mellow.
And we've only had 50 car accidents this month, that's not so bad.
Oh, I see that's made you kind of sad.
Well, I'm sure that when I'm done you'll just be fine.
Because a gallon of gas here is only 15 dimes!
Now I can see a slight grin on your face.
So now allow me to talk about Springfield Elementary; it's a marvelous place!
There are some cool things here and there
Plus the teachers here will give you love and care.
So what do you think?
It's great right?
O.K. you'll be moved in by tonight!

Grant Rickman, Grade 7
Holy Family Catholic School

Tropical Rainforest

Green grass with fresh dew
Tall Redwood trees, with monkeys swinging from branch to branch
Shadows lurking in the dark, looking for their prey
Beautiful waterfalls hitting the ocean's floor with a huge splash
Rain trickling to the ground with soft thumps
Birds chirping their songs of joy, in the early morning
Sweet juicy strawberries picked at perfection
Hidden treasures in the heart of the jungle
Treasures of joy, happiness, and pure bliss
Native animals exploring their homeland
Rich and diverse
Undisturbed peace
A dreamland, filled with paradise.

Isaac Halasa, Grade 9
Gunderson High School

The Samurai

The samurai stood in the war fronts with their saddle, horse, and sword
Armor made of strong metal scales laced together with the finest silken cord
A fierce gaze lined their faces as they prepared for combat
Ready to die,
Willing to fight,
And hoping to win,
The samurai announced the war call
The bow casters shot with skillful aim
The horsemen attacked with all their might
The enemies won and lived but the samurai did not
They might have died,
But their legacy lives on with us
Of the fearsome and brave samurai who were
Ready to die,
Willing to fight,
And hoping to win.

Mahnoor Saleem, Grade 7
Sinaloa Middle School

Friendship: The Ship That Never Sinks

Sometimes when I am all alone,
As I lay motionless just like a stone.
I decide to talk to my friend on the phone
And from then on I never start to moan.

Have you ever been alone and had no fun?
You can call a friend and your life has begun.
Friends are the people you can trust,
Your bond of trust will be a must.

When you stand up and look in a mirror,
You will see your friend as a brother.
All the happiness a friend will bring,
Will make your joyful heart ring.

Friendship will help you understand life,
And help you if you are in a severe strife.
Friends are generous, cheerful, and kind,
They give suggestions from the top of their minds.

Though friends will not always be together,
The memories of them will be forever.
The connection of friendship will always have many links,
After all, friendship is the only ship that never sinks.

Harish Shanker, Grade 8
Challenger School – Ardenwood

Day After Christmas

December 26th was the day,
when everything was still and gray.
Nothing here seemed to be right.
I felt something go down my cheek,
it seems as though my eyes can leak.
Someone is no longer here,
I feel my heart begin to disappear.

My heart is now like a sinking boat,
everything goes and nothing floats.
Who it is that I have lost,
it's someone who's without a cost.
I know that they wouldn't want me to cry,
but if I say I won't then I would lie.
But because I miss them way too much,
my stomach sometimes begins to bunch.

So to my grandpa up in heaven,
since I think I was eleven.
Just to remind you,
unless you already know,
that I still really love you,
but never wanted you to go!

Rebecca Alvarez, Grade 8
Almondale Middle School

My Passion

The lights dim down, as my nervous hands come up
A fast beat song turns on, and my feet jump up
But it is not just any old song that I dance to
It is my culture, my tradition, my life
There are hundreds of varieties you could choose to dance
Yet I chose to do Indian, Bollywood, dancing
This represents my religion, as well as me
I show who I am through dancing,
With sharp facial expressions through fast movements
Along with jumps and skips, as well as turns and spins
I dance for me, not because I am told to
At parties and ceremonies, you will see me perform
There is no word to express my feelings about dance
Maybe some phrases, but no exact words
When I dance I feel free
No slights could bring me down
Dance is a part of me
If there was no dance, I would not be who I am today.

Abi Raja, Grade 9
Hemet High School

Electricity

Electricity, how it powers everything,
How we depend on it so much.
We use it for many things,
Like our houses and such.
It is very important in our daily lives,
But what should happen when the electricity dies.
A great pandemonium may break out in the streets,
Or some may go crazy, whomever you meet.
A blackout can happen anytime, anywhere,
So always be very prepared.
Electricity is like an addiction of power,
It makes us want to use more and more.
So there is no real downside to electricity,
But be careful because you never want to get addicted.

Aaron Fortelny, Grade 7
St Hilary Elementary School

Conversation with an Angel

A diamond illuminating the shady cliffs
It is an angle in gray robes, with heavy wings it lifts.
Moving towards sky, moving toward the rising sun
Your journey is far from done.

Where were you going? Where have you been?
Will I ever see you again?
Moving toward the sky, moving toward the rising sun
Your journey is far from done.

You are headed toward your destination.
I won't forget our conversation.
Moving toward the sky, moving toward the rising sun
Your journey is far from done.

Daniel Kodama, Grade 8
Santa Rosa Technology Magnet School

Why

Why am I alive breathing today? Heading in paths of sin looking and talking the wrong way
Why do I see things in a perspective that no one else can? Just living for the next day going through life without a plan

Why am I so depressed and filled with sorrow? Trapped in the dark with no light to follow
Why has my life had such a downfall entering in a teenage world? My uncle says it is more to life than trying to be the bad girl

Why isn't it so easy to do right? Fear hits me every day telling myself I will make it if I hold on tight
Why do I say things I don't want to say or think? Since my grandpa died my ship of hope has started to sink

Why do I fear of being alone up above? It's like I don't have anyone to look up to, no one to love
Why don't my family try to understand knowing they have turned away leaves me with my heart in my hand

Why can't someone hold me and help me achieve tell me they care, show me so I can believe
Why do I hold so much anger inside? Sometimes I wish that I could just curl up and hide

Why when I look for a way to get by?   Something hits me with thunder, hard enough to make a grown man cry
Why is my days going by so fast? Thinking of the next day unable to forget my past

I'm still waiting for the day when I can answer my whys and loosen the chain so I no longer will have to suffer the pain

Vernia Short, Grade 7
Stephens Middle School

Faith

Cold water splashed against my bare feet, I could feel the terror rise in my throat
As if telling me to run to the beat, of the rain crashing down on my ragged coat
While the Jewish never gave up their faith

At the camp, we have lost all of our hope, families are separated as if they were slaves
When you take showers, you don't get water or soap, instead you get gas in order to stop the raves
But the Jewish never gave up their faith

The Star of David cries out with a plea, it is like a symbol of their suffering
The Nazis continue to watch with glee, as the innocent Jews continue their marching
But the Jewish never gave up their faith

As tired as one could possibly be, branded like cattle but too exhausted to rage
Everyone paid the immense racism fee, it did not matter your gender or age
But the Jewish never gave up their faith

I stare into the distance, the incarcerating gate is ahead, I hear the murmured shouting from those who are around
All I am thinking about is my old warm bed, then loud shots go off and I fall to the ground
But I never gave up my faith

Lauren Trambley, Grade 8
Sacred Heart School

Grades, Grounded, Graduation, God!

Staring at the rain pouring down my window wishing my grades wouldn't have gone so low. Wishing I would have listened and studied. Being grounded isn't the funnest thing, staying out of trouble is the hardest, but at least I was honest. I had been getting into trouble and flunking tests, but now I'm facing the end. Graduation is almost here, a time to be happy and thankful for everyone who has helped you get this far. Study harder, do all of my homework and keep focused is what I'll do. So when the day arrives I'll graduate just like you. God will help me too. God will stay by my side to guide me through my last days as an eighth grader.

Bianca A. Henderson, Grade 8
St Mary's School

A Soul Without a Path

Forced through the devil's gate
Marked with the numbers of death
Going through constant pain
Without a person to blame
Standing in line, with no decision to live
Waiting to breathe that glorious relief
With no name for this hatred
The cries, the struggles, the journey of neverending
Leading to their tragic slaughter
All caused by the devil's promises
Who accomplished his desires
Of locking their souls forever in their graves

Esmeralda Escarzaga, Grade 9
Francisco Bravo Medical Magnet High School

Twilight Once More

The darkest moiety through thy inner day's worth,
Troubled by the honor of another
Prevailed upon, turned to the lambent sun
But success shall not proceed

As arrogant as my inner part
Determined to refrain —
None so lacked as the piece I'm missing
The incandescent darkness yet blinded by light

Change, for change's worth —
Perceives as no more than a folly
Why correct the one all so wholesome?
The one that puts the sun at dusk

Yet there always has been the time of dawn
Penetrating each and every fragment of dark
Tearing a hole through my body's worth
And letting the lustrous light ramble through

Have your time before twilight comes once more.

Laura Farris, Grade 7
Holy Family Catholic School

Beauty of Nature

Flowers bloom in the rays of light,
Colors amazing, a wonderful delight,
On the ground or in the trees,
They float slightly with a little breeze,
It's amazing how fast time goes by,
When you're just lying there watching with human eyes.

You watch the flowers and hear the sounds,
The music of nature is all around,
Birds singing the songs of day and night,
Songs far more colorful than black and white,
It's hard to believe how amazing it can be,
All you have to do is listen to be set free.

Alexa Robinson, Grade 8
St Hilary School

Enjoying the Journey Ahead

Two paths, two choices
Which will I choose?
One leads back home
The other shows no clue
Should I take a risk?

Do I want to enjoy each passing day?
or live life regretting my decision?
Which will I choose?
Pondering, pondering on this thought,
I look down the old, but unused road.

Seeing only as far as the dense forest allowed
Down the other, the sun shines bright
beckoning me to lay in its warmth
I make my decision, my choice.
Trotting down the mysterious path

Ignoring the shining sun
Moving forward with my life
Strong and free, I take the path I choose,
Following it until the end.
Enjoying the journey ahead.

Karissa Cristiano, Grade 9
Westview High School

Touch of Love

Love, described as the rollercoaster of our lives.
It has its ups, its downs, twists and turns
Yet, it is often what we all yearn to have.
The infatuated feeling leaving us breathless.

Every beginning has an end, but love has much more to teach.
Fragile as a broken heart, it can stab you, shatter you, and yet,
Make you giggle.
For love, it gives many emotions.

It's the wounds that won't seem to heal
From the rise and fall of the ride.
Time cannot erase
The pain that's just too real.

You must overcome the obstacle drops,
Strive to stay strong, forgive but don't forget
All the memories we hold deep in our hearts.
It's love that makes us that much vulnerable.

The morose will conquer the joyous state of mind
Which leaves us back in sorrow.
Hatred and regret come pouring in.
For it's love that can kill us in just one moment's time.

Grace Huang, Grade 8
Madrona Middle School

Basketball

A basketball is always in my hands
It is never out of sight
You can complain after a loss
Or can celebrate after a win
But it depends on how much you want it
And that is why I like it

Jared Biggs, Grade 7
Holy Family Catholic School

Sunlight

A bright ball leaps
Over the morning clouds
As the sun descends to earth.

Pure heavenly fire comes
Pouring out unceasing light
Over the tallest mountain tops

Light pierces through the sky
Painting the world with colors,
All around the passing water.

Bringing brightness everywhere
To all the things that matter

Derek Huddleston, Grade 8
Madrona Middle School

Ode to Hockey

passing the puck
don't skate like a Duck

swerve through the defender
fire at the goal tender

puck sails
crowd wails

hit the pole
NO GOAL!!

goalie has it
the standing fans sit

face-off, pass, score
fans stand and adore

the players skate 'til they were in pain
but it was all in vain

the score was 1-nil
at the buzzer's shrill

another hockey game
this sport is anything but lame

Derick Baker, Grade 8
La Joya Middle School

My Office

They come into my office every day
earaches, backaches, stomachaches
I give them some Advil and send them on their way
they complain over nothing
There are little kids
with pinto beans in their ear
I pull them out
they may shed a little tear
others have broken ribs, what a blast
broken tibulas, fibulas
I take their x-ray and give them a cast
they got lucky
others aren't too lucky and come in my office too late
their symptoms have one dreadful fate
But there is one thing I can do
Make them feel loved and comfortable as I watch and view
Their slow and painful last breath
Through my job I have learned to appreciate what I have
I have watched people lose the best things in their lives before their eyes
And they finally realize when their heart is numb and torn in two
that they should have appreciated that person a little more

Elise Anderson, Grade 8
La Joya Middle School

Nature's Bulldog: Water

Covering almost three-fourths of the entire planet Earth,
Water flows to and fro with such an enormous worth.
Being destructive throughout the whole of Earth's entire days,
It carves out valleys, canyons, and removes silt with large display.

Yet this is an important part of all of Earth's long life.
It may be destructive alone, but without it there is strife.
All animals need it, mammal, reptile, fish and bird.
For living things to live without it, it would be absurd.

Man, though, depends on water more than animals for everything.
So much so that people worship water like a popular king.
Civilizations grew near water over periods of Earth's entire time,
Thriving on the silt for farms, making the economy slowly climb.

But, when all the water stops flowing to men altogether,
People fight each other and pray to gods for rainy weather.
Will that work? We cannot say at all, yes or even no.
As you can see, we are slaves of water, Nature's strong dynamo.

Water is a very important substance to everything and everyone.
This substance, water, is, I think, even better than our glorious sun.
Even though all life treats water as a strong and exploited slave,
Water is man's master, for without it, people misbehave.

Mark Chen, Grade 7
Challenger School – Ardenwood

Juanita the Tortilla Girl

I see you in your corner making delicious tortillas
And I know in my heart you're no novice tortilla maker
And you make them warm and special for me
There are irresolute feelings between us
For you I feel adulation
You resuscitated my heart and my taste buds
Your tortillas make my hunger abate

Juanita the tortilla girl
At the tortilla station
You give me the deal
And tell me how you feel
Warm and buttery delicious and delicate
Flaky and flavorful
Tortillas transcending time itself

Juanita the tortilla girl
At the tortilla station
They melt in my mouth
On every occasion
Juanita the tortilla girl
This is coming to an end but I know that in my heart
You'll always be my special tortilla girl

Eric Aberbook, Grade 7
The Mirman School

Soccer

My favorite sport is soccer
I play it all the time
I try to keep school in my head
But I'm even thinking about soccer while writing this rhyme

The thrill of when you kick a goal
It is the best feeling ever
You feel so very tall
And also proudly clever

My team is the Loomis Lightning
We may not always come out on top
But we never get too rowdy,
They have never had to call a cop

It's exciting when you are dribbling down the field
And defeat is looking you straight in the eye
Then you score the winning goal
And after go for a pizza pie

So in conclusion, everyone should play soccer
Every day, every day
It doesn't matter where you are
Just get out and play!

Connor Ward, Grade 7
Holy Family Catholic School

Champion

I step onto the block,
Everyone watches.
Like a train speeding through my head,
I worry.
I hear the beep and dive into the pool,
Fast as lightning,
Graceful as a ballerina.
A sudden rush of cold water covers my body.
I swim my heart out.
So many hours of training,
Such a swift sport.
Nothing feels exactly like I do when I step out of the pool.
Passionate, happy, a champion.
You can never take that away.

Shelby Soltau, Grade 8
St Joseph's School of the Sacred Heart

The Desert

The desert is a very silent place
No one is around to share the wonder
Of a vast, star-studded sky.

Snakes slither in the warm sand
While coyotes howl at the glistening moon
Daylight will be coming soon.

There is much desert land
Mile after mile of space
Sandstorms swirl round and round
Tumble weeds twist and turn upside down
The desert is a very silent place.

Jared Allred, Grade 8
Madrona Middle School

I Love You

I never said I love You
I never said I cared
Even though I miss you
I know you won't be there

Forgetting you I will never
Even though it bothers me that you're gone
I know it's just the beginning
Loving you so much hurts to see you gone

Wondering if you can hear me
God answered my prayers that day
He took you out of your pain
but you won't be here to stay

I will always love you
No matter what I say or do
You will always be in my heart
I just wanted to let you know "I Love You"

Isela Retana-Torres, Grade 7
St Hilary Elementary School

A Figure of Your Imagination

I am your imagination
I wonder why you think of me
I hear your thoughts
I see nothing but your happiness
I want you to free yourself from dread
I am your imagination

I pretend nothing wrong will happen
I feel joy
I touch everything you dream
I worry nightmares will take over
I cry you to sleep with happy dreams
I am your imagination

I understand you want anything but bad
I say 'go for it'
I dream your dreams
I try to see the real you
I am your imagination

Ariel Martin, Grade 7
Lawson Middle School

A Day in the Park

Dark, lonely park,
Its trees as tall
As skyscrapers
A woman fed birds
Handfuls of seeds
Birds chirped happily
Excited about all the food
They were given.
Morning, new day, new life
Sunshine gleaming in your eyes
Children running, yellow
But not in the now-deserted park
It has been dark now for hours.

Ricardo Olivares, Grade 7
St Alphonsus School

Someday

Someday there will be no wars,
We will settle with words.

Someday there will be no hunger,
All children will eat a hamburger.

Someday there will be no crime,
All people will be nice.

Someday there will be no illegal drugs,
We will be safe on the road.

It will happen, someday,
Not so far away.

Arturo Sanchezdiaz, Grade 7
Linfield Christian School

Traffic Cone

I am a traffic cone red, orange, white.
I block off trouble zones in the dead of night.
I work day or night an emergency worker's friend.
Isolating people from the blight of humanity's self-destructing trend.

The rain are my tears flowing down my paralyzed form.
Alerting you of brutal fears from the streets to the dorms.
Knocked over, left to rot in the roar of a frantic race for survival.
Years of service, for naught watching humanity fight for revival.

Cowering like a prisoner in the mud unable to alert you.
Of the danger in each man's blood, the danger that never seems to be few.
However, I am finally in peace. No noticeable need to be in constant sight.
But if you ever search east don't pull out the red, orange, and white.

Francis Libiran and Sean Tsai, Grade 7
St Patrick Parish School

Gone*

He is holding me
Drying my tears,
As I cope with the fact that you are no longer here,
As I face my fears.

His hands are big and gentle
As He coaxes me to state what I feel
And I feel better knowing that you're in a better place
Away from the chaos and pain.

He is my leader
And I am His follower;
He is my lord
And I am His believer;
He is God
And He stood by me as I dealt with the fact that you were no longer here…

Katie Rios, Grade 7
Rogers Middle School
*Dedicated to Danny

Splinter

Running on the deck, a shade of light cocoa powder
Running not knowing what lurked in the wood
Pit pat pit pat my feet lightly touched the ground
One step too soon, a slish, a shard of wood slid easily into my foot
Then the pain, first just a poking then as I looked down
An incomprehensible pain gripped me
Which increased as my fear heightened
I grabbed my "blankie"
Squeezing it tight as tears effortlessly slid down my face
1…2…3
The splinter slowly pulled out of my foot
Resisting to let go of its new home
With one final tug it came out and I relaxed
The piece of wood would have to find a new home soon

Katrina Nibbi, Grade 8
St Joseph's School of the Sacred Heart

My Mother

My mother is the world
   the sun
   the stars
   and the moon
she is the world for that's how much she loves me
she is the sun for how she warms me when I'm in her arms
she is the stars for the twinkle in her eye when she looks at me
she is the moon for watching me when I sleep.
My mother is all these things and so much more.

Desiree Luna, Grade 7
Almond Tree Middle School

I Am So Sorry

I am so sorry,

Sorry that I drew all over your face
but you should've seen your silly smile,
you looked like a crazy clown,

Sorry that I tied your shoes in a knot
but you should've seen how clumsily you fell,
you were like a toothpick trying to stand,

Sorry that I hid all of your toys in your backyard
but you should've seen your face in so much horror,
you were like a tiny toddler who just lost his mom,

Sorry that I have done all of these horrendous,
horrible things to you
but can't you forgive me?

Jesse Gi, Grade 8
Madrona Middle School

Hatred

Hatred is a demon.
He is a master of demise.
He lures you to do things
That are not very wise.
Hatred builds up inside you.
It creates stress and makes you feel blue.
When you can't hold it in any longer,
Boom! It explodes right out of you.
Unkind things burst out of your lips.
You can't control what you say or do.
Finally, you calm down,
And realize hatred had taken over you.
Hatred tears you apart.
It destroys you inside out.
Get rid of it as soon as you can.
Otherwise you'll become an evil man.
Hatred's face shines to those of immense evil,
Yet does not appear to those free of enemies.
Getting rid of your hatred
Is like getting a great trophy of glory.

Sujay Tadwalkar, Grade 7
John F Kennedy Middle School

Fear

Fear is a place between heaven and hell
Where we really are, we really can't tell
Fear is a thing inside of us all
Sometimes we can hear it, its loud frightened call
And sometimes the fear is as lost as can be
But once you tell it, we can all see
A little white angel with silky black wings
Is the fear inside us, and it always sings
"Wherever we are it's so hard to tell
But we know it's between heaven and hell"

Paige Valentine, Grade 8
Eagle Peak Middle School

Tomorrow

Why wait until the end is near?
Don't let death become your greatest fear
Don't wait until the end comes close
Until you realize what you love the most

Never forget the days you had
Even though they were really sad
Hold dear life with all your might
Because you'll never know when you'll see the light

Not knowing what will happen next
That's truly knowledge you know the best
Counting days is wasting time
Loving people doesn't cost a dime

Even though life's unfair
At least you're living with people who care
Stop clouding your mind of hatred and sorrow
Don't waste your time, there's always tomorrow

Julie Takigawa, Grade 8
Madrona Middle School

Right vs Wrong

You may think you're always right
They may think you're always wrong
But when it comes to fight
Everything will just go wrong

It's always hard to say I'm sorry
To the person you have hurt
Because it might make things worse
With words you just blurt

It always hurts a person with what you say
And it always hurts with what you do
That's why, you think before you say
And think before you do

Kara Tiqui, Grade 8
Calvary Chapel of YL

Away!*

I am going away,
I don't know how long.
It may be forever
but I just don't know.

I leave behind all my
friends and family in town.
Let them be free
and let me be free too!

Don't think I leave for good,
I will be back from
my trip away.

When I am back I will
bring you something good
from my experience on my
trip away.

Unless I am wrong
I may never be
back, but you might
find me wherever you are.
Desiree Seng, Grade 9
The Winston School
*Inspired by Robert Frost

Little Kitten

Little kitten sleeping tight,
Longing to be a cat,
Dreaming of being free,
Roaming in night's light.

Little kitten drinking milk,
Wishing to be loyal,
Wants a lady that's nice and friendly,
Wraps him in silk.

Little kitten chewing fish,
Wanting to catch his own,
Washing it down with milk,
Then the lady cleans the dish.

Little kitten loves the lady,
He purrs in her lap,
He will take a short nap,
Now pets her baby.

Little kitten has grown up,
Little lady has become old,
Cat now sits in her lap,
Little old lady loves him from bottom up.
Balentin Lugo, Grade 7
Almond Tree Middle School

My Tragic Love Story

I was in love,
Whenever he passed by,
My heart would race.
He was my natural high.

He'd always call me
To see how was my day.
When I was sad he'd hold me
And ask if I was okay.

But then he likes someone else
And my whole heart shatters.
I'd spend all night crying because to me,
He was the only one that matters.

After going through
All of this agonizing pain,
I realized that without him
I'd be lost, I'd go insane.

My days were quiet and gloomy,
With no more fun and laughter.
For me this was the end
Of my happily ever after.
Kathy Bach, Grade 8
Meadowbrook Middle School

What I See in the World Today

What I see in the world today
Is horrid, which could be understood
I wish that I could change it all
If I only could

It's like darkness has taken over
And has blocked out the light
Turning happiness into hatred,
Making everything a fight

I see a funeral for a green woman
For she was killed by a green man
Who seeks the greed in people
In every single way he can

I see horror, I see blood
From an innocent soul
I see people with a heart
That is as black as coal

So what I see in the world today
Are all these horrid nightmares
Hurting, frightening, and killing
All the people whom they scare
Monica Hart, Grade 7
Serrano Middle School

Vacation

Tropical sunshine
Waves crashing onto the beach
Vacation awaits…
Jessica Atha, Grade 8
Citrus Hills Intermediate School

Fun Times

Fun, fun times
We had together.
My family as strong
As leather.
Through the rough
Times you can't see.
Fun, fun times
You see so well.
My family is a shooting star
But it's the brightest one
There can be.
Smiles on our faces
Like we had just won a million dollars.
We were together and happy
That's all that counts
Branches reaching out and
Trying to tear us apart.
But we were strong
We held together.
Fun, fun times
We will always have forever and ever.
Candace Fernandez, Grade 8
Valley Oak Middle School

Nature

Flowers blooming
Lush, green forests
Seem to never end,
Walking through the deep grass
With a friend
Never ending field

Leaves are gone
Here comes the winter
Still there is nature,
It is all around you
Even if trees seem all dead
The white fluffy snow is now there.

Nature is great
It is year round
Here comes spring again,
Flower's blooming
Lush green forests
Seem to never end…
Riley Torres, Grade 8
Santa Rosa Technology Magnet School

I Do Not Understand

I do not understand
why people harden their hearts
why they don't care
why our world has so many problems.
But most of all
I do not understand
why people strive for material things
(all this will amount to nothing when Jesus comes again).
What I do understand most are outreaches
they give a good feeling
when you help one another
you are fulfilling your call to be a light in a dark world.

Mitchell Johnson, Grade 8
Linfield Christian School

Heaven or Hell?

Heaven, where God lives and angels sing
Hell, where Satan reigns and people scream
Heaven, where we will walk on streets of gold
Hell, where people wish the streets were cold
Heaven, where we'll all be singing
Hell, where Satan is taunting, mocking, and laughing
Heaven, where we will all be given new bodies
Hell, where people's bodies are burning
Heaven, where mansions will be our next home
Hell, where there is no place to be called "home"
Heaven, where angels will be our friends
Hell, where demons are torturing people till the end
Heaven, where people are rejoicing
Hell, where people are begging for mercy
Heaven, where God will say,
"Come thou enter the joy of the Lord"
If you're on your way to Hell
Angels are commanded to throw you in there
Knowing that there is no way out
Where will you go?
Heaven or Hell?

Chloé Lynn Roland, Grade 9
Lighthouse Baptist Academy

A Child, the Butterfly

The blue and purple blending while they fly
The family, the trio, dreaming in the skies
The vast plains contain endless possibilities
Their eyes glitter with a spark of creativity
Educate themselves while they're away from the Earth
Again they learn to walk after the rebirth
Children laugh as days pass
They grow old, so old, really fast
The blue and purple blending while they fly
The family, the trio, dreaming in the skies

Adrian Garcia, Grade 9
Valhalla High School

Life Is a Waste of Death

Life is a waste of death
some brave enough to end their breath
We ignore him through our life
in the last hour we are filled with strife
Digging our nails on mor-tal-it-y
just to live once more in this wretched city
Alas no mortal can defeat him,
there is another deprived of sin

One in black — one in white
one to welcome, another to fight

He is two-faced, good and bad
though he is always sad
He sees his children sinful and killing
for all but him very thrilling
When horses and riders ride from the depths
there shall be many deaths
But not so cruel as solemn
when all, but me — have fallen

William Coulter, Grade 8
Green Acres Middle School

Ordinary

In the corner of a road, a single shoe rests,
Worn ragged from the ages
Bearing a number of mysterious adventures
Like a book with unread pages.
Maybe it was the polished boot
Of a general fighting a war
It could have sported the shiny spurs
That only cowboys bore
It's possible that its owner
Was a haughty, spoiled brat
That threw it out the window
In a fiery, screaming spat
Perhaps a homeless person
Then picked it up; it was almost new!
And used it as a homey friend
Until the soles were all worn through.
So many different exploits that
A single shoe could've traveled!
No careful observations
Can have all its journeys unraveled
A simple glance at the ordinary has me bedazzled.

Dahsohl Im, Grade 7
Pleasanton Middle School

Ode to Dogs

Dogs they are, dogs to me, I honor you.
Loving, strong, helpful, courageous, and man's best friend.
They help, they hunt, and best of all they hug.
When you're all alone remember the best of all friends
has four legs and wags his tail.

Gabe Gold, Grade 7
Santa Rosa Technology Magnet School

As I Stand Here

As I stand here,
Surrounded by a million people,
I wonder why I feel so alone.
The people around,
Don't seem to know
How I feel.
They may talk to me,
But I still feel alone.
They don't seem to know who I am.
I feel like a stranger or maybe a ghost,
Just wandering 'round
Not knowing who I am,
Nor what I want.
Nobody really knows me,
Even though they think they do.
I always have little secrets —
That are really not that little.
As I stand here,
Surrounded by a million people,
I wonder why I feel so alone.

Pilar Vasquez, Grade 7
Almond Tree Middle School

Surviving

My heart was racing
And my knees were trembling.
Then the judge called my
Name.

Butterflies were in the
Pit of my stomach.
All eyes were on me.
I had the fear of forgetting my poem.

I sped through my poem,
Trying not to forget anything.
At the end I got a huge applause.
It was over.

Taylor McCowan, Grade 8
La Joya Middle School

The Big Chance

I practice 24/7
In three days we do it
We figure out the song
"Let's get to it"
I'm nervous and scared
One hour to go
Can I do it
"Lets put on a show"
I get on stage
I got in line
The curtains flew open
And I did pretty fine

Alisa Caro, Grade 7
South Tahoe Middle School

I Love Everybody

You scream bloody murder and Hail Mary,
The tired and the timid crawl away, limp and dead; gnarled trees of the seasons of time
And you say I love everybody.
Raining so sweetly; tears of mine they are reaping.
I am not bullet proof,
Human like you; I kill too
Suicide, genocide, it's all inside
Their catharsis is tainted and unspoken; All for the gory
And I love everybody
Clipping and yelling: shoving and shouting
Your words don't affect me.
That foreign liquid dribbles from hidden scars; laughs of apathetic ridicule
Sick with guilt for the one taunted; oh haunted
No pity, unshakable like slabs of granite; frigid, hard of the heart
I rise for revenge of the fallen: oh so relentless and regrettable.
I love everybody. (yet I will not regret)
Chaos, the viper moves behind the pearls of teeth.
Ban of holy terror, sun rising in the east.
Ignorant rats dancing in filth, their pestilence, under the setting sun of the west
Vacant, white, don't stare back at me; my future regret; past ever fulfilled
And I said I love everybody.

Amanda Uyesugi, Grade 9
Presentation High School

Going Down Memory Lane

The end of middle school, it is a time for laughter and a time for tears,
Going down memory lane, cherishing experiences of past years.
I first came to this school, when I was a mere four years old,
From a shy little boy, I've grown more confident and bold.

The first time I received a scholarship was certainly sweet,
For the next four years, I continued to accomplish this feat.
Participating in school contests and programs sure was swell,
I hope these experiences will help me grow and excel.

I have had great companions that make me laugh and smile.
I know our strong friendships will definitely last a while.
Through my school, I have learned how important hard work can be,
I have always tried my best, and it has paid off for me.

To all my amazing teachers, I shall forever be in debt,
Constantly patient, and giving memories I'll never forget.
I consistently felt comfortable, esteemed, and cared,
In this school, I always felt safe; no reason to be scared.

Every time I begin to think of this wonderful place,
A smile of fond memories starts to creep onto my face.
And I know I'll truly miss this school as I begin to move on,
But I will always have my memories; they will never be gone.

Vijay Singh, Grade 8
Challenger School – Ardenwood

Funeral Bells

Hear the tolling of the funeral bells.
Iron bells!
What a feeling of despair
The ominous sounds entail.
On a cloudy, cloudy day
They emit a feeling of dismay,
These bells, iron bells.
Those who in black are adorned,
Those who sorrowfully mourn, mourn
In disarray.
They are too sad to do aught but wail
At the end of a young one's bittersweet tale
Cut far too short by many a good day.
Such a story some sorrows show
Of distress.
By the waxing or the waning in the sorrow of the bells
In the booming and the tolling of the bells.

Michael Carton, Grade 9
St. Michael's College Preparatory School

Nature

Mother, mama, mom,
Wilderness and colorful,
Contributes resources,
To humans and animals,
Food, water, and life,
In the sky, she makes clouds,
That drop rain in the dirt,
Growing trees that form apples for eating,
Tickled by creepy, crawly insects in the dirt,
Producer to the world.

Nicole Bailey, Grade 7
St Alphonsus School

I'm Blue

I wake up to find a sunny day,
Even though it was rainy last night,
As I walk towards the bay,
I am blue though everything is bright.

I hear birds chirp nearby.
I see butterflies flutter.
I think of how I had to let you fly.
Now every day will not be as smooth as butter.

Love is in the air,
But I feel blue.
My heart will always be bare,
But I somehow will make it through.

I hate how this is the way it is,
I thought we were meant to be
You will be greatly missed
And everything I see and do reminds me of your love for me.

Stephanie Ha, Grade 7
Citrus Hills Intermediate School

Dark Shadows

The dark death shadows stare me in the eye
And fills me with fear in the darken night
My life closes its eyes and gives a sign
My heart and lungs turned cold as of death
On bed I crumple like an autumn leaf
I still wait for my last breaths to leave me
Living or dying is a great relief
I had hoped to live as long as a turtle
I stare out the window for the last time
But the shadows of horror blocks my way
I try hard to block out my memories
But they make my mind begin to worry
My eyes goes blank and my heart begins to beat
And leaving forever, I go to sleep.

Alexis Pena, Grade 8
John Adams Middle School

Break Through

Why can't my thoughts come clear?
I am surrounded by an ocean of frustration.
Ideas are distant — afar, not near,
My only salvation is determination.

As pressure mounts to find my way,
My journey toward the answer is not in sight.
The setting sun signals the end of the day,
And darkness overpowers the fainting light.

Yesterday's failures that tormented me so,
Have left me for today's new beginning.
The challenges lessen, and optimisms grow,
My thoughts of defeat now turn to winning.

The barriers to my goals are now long faded visions.
I realize the answer was always within me from the start.
When the future brings me difficult decisions,
No farther will I look than deep inside my heart.

Megan Massoud, Grade 8
Holy Family Catholic School

Going to War

So here I am,
In a place where no one wants to be
In a very hot place with very little food or water.

A place where there's no fun, only death.
And sadness all day long.
So many days in the heat will make you forget about things.

So remember all those days and nights.
I am out there fighting for our country.

Margarita Gomez, Grade 8
Shadow Hills Intermediate School

Friends

Friends.
Honest, kind, caring.
There when you need them the most.
Always trustworthy and eloquent.
Always willing to share parts of their lunch or snack if yours is absent.
Always trying to help with anything possible.
When you are down they are there trying to cheer you up.
When you don't quite understand your homework, they are the first to help you.
When you are sad about something, they are there for support and you can lean on them
and talk to them with total confidence that they will help you no matter what.
Thinking back, I realize that without friends, I couldn't have made it to now without them.
Like a psychologist, they will listen and think of what to do then express.
Thank you for all you friends that have done anything for me at anytime, anywhere.
Here's to you, all of you,
Friends.

Stefan Valenzuela, Grade 7
Santa Rosa Technology Magnet School

The Important Thing

The important thing about life is to live it to the fullest and have no regrets.
       It has countless memories.
       You may wish you could regret, but they are just mistakes that you are learning from.
       You meet new people and explore in life,
              and there are tragedies,
              and not *true* friends and heartbreaking moments,
              and you may wish that you were never born because life turns on you.
But the important thing in life is to live it to the fullest and have no regrets.

D'Vana Vasquez, Grade 7
St Mary of Assumption School

My Passion of the Ice

Walking into the ice skating rink feels cool.
The aroma of cold Dippin Dots along with cocoa and cinnabuns that are both hot
Now looking onto the rink, it resembles a giant frozen pool.

The first steps onto the ice are always the best ice against blade and blade against ice
The zambonied smooth ice feels crisp and nice perfect for practicing for my big ice skating test

As I look around the rink, so many skaters are already in
It's time to take lessons from my coach Susan now we'll start off practicing a Salcau
After my jump I go for a scratch spin

She said "Stephanie spin with speed and swiftness"
As I stood there listening the ice was glistening
This time I spun with a lot more gracefulness

Time to jump down for a squat spin twirl
Constantly having to whirl almost time to return back to my won town

The last move to practice is back crossover around the cones it feels like along the ice, I glide
I try to do a waltz jump, and if I fall than at least I tried
After class is over all the ice skaters return home

Stephanie Strahl, Grade 9
Fountain Valley High School

Our Hearts*

Our hearts were once lost in the darkness
Not being able to find a way out
Until they found each other
Now found and so in love
All take your heart
Keep it safe
As long as you do the same for mine
There are many places in this world
But they all have the same sky
So with two hearts
One sky
A destiny for two
Intertwined together
Always shining bright
Because I have you

Daniel J. Strickland, Grade 9
Shadow Hills Intermediate School
*Dedicated to my love Kory Galvez

I Know He's Out There

One day I'll find a guy that'll blow my mind
I can already imagine him now
Everything from his height, to his sad frown
We'll have love that's truly one of a kind
We'd always be together, forever intertwined
With a voice fit for a king in his crown
A smell that would drive me crazy deep down
And dimples that are perfectly inclined
We'll have unconditional love; real love
Filled with mistakes and nights I'd want to cry
Still, it'll shine stronger than the stars above
It'll be as if we were in junior high
I'd be that girl he can't stop thinking of
I know he's out there, the ultimate guy.

Cynthia Moreno, Grade 8
Henry T Gage Middle School

The Love of a Dog

Dogs are our friends,
They stick with us until the end.
When our hearts are broken and need to mend,
They come to be a helpful friend.
They cuddle, play, and chew on toys,
Sometimes they make lots of noise.
Every once in awhile they'll pee on your carpets,
And make you want to throw them in the tar pits,
But when they give you that loving face,
And kiss you in that place,
The memories of their wrongs are erased.
All in all, dogs are great,
Plus they make a good playmate.

Kevin Cruz, Grade 7
Linden Center

Why?

"Faster! Faster! Move you lazy good for nothings"
The Germans hate us.
The Hungarians hate us.
The Italians hate us.
Why do they hate us?
Is it what our beliefs are?
Is it our traditions and holidays?
Is it because we do not have blue eyes?
Is it because we do not have blonde hair?
Is it both?
Why do they hate us?

Zack Lautmann, Grade 8
St Joseph's School of the Sacred Heart

Where I'm From

I am from GI Joes
from Fisher-Price swing sets
and trampolines.
I am from skyscrapers way up high
and the statue that stands for my liberty.
I am from the beautiful orchids,
and the palm trees.
I am from big parties and Italians,
from Gladstone and Quatraro.
I am from Pasta and Pizza.
From "Sit down!" and "Be Quiet!"
I am from a Christian upbringing.
I am from the armpit of New York,
from the *Penne a al Vodka*
and *fettuccini alfredo*.
From the helicopter in WWII,
from the bomber sent out
to do what was needed.
I am from the deserts where water is scarce,
and cactuses grow everywhere.
I am from GI Joes.

Dean Defuria, Grade 7
Linfield Christian School

Back Stabbers

Days go by and I feel so lonely
Friends seem to be everything but daisies
They seem to be cool yet they're phony
To call them friends I'd have to be crazy
Back stabbers are not my type of people
I'd have to deal with lies until the end
My so called friends think they make me feeble
I'll try to clear my head while they offend
But it'll be over soon when I leave
They cheat and lie and claim to by my friend
The lies they tell me I will not believe
The wounds they've created I cannot mend
I'll live my life happily till I die
"Friends" will not get me mad or make me sigh

Brisa Hernandez-Carbajal, Grade 8
John Adams Middle School

Sky

You are not sad or mellow,
As if you were gray or yellow.
The sun smiles down at you,
The clouds just grew and grew.
Flowers glorify you with
Faces turned toward your bliss.
Even the green, green grass
Stares at your mass.
The pinks, oranges and reds
Are forced to bow their heads.
For you are the cool,
You, the many shades of blue.

Miranda O'Connor, Grade 8
EV Cain Middle School

Motorcycles

Motorcycles are awesome,
everyone wants one.

The prices are going up fast,
buy one so you can have a blast.

My dad's motorcycle is black,
with a little red in the back.

He lets me ride with him,
and sometimes my older cousin Kim.

Angel Chavez, Grade 7
St Vincent Elementary School

The Power of a Word

One word of vengeance
May find its way to your heart
And become a war

One word of kindness
May soften a heart of stone
And become true love

Alaura Royce, Grade 8
Middletown Adventist School

Music

Listen to music
Sing out loud
Check out a band
And join the crowd
Know the lyrics
Hear the song
Get in the rhythm
And beat along
Feel the music
Get on stage
Give it your all
The crowd will enrage

Vincent Rulli, Grade 8
St Ferdinand Elementary School

What's Outside Our Windows

As I watch the world pass by, I often ponder through
The ever growing conflicts, and we without a clue
Propose our heart's desire oblivious to what's outside
Our little private window we set our minds to hide

Children carry bearings of burdens never shared
Hunger, pain spread in the streets bodies thinly layered
Adults mistreat each other to a point beyond belief
Abuse and hate come into one shame, oppression, grief

All that we can prevent past mistakes erased
I glance outside my window and find the world enlaced
With all our shameful doings my nervous fears confirmed
Nothing will be done nothing will be changed, I learned

Until we mend this scar, something needs to be done
If no one looks beyond their glass the change…there will be none.

Elizabeth Ye, Grade 9
Westview High School

Broken Heart

When you get a broken heart
You feel empty inside
You just can't believe It happened to you
You feel lonely and even begin to cry
You just don't know what to do

You sit on a your bed and drown yourself in tears
Thinking about what you did together
Then every day you see him and you just can't stop staring at him
How do you fix a broken heart
Well only you know the answer

Samantha Caballero, Grade 7
Sarah McGarvin Intermediate School

Roller Coaster Life

The clink against your chest
The vehicle starts the beginning of life
It mounts its way up like a bird climbing the wind
A child growing, thriving, the sight from up here
Hot dog stands, cotton candy, lemonade, the joy of life
The stillness for a second as though time had stopped itself
The next second diving downwards against the wind like an eagle
Wind brushing against my cheeks, the moments of a bird flying
Another joy to cherish
The jolt of the vehicle's gears shifting
Problems in your life
Another jolt, another turn, another problem
Then a circle
Big confusion in your life
As though a plane is about to crash
The vehicle glides to a stop
Again the clink, the relief on your chest

David Cheuk, Grade 7
Purple Lotus International Institute

Friends

I really love all my friends to no end,
Because they have always been there for me.
Showing love day to day, friend to friend;
And no matter what, that will always be!
Leaning on each other isn't a crime,
Always sharing laughter and sharing tears —
When we're together we have a good time!
I am always reminded that they're near,
During tough times, we protect each other.
We don't pretend to be someone we're not.
With much laughter, we tease one another.
This kind of friendship could never be bought.
I truly love my friends with all my heart,
And hope that we must never have to part!

Ali Cornish, Grade 8
CORE Butte Charter School

What Death Brings

I am most scared of death
When it falls upon my steps
Knocking at my door
Taking away my breath
Crawling, creeping up the shore
Always taking more
A widower I may be
Loved ones fall to the floor
It's hard to see
That it will one day happen to me
I feel as if I am all alone
The doorbell rings, rings
But no one is home
You never know what death brings

Hannah Cummings and Kathleen Dooley, Grade 7
St Patrick Parish School

My Best Principal Always!*

You were always there for me.
When I needed you,
You were there.
You knew what to do.
Everywhere you go,
The love and comfort follow you.
But now that you're no longer here,
Things have changed.
You were the only one
Who knew the way.
I miss you! If I could stop time,
I would put you back.
You gave us our chance to change.
I miss the way you smile at me.
Your smile gave me the warm feeling of home.
You were like a mother to me…
My Best Principal Ever!

Vivian Yu, Grade 7
Corpus Christi School
*Dedicated with love to Sister Anna Bui, FMA

Sister

Loud…like the sound of music blasting from the radio…
Or a kid jumping in the pool with a splash…
All I hear is sound…
Just a baby crying frantically…
A slamming of doors continuously…
The angry honking of cars in traffic hour

Loud…like a pack of friends at the mall…
Laughing every second…
Yelling that lasts forever…
Running into every store…
Clothes being torn to shreds

Loud…like parents yelling at kids…
Teachers reminding students to be quiet…
Students ignoring them…
They keep on talking

Loud…
A word that definitely
Describes
A sister

Tatum Dobalian, Grade 8
St Sebastian School

My Fading Grandfather

The words crushed my grandpa's
Spirit like a crumbling wall.
Four years ago, the doctor
Told him that cancer was attacking him.

He took it hard,
But he bounced back like a ball.
Tick, tick, tick, tick.
Time is short.
Time to travel and enjoy.
His visits to California brought
Warmth to my house like sunshine in the garden.

Tick, tick, tick.
The disease consumed him, little by little.
Losing hair, weight, and appetite, but never his spirit,
His radiance dimmed with each passing hour.

Tick, tick.
Weak and weary, frail and fragile
Like a fallen autumn leaf,
His voice whimpers only a whisper,
And his eyes' sparkles are long gone.
Soon he will fade away like the setting sun.

Alan Soetikno, Grade 7
The Harker School - Middle Campus

Seasons

Autumn
Breeze, winds
Leaves falling down
Cheerful, playful, happy, excited
Fall

Summer
Warm, sunshine
Flowers popping high
Happy children playing outside
Spring
Elizabeth Diaz, Grade 8
Almond Tree Middle School

Teens

Being a teen
Not all fun and games
Friendships and fights
Most importantly, changes
All of us have.
Start growing up
One way or the other
Peer pressure makes us more mature
Because of decisions we make
Friendships — the saddest or best part
One day you can have a friend
Another day an enemy
This is a risk we all take
If we make the right gamble
Our friendships will last forever
We use this time to build the person
We'll be the rest of our lives
Being a teen is fun I can't complain
But when I grow up
These are the memories
No one can take from me.
Heidi Aquino, Grade 8
St Alphonsus School

Waterfalls

Big blue waterfalls
Making so many splashes
Aren't they cool to see?
Jheena Arellano, Grade 8
Almond Tree Middle School

Taken

Because of this
Because of that
Because of whom we are
Because of what we are
We are taken
Hannah Lutke, Grade 8
Buchser Middle School

Do I Want a Choice?

My mom says,
"Mackenzy, it's all up to you."
I freak out,
I panic.
What should I do?

But then she says, "No."
And oh, here I go.
"Did she just make a choice for me?
That is so unfair!"
But then I realize
all she ever did was care.

Choices are frightening matters,
that are confusing too.
But tell me that
I cannot choose,
and it's over for you!
Mackenzy Taylor, Grade 8
Visalia Christian Academy

Water Falls

Water hits the earth
like spring showers in the garden
mist comes to greet me
Alexis Morales, Grade 7
South Tahoe Middle School

Running

The air is rushing past
I'm going really fast
I'm having such a blast
I definitely won't be last.

What is that sound
My feet hitting the ground
There's no turning around.
My love was just found!
Cassie Widdison, Grade 9
Shadow Hills Intermediate School

Fireworks

Independence Day has come.
The air is sweet.
The sky is calm.
I'm sweating in the heat back home.
And the fireworks are loud.
Bright and colorful.
In the park they go bang!
Loudly and proudly
Showing off their colors.
Independence Day has come.
Danny Oh, Grade 8
Madrona Middle School

Promises

Promise we'll be friends forever.
Always. No matter what. Whenever.
You need me and I'll be there.
Promise me you'll truly care.

Promise we will always be tight,
Even though we may get in a fight.
And I know this may sound odd,
But we're like two peas in a pod.

Promise you will stay in my heart,
Together, we'll never grow apart.
Promise you'll be a good friend,
And we'll be friends until the end.
Lauren Weidler, Grade 8
Calvary Chapel of YL

Dream

When I close my eyes
I can fly for miles
Upon scented clouds full of schemes
And scarlet dragons fly beside me
Breathing new clouds of dreams
Filling them with fire
So that the angels riding them perspire
As the night winds whistle and sing
Until the moon leads the choir
I want to disembark and be set free
Gliding with wings of peace
And let the sights tickle my imagination
And feed fuel to the fire that heats
The water filled with my dreams
So that when I close my eyes
I can fly for miles
Hannah Haley-Granados, Grade 8
Valley Oak Middle School

Ode to My Dog Foster

My old boy Foster
Acts as if he's a puppy
Playing with a new toy
Running the field, playing tug o' war
As tender as a blade of grass
Running for treats
Tongue lolling out
Lapping up water that falls
softly from his tongue
Playing as if not nine years old
But as if only two
Hair getting grey, legs are getting stiffer
He is my old boy
That will be with me forever more
Cameron Gardner, Grade 7
Santa Rosa Technology Magnet School

A Candy Bar

The important thing about a candy bar is that it is *delicious*.
It is brown and sometimes pure white.
When I take a bite I taste the chocolatey goodness,
it is the thing I crave when I want sweets,
but if I consume too much I get sick.
It feels satisfying and filling and it comes from many places.
The important thing about a candy bar is that it's *delicious*.

Kaitlin McNeil, Grade 7
St Mary of Assumption School

My Heart and Joy*

My mom was my heart and joy,
My mom loved her little boy.
My mom was one of the best,
My mom was better then the rest.
But I knew my mom was not going to be here for long,
I knew that she would be gone,
She spent her life with me,
She always filled me up with happiness and glee.
But one day she was gone,
No goodbye, nor a so long
My heart exploded no blood, no love,
No kisses, nor any hugs.
No more seeing her joy,
No more seeing her little boy.
As days go on and time past by,
I still don't have a real mom to say hello or goodbye.
And now I sit down alone cry,
And tell God why He took half of my heart and half of my life.
But as I grow I'm not a little boy,
But I still go back to when I had my heart and joy.

Antonio Carrasco, Grade 9
Henderson Community Day School
**R.I.P. Sylvia Corrales*

Mr. A's Ties

Many colors I come,
With many shapes and size.
I can be purple like a plum,
Each day I am a surprise.

Looking out at the crowd,
I am a pretzel tied in a knot.
Listening to the voices aloud,
I can come in polka dot.

My master's never seen without me,
Sigh, sometimes I make the students cry.
To happiness I am the key,
For I am Mr. A's Tie!

Paige Leonard and Cassidy Klovanish, Grade 7
St Patrick Parish School

Get Back on Track

I've lost my way
I've got no where to run
It scares me, where will I end up?
There's always strangers around
I've lost sight, and it's time to fight
I've got to go now
take a different path, on a road I've known
I wanna see faces I know,
and get hopes that aim high
and never have to say goodbye,
because today is the day
to make sure it all changes
and you were the one to blame
and I'm positive I'm done playing your games
now all you can do for me
Is just realize that I beat you
at your own playing field.

Samantha Fitzgerald, Grade 9
Lucerne Valley Jr/Sr High School

Ode to Strawberries

Strawberries, the best of all the berries
Its red beautiful color to be shared for all
With its perfect countless seeds
Its green leaves with seeds far and wide
Its special unique shape with red all over
Its delicious taste that none can match
When you take a first bite, you meet a new world
Strawberries, are the king of berries

John Vega, Grade 7
Santa Rosa Technology Magnet School

Raindrops

I wake up by the sounds of raindrops
It's raining! And the sky is dark
Finding a light in my room is hard
But harder is finding a light in my soul,
Cannot see whether morning or night
Cannot see the sun has gone
Perhaps I wake up at the wrong time
Perhaps it is my dreams
That carry me away, it really seems…
I feel rain is pouring in my heart
I feel lost when wanted to talk
To somebody and say how empty the raindrops fall
How complex life is for all
How I taste my maturity
By waking up alone, and count every drop of rain
In all its purity, I just want to see
If tomorrow comes again
No more raindrops waking me
No more confusion whether day or night
No more dark clouds in the sky
No more wandering thoughts, sadly will subside.

Valentina Le, Grade 8
Horace Ensign Intermediate School

Moving On…

No matter what the hard times
No matter what the addictions
They're working hard now
My family abused and used
But I'm not mistaken
What they did will always be forgiven
Most people were forced out
Then I reached out
For those who have always been there
Maybe not foster parents
But at least my friends care
Now I've made a mistake
I want it to be okay
I scream go, go, go away
I'll try to laugh
Only with my best friends
My mistake definitely cost me
People tell me it's not your fault
I don't care what they say
I need to know, like my family
That I'll always be forgiven

Kayli Bland, Grade 7
Juan Cabrillo Middle School

Music

Music
Crazy, relaxing
Singing, laughing, dancing
Makes me feel happy
Loud

Taylor Alvarez, Grade 7
St Mary of Assumption School

The Sky

The sky is a palette
Of many colors
Morning is yellow
Noon is blue
Evening is orange
Night is black

The sky is an ocean
Wide and blue
Very quiet
I can't hear any noise
I can relax near the sky
It is very beautiful

The sky is a family
Sun, cloud, snow, and rain
They are the family of sky
Sometimes they quarrel
But mostly they get along well
They are a good family

Natsumi Kumagai, Grade 8
Madrona Middle School

At the Water's Edge

The smooth ocean waves that overlap on the silent sand,
Oh how awfully quiet and peaceful this beautiful land.
This beach with its tropical scene cannot be described in books.
Come on enjoy the fun, put down your comics and take a look.

Splashing and clashing all over the place, in the water, is that your case?
The sky blue water all calm and shiny over looked from the mountain's base.
Or are you just surfing the water of the cool blue ocean,
Or are you just bobbing your head to the water's motion?

Sitting on the beach with exactly no thoughts or care,
Enjoying the glamorous view of the sunset from your beach chair.
If you are a surfer the most impossible occurs on a wave,
And all spectacular performances are what the audience crave.

In the far distance you may see the elongated jagged peaks,
You may even stare into it for many, many weeks.
Gathering darling and charming sea shells from near and far,
We are making memories so it does not matter if they are bizarre.

Staring into the endless ocean you wonder if it ever has an end,
You see all the pretty colors that start to form one color and blend.
As this awesome day seems to end you stare into the sky,
And wonder how all that time today had easily gone by.

Ruchita Patel, Grade 7
Challenger School – Ardenwood

Nocturnal Negotiations

When the dark is thrown upon the sky
The bustling day seems to end,
But for many nocturnal animals that play
Their hard work just begins to ascend.
Owls hoot with vigor and vivacity,
Look for delectable in full capacity,
And maintain full peace and tranquility,
Lest their location loses obscurity.
Raccoons with heads as big as balloons
Glistening yet dark eyes, more circular than moons
Search silently for scouring snakes and slumbering snails
Cautious not to crunch the leaves, and create a thunderous uproar.
The night is an ambivalent market,
Gridlocked with wandering animals.
Each hurrying to complete its project
Vying for all there is, from their rivals.
They return to their dens,
As the moon wanes,
And darkness in the sky transcends.
The creatures silently sleep, awaiting for the sun to set,
In order to begin another exciting adventure, in the moonlight.

Sulekha Ramayya, Grade 8
Rolling Hills Country Day School

Darkness Incarnated

On the albums, I play each track
Music plays that is purely black
Guitarists playing at a speed of fast
Drummers slamming on a set for blasts
Lyrics detailing the worst of fears
Melodies drawing from men their tears
With every song, they call on their rage
Wars of deep passion and fury they wage
The art they create is overly dramatic
Their symphonic dissonance sounding sporadic
Magically mighty musicians of metal
Mercilessly mystify many with their mettle

Dennis Wong, Grade 9
Fountain Valley High School

Marshmallow

It's fluffy. It's white.
It's always a delight.
It's smooshy. It's gooshy.
Like a cloud that's very bushy.
I'm always dying to eat it and when
I do I want to repeat it.
It's ewy. It's gooey.
Did I mention how it's very chewy?
When we're sitting by the campfire and we're
very, very, cold it always warms me up and it
deliciousness never gets old.
When I have it I just want more and more, and
without it there would be nothing so delicious as a
S'MORE!

Camille Hoffman, Grade 7
Holy Family Catholic School

The Way It Should Be

There is this boy
And he's so nice to me
We've known each other forever
And I wish he liked me
I'm afraid to tell him about how I feel
But I don't want to ruin what we have
Because our friendship is so real
He makes me smile every day
And he's so funny
But in his own special way
He asks me who I like
But I always have to lie
Because I don't want him to know
I would just die
This whole thing may sound cliché
But this is how he makes me feel
Every single day
So maybe just friends is the way it was meant to be
But, baby, I'll always love you
Even if you don't love me

Natalie Cully, Grade 8
Holy Family Catholic School

Sunrise

In the pitch black darkness I wait
For the soon coming morn.
I'm in such a state;
It cannot be borne!
I hate this darkness, I need the light.
This inky blackness around me
Is giving me quite a fright!
But wait, is that the sun I see?
Of the bright light I drink my fill.
I shout happily with glee,
For the sun is rising o'er the crest of a hill!

Chelsea Hanifin, Grade 7
Chino Valley Christian Schools

AJ Is Here

I was in school for two hours
Telling everybody my nephew would be born
I got picked up and went to the hospital
At 12:57 PM AJ arrived and was as small as a piece of corn

His mom is only fifteen years old
Has she made a mistake?
Will she be able to raise her new baby?
Or will it be a piece of cake?

So far everything has gone nice and smooth
AJ's mom will soon be back to school
I wish AJ and his parents the best
I can't wait to be able to take him to the pool

Nemesis Ramirez, Grade 7
South Tahoe Middle School

My Life

Why am I feeling so blue and lonely,
In this house filled with many luxuries,
Hoping that something could be found in me,
Except my old and boring history?

No one seems to notice me anywhere,
Only when I do something foolishly.
It just does not seem to be really fair,
As if I was stuck in a dark alley.

Yet, then I see someone's shadow of light,
Trying to get me back on my two feet.
It was my loving family all right,
Filling all my fantasies so complete.

And my family makes me truly blessed,
To put my question to a final rest.

Yesenia Melgar, Grade 8
John Adams Middle School

Reflections of a Princess
Princess gets caught in a stormy situation!
While the princess sits in her room with her older sister, she sees two people.
But instead of running to greet them, like she used to do,
She sits quietly and waits for them to appear
And for the signal to go eat dinner with her family and younger sisters.
They talk about dreams and thoughts
All of the children have about the world before they all go to bed.
She sees her sister in the diamond mirror looking more like
A nice witch than a princess.
"Oh no!" she exclaims, while curiously looking around her room
"I don't know what was wrong with my mirror!"
She figures out that her sister messed up her mirror.
She listens intently for the sound of footsteps
Climbing up her stairs, giving herself a scare, and laughing at herself.
She listens as the rain comes pounding like a tsunami.
She hears the wind whistling in the dusky day
And the tree's leaves falling in the open air.
She smells the lusty air of the ocean breeze.
She hears a buzzing bee coming to sniff at a flower.
It was a great day in the morning, but look at the clouds coming in,
It will rain hard tonight. It was a great day to just stay inside and look around the house.

Kristy Gee, Grade 8
Rolling Hills Country Day School

What Is Love?
What is love? Is love the weird feeling you get anytime you're with the one you like? Is love how you feel every time you see your crush? Is love the way you talk, talk, and talk to them about nothing? Is love when you cry over them, but you don't know why? Is love what you feel every time you close your eyes and think of them? Is love the songs you listen to that make you think of them? Is love the movies you watch and wish that the one you had feelings for would treat you that way? Honestly, it makes me wonder, when young adults and teenagers who clearly have no clue what love is say, "I love you." Those people probably don't know what they're really saying. I have no clue what "that" kind of love is and I want to wait to find out, but for now I'll just keep on guessing.

Allison Blazona, Grade 8
Holy Family Catholic School

As the Cherry Blossoms Fall
As the cherry blossoms fall she looks over her shoulder
At the place she would never see again.
As the cherry blossoms fall she looks back at the faces of people
So dear to her that had helped her through life.
She sees tears slide down their cheeks and their lips tremble.
As the cherry blossoms fall she tells them without words
That she loved them more than life
And that she would remember them always.
And as the cherry blossoms fall
And with the sun at her back, she turns away from her life to a new one.
As the cherry blossoms fall life ends.
As the cherry blossoms fall life begins.
And as the cherry blossoms fall she feels the warmth of something warmer than the sun.
The warmth of her love.
The warmth of the person she was starting a new life with.
And as the cherry blossoms fall she gathers herself and move forward to new life.

Alex Dugan, Grade 7
Ruth Paulding Middle School

Sunset in the Desert

The setting sun, red and orange,
Behind grand shadows of cactus.
A long, flat horizon borders the sky,
Gently glowing with light's last goodbye,
Before the moon, stars, and navy blanket swallow all.

An owl hoots, quickly silenced,
A coyote howls its long sad song,
Rocky, barren ground swiftly comes alive,
When all the creatures of night arrive,
Once the ever watching, always seeing moon has risen.

Burning light, to freezing darkness,
Hot, dry afternoon,
Becomes cool, crisp night,
Rocks and rough shrubs the only things in sight,
Farther than the eye might see.

Here can be found,
The brightest of any stars,
Without a cloud or city nearby,
Sky's glimmering freckles, completely un-shy,
Such a calm, quiet place to be.

Adelle Park, Grade 7
Dorris-Eaton School

Change the World

I wake up in the morning and go to brush my teeth.
I see the sun's warm rays upon the sky and everything beneath.

The day's just begun; I am filled with delight
I must hurry now, so little time 'til night.

In a rural neighborhood,
I walk along the streets, you see.
And what brings me sorrow.
I glimpse starvation and poverty.

Many people may ponder.
What can one adolescent do?
She can't change the way things are.
She doesn't know what she's getting into

But it merely takes one brave soul to evoke change.
I promise you, it only takes one
Anyone can make a difference.
Mother, daughter, father, son?

I chose to be part of these ones
We're going to change the world.

Joy Liu, Grade 9
Westview High School

Future Love

Smiling and laughing he will hold me tight,
Loving me and staring into my eyes,
He holds me closer and the world is right,
Trust will be key and we'll never share lies;
Strong and unbreakable our love will be,
Growing with happiness each coming day,
Once our eyes meet that shall be our decree,
Of passion and faith in all that we say;
Laughter will always be something we share,
Honest and true we're forever sincere,
My heart in his hands I know it won't tear,
Love will grow stronger with each passing year;
Our two hearts will be one and together,
The love we will share shall never weather.

Taylore King, Grade 8
Las Flores Middle School

Ode to My Catfish

Swimming through the water
Hook baited with a worm
Twitching in pain
Hook as sharp as a razor
Do I get a bite?
ONE HOUR
TWO HOURS
Change of bait
Worm to liver
A bend of rod
A zing of reel
Fish on
Fish on
Meeting face to fish face with a catfish
A catfish the size of a truck
Gasping for air
Asking me to put him in the water
Calling my mom to tell her "CATFISH FRY"

Tanner William Burgess, Grade 8
Valley Oak Middle School

Revealing a Mystery

It's a mystery to everyone on how to get it perfect
Biolage is the answer
Sometimes unmanageable, always thick
The aroma is of orchids and coconut milk
Reminds me of an endless motion
Always putting me in an endless commotion
I would never survive with it short
It dances when the wind blows
As if it was a twirling ballerina
Equal to the ocean on a perfect day in Hawaii
NEVER BLONDE, ALWAYS BROWN
The way I go is ALL NATURAL
It makes me frustrated
But my hair's the best because it's not boring

Taylor Barlow, Grade 9
Fountain Valley High School

Imagine Life!

Imagine the world tiny.
Imagine us very big.
Imagine our universe as a tiny particle!
How would we have been?
What if we had no air?
What if we had no hair?
Imagine our trees purple…
Imagine our plants brown…
Our world would be up side down…
Imagine the bees big and sweet.
Imagine our dogs in two feet.
Imagine all of this all cool and funny…
But just remember the bunny!

Sarah Maria Padilla, Grade 7
St Mary's School

Poetry

Freedom expressed.
Beauty suppressed.
In minds, in hearts
Through letters freed.
Brilliant thoughts
Which so exceed
Any words or muttering
They leave us shuddering
Because of so much freedom
Expressed
From inner beauty
No longer suppressed.

Sandra Limon, Grade 8
Tenaya Middle School

Ocean

Sea water is blue
There are creatures living there
Peaceful like the clouds

Mary Joy Membreve, Grade 8
Almond Tree Middle School

Knight in Shining Armor

You're my knight in shining armor
I'm a damsel in distress
I'm a maiden who's quite poor
Forever cleaning up a mess

Locked up in a horrid tower
With a dragon guarded key
I have little but a flower
Oh please come and rescue me

My heart is crying out
So come and slay the dragon
And with a mighty shout
Carry me off in your wagon

Katelyn Larson, Grade 7
John Muir Middle School

Classroom Speeches

Today was my classroom speech
When I got to school, my face was as white as laundry bleach
As soon as the bell rang, I knew it was my turn.
My stomach felt as if it was going to churn!
Although I sit in the back of the class,
I wish I was invisible just like glass.
Suddenly when the bell rang my first fear came,
I walked up the aisle to the front of the class as if my legs were lame.
As I started to say the first word in my speech,
The whole class was as quiet as if a priest was ready to preach.
I never knew what happened next,
Because I awoken to my sore foot from not trying to flex.
I found out I was in the ER room from fainting in school,
But I still got a B in class and that's really cool.
I knew I tried my best,
But I do not think I could pass another test.

Cindy Tran, Grade 7
Sarah McGarvin Intermediate School

Deceived

I have been deceived, only, I am the deceiver.
The great crime, though seemingly small, hast become larger and larger.
He hast revealed to me what I in my blindness could not see.
The other hath inflicted a small disease upon me.
This small disease, I reasoned, when I look't at it in thought,
Must be very small, if is't; if is't not, then is't not.
Then slowly, began I to think, 'tis no disease at all!
This thing which is inside me need not be so very small.
Then eagerly I awaited it each and every night,
It was a joy to me, this contusion, I thought, is't not that it's not right.
This infestation cultured and throve inside my soul
And despair, had I known it, began to take its toll,
Is't him? Is't me? We're the deceiver and the deceived!
We both are solemn enemies, yet work together as a team.
But in the midst of my destruction there shone a valiant light;
'Tis Him! The Undeceived! He then pulled me up to right.
Just when The Deceived almost had ta'en me o'er, thought he, I he had receiv'd;
The Deceiver, wretched being, was deceived.

Karis Tanksley, Grade 8
Living Waters Academy

Baseball

Ninth inning two outs you're up
Down eight to nine got a man on third and second
If you can just make contact, you can win
You step up to the plate
First pitch flies right past you, it's a strike
Second pitch curves in at you, it's another strike
Third pitch comes straight down the middle, you swing
You miss, you're out, but wait
The catcher dropped the ball you're running to first
The catcher overthrows it, and third, and second, come running home
You won the game all because you didn't give up

Erik Cirujano, Grade 7
Monte Vista Christian School

The Meaning of Music

So she's finally gone,
After years of waving goodbye.
You knew it would happen for so long,
But you still feel so dead inside.
She left her music behind,
All of it, just for you.
All the words she couldn't find,
In these lyrics so few.
She loved you like sappy love songs,
She needed you like those friendship tunes.
She smiled like the fire in metal songs,
She laughed like Christmas carols in June.
All the music she left behind,
They made you listen,
To the words she couldn't find.
So let the music play.
Let it take you away.
Her death, you must put it aside.
She made you listen,
So you wouldn't feel dead inside.

Kylee Katsumata, Grade 8
Madrona Middle School

My Home

I get up every morning to surf.
The waves are like gigantic beasts.
They are always trying to feast.
The big ones especially.

Every morning I hear the wind whistle.
It goes smoothly through my ears.
I always love walking on the pier.
Ruby's always brings me excitement.

The barrels are like never ending tunnels.
They are always smooth and clean.
But sometimes they can be mean.
Like a blender tossing you around.

The sand is chilly in the morning of the winter season.
It always numbs my feet.
So I run for awhile and then have a seat.
But the sand is always soft.

Jordan Frazier, Grade 9
Fountain Valley High School

Family

They protect you.
No harm will come to you.
Never give up and they will look up to you.
Say thanks and they will welcome you.
You get hurt and they will comfort you.
Day and night they will love and pray for you.
And people will know they love you.

Jonathan M. Zepeda, Grade 7
Our Lady of the Rosary School

Guitar and Music

My guitar is made out of wood.
When polished, it's looking real good.
Wake up every morning my guitar is there to greet me,
It creates beauty that you cannot see.

It creates something so beautiful, it's called music
Music so awesome, you will just about lose it.
From loud, heavy low sounding chords
To the soft, sweet, high sounds of harmony.

Slow, steady, single played notes
To the fast, rhythmic solo's that may promote.
This guitar has it all
The looks, sound and beauty that can only awe.

Jake Callahan, Grade 8
Santa Rosa Technology Magnet School

See You Once More

If I could see you again,
What would I say?
Would you remember me,
Would things remain the same?

I wish I'd been there when you left
Or been there for your last breath
Because life is too short to live with regrets
Because tomorrow is a gift we haven't opened yet.

I try to live each moment as my last,
Because when I think about you I cry.
So to all the people I love and meet,
I always make sure to say goodbye.

Angelica Castro, Grade 9
Shadow Hills Intermediate School

Breathe

Love as they say, can send hearts aflutter,
As I met your eyes, I took a sigh,
They bring me warmth and glee like no other,
That smile of yours, I could almost die:
Through rain or shine you will always be mine,
Your words never leaving me at bore,
You beam and inside I melt, it's a sign,
Love, you brought the rain's romantic pour:
We hold hands as we walk place to place,
Causing onlookers to gaze at us and grin,
And in that moment, I look towards your face,
And see that I truly love you within:
Knowing you're there, I can't help but stare,
I am your heart and you are my air.

Nicole Pannebaker, Grade 8
Las Flores Middle School

Middle School Jungle

Middle school is like a jungle
Waiting for you to see
The craziest things a middle schooler
Can scream!
A lion is like a principal
Stalking its prey
Waiting to catch a kid saying
Rude and ridiculous comments.
Teachers are tigers
Roaring at their kids.
Scaring and telling them
Do your work now!
Children are like flies
Caught in a web
Waiting
For the time (3pm)
Flying right through the
Sticky, icky web
They are out to freedom
But
So soon it starts again.

Juan Carlos Romero, Grade 8
St Sebastian School

Summer

Summer
A time for friends
Swimming and eating Popsicles
Playing in the sprinklers
Selling lemonade
We wish it would never end

Colleen Nawn, Grade 8
St Joseph's School of the Sacred Heart

Lemon

I found a treat
That you can eat
Some say
It is very sour
Others say sweet.
I cannot say but
What color?
It is bright
Almost like the
Bright sunlight glow
some say the sun
Helps it grow.
It is a citrus,
Citrus filled
With sunlight
It's gone for good
But it was good.

Daniel Contreras, Grade 8
St Alphonsus School

Hamster

Furry, soft, hamster
Running in the cage.
Stops
Looks up at me
So cute.
So tiny, yet with a huge heart.
Out of the cage
Into my hands,
Giving me comfort.
I lay the small fuzzy creature
On the bed.
It runs so fast
As if it was free,
It knows that it was free
Until it goes back into the cage.

Esperanza Saavedra, Grade 7
St Alphonsus School

Lake

Smooth as glass, cool and crisp
When the wind blows
Ripples of laughter echo
From beneath the lake
Causing the reflection to swirl
Into a mixture of colors
Dancing on the lake's surface
To the beat of the wind

Winter covers the mirror
In a crystallized cloak of white
In autumn, the leaves
Form a ring of gold and brown
Along the lake's shore
For summer, the lake is a haven
From the sun's beating rays

Through the years
The lake shrinks and swells
But always remains silent,
Soothing and serene

Marissa Rodriguez, Grade 8
Madrona Middle School

Stand Still

Standing there with nothing
But long ashy hair
And eyes of emerald green
From her lips left a scream
And while a tear left an eye
She came to realize
She was absolutely
Out of her mind

Emily Kennedy, Grade 9
Opportunities for Learning Center

Summer

Summer so calming
Summer so hot, dry, and free
Summer is so free

Rosa Cortez, Grade 8
Almond Tree Middle School

Alone

Alone
Is being in the dark
Alone
Is loving someone and them
Not loving you back…
Alone
Is feeling empty
Alone
Is loving someone you lost
Alone
Is fighting with your best friend
Alone
Is being invisible
Alone
Is a part of life

Sydni Miles, Grade 8
Citrus Hills Intermediate School

A Recipe for How to Fake Sick

You need a bucket of blankets,
Tons of blow-drying.
A pinch of hot peppers,
A dash of coughing and sneezing.
Mix it until you feel really sick,
And add a teaspoon of happiness,
That you missed school.

Tracy Kieu, Grade 7
St Barbara School

If No One

If no one knows
If no one sees
you underneath
If you hide yourself,
like a cat in a storm
If no one hears
the cry in your mourn
Yet they hear the whispers
of their peers
If no one knew you hide
yourself with a blanket of fear
If no one knew
If no one hears
If no one shows
No one knows…

Macayla Morse, Grade 8
Valley Oak Middle School

My Love

If you leave me now rain or shine
You will always be my true love
Face to face forever I'll always love you
That's how I know you're my love
My one and only love,
This world doesn't know
What I feel about you drives me crazy
How my heart beats for you
Hearing your voice really puts a smile on my face
Now I don't know how I feel anymore
I just want to tell someone how I feel
Because I'm just a mess without you

Jose Rivera, Grade 7
Almond Tree Middle School

Music

The sounds go through our ears like a zesty touch.
It's a smooth breeze.
Music is an avalanche cascading down the mountain.
When I listen to the music,
I hear its message.
Music plays 10,000 times a day in my mind.
It's flickering dream coming to life.
It's all over the world.
It calls to me.
Music feels like the finest sand.
Tastes like the finest meat.
It looks like a tropical island.
If it were a body part it would definitely be the feet.
Music puts the dance in my life.

Clayton Smith, Grade 7
Rolling Hills Country Day School

Ode to My Cousin

Smile shining as bright as the sun,
Always so carefree and loving
When she laughs all of my problems go away
She's more of a big sister than a cousin,
From the same family tree
Cousins by blood, friends from the heart,
Forever, you and me
Always helping with problems
Cares about what I do and when I do it
Even though she lives an hour away
She always is close to me,
One of my favorite poems is to you and to me:
"Cousins are many, best friends are few,
What a rare delight to find both in you."
You will always be a part of my life, my cousin,
You'll always be special to me.

Annalea Fusci, Grade 7
Santa Rosa Technology Magnet School

Foliage Tail*

Climbing up the walls of a moist, mossy tree,
It is truly a sight, something to see.
Sticking on a branch is this twelve-inch creature,
So much to describe, even so for a preacher.
This reptile so exotic and truly so strange,
Is not commonly found throughout its range.
Its range through the forest away so far,
Its range in the forests of Madagascar.
It's a reptilian creature calm indeed,
It's something to observe, which I'd surely heed.
It has a calm nature, deep within,
And there's something to mention about its skin,
It looks very mossy and leafy also,
And has large eyes to greet you, when saying hello.
Its tail is probably the most tremendous of all,
And if you try to grab it, down it will fall.
It is wonderful when it comes to camouflage,
You don't know what you're seeing, perhaps a mirage?

Rory Muldoon, Grade 9
Balboa City School
*Uroplatus Fimbratus discovered 1797.

As I Pass You By…

I can hardly breathe
Simply can't help myself, it makes me want to scream
I'm ready to burst out
This aching, is what I dread the most
I cannot speak, I cannot hide
I've lost control

As I shed tears of pain,
The bleak wind of change surrounds my every move
Breathing swiftly across my face leaving me with nothing to say
Yet, dazed by the grace it's given me

In a moment I seize this bliss
Never letting it escape me, not ever…
As I treasure every moment, embracing every second
It leaves me with nothing but hope
Hope for today, hope for strength
Hope, to live

I've found my place
Not a single tear runs down my face
For the first time in my life it's made me feel safe
It's where I belong, it's where I hide, it's where I lay
Sincere Inside

Janeth Garcia, Grade 8
St Anne Elementary-Jr High School

Waiting

Waiting for time to pass
Without a response not even one call
A loneliness of a no one

Diana L. Santana, Grade 7
John Charles Fremont Intermediate School

Please Lady

"Please lady,
I don't have a dime
It is too shady."
"I don't have the time!"

"Please little boy,
I'm out of money,
I have no joy."
"All I have is my toy bunny…"

"Please sir,
I have no cash,
would you care to give?"
"Get away from me you pile of ash!"

They all came back the next day…
Only to find
The man had passed away.
They realized they weren't kind.

Andres Gutierrez, Grade 8
La Joya Middle School

On and On

As the many days go on,
And life goes by,
The world moves along,
And lets the time fly,

The young are ignorant,
Incompetent and youthful,
Yet they show so much promise,
But they are still so untruthful,

The elders are wiser,
Leading our many nations,
As common day advisors,
To meet their expectations,

And though the time flies,
And the world moves along,
We all stay in our small time,
For though many days go on,
Not as many as we'd wish.

Mayookh Siramdas, Grade 7
Thornton Jr High School

White Wings

Beautiful white wings
Flying through the crisp night air
Soaring and gliding

Their wings unfurled
The world like a spec below
The birds will fly on

Brandon Harris, Grade 7
South Tahoe Middle School

If You Want to Be My Teacher

If you want to be my teacher,
You must become a ballerina,
Strap me in the shoes that force me to dance on my toes,
Steal my sneakers form me,
So I must forever leap on my toes,
Chasing after you so I can get them back.

Megan Yang, Grade 8
St Joseph's School of the Sacred Heart

A Day in the Life

The miserable morning
Awoken by the sound of the bird's beak
It's just another sock I seek
There is no point in mourning
The day seems bleak
The car window stuck open leaves a nasty little leak
I arrive at school my hair sopping wet
The pattern of my day is set
One class after another, the bell repeatedly rings
The stress just builds and builds, but 5th period is finally finished
Now it is time for volleyball, diving suicides and hitting lines
The floor boards of the gym are unforgiving
The scent of the gym constantly rising, volleyball is finally finished
My day is nearly over, I go out to eat
How easy it is to waste what wealth we worked for
My momentary break from stress is finished
The piles of homework I've put off until now, are now something I must work on
Hours are spent merely hearing the pencil scratching, homework is finally finished
I walk upstairs to my room
I lie in my bed enjoying my restless rest
As I drift off to sleep the stress is relieved until tomorrow. My day is finally finished

Justin Speak, Grade 9
Fountain Valley High School

Behind the Perfection

She's the girl, who won't accept anything below perfection,
With her way there's no mistakes, no sense in pointing her the direction,
Nothing she can't learn, nothing she can't fix, nothing she can't do,
She's there on time, she's got the main part, and you know she'll be right on cue.

Everyone admires her and thinks she's got the best life,
She may joke and laugh but deep down inside there is always a strife,
Her walk is confident and nothing seems to bug her calm mind,
He smile lies and fools you all because you don't know what lies behind.

She'll make it look simple but it's hours of tough work and stress,
Don't think for a second that she didn't work hard to get to success,
You've never seen a tear but there are moments where she broke down,
Weak inside yet stronger than ever, her endless hope will never drown.

She hides her feelings because she doesn't need your sympathy,
Nobody's perfect because perfection stops at certain degree,
So go on and believe that every day for her is a light breeze,
Just remember that nobody's life comes easily with ease.

Yifei Ding, Grade 7
Challenger School – Ardenwood

Out of My Inner Igloo

Everything hypnotizes my senses
In the morning's dark.
Your smile, your touch
Gives my day a silver crown.
You'd expect it to crumble by now
Yet my silent tune of hope keeps playing on.
The small twists of the day
Remind me of nothing, but you.
As I walk gently on the fallen powder, my December slumber
Sighs and breathes in memories, from a July lover.
It trades in pain with more light
And can sparkle everything from its slick ice.
Change says it will take a break for now
Till next spring if you still care for me.
I remember the kisses you gave generously away
And on my face they will stay.
I can't say it more plainly
But now I wish you were with me more than anything.
The mountain could shorten
Time elapse and with a grin as wide as can be
I could then shout, "I AM SMITTEN!"

Makani Speier-Brito, Grade 8
Trinity Center Elementary School

The Child's Tears

A world of time passing by,
the silence of every night.
So many dreams broken apart,
memories lost and tormented his life.
The child weeps many moons
and listens for the voice, calling his name mid-tune.
The Child's tears,
filled with hunger and pain
as his smile fades in the midnight air.
The sparkling tears bitter and nay,
his ghoul wanders off far away.
To embrace the past fears, he does not reach,
he stays in the shadows of the dark streets
worthwhile his future sinks
the darkening sky, turns black as ink.
The Child's tears
fall down to Earth,
seasons passing to change the world.
You may not see, he is always there,
helping thee and turning sights green.
The Child has not a path, no ending, only a new beginning.

Angelica Palomares, Grade 8
Shorecliffs Middle School

Skit

S he loves to perform,
K eeping every skit sheet with her lines,
I t helps her when she's nervous,
T o know that it's just another audition.

Katrina Jacinto, Grade 7
John Charles Fremont Intermediate School

Graduation

The sun rises,
As do I,
This is the best day of my life,
But soon I will say good bye,
Goodbye to the people who gave me a good education,
And also the people who gave me inspiration.
It is time to walk down the aisle,
And as I walk I smile,
I can see my future,
It starts to become clear,
That everyone doesn't want me to have fear.
Fear of a new school and faces,
I walk up to get my diploma.
I look up and see everyone staring at me,
And now I'm ready to take whatever life throws at me.

Adrianna Garcia, Grade 8
St Joan of Arc School

In the Meadow

In the meadow, I walked for hours,
Gazing at the birds and flowers,
The busy ants, the buzzing bees,
Bustling through the sturdy trees,
A world discovered, it's not so new,
In ancient times they existed too.

In the meadow, I looked about,
I found trees slim and stout,
Squirrels scamper here and there,
On the bark that's not so fair,
It's rough and rigid, this I know,
But on its branches, blossoms grow.

In the meadow, I found myself,
I broke out of my hollow shell,
Dared to be real, dared to be bold,
Dug through the dirt, what I found was gold,
And on this field, on this sod,
In my heart, what I found was God.

Tressa Mikel, Grade 7
Chino Valley Christian Schools

The Important Thing About Living

The important thing about living is that you must breathe.
    It is fun to live.
      You dance and sing, you play with friends,
      and you party every day,
      and it feels great and sometimes miserable,
      and comes from our parents.
But the important thing about living is that you must breathe.

Vincent Bucayu, Grade 7
St Mary of Assumption School

Earth's Crisis

Convenient is to let it go
Tomorrow I shall change the world,
Today, let fresh water supplies run low,
For a hundred years later, why is gray, filthy smog stuffing the air, my problem?

Every day, there is constantly problems anew,
About global warming and how it affects the *one* Earth we live on,
However, the care about our Earth is only given by few,
So where are our moral values, the ones for respect?

Ideas for saving our Earth,
Are all around, still only the few take a look,
It is said that if everyone does his or her part, much is the total worth,
Nevertheless, few do the minimum, truly required, amount.

So now what?
Take part in changing the future of the planet where we all must reside!
Shall we *not* all see the Earth spoil like an overripe nut?
Instead we will see beautiful black solar panels top our houses, making the difference.

Remember, that from oil spills causing global hazards,
To beach clean-ups with numerous people working together to make it matter,
Anything can happen!!!
Make sure you are *ONLY* a part of the latter.

Karishma Kodia, Grade 7
South Lake Middle School

Love Every Second

Remember when
Bath time was a play time
You never wanted to wash your body or hair just play with the toys
Or just fill up the tub with more bubbles than water
Remember when
Mom did your hair
She never pulled too hard, but got all of the knots out
Or she would do braids and put pretty hair bands on the end
Remember when
You wanted to stay up all night long and hated when your parents forced you to go to sleep
But you loved the feeling of when they tucked you in
Said good night, I love you, and then put the radio on for you to fall asleep to
But now
You take showers in the morning
Mom can never do your hair because it looks like a dumb little kid
You go to bed on your own, close the door and don't wake up till afternoon the next day
It seems to go by so fast, in a blink of any eye
You can do everything yourself
And never need Mom or Dad
Don't grow up too quick, take your time enjoy childhood
Love every second

Brooke Nagel, Grade 9
Linfield Christian School

The 4th of July

The Fourth of July is a great day,
where people get to laugh and play.
And give thanks and honor for those above,
who gave their lives for the ones they loved.
Celebrate the lives of those who fought, and
celebrate the things they've accomplished.
By having fireworks and waving our flag
the fourth of July is not just a holiday,
It's a holiday of Freedom and Independence, so
on this day Independence day we say hooray!!

Cameron Jones, Grade 8
Grace Christian Academy

My Great Grandma

Her lively spirit, and her charming appearance.
Her rosy pink cheeks, and her soft pale skin.
Her laughter lighted up any dull type world.
Now being gone I'm sure she misses her girls.
Above these clouds without worry or harm.
In a place called Heaven, the sound is charm.
She dances all day and sings too, all of this and still,
She watches over you.
In a flowing white gown and a golden halo too,
The sound of her voice is reassuring you.
My great grandma.

Kalani Oatney, Grade 8
Almondale Middle School

As the Seasons Go Past

A wide smile full of love and sweet innocence
Is the warmth that comes with the spring morning.
Thoughts of play are simple
Like the life of a small child.
She rushes home to tell Mom about her adventures,
Swelled with energy and overflowing with pride.
The days seem to grow longer with each passing week.
Spring begins to slowly fade…
Her head is held up high with confidence but no fears,
Like the sun at its peak in the summer afternoon.
She has grown over the years
Into a strong girl with opportunities ahead.
Hopes and dreams can never be too perfect,
But the fall days seem to drag on endlessly.
She is determined to never give up,
But with age comes more responsibility.
Broken promises and shattered dreams
Are what is left of the merciless winter storm.
What remains is the hope in her heart.
After all, spring never fails to return
As the seasons go past.

Kathryn E. Melendez, Grade 7
St Luke the Evangelist Catholic School

The Morning

I wake up, the sky is blue
The sun is shining and it looks like a beautiful day
There is dew on my lawn
The birds are chirping, the dogs are barking
I get ready to start another day

David Kelm, Grade 8
Tierra Linda Middle School

Speech

Speech is like the wind
Unseen but heard
Carries hidden meanings in its flow
Twigs and leaves and petals are carried in a word

Speech is like a river
Trickling and gliding
Takes twists and turns with a gentle swish
And under the water shells and pebbles are hiding

Speech is like the sun
It can be felt but it's hard to see
Seen reflecting off things it reaches
Its golden splendor allows ability to be free

Speech is hard to compare, to anything
Brings understanding to everything
Like a joyful song waiting for lips to sing
From wings of flight, roars of the ocean,
The top of a mountain, we hear it ring

LilyAnne Rice, Grade 8
Community Home Education Program

The Artist

I paint on my canvas
most of the day.
I watch all kinds of people
going on their way.
I see most expressions:
depressed, joyous, and berserk.
This is the emotion expressed in my work.
I paint with every color
to show what I feel.
The whole world has feelings
they're waiting to reveal.
People stop and stare
at my canvas so square.
They ask how I create
my paintings so great.
I tell them how it comes from my heart
and that they too can do their part
Just let out their emotion
let it flow like the ocean
The whole world has feelings
they're waiting to reveal.

Kathryn Vander Molen, Grade 8
La Joya Middle School

The Golden Eagle

A golden eagle
It flies very high and proud
It is majestic
Leighton Cook, Grade 7
South Tahoe Middle School

The First Time

The first time I
saw you
I heard fireworks
My whole world
turned
upside down
Time for me
had slowed
down
Because I fell
in love
with you
Faye Tan, Grade 7
Corpus Christi School

Through the Desert I Travel

My Life
through the Desert
I travel
trying to find the lost idea
that is Who I Am

we all go through rough spots
where the weather seems to be
the Driest and there is no water left
but still my life sometimes seems
more complicated than the rest

Twists and turns
no map to follow
only guidelines and hints

An Oasis I do periodically find
green Grass
palm Trees
clear-water Streams

through the Desert
My Desert
My Life
Gabrielle Bustamante, Grade 8
La Joya Middle School

Peace and War

field of blackened trees
sitting on a plain of green
contrast; peace and war
Miranda Gomez, Grade 9
Patriot High School

Winter

December begins when the lights disappear,
When the sun plays hide and seek with the frosty breezy air.
The woods undress with nothing to wear
And with no strength to shine, the sun sheds a tear.
Pure white snow lay sleeping here
And there, melting like ice cream, being completely unaware.
Oh! The sweet pain of which nothing to compare,
And everywhere and anywhere only few things appear.
When, suddenly, spring comes and the clouds move out of the way,
The sky, the sun, and the birds fly up high
And only happiness, love, and excitement show.
A streak of all colors comes out to play
And to sing and to never say goodbye
Because now everything and anything will say hello.

Angela Oh, Grade 9
North Hollywood Sr High School

Beach

It's sandy,
It's full with people,
There's water nearby.
People go there to enjoy themselves,
Others to get wet when it's really hot.

I love going to the beach!
I love writing on the wet sand, "Vanessa was here,"
But then it gets washed away.
I love getting grossed out when the seaweed touches my feet.
I love seeing people under their umbrellas making sandwiches or other good stuff.

Hearing the annoying sounds of the birds is the best thing of all.
Vanessa Campos, Grade 7
St Vincent Elementary School

Electronics

All the iPods and mp3s, full of sounds putting music in your ears.
And the TV for you eyes, making your eyes full of joyful tears
iPod video, iPod Nano and iPod Mini.
They just keep getting small and smaller and also very skinny.
The music goes to your head and it makes you want to bop.
The sea walk, the moon walk, just keep goin' until you drop.
Then there is the amazing computer that looks like a cube.
You just keep checking your e-mail and going on YouTube.
But you know what's even more amazing, it is a cellphone.
Although I don't have one, it's fun to press a button and hear a little tone.
All of electronics keeps getting more and more complex.
I have to buy it all, should I pay in cash or maybe just with checks!
Cash will actually be better, but the only problem is, look at the price!
Here's something smarter, ask your parents, you should take that advice.
Every single day it is impressive to see a brand new device.
I think it's so cool, in face, it is even cooler than ice!
I think you got the point on how much I adore this stuff.
The greatest part is these electronics are endless, that's sure enough!
Kearney Singh, Grade 8
Challenger School – Ardenwood

My Dog

He is a dog who likes to play then drink.
He sleeps like a teenage boy; it's insane.
He is stubborn and never stops to think.
He runs like Seabiscuit while in the rain.
He bites, scratches, and lifts up his right ear.
He's a happy soul if he gets a bone.
He barks at strangers and chases the deer.
He lives to be petted by anyone.
He takes large risks but receives big rewards.
He jumps and gets into the creme brulee.
He tries to face away but ends up towards.
He is always ready for the next day.
He is friendly, therefore, will never fight.
He's after all, the joyful Dunkin White.

Kyle White, Grade 8
Las Flores Middle School

The Ocean

The world has many wonders both big and small,
But the ocean is the biggest one of all.
From its murky depths to its sandy beaches,
There is so much that it teaches.
Yet the ocean is unreliable,
And can never be trusted,
For if you do,
You just might get busted.
It has no feelings or emotions,
Just a life long devotion.
As many generations have gone and past,
The ocean has always been there,
Completing its life long task.

Westyn Herscovitch, Grade 8
Martin Murphy Middle School

Please Always Remember Me

Open my box and what do you see,
a really old picture of you and me.
We have no teeth, just smiles and joy,
and way too young to think of that boy.
Lift up the paper and behind it you'll find,
a unique golden key that is one-of-a-kind.
If you think you know me and are pretty smart,
you will eventually find out that the key belongs to my heart.
I give you the key for you to keep,
in case you are sad and need to weep.
Place the key back into the box,
and please attach to it one of those special locks.
This is our secret, so treat it with care,
don't leave it lying somewhere so lonely and bare.
The best place to bury the box is deep in the dirt,
but if you forget I will eventually hurt.
Please don't forget me when we depart,
I would hate to drift further apart.
So, please always remember me.

Angela R. Zaniboni, Grade 8
Holy Family Catholic School

How We Roll

Getting up early
Staying up late
Rigging up my rods with my go-to bait.

Driving my truck down the road
Hauling and pulling a thousand-pound load
Unhooking and backing her up
Then running to my car for my coffee cup

In my Nitro
Igniting my passion
Getting the feeling of a fresh new fashion

Got the Z-9
The top of the line
A red and black flake that looks so fine

Living my dream and bringing the steam
Zooming in my boat like a lazer beam
Fishing from day and into the night
We are the ones the big bass fright

Whether it's casting those cranks or pulling the Carolina
Watch out hawgs! We're right behind ya!

Hitting those points, fishing that grass
Hauling up serious, well-fed bass!

Leo Andrada, Grade 7
Southpointe Christian School

I Know My House

I know my house in the morning when I hear
my brother crying
or when I hear the television on

I know my house in the morning when I see
my brother getting ready for school
and my sister brushing her teeth
and my mom combing her hair

I know my house in the morning when I smell
cereal in the kitchen
and the smell of burnt toast
and the smell of toothpaste

I know my house in the morning when I hear someone say
get ready for school
or hurry up and eat
and before I leave my mom tells me she loves me
I know my house in the morning

Tyler Nusz, Grade 7
Richland Jr High School

Denise Escobar

Attitude
Nice happy
Wishes to go to Six Flags
Dreams of being a teacher
Wants to have a dog
Who wonders about my family
Who fears of getting a referral
Who is afraid of not graduating
Who likes hearing music
Who believe in myself
Who loves my family
Who loves music
Who loves my friends
Who loves boys
Who plans to be a teacher
Who plans not to smoke
Who plans to be a better person
Whose final destination is
Graduating

Denise Escobar, Grade 7
Almond Tree Middle School

Teamwork

The light is fading out
So we come together,
We each hold our own candle
To form a better way,
As you can see
Teamwork is the best game.

Masuda Sharifi, Grade 7
Thornton Jr High School

Ode to Nodachi

The glistening shine
The wondrous design
The greatness as you can see
The Nodachi

The sharp blade
The significance it has made
This is the creed
Of the Nodachi

The remarkable swiftness
The blinding quickness
The movement so free
The Nodachi

Edmund Garrett, Grade 8
Santa Rosa Technology Magnet School

Thunderstorms

Thunderstorms are loud
they're dangerous and scary
their light shines the night

Cynthia Hernandez, Grade 8
Almond Tree Middle School

In My Garden

I can see the flowers blowing in the harsh wind,
Bending them all the way to the ground.

I can smell the scent of the lovely roses going through my nose.
It is the most wonderful smell in the world.

I feel the petals of the flowers; they feel like red velvet.
The feeling is remarkable.

I can also hear the wind pushing against the flowers.
The sound is soft and pleasant to hear.

Everything is electrifying.
My senses come alive, in my garden!

Reina Black, Grade 7
Chino Valley Christian Schools

Stop the Madness

Stop the madness of this retched killing.
Stop the sadness my heart is feeling.
End the war, don't destroy
This will solve no problems nor give any joy.
Reach out to the so called enemy, try to make friends.
Believe in one another no matter how different.
Good people come in many ways and forms.
Race is but a word.
You never know what to expect from a person you don't know.
Don't assume the worst, take a chance.
Reach out and learn from one another.
Things may not always be as they seem.

Michaela Kremer, Grade 7
Sutter Middle School

Tedious But Important

Homework is monotonous, tedious, and quite boring.
It's hated and abhorred; children dislike that "scary" thing.
I know some people consider it as a waste of time,
And I know some people do not even do it sometimes.
Most people would rather play with their friends and have some fun
Than research the life of the wonderful George Washington.
And many people would much rather fly a kit outdoors
Than learn all the causes of the terrible Civil War.
Who would prefer a few theorems or inscribing a circle?
Wouldn't you rather go play a game of basketball,
or turn on the TV and watch a good game of football
Than learn how to use pronouns, clauses, and punctuation,
Or read *Animal Farm* to further your education?
Although just the mention of homework may make your smile fade,
It helps you learn and is very important for good grades.
Even if you hate them, you may eventually repent.
Why is it that things that are tedious are often important?
Homework is the perfect example: it's dull, but significant.

Grace Liao, Grade 8
Challenger School – Ardenwood

My Piano

The instrument I play has a keyboard
A panel over which many fingers soared

My piano makes a beautiful sound
The sound produced can be quiet or loud

When played, anyone's fingers dance over the keys
My piano is worthy of any piece

My piano is a speaker, producing anything pleasing
My piano is like a sacred being, greatness ever-increasing

My piano has a certain kind of beauty
An aspect everyone finds eluding

My piano is not all-together great looking
But the sound created is very hooking

The instrument I play has a keyboard
A panel over which many fingers soared

My piano has characteristics perfect for anyone
Even me

Maxton Vieira, Grade 8
Valley Oak Middle School

Ode to My Cell Phone

Ode to my cell phone
Without you I feel alone

You're what wakes me up in the morning
So I don't have to hear my mom yelling

You're what lets me call my friends
So I can hear who is cheating on their boyfriend

You're what plays my music
So I show you off in public

People say you're the coolest thing
But it isn't that shocking

The day I got you I was so excited
Now I use you to text every period

I love you so much, you're like my lifeline
Whoever made you is as smart as Einstein

If I ever lost you
Well, I wouldn't know what I'd do

Elizabeth Halstead, Grade 8
Valley Oak Middle School

A Holocaust Horror

The Holocaust.
A worldwide fear,
The danger is near,
The Holocaust.

The Star of David is sad,
Surrounded by all that is bad.
It cried for all the dead and dying.
It cries for horrible Nazis, lying.

Camps are like big, black holes.
People burning on smoking coals.
No hope, all despair,
There was no joy that Jews could share.

Some had died of starvation.
End of war brought mass jubilation.
Soldiers couldn't believe their eyes.
Finally, the end of a great demise.

The Holocaust is like a terrifying nightmare.
It could be woken up from but never forgotten.

Lisa Popylisen, Grade 8
Sacred Heart School

Special Person

Everyone has a special person
In their lives
Whether they're dead or alive
A crush a lover
Or even a family member
No matter if they love you back or care
And we know there are heroes
Like Mom and Dad
It could be anyone on TV
It could be a cartoon
But remember if someone special
Does not care
And you're the one crying
The one who helps you when you're down
Should be your hero too!

Kamisha Williams, Grade 7
MIT Academy

The Fourth of July

Everyone was dressed in red, white or blue
It was hot and humid, yet dry and sticky
My grandparents were ready, with many sparklers in hand
Grandpa lit the flame, and off it went
Shooting sprits of flames crackled off the sparkler stick
Glowing as it went
Grandpa, holding the stick behind me, in case I was to drop it
But later, he dropped me, no longer holding my hand
He was gone, never to come back.

Mackenzie O'Holleran, Grade 8
St Joseph's School of the Sacred Heart

Learning French

Learning French is so great,
Although you have to wait,

Until you learn it very well.
Then you can just shout out and yell,

"French is easy!"
Until then you are busy.

Working and studying hard,
Until you receive your reward.

French may take a lot of time,
But it's easy if you're not a mime.
Nathalie Recendez, Grade 7
John Adams Middle School

Home

In the beginning
Hopeless and helpless
I was bad
I was sad

I came here
Depressed and scared
Met some friends felt better
I realized my life isn't so bad

I miss my family
My dog Sydney
My friends, my school
I miss home

It's time to go home
Isabel Ortega, Grade 9
Jack Weaver School

Butterflies

Butterflies are the flowers of the sky
See them as they flutter by

Bright color of pink and blue
Yellow, orange, and violet too

Watch them fly with all their might
Oh wow, what a beautiful sight

Butterflies are free to roam
Anywhere and find their way home

I wish one day I could fly
Like a soaring butterfly
Lauren Martin, Grade 8
Madrona Middle School

A Great Putt

A perfect putt
The ball goes straight
The ball hits a nut
And drops in hole eight

The crowd says boy o boy
The ball hits the green
The announcer is filled with joy
The first hole in one has now been seen
John Erhardt, Grade 7
Sarah McGarvin Intermediate School

Morning Rain

Pit-pat
Pit-pat
Morning rain
Falls on the dirt-stained window pane
Crash!
Ka-boom!
Violent thunder
Crashing
Clashing
Shhhhhh!
Drip
Plop
Then silence…
Cold, bittersweet silence…
Pit pat
Pit-pat
Here comes the rain
Splishing
Sploshing
On the dirt-stained window pane
Alyssa Ferrer, Grade 7
South Tahoe Middle School

The Lonely Tree

In the whispering meadow
There was a lonely tree
Whose spirit wanted to be set free
Along came a man
With a bunch of tin cans
At night he slept beside the trunk
With all his junk
It tickled the tree
And the leaves began to flee
The man thought he was alone at last
A place where nobody knew his past
Under the trunk there was a key
That would finally set the tree's soul free
Now the man and the tree are friends
Now and forever till the very end.
Sarah Magdaleno, Grade 8
Madrona Middle School

A Little While Longer

I hate you
I love you
I loathe you
I'll kill you
You may think they mean what they say
Yet…they don't
All words of love
Never of hate
They cherish your heart, soul, and mind
They couldn't live without you
When your heart beats so does theirs
So don't stop beating
I can't live without you
I hate you
I love you
I loathe you
I'll kill you
But not now
Stay a little while longer
I live while you live
I beat when you beat
Dawn McCladdie, Grade 7
Bancroft Middle School

The Shiny Moon

I wonder how the moon goes down
The moon will come back again
But now I see the sun
Sometimes I think how many stars
Are in the sky
Raul Alanis Jr., Grade 7
Richland Jr High School

Little Girl

My name is Emma
I am thirteen years old.
I live in a world that's so cold
so cold.

I pick cotton by day
get beat by night
I'm black
but beautiful is what I lack.

Momma said black is beauty
Master said it's a lie
black is just a working slave
who will soon die.

It's 1862 and all's well to come
I'll be free soon
and so will everyone.
Dani Washington, Grade 7
Odyssey Charter School

I Am

I am young and ignorant
I wonder how birds see the world
I hear sounds of the ocean
I see the great beauty of nature
I want to travel to imaginary places
I am young and ignorant

I pretend that no one can see me
I feel quivery all over
I touch the blades of grass below me
I worry that the world won't see me for who I am
I cry at the thought of broken friendships
I am young and ignorant

I understand the meaning of life
I say health and happiness is more valuable than money
I dream that life can end in a blink of an eye
I try to make it seem worthwhile
I hope it'll last forever
I am young and ignorant

Ngoc Ly, Grade 7
Sarah McGarvin Intermediate School

The Way You Smile

Your contagious smile brightens my day,
Your smile helps me in seeing the light.
Holds as much sunshine as the month of May;
Glows like the moon on a bright summer night:

Through your smile, I'm let into your soul;
Out of there comes a great healing power.
To help mend a broken heart, to console,
Enough to repair a wilted flower:

You light up my face with such happiness,
Although falling tears may be very near:
Somehow you clear every bit of sadness;
You inspire me to conquer my fear:

You make me remember life's worthwhile,
With one big grin, one beautiful smile.

Simone Teitelbaum, Grade 8
Las Flores Middle School

The Sun

The sun is shining over the ocean
Its reflection is a clear picture of a beautiful sea
I look upon it as if I was picturing a glorious field of flowers
I wish I could float away on a soft current
The sun is shining and now it is setting out of sight

Ali Welisch, Grade 7
St Hilary School

Passion and Adventure

As I get ready to begin my adventure, I feel the
Flow of the wind in my hair.

The sun is setting and everything stops
Around me as time stands still

Then I feel a rush of power and I begin

As I gallop off into the valley I feel the strength
Of our two hearts beating together.

The feeling is mutual.

Others may think that horseback riding is just
A sport, but to me — it is a passion…it is my passion.

When I am riding, I feel like nothing else
Around us matters.

What matters is that I know I can do this every day
For the rest of my life.

This makes me happy because it makes me feel free,
and most of all…alive

Morgan Robledo, Grade 7
Holy Family Catholic School

Confession of a Brokenhearted Lover

Can't breathe, won't try;
Don't want to see again.
Can't speak, won't lie;
Don't want to move again.
Can't cry, won't die;
Don't want to laugh again.
Stand still, don't breathe,
And I'll tell you how I feel.

Bones melting, heart's aching
Eyes blinded, sight blackened
Hands frozen; time's fading
Fire's freezing and ice is burning.
Wind's still; smoke's raining
Colors bleeding, shadows hiding
Cold and lost, scarred and screaming;
Faithfully yours, forever doubting the warmth…
The comfort your soul provides for mine.
Please don't go, please stay with me,
Forever now and till always won't be —
Eternity; it's ours, so don't walk away from me.

Ashley Williams, Grade 9
Palo Verde High School

The Ocean Blue

I lie on my back
Silence falls over the horizon
I don't know where I am
I open my eyes
I am underwater
I have never seen anything so beautiful
Fish of every kind swim past me
As if nothing is out of place
I suddenly feel I am home
I watch as bubbles release from my mouth
My hair is flowing in the soft current
I know this is where I belong
The pressure is rising as I go deeper
But I don't seem to notice
I am mesmerized by the world around me
I stroke the dolphin's rough skin
As he talks to me in hushed tones
He is beautiful
I am slowly reaching the horizon
My epic journey has ended
The sun shines brightly on the ocean blue

Britt Lindberg, Grade 8
St Hilary School

Sounds of Football

The smashing bodies,
The crashing helmets.
The yelling coaches,
And exuberant fans.
Cheers their teams to victory,
Do whatever it takes.
The click-clack of their cleat,
Blowing by defenders.
Battle scars show on their faces, arms, and legs,
A sign of toughness needed for this game.
The swoosh of the spiraling football,
The smack when it hits the wide out's hands.
The roar of the crowd,
The falls that shake the ground.
The rain falls and moistens my head.
But this doesn't stop the determined players,
To make it to the end zone.
The whistle blows,
Play is over.
But for me it is just beginning again.

Jack Larson, Grade 8
St Joseph's School of the Sacred Heart

Colors

Colors are everywhere you look,
In a painting, picture, or in a book.

They make our days full of life,
Cuts deep through our souls, like a white-hot knife.

Without them our life would be gray,
Making our imaginations drift off and away.

When mixed together, they create such a sight,
You can easily see them day or night.

I'm really glad that colors are here,
I look forward to seeing new ones every year.

Dominique Mendoza, Grade 8
Madrona Middle School

The Race of a Lifetime

Five, four, three, two, one beep!
The horn blows as Paige Railey
finds her way to the head of the fleet.
Starboard!
Yells another racers she swerves past them
and effortlessly lee-blows others.
Bystanders cheer from the land and other boats.
Their yelling like neighs of a horse, loud and long.
Tacks, gibes,
turns around marks,
racing to the finish,
she makes navigating through the race course look easy.
The water crashes against the committee boats
as she nears the end of the race.
She zooms through the finish line like lightning,
the horn blows, the crowds cheer, and Paige smiles.
She has finally finished an intense day of racing she is proud of.
No matter what place she receives,
she did her best and no one can ask for anything more.

Sarah Mackey, Grade 8
St Joseph's School of the Sacred Heart

Index

Author Autograph Page

Author Autograph Page

Author Autograph Page

Author Autograph Page

Author Autograph Page

Author Autograph Page